Of Marshes and Maize

**Preceramic Agricultural Settlements
in the Cienega Valley, Southeastern
Arizona**

ANTHROPOLOGICAL PAPERS OF
THE UNIVERSITY OF ARIZONA
NUMBER 59

Of Marshes and Maize

Preceramic Agricultural Settlements in the Cienega Valley, Southeastern Arizona

Bruce B. Huckell

CONTRIBUTORS

Lisa W. Huckell
Penny Dufoe Minturn
Lorrie Lincoln-Babb

THE UNIVERSITY OF ARIZONA PRESS
TUCSON
1995

About the Author

BRUCE B. HUCKELL is Senior Research Coordinator for the Maxwell Museum of Anthropology at the University of New Mexico in Albuquerque. Educated at the University of Arizona, he completed a Master's degree in Anthropology in 1976 and a Doctoral degree in the interdisciplinary Arid Lands Resource Sciences program in 1990. He worked at the Arizona State Museum in various capacities from 1972 through 1990, including Assistant Highway Salvage Archaeologist and later as Project Director for the Cultural Resource Management Division. Prior to moving to New Mexico in 1994, he was a Research Archaeologist at the Center for Desert Archaeology in Tucson. His research interests in the archaeology of hunter-gatherers, Quaternary geoarchaeology, lithic technology, and traditional agriculture were developed during many projects on sites in southeastern Arizona that ranged in age from Clovis through Upper Pima. Buried sites in the arroyos of the region hold a particular fascination for him, because they offer detailed records of the interaction between people and their environment. Current research efforts include continuing study, with Lisa W. Huckell, of the establishment of agriculture in the southwestern United States.

Cover: Maize plant and a Cienega style projectile point superimposed on a scene of cottonwood and willow growing along Cienega Creek, Arizona (*see* Figs. 2.4, 4.1). Some 2500 years ago, marshes and maize fields were scattered along this channel.

Contributors

Lisa W. Huckell
  Maxwell Museum of Anthropology, University of New Mexico, Albuquerque.

Penny Dufoe Minturn
  Desert Archaeology Inc., Tucson, Arizona.

Lorrie Lincoln-Babb
  Department of Anthropology, Arizona State University, Tempe.

THE UNIVERSITY OF ARIZONA PRESS

Copyright © 1995

The Arizona Board of Regents
All Rights Reserved

This book was set in 10.7/12 CG Times
♾ This book is printed on acid-free, archival-quality paper.
Manufactured in the United States of America.

99 98 97 96 95   9 8 7 6 5

Library of Congress Cataloging-in-Publication Data

Huckell, Bruce B.
  Of marshes and maize : preceramic agricultural settlements in the Cienega Valley, southeastern Arizona / Bruce B. Huckell ; contributors, Lisa W. Huckell, Penny Dufoe Minturn, and Lorrie Lincoln-Babb.
      p. cm. -- (Anthropological papers of the University of Arizona ; no. 59)
    Includes bibliographic references and index.
    ISBN 0-8165-1582-4 (acid-free paper)
    1. Indians of North America--Arizona--Cienega Creek Valley--Antiquities. 2. Cienega Creek Valley (Ariz.)--Antiquities. 3. Arizona--Antiquities. I. Title. II. Series.
E78.A7H833 1995
979.1'53--dc20   95-32510
                                                        CIP

1904–1992

Emil W. Haury at Los Ojitos in Matty Canyon
June 1983

To Doc

With deep appreciation for his support,
scholarly example, and friendship

Contents

FIGURES

TABLES

Foreword

The invitation to write the foreword to Bruce B. Huckell's long awaited monograph on preceramic agricultural development in southeastern Arizona is a distinct honor, and one that I assume with great pleasure. As an original participant (okay, a shovel bum) in the excavations at Matty Canyon in the spring of 1957 under the supervision of Frank W. Eddy, I developed a life-long interest in the area and its archaeological intrigue. As a consequence, I have revisited the Cienega Creek Basin at frequent intervals and, perhaps even more frequently, have discussed the experiences of that spring with friends and colleagues who share an interest in the prehistory of southern Arizona.

Frank and I were roommates that year. We both developed, perhaps in a blush of innocence, a passion for southern Arizona prehistory. Frank, influenced by Emil W. Haury and even more especially by Ted Sayles, our constant companion in the bowels of the old Arizona State Museum, turned his interest to the preceramic period. I, challenged by Haury in a different direction, was drawn to the proto-Historic period. We both participated, however, in Haury's traditional seminar field trips to the Cienega, Lehner, Naco, and Whitewater sites in the mid 1950s. And those trips surely led to Frank's choice of the Matty Canyon site (AZ EE:2:30 ASM) as the centerpiece for his master's thesis (and subsequent publication).

The results of those excavations, conducted with the assistance of fellow graduate students and, thanks to a small grant, a few weeks of hired shovels, exceeded, I believe, Frank's greatest expectations. But those results, at the same time, presented him with some rather vexing interpretive problems (problems that became the subject of late night discussions both at the site and later in our careers). As outlined by Bruce Huckell in Chapter 1, first Sayles in 1941, then Eddy (and I as a fellow graduate student and participant) were fully aware of the conflict that the physical dimensions of the midden presented to the then conventional understanding of the San Pedro culture as a mobile hunter-gatherer society. This midden represented a deposit rich in artifacts and carbon residue that must have built up from cultural activities lasting hundreds of years. On the one hand, we tended to dismiss the "conflict" as perhaps artificial because of the limited excavations. At the same time, limited excavations or not, the shovel was telling us that we were involved with what would, in ceramic contexts, be considered a sedentary community. Bear in mind that flotation analysis was not in our toolkit and, as Huckell reviews, there was not enough "hard" evidence to challenge the current interpretations of San Pedro Cochise.

Thus, I was enthusiastic to face that conundrum again when, in the spring of 1983, Bruce Huckell invited me to revisit the site with Emil Haury. We observed the great lateral extension of the midden being exposed by the 1983 excavations, far more than we had a hint of in 1957; the physical evidence of corn, both cobs and kernels, that had eluded the earlier excavations; and the continuing confirmation of the absence of pottery. Our intuitions of 1957 were now taking on the substance of empirical evidence. And as I observed then, and in the subsequent weeks as the excavations progressed, I blessed the circumstances that allowed much of the site to remain available for future excavation. New techniques that were unavailable in 1957 had been developed, such as flotation analyses and accelerator dating, which now could be applied to the long protected archaeological materials. Importantly, Huckell's experience, formed by a decade or more of excavations in late Archaic sites in southern Arizona, including his later reexcavation of the San Pedro type site at Fairbank, allowed him to view these late preceramic remains without forcing the evidence into the explanatory model of Eddy's time. Thus the stage was set for a truly significant contribution to our understanding of the development of agriculture in southern Arizona.

Of Marshes and Maize presents the results of the 1983 excavations at two sites in the Cienega Creek Basin, information that necessarily forms the framework on which an understanding of process, of history, is built. These data are succinctly summarized by Huckell, but let me emphasize the major points that permit him to expand the descriptive material to suggest a fundamental taxonomic shift in the cultural systematics of the late preceramic period in southern Arizona. First, there is the midden! Oh, what a midden! Huckell could only estimate two dimensions, length (along the stream axis) and depth. The width dimension was effectively masked by some five meters of overburden. This midden was 140 m in length and nearly 0.50 m in depth. It must be obvious that few, if any, early ceramic sites in the Southwest can claim dimensions even close to these.

Second, there is the now indisputable evidence for an abundance of early cultigens, especially maize, but also perhaps squash, presented by Lisa Huckell in Chapter 5. The results of flotation studies from the Matty Canyon sites once and for all put an end to any doubts regarding the presence of agriculture in preceramic communities.

Third, the study of the bioarchaeological remains, an incredible number for an "Archaic" site, presents dental and skeletal analyses that support the conclusions of the physical and macrobotanical data, namely that the population of the Matty Canyon settlements was, in fact, dietarily dependent on agricultural products.

The results of these investigations, combined with Huckell's previous excavations of late preceramic sites in the San Pedro and Tucson basins, have brought together this most timely monograph. While reading the concluding chapter, I was drawn to reread, for the nth time, *The Cochise Culture* by Sayles and Antevs. As I did so, it slowly but forcibly dawned on me that all of these excavations, at Matty Canyon in 1957 and 1983, in the San Pedro Valley, in the Tucson Basin, and elsewhere in the last 10 years or so, provide a data base that exceeds, probably by tenfold, the information that was available and used by Sayles in the original definition of the San Pedro Cochise.

Huckell concludes that the term Archaic as applied to late preceramic sites in southern Arizona is both inaccurate and confusing. He presents, as an alternative, the term Early Agricultural period, divided into the San Pedro and Cienega phases. The argument is persuasively presented and I, for one, find that this shift in taxonomies fits the 1995 state of knowledge admirably. My only regret is that I may be forced to invent new subjects for late night discussions!

William J. Robinson
Tucson, Arizona
June 1995

Preface

The Cienega Creek Basin of southeastern Arizona is a rare gem in an arid land, an almost pure grassland surrounding a perennial stream in a broad valley bounded by mountain ranges clad in junipers, oaks, and pines. At its southern end, it looks more like a misplaced piece of Wyoming than part of Arizona. This richness of the land first drew people to settle in this valley some 3000 years ago and has continued to attract others to this day. Among those who have found much of value here are archaeologists from the University of Arizona.

This monograph concerns the late preceramic people who settled in this valley during the last millennium before Christ. Much of the valley that they knew and lived on lies 5 m beneath the waist-high sacaton grass and mesquite forest that cover the Cienega Creek floodplain today. We might not know of this buried world without the livestock industry and the pioneering ranchers, who saw in the vast green expanse and running stream pastures and water for thousands of sheep and cattle. History has recorded the subsequent late nineteenth century calamities resulting from too many animals and too little rain; among them was the transformation of Cienega Creek and its tributaries from broad, shallow streams to deep, steep-walled arroyos. By the mid-1920s, ranchers, chasing cattle through these entrenched channels, began to find traces of the former residents of the valley protruding from the banks; they brought archaeologist Byron Cummings of the University of Arizona to see what they had discovered. He in turn introduced a young student named Emil Haury to the Cienega Basin, and for more than 50 years he, too, shared this beautiful land with his students. With him, they surveyed much of the valley on weekend or vacation trips, marveling not only at the remains of villages on the terraces along Cienega Creek, but also at sites that had not seen the sunshine for thousands of years.

In the middle 1950s, one such deeply buried settlement in Matty Canyon, a tributary of Cienega Creek, became the centerpiece of an ambitious multidisciplinary project conducted by Frank Eddy as research for his Master's degree. The unexpected complexity and bounty of this late preceramic site, known simply as AZ EE:2:30 (ASM), was both fascinating and disconcerting.

It yielded a wealth of detail about life during the period, but it clearly did not fit prevailing views about the mobile, hunting-gathering culture archaeologists presumed had produced it. For nearly 25 years after Eddy's work, AZ EE:2:30 saw few visitors except for cattle, but slow, inexorable erosion continued to deepen and broaden the exposure of the site. In 1982 the lessee of the Empire Ranch, John Donaldson, called Emil Haury to report a burial. Haury's visit to inspect it led to the "rediscovery" of AZ EE:2:30 and to a second site of similar culture and age downstream. It was clear that both sites could contribute much to the understanding of the late preceramic period and that investigations were warranted. The torch thus passed has enabled further expansion on the accomplishments of Frank Eddy and Emil Haury.

The Matty Canyon Project, as this most recent effort was christened, was directed toward acquiring new information that, through use of the theoretical and methodological gains made since 1960, would expand our archaeological perceptions of that critical period when hunting-gathering societies settled into a more sedentary lifestyle with some agricultural stability. This monograph describes small-scale investigations at two deeply buried preceramic sites in the Cienega Creek Basin of southeastern Arizona and considers in both theoretical and empirical terms the consequences of the adoption of agriculture by late preceramic societies in this portion of the Southwest.

Excavation of the Donaldson Site and of Los Ojitos was conducted during the summer of 1983. A large portion of this manuscript was written by 1989, but a variety of other commitments prevented its completion. Late in 1993, William J. Robinson, former Director of the Laboratory of Tree-Ring Research at the University of Arizona and a participant in the Matty Canyon work by Frank Eddy, generously offered his organizational skills to raise funds to cover the costs of publication, and a final flurry of writing and analysis has resulted in this final report in 1995.

To place the work in historical context, I begin with a general overview of the terminal preceramic period of the southern Southwest to convey the state of knowledge of preceramic prehistory in the region as it existed in 1957 when research was undertaken in this area. Investigations between 1955 and 1957 at a series of late preceramic archaeological localities in and near Matty Canyon, a major tributary of Cienega Creek, are reviewed, followed by subsequent empirical studies of late preceramic archaeology with explanatory models of the adoption of agriculture. Chapter 2 discusses the physiography, biota, and history of Matty Canyon and the Cienega Creek Basin. The 1983 investigations conducted at two Late Archaic sites in Matty Canyon and the results of that fieldwork are then presented in Chapter 3, followed in Chapter 4 by a consideration of the artifact assemblages from these sites and comparisons of the flaked and ground stone assemblages with samples obtained from earlier work in the area. The analyses of macrobotanical remains from both sites and animal bones from one are described (Chapters 5 and 6), and in Chapter 7 a detailed examination of the human skeletal remains from the 1983 investigations is presented. The concluding chapter considers the implications of these archaeological findings for our understanding of the importance of agriculture in the late preceramic period and for our perceptions of the rise of village life in the Southwest.

Acknowledgments

The Arizona State Museum Matty Canyon Project has benefitted from the combined efforts of numerous individuals and organizations. After the passage of more than ten years since the original fieldwork, it is a pleasure to thank in print all those who worked so hard to make it possible. First and foremost, I express gratitude to Agnese Haury, whose unfailing generosity provided the financial means to conduct much of the fieldwork and most of the analyses. Significant funds for fieldwork were also granted by the University of Arizona Foundation and the former ANAMAX Mining Company. At the time of the excavations, ANAMAX owned the Empire–Cienega Ranch property and kindly granted permission to excavate. In particular, thanks are extended to Gene Wyman, then President of the company, and Wilson McCurry, then a geologist with ANAMAX, for their interest in and support of this research. The present owner, the Bureau of Land Management, has continued to grant access to the sites since acquiring the ranch in 1988.

The field crew spent six weeks during the hottest part of the year excavating the two sites. Kenneth Rozen was an excellent crew chief, ably assisted by Ronald Beckwith, Richard Ervin, Cynthia Graff, and Martyn Tagg. All of them were veterans of the ANAMAX-Rosemont Archaic excavations, and a better crew for digging preceramic sites could not have been assembled. When the work was extended for another week, Nancy Bannister, Allen Dart, and Ronald Maldonado capably took the places of Ken, Marty, and Rick. We were also fortunate to have the services of many volunteers, including Jon Czaplicki, Christian Downum, Alan Ferg, David Gregory, Lisa Huckell, Fred Huntington, Richard Lange, Norman Little, Emma Little, Rick Martynec, and Adrian Rankin. The artifacts were processed under the direction of Arthur Vokes. I am also indebted to Michelle Napoli and Walter Birkby, Director of the Arizona State Museum Human Identification Laboratory, for their handling of the burials. Michelle did the initial inventory analysis of the remains. Dr. Birkby also arranged working space for Penny Minturn and Lorrie Lincoln-Babb in 1994.

Raymond Thompson, Director of the Arizona State Museum, and Gwinn Vivian, then Associate Director, provided constant support and encouragement for the project from beginning to end. Dr. Thompson secured funding for the fieldwork from the University of Arizona Foundation and for photography and drafting from the Arizona State Museum. Other individuals from the University of Arizona visited frequently while we were in the field, and they provided much-needed help in identifying where earlier excavations had been conducted at the Donaldson Site. They included Matty Canyon veterans William Robinson, Bryant Bannister, and Alexander Lindsay. Frank Eddy, of the University of Colorado, who first excavated in Matty Canyon, spent a day in the field with us and later sent me all of his original field notes. I hope that his generosity will be repaid by seeing this report reach printed form. Lynn Teague of the Arizona State Museum supported not only the fieldwork, but also helped coordinate discussion regarding the illustrations that appear in Chapter 7. Particular thanks go to Joseph T. Joaquin, Chairman of the Tohono O'odham Cultural Committee, for considering and approving use of the drawings of the skeletal and dental attributes.

It is a pleasure to acknowledge gratitude to my collaborators in this publication: Lisa Huckell, Penny Minturn, and Lorrie Lincoln-Babb. Penny and Lorrie volunteered their time and skills to study the human remains from the sites, and Lisa tirelessly pursued the study of the carbonized plant remains. Doc Haury assisted in the analysis of the flaked and ground stone and wrote the section on the ground stone artifacts from the Donaldson Site.

My appreciation is expressed to Christine Szuter for her aid in identifying many of the Donaldson Site faunal remains and to Amadeo Rea for examining the three bird bones from that site. Jennifer Strand aided with some last-minute identifications of rabbit bones. Tom Van Devender kindly identified the toad remains.

Ron Beckwith's drafting talents are reflected in the maps, figures, and artifact drawings in this volume, and I am indebted to him for skillfully reproducing my squiggles. Robert Caccio provided the drawings in Chapter 7. I also thank Ken Matesich for the artifact photographs reproduced as Figures 4.3, 4.4, and 4.13 and for his special efforts in producing the fine print, from an old negative, of Bill Robinson at the Donaldson Site in Matty Canyon on the following page. The photograph of Emil Haury on the dedication page was taken by Helga Teiwes and also printed by Ken. Kathleen Hubenschmidt tracked down photographs in the Arizona State Museum photo archives of Frank Eddy's original excavation and helped to arrange the printing of the field and artifact figures.

Much of this manuscript was revised while I was employed at the Center for Desert Archaeology, and I am deeply grateful to President William Doelle for his fiscal and intellectual support of this endeavor. Catherine Gilman of Desert Archaeology skillfully pulled together the bibliography for the book.

Many other individuals made the project an enjoyable experience, particularly John Donaldson and his son Mac. Their interest in these sites brought them by for frequent visits during the fieldwork, and it was in their honor that one of the sites was named. Bob Foote maneuvered his backhoe into places where I was not sure backhoes could go in order to give us a better look at the buried cultural deposit at the Donaldson Site. Ed Lehner visited us in the field on more than one occasion, sharing with all of us his wry sense of humor and some cold drinks. Arthur Jelinek, Bryant Bannister, Emil Haury, and Agnese Haury visited frequently to check on the progress of the work and offer sage advice. Helga Teiwes usually accompanied them and took a number of excellent field photographs. Several of the artifact photos that grace the pages of this monograph are by her. Vance Haynes, Mike Waters, and Fred Nials provided some valuable insights into the alluvial stratigraphy during field visits. Appreciation is expressed to the NSF–Arizona AMS Facility for dating four radiocarbon samples at no charge to the project.

Without the support and encouragement of Bill Robinson and editor Carol Gifford, this volume would never have been completed. Bill raised money to cover the costs of publishing the Matty Canyon research, and he also reviewed and commented on previous drafts of the manuscript. Matty Canyon and the Cienega Valley have been among his favorite places for many years, and he has freely shared his enthusiasm for and knowledge of the local history, archaeology, geology, and natural history. In September of 1994 he helped to relocate AZ EE:2:35 and, with his wife Priscilla, treated Lisa and me to a wonderful going-away picnic under the cottonwoods of Cienega Creek.

To my colleagues who have pursued the story of early Southwestern agricultural societies I also offer my appreciation for many stimulating ideas and conversations during the past several years. There are many, and for now I would like to acknowledge Chip Wills, R. G. Matson, Paul and Suzy Fish, the late Don Graybill, Kim Smiley, Bill Parry, Barb Roth, David Gregory, Jonathan Mabry, Jim Holmlund, and particularly my wife, Lisa. Two anonymous reviewers of the manuscript offered insightful and beneficial comments.

My deepest professional and personal debt is to Emil Haury; it was a special privilege to be associated with him over the course of my career at the Arizona State Museum. He offered me the opportunity to be involved in this project and so unstintingly believed in the value of the work that he donated a considerable amount of his time and financial support to ensure its completion. His long-standing interest in the Cienega Creek area and in the problems of preceramic archaeology and early agriculture was inspirational. I regret that he did not live to see this work published.

William J. Robinson at the Donaldson Site (AZ EE:2:30 ASM) in 1957. The overburden of Test 2 has been stripped down to the level of cultural material. (ASM photograph 4201 by Frank W. Eddy.)

CHAPTER ONE

Archaeological Research in the Late Preceramic Southwest

The transition from foraging to agriculture is one of the most significant chapters in the story of human cultural development. The nature, causes, effects, and timing of this shift in subsistence have received a profusion of theoretical treatments and considerable archaeological research in several areas of the world where agricultural economies rose to prominence. In particular, the past four decades have witnessed a tremendous surge in interest by scholars attempting to understand and explain this fundamental change in human ecology (Binford 1968; Ucko and Dimbleby 1969; Flannery 1973, 1986; Cohen 1977; Reed 1977; Rindos 1980, 1984; Harris and Hillman 1989; Cowan and Watson 1992; Gebauer and Price 1992, to cite but a few).

Prehistorians have devoted most of their efforts toward understanding the origins and rise of agriculture in the places where it is believed to have first appeared. Despite the fact that the southwestern United States was not an area in which food production originated, the addition of cultivation to a hunting and gathering subsistence in this region has attracted special attention from archaeologists. Research conducted during the past 40 to 50 years has resulted in the identification of a general dichotomy between the preceramic (Archaic) hunter-gatherers and the later ceramic-producing agriculturalists. Archaic period economies entailed hunting and gathering, with frequent residential moves by relatively small social groups to take advantage of seasonally available wild plant and animal resources in spatially separated ecozones. In contrast, later ceramic period economies revolved around sedentary village life in large or small social groupings supported by a varying but substantial dependence on agriculture, supplemented by hunting and gathering. Only during the Late Archaic period did this dichotomy tend to blur slightly, when archaeologists recognized evidence that agriculture had arrived on the prehistoric scene but perhaps had not yet become an integral part of the economy.

Many researchers concluded that a mixed farming and foraging economy existed from approximately 1000 B.C. until A.D. 200, at which time true villages, pottery, and perhaps a greater reliance on agriculture became commonplace. Several scholars suggested that the adoption of agriculture had minimal effects on foraging economies (Haury 1962; Dick 1965; Whalen 1973; Irwin-Williams 1979; Woodbury and Zubrow 1979; Ford 1981), and that the full productive potential of agriculture was not realized until improved cultivars or technologies permitted the development of more intensive crop production. This was the general state of affairs in 1983 when archaeologists from the Arizona State Museum were presented with an unanticipated opportunity to renew their research in a remarkable area of southeastern Arizona first discovered and investigated some 30 years earlier.

I begin the story of this subsistence transition in the southern Southwest with a brief overview of the state of knowledge of preceramic prehistory in the region as it existed in 1955 when the first excavations were undertaken in the Cienega Creek Basin of southeastern Arizona. Within this context, attention is focused on investigations made between 1955 and 1957 at a series of late preceramic archaeological localities in and near Matty Canyon, a major tributary of Cienega Creek. The results of that research and its impact on perceptions of late preceramic subsistence settlement systems are presented, along with a review of the subsequent development of empirical knowledge and theoretical models about early Southwestern agriculture. Together, these discussions provide an intellectual context for the 1983 research described herein. A proposed revision of the designation of the late preceramic period is offered.

DEFINING THE PRECERAMIC PERIOD IN THE SOUTHERN SOUTHWEST

The existence of preceramic cultures in the Southwest was established before World War I in the region's northern sector, where both amateur and professional archaeologists excavating in rock shelters discovered the storage cists, caches, and burials that led to the definition of the Basketmaker culture (Pepper 1902; Kidder and Guernsey 1919; Guernsey and Kidder 1921; Nusbaum 1922; a history of Basketmaker research is given in Matson 1991). These shelters were located in south-eastern Utah and northeastern Arizona. Basketmaker II subsistence was clearly based in part on agriculture, as demonstrated by the maize, beans, and squash recovered from the shelters, but an earlier Basketmaker I stage, supported by a purely hunting-gathering economy, was proposed by Kidder (1924) on theoretical grounds.

Although it was recognized as early as the mid-1920s that southeastern Arizona was home to early hunters and gatherers, it was the research undertaken by the Gila Pueblo Archaeological Foundation in the mid-1930s that provided the baseline of knowledge concerning these preceramic foragers. In 1935, E. B. Sayles and Emil W. Haury initiated an intensive search for traces of ancient camps, focusing in particular on exposures of artifacts in the banks of deep arroyos in the San Simon, Sulphur Spring, San Pedro, and Santa Cruz river valleys (Fig. 1.1). They were joined in 1936 by Quaternary geologist Ernst Antevs in one of the first collaborative efforts by archaeologists and geologists to solve problems of mutual interest. Haury's departure from Gila Pueblo in 1937 left Sayles and Antevs to bring the work to completion. Their landmark publication of *The Cochise Culture* in 1941 reported the existence of a nearly 10,000-year-long record of the activities of these early Southwesterners. The Cochise culture was identified from surface collections, geologic mapping, and limited excavations at several key sites. The authors defined three subdivisions or stages on the basis of material traits and relative ages as determined from stratigraphic position and sedimentological characteristics of the deposits yielding the artifacts: Sulphur Spring, Chiricahua, and San Pedro.

The Sulphur Spring stage was linked to the close of the Pleistocene, based on the occurrence of simple ground stone milling equipment (handstones and grinding slabs) and of crudely flaked stone tools stratigraphically beneath geologic units containing the remains of mammoth, horse, bison, and dire wolf. The succeeding Chiricahua stage was bracketed between 8000 B.C. and 3000 B.C. It was marked by the appearance of typologically more advanced ground stone implements (basin metates, a wider range of handstone forms, and pestles) and of flaked stone implements similar to those present in the Sulphur Spring stage. Projectile points were recovered at some Chiricahua stage sites but were interpreted as intrusive on the basis of their manufacture by pressure flaking, a technique that Sayles presumed was not part of the technological repertoire of the Chiricahua Cochise people. Instances of direct superposition of

such artifact assemblages above Sulphur Spring stage sites and their occurrence in the fills of erosional channels truncating Pleistocene deposits indicated a mid-postglacial age.

Sites of the San Pedro stage represented an anomaly compared with known Chiricahua and Sulphur Spring stage sites. Some San Pedro sites exposed in arroyos were characterized by thick, well-developed, highly organic deposits that extended laterally for considerable distances and that contained abundant artifacts and fire-cracked rocks, large pits, hearths, and possibly pit houses. Sayles conducted small-scale excavations in a portion of one such site near Fairbank on the San Pedro River (Fig. 1.1) and designated it the type site for the stage. He mentioned that "neither the excavation nor frequent and careful examinations of the exposure produced a single sherd" (Sayles 1941: 21–22). Clearly the overall impression created by the deposits at this site and others like it was their strikingly similar appearance to younger ceramic period sites.

The material remains of the San Pedro stage consisted of ground stone implements like those at earlier sites, except the handstones were generally larger. The flaked stone artifacts appeared to be more varied and, relative to the ground stone tools, more abundant than at sites of earlier stages. Projectile points with broad lateral notches were part of this assemblage. In concert with the relative abundance of flaked tools, these points suggested the possibility that hunting was of greater importance during this interval than previously. There was no archaeological evidence that agriculture was practiced. The deposits containing San Pedro stage sites were determined to be of late postglacial age by Antevs, who suggested that the stage encompassed the period from approximately 3000 B.C. to 500 B.C. Sayles noted some resemblance of San Pedro artifacts and features to those reported for Basketmaker II.

As later observed by Haury (1983), in 1941 the Cochise culture was greeted with some skepticism. Despite the reservations held by a few people about the Sulphur Spring stage (Kelley 1959), the Cochise culture became established as the only cultural-historical framework that encompassed the entire preceramic, post-Pleistocene epoch. Haury's (1950) own investigations at Ventana Cave in southwestern Arizona did much to refine the age and validity of the Cochise culture and to expand the material inventory of the stages.

Although the dating and material composition of the Sulphur Spring, Chiricahua, and San Pedro stages have been debated and modified over the half century since the Cochise culture was first presented by Sayles and

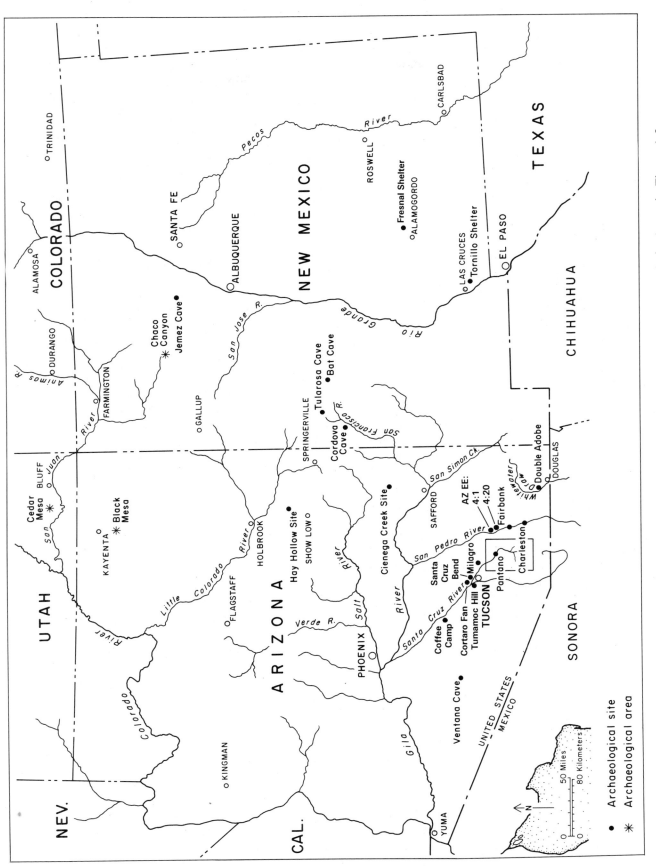

Figure 1.1. Locations of late preceramic sites in the American Southwest. Area in rectangle is shown in Figure 1.2.

Antevs, these comments indicate our understanding of it by the mid–1950s. With this foundation in mind, we focus our attention on the development of knowledge about the youngest part of the preceramic period up to the initial research by the University of Arizona and the Arizona State Museum in the Cienega Creek Basin.

INVESTIGATION OF THE LATE PRECERAMIC PERIOD PRIOR TO 1955

The San Pedro stage of the Cochise culture was accepted as representative of the late preceramic period, and most of the archaeologists working in the southern portion of the Southwest supported the concept. Sayles continued his research on the San Pedro stage and established that pit houses were indeed present at San Pedro sites in the Sulphur Spring and San Pedro valleys (Sayles 1945). San Pedro stage deposits were identified at Ventana Cave, although they occurred in the moist midden and thus yielded only stone artifacts (Haury 1950).

A second cave site excavated in the late 1940s, Bat Cave in west-central New Mexico (Fig. 1.1), contained dry deposits with indications that the San Pedro stage people of that region had been farmers of maize, squash, and beans. However, the impact of the arrival of agriculture apparently had an imperceptible effect on the material culture and lifeway of the San Pedro people: villages did not appear, ground and flaked stone tools showed no significant morphological change, and life in general seemed little changed from the preceding Chiricahua stage when maize apparently made its initial appearance in the Southwest (Dick 1965). The inference drawn from these observations was that agriculture was but a minor "dietary supplement" to an otherwise hunting and gathering economy. Investigations by Paul Sydney Martin at Tularosa Cave, Cordova Cave (Fig. 1.1), and other nearby rock shelters only 40 km southwest of Bat Cave produced further evidence of late preceramic agriculture but did not contradict the general impression that agriculture was of minimal importance (Martin and others 1952, 1954). Martin labeled these deposits simply as "prepottery," eschewing use of the San Pedro and Cochise culture systematics.

Surface sites in central New Mexico (Campbell and Ellis 1952; Agogino and Hibben 1958) and east-central Arizona (Wendorf and Thomas 1951) yielded artifacts similar in morphology to those of the San Pedro stage. Morris and Burgh (1954) excavated two late preceramic sites near Durango in southwestern Colorado (Fig. 1.1)

that contained large structures, storage pits and cists, and burials. They identified the sites, Talus Village and Falls Creek Shelter, as Basketmaker II, but pointed out their resemblances to San Pedro stage sites. These similarities hinted at the existence of broad, regional relationships among late preceramic cultures.

A far-reaching development in the late 1940s and early 1950s was radiocarbon dating, which permitted for the first time the direct determination of the ages of preceramic remains. Some of the first samples to be dated were from preceramic sites in the Southwest. Dates between approximately 500 B.C. and A.D. 200 were obtained from samples collected at the San Pedro type site at Fairbank and at another San Pedro site in the Sulphur Spring Valley (Libby 1955: 113, C–518, 519). San Pedro deposits in Bat Cave, also among the first archaeological samples dated by Libby, ranged from approximately 900 B.C. to 100 B.C. (Dick 1965). Maize cobs provided two dates for the prepottery levels of Tularosa Cave, approximately 300 B.C. to 200 B.C.

Thus, by the mid-1950s, sites dating to the San Pedro stage, or what is referred to as the late preceramic period, were known to be widespread in the southern portions of Arizona and New Mexico. In ecological terms, these people were viewed as hunters and gatherers who practiced a kind of desultory agriculture that produced little or no change in the mobile life-style they had inherited from their predecessors. It was in this intellectual environment that the first work was done in the Cienega Valley of southeastern Arizona.

THE LATE PRECERAMIC PERIOD IN THE CIENEGA VALLEY

Shortly after the discoveries made in the highland rock shelters of New Mexico had been published, the University of Arizona and the Arizona State Museum launched a program of studies in the Cienega Valley of southeastern Arizona. After moving to the University of Arizona in 1937, Haury remained interested in the problems of preceramic archaeology. Sayles was hired by Haury as Curator of the Arizona State Museum in 1943, and the two of them collaborated on several studies over the next two decades.

Both Haury and Sayles were united by a strong belief in the value of archaeological sites buried in alluvial contexts for understanding the lifeways of early foragers and the environments in which they operated, and both shared an enthusiasm for fieldwork. Haury, in particular, strongly encouraged interest in such problems by taking students on field trips to view archaeological sites in alluvial contexts. Often the students provided both survey and shovel labor during extended trips on holidays and weekends. Only 30 airline miles from the University campus and possessing numerous alluvial exposures with deeply buried sites, the Cienega Creek area was ideal for research and teaching (Fig. 1.2). From the late 1940s on, field parties from University classes visited the area and recorded sites up and down the creek and its tributaries. A more formal survey of a large portion of the basin was conducted from 1948 to 1951 by Swanson (1951). His survey revealed 15 preceramic sites, 7 of which were exposed in arroyos, and it laid the ground work for subsequent investigations.

The Cienega Creek Basin may be briefly characterized as a broad valley bordered on the east by the Whetstone Mountains and Mustang Hills, on the south by the Canelo Hills, and on the west by the Santa Rita Mountains and Empire Mountains (Fig. 1.2). The headward reaches of Cienega Creek are ephemeral, but perennial flow occurs throughout most of the lower half of its course. Its name derives from "cienega" or "cienaga," a Spanish word generally applied to groundwater supported marshes. Such marshes occur in several locales along the stream today. Cienega Creek flows through a grassland or semidesert grassland; mesquite and other shrubs have extensively "invaded" this community in the lower one-third of the valley. Numerous ephemeral tributaries join Cienega Creek from the surrounding mountain ranges. Along with many parts of Cienega Creek, these drainages have been deeply trenched by erosion over the past century or so, revealing long histories of alluvial deposition exposed in banks up to 5 m or 6 m high.

The Discovery and Investigation of AZ EE:2:30 (ASM)

In 1954, an exposure of dark gray sediments containing abundant artifacts, fire-cracked rocks, and animal bone was discovered in the floor of the 5–m-deep arroyo of Matty Wash, a major tributary of Cienega Creek (Fig. 1.2). The site extended along the outside of a bend in the channel, and the continuing erosional deepening of the wash there showed that the deposit had considerable lateral extent. The deposit was assigned number AZ EE:2:30 in the site survey system of the Arizona State Museum and was tested in 1955 during three days of the Easter break by Haury, Sayles, Edward B. Danson, and five University of Arizona students.

In 1956, Frank W. Eddy, then a graduate student at the University of Arizona, became interested in pursuing work in the Cienega Creek–Matty Canyon area for his master's thesis. The goal of his research was the study of "interrelationships between culture and environment through time in a selected portion of the Cienega Creek basin" (Eddy 1958: 1). An implicitly cultural-ecological theoretical base guided the study, which consisted of three major tasks: (1) excavation of AZ EE:2:30, including integration of information from the 1955 testing; (2) limited excavations at a small number of other preceramic and ceramic period sites; and (3) archaeological survey and geologic mapping of the arroyo walls and surrounding terrace surfaces.

Eddy's research followed the interdisciplinary pattern pioneered in southeastern Arizona by Haury, Sayles, and Antevs, and culminated in 1958 with his master's thesis, "A Sequence of Cultural and Alluvial Deposits in the Cienega Creek Basin, Southeastern Arizona." It contained appendixes by M. E. Cooley on the alluvial geology of the area; wood charcoal identifications by Terah L. Smiley; identifications of animal bone and an assessment of mammal habitats based on work by William J. Schaldach, Jr., and James J. Hester; and an examination of the nonmarine molluscs by Robert J. Drake. Drake later published his findings separately (Drake 1959). Subsequent to Eddy's work, both Paul Schultz Martin (Martin, Schoenwetter, and Arms 1961; Martin 1963) and James Schoenwetter (1960) conducted intensive studies of surface and alluvial pollen in the same area. Twenty-five years later, Eddy's thesis was revised and published as an *Anthropological Paper of the University of Arizona* (Eddy and Cooley 1983). Although that monograph addressed the full spectrum of local prehistory and history, it is the research at the late preceramic sites that is of particular importance to this study.

The 1955 excavations in Test 1 in the "midden," as the cultural deposit at AZ EE:2:30 was termed, had exposed four large pits, a dog burial, and a cultural deposit some 30 cm to 40 cm thick, all in an area less than 3.5 m long by 2.0 m wide (Figs. 1.3–1.5). Eddy's own excavations included work in three more areas to the south, east, and northwest of the initial testing. Test 2, located about 16 m south of Test 1, produced seven pits and three burials; four additional, partial burials were recovered from the arroyo bank immediately north of Test 2. Midway between Tests 1 and 2 was yet another burial exposed by the arroyo; it was excavated as an isolated feature. Test 3 was placed on a point bar on the inside of the arroyo channel bend, about 7 m east of

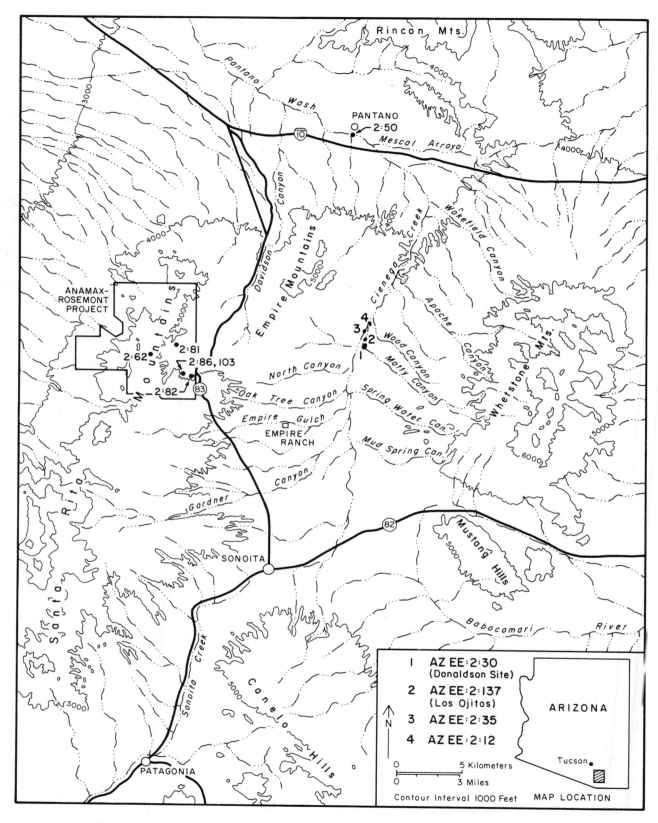

Figure 1.2. The Cienega Creek Basin and surrounding topography, showing the locations of late preceramic sites that have been investigated (all site numbers preceded by AZ EE:).

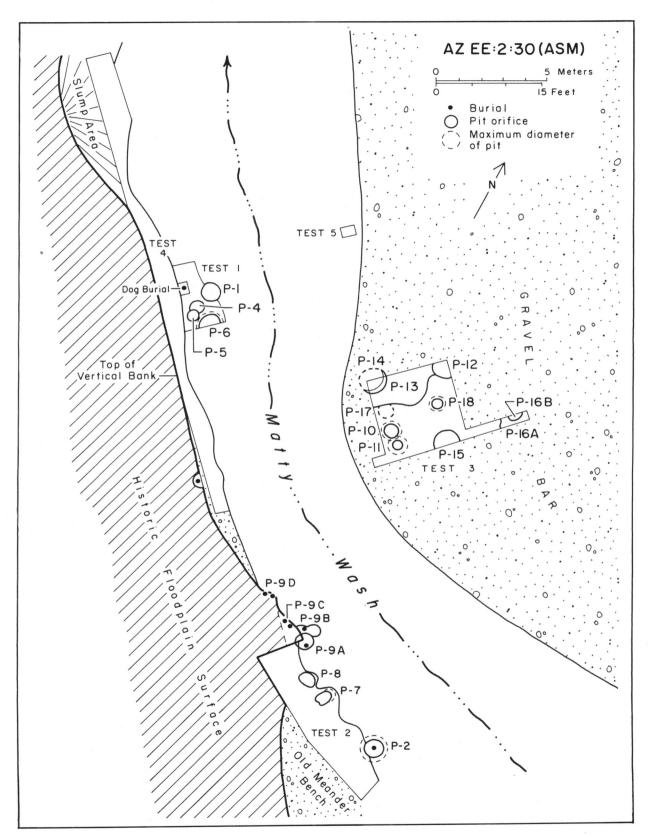

Figure 1.3. Site AZ EE:2:30 (ASM), showing the locations of archaeological excavations reported by Frank W. Eddy. (Redrawn from Eddy 1958, Figure 4.)

Figure 1.4. The appearance of AZ EE:2:30 in 1955 during initial test excavations. View is downstream. People at the center are at work on Test 1; Test 2 was later excavated just behind the man in the foreground. (ASM photograph 3985 by Emil W. Haury.)

Figure 1.5. Excavations at AZ EE:2:30 in 1955, looking upstream. The crew on the right is working in Test 1; the man at far right is E. B. Sayles. The person at far left is digging in the vicinity of Eddy's 1957 Test 3. (ASM photograph 3988 by Emil W. Haury.)

Test 1. It revealed 10 more pit features. Two additional areas of work, Tests 4 and 5 (Fig. 1.3), produced no features. The 5-m-high west bank of the arroyo was profile mapped in continuous fashion, approximately from Test 2 to Test 4. The combined areas of all test units totaled about 65 square meters. Eddy determined that the deposit was at least 41 m long by 15.5 m wide, but cautioned that these were minimum figures.

The abundant cultural remains in this limited exposure included some 141 "intentionally fashioned tools" of flaked and ground stone, and an additional 268 "flake knives and scrapers" that were not included in the tabulation of implements because they were not perceived to be an "intentionally fashioned tool form" (Eddy 1958: 47). Also recovered were bone awls, tubes, and ornaments, and antler flintknapping tools. Eddy concluded that the "tool complex agrees in its overall form" with that of the San Pedro stage of the Cochise culture.

Several radiocarbon dates were obtained from AZ EE:2:30, all assayed at the University of Arizona's then new Carbon-14 Age Determination Laboratory. Wood charcoal from three pit features yielded the following results (Eddy 1958, Table 8): from undercut Pit 14, three subsamples dated to 3080 ± 300 B.P. (A-86a), 3660 ± 400 B.P. (A-86b), and 3180 ± 300 B.P. (A-86c), giving a three-assay average of 3307 ± 400 B.P. (A-86av); from undercut Pit 11, a date of 2550 ± 300 B.P. (A-85); and from straight-sided Pit 1 a date of 1950 ± 200 B.P. (A-74). Of this 1,357-year span, he observed that it was "unusual to find such an extended period of time involved in a single site" (Eddy 1958: 92). All of the dates were solid carbon assays.

The Alluvial Record

In conjunction with Spade Cooley, then a graduate student in the Geology Department at the University of Arizona, Eddy worked out a general stratigraphic framework for the alluvial deposits in the area (Cooley 1958; Eddy and Cooley 1983: 6-9). These deposits are described in detail in Chapter 3 (Figs. 3.2, 3.3).

Dating of the alluvial deposits was accomplished primarily by archaeological associations. Preceramic remains were contained within Units 4, 5, and 7 and were resting on top of the paleosol that had developed on Unit 100, the oldest alluvium in the area. Unit 3 contained ceramic period sites and features attributed to the Hohokam. Historic artifacts were on top of Unit 2 and within Unit 1. Cooley produced an isometric fence diagram that showed the interrelationships of these units to

one another along Cienega Creek and Matty Canyon and projected correlations between the two drainages (Cooley 1958, Fig. 22; Eddy and Cooley 1983, Fig. 5.1).

Eddy (1958) noted that throughout the entire sequence of alluvial deposits there was evidence of human presence, ranging from scattered artifacts to well-developed settlements. Moreover, the complex interaction of ephemeral tributaries such as Matty Wash with the perennially wet Cienega Creek created an intricate suite of depositional environments and opportunities for human use of the landscape. Cienegas seemed to appear early in the sequence and to persist throughout it.

Investigations at Other Preceramic Sites

In addition to the Donaldson Site, Eddy's research in the Matty Canyon-Cienega Creek confluence area (Eddy and Cooley 1983, Fig. 1.3) included survey and geological mapping of archaeological and alluvial deposits. He conducted limited excavations of features and deposits at three other buried preceramic sites.

One of these sites was AZ EE:2:35 (ASM), located at the base of the east bank of Cienega Creek approximately 1.2 km (0.75 mile) due north of AZ EE:2:30 (Fig. 1.2). Described as a buried "trash zone" with five pit hearth features exposed over 60 m of the bank, this occupation occurred in a deposit of sand (Unit 5) stratigraphically below Unit 3, which overlay AZ EE:2:30. In the published version of his thesis, this site and its stratigraphic context are shown in a pair of photographs (Eddy and Cooley 1983, Figs. 2.5, 2.6). Two of the features were excavated, and the overlying trash zone was sampled. The bones of mule deer, antelope, and jackrabbit were recovered from the trash zone, and the two hearths yielded charcoal, fire-cracked rocks, and two milling stone fragments. One of the excavated pits (Lens 4) yielded sufficient charcoal for radiocarbon dating by the solid carbon method. A date of 2610 ± 250 B.P. (A-87) was obtained, and three assays were made of subsamples of a large mass of charcoal (Eddy 1958, Table 8): 3180 ± 300 B.P. (A-89a), 2620 ± 200 B.P. (A-89b), and 2520 ± 300 B.P. (A-89c). Averaging the three produced a value of 2773 ± 300 B.P. (A-89av).

Subsequently, Paul Schultz Martin collected charcoal from this site during his alluvial pollen research and submitted it to the Shell Development Laboratory, which used the CO_2 gas method. The resulting date, 2800 ± 190 B.P. (Sh-5356), was not available for Eddy's use at the time he completed his thesis, but was included in his later publication (Eddy and Cooley

1983, Table 3.1). Although no temporally diagnostic artifacts were recovered from AZ EE:2:35, the solid carbon dates placed it within the broad range of dates from EE:2:30, and Eddy classified it as a San Pedro stage site. Martin's date supported this assignment.

About 2 km (1.3 miles) north of AZ EE:2:30, along the east bank of Matty Canyon and continuing into a small tributary arroyo, was another buried preceramic site containing artifacts and features in four superposed strata (Eddy 1958, Fig. 12). Designated AZ EE:2:12 (ASM), this locus had been discovered in 1948 by Haury. Eddy mapped the profile of the deposits, excavated one hearth, and collected artifacts. It was an important site because it contained scattered artifacts in the oldest of the post-Pleistocene alluvial deposits, Unit 7, and revealed artifacts and features above Unit 7 in a sand facies of Unit 4. The uppermost traces of occupation, fire-cracked rock clusters, were in the basal part of Unit 3. Eddy excavated one hearth in upper Unit 4, recovering fire-cracked rocks, four handstones, a milling stone fragment, a ground stone disc, debitage, and a deer antler tine. Small pieces of charcoal were present in the feature but were not collected. Fortunately, a complete San Pedro projectile point was discovered near a second hearth in the lower part of Unit 4 (Eddy 1958, Fig. 14c; Eddy and Cooley 1983, Fig. 2.1c), establishing a late preceramic age for the material in Unit 4. The scattered artifacts in Unit 7 were thus at least of San Pedro stage age, and perhaps earlier.

Two other buried localities containing preceramic remains apparently also received some investigation, but unfortunately, neither site was described in detail by Eddy. One, AZ EE:2:13 (ASM), was in pre-Unit 4 deposits. The other, AZ EE:2:33 (ASM), lay near the base of Unit 3 sediments in a stratigraphic position similar to that of AZ EE:2:30 (Eddy 1958: 56–57).

LATE PRECERAMIC ADAPTATIONS TO THE CIENEGA CREEK BASIN

Eddy discussed the socioeconomic aspects of the late preceramic occupation in the Cienega Creek Basin by using Julian Steward's (1955) description of the Great Basin Shoshonean lifeway as a reasonable analog. He suggested that AZ EE:2:30 might represent an encampment occupied by an "association of families (band)" similar to ethnographically known Shoshonean winter camps. Historically, such temporary large settlements were made possible by stored surpluses of piñon pine nuts and the presence of sufficiently large populations of jackrabbits or antelope to make communal hunts pro-

ductive. By analogy, the habitation at AZ EE:2:30 perhaps existed because of a "concentrated food supply of sufficient quantity to allow settlement in a restricted area" (Eddy 1958: 59). Eddy suggested that communal hunting of rabbits and antelope by members of a band would have been an activity of primary economic importance. Collecting local grass seeds and mesquite beans, and perhaps marsh greens and tubers from the cienegas, would further support such a settlement. From this base, foraging expeditions by individual families to the nearby mountains to procure deer, bighorn sheep, elk, and acorns were feasible. Procurement of desert resources such as cactus fruit could have been achieved in the same way. Because there were no archaeological indications of agriculture, Eddy assumed that hunting and gathering were the principal subsistence tactics. Despite the attractiveness of the analogy, Eddy (1958: 54–55) noted that the midden deposit at AZ EE:2:30 was somewhat at odds with the expected appearance of a Shoshonean campsite:

> The vertical growth of the midden trash debris is highly unusual in an open camp site. In such a situation, accumulation of debris is generally in a lateral fashion. This factor suggests an annual visitation to one particular spot for camping purposes or even the semi-sedentary occupation of a habitation area by an assumed pre-agricultural group. Whichever situation actually existed, a reasonably permanent nature of the food quest is implied. Such a situation is not generally found associated with an economy featuring solely the hunting of large mammals or the trapping, netting, or snaring of smaller rodents. However, these techniques, coupled with activities focused on the gathering of plant foods, might account for a more stable settlement. This balance in subsistence activities could be accounted for by both a wide range of easily accessible life zones and the even more convenient local cienega areas containing what may have been an abundant source of wild foods.

Eddy interpreted the archaeological record as precisely as possible with the information at hand, but recognized an apparently contradictory relationship between the extensive, artifact-rich deposit at AZ EE:2:30 and the lifeway inferred to have created it. Such a deposit suggested a far more intensive, stable occupation of a single locality than was known for any arid lands hunting-gathering group. Eddy's thoughts echoed those of Sayles, who was similarly perplexed by the San Pedro stage type site near Fairbank.

DEVELOPING PERCEPTIONS OF THE LATE PRECERAMIC PERIOD

Following the investigations of Frank Eddy, Paul Schultz Martin and James Schoenwetter of the University of Arizona Department of Geosciences initiated palynological research at a series of localities in southeastern Arizona. They were the ones to actually provide the first evidence that the late preceramic foragers of the Cienega Creek Basin had also been cultivators. From two separate alluvial sequences, one in Matty Canyon and one along Cienega Creek, maize pollen was identified from nonsite deposits (Units 4 and 5) radiocarbon dated to the last two to three centuries B.C. (Schoenwetter 1960; Paul Schultz Martin 1963: 31–34, Figs. 17, 18; 1983b). In the revised version of his thesis, Eddy (Eddy and Cooley 1983: 46) integrated this information, recognizing that agriculture had been part of the San Pedro stage subsistence system. The implications of this addition for understanding the nature of settlement at AZ EE:2:30 were not considered, however. With the close of Martin's research, archaeological activities in the area essentially ceased.

From the late 1950s until 1980, the growth of information on early agriculture in the Southwest was slow. Discoveries of maize continued in preceramic deposits in caves or rock shelters. Jemez Cave in northwestern New Mexico was first reported by Alexander and Reiter (1935), but not dated until much later (Crane and Griffin 1958; Ford 1975). Other reported rock shelter sites included Swallow Cave in northeastern Chihuahua (Mangelsdorf and Lister 1956; Lister 1958), En Medio Shelter located a short distance northwest of Albuquerque (Irwin-Williams and Tomkins 1968), and Fresnal Shelter in central New Mexico (Human Systems Research 1973). Open sites also yielded maize pollen in preceramic contexts, including the Cienega Creek Site near Point of Pines in east-central Arizona (Haury 1957; Paul Schultz Martin and Schoenwetter 1960); Double Adobe IV (Paul Schultz Martin 1963) and the Pantano Site (Hemmings and others 1968) in southeastern Arizona; the Rio Rancho phase sites near Albuquerque (Reinhart 1967); and the Hay Hollow Site, a pit house village in east-central Arizona (Bohrer 1972; Paul Sydney Martin and Plog 1973; Fritz 1974). Except for the sites in southeastern Arizona and near Albuquerque, all others were in the mountains (Fig. 1.1).

The Haury Model

Interest in the initial appearance of agriculture in the Southwest increased during the 1950s and 1960s, and explanatory models for the transition from hunting and gathering to agricultural economies were developed.

One particularly influential work was the theory advanced by Haury (1962) concerning the entry of maize into the Southwest via the "highland corridor." Observing that virtually all of the known Southwestern sites with evidence of preceramic agriculture (Bat Cave, Tularosa Cave, the Cienega Creek Site near Point of Pines) were at elevations above 1,850 m (6,000 feet), he inferred that early maize and other crops must have been adapted only to the more mesic conditions existing in the Mogollon highlands of east-central Arizona and west-central New Mexico. Although arriving by approximately 2500 B.C. from the Sierra Madre uplands of Mexico, early agriculture "left no measurable effect upon the recipients" for a period of nearly 2,000 years. Further, dispersal of agriculture to the lower elevation, more arid environments of the Colorado Plateau and southern Basin-and-Range province was delayed until around 500 B.C. Haury was careful to point out that earlier Cochise culture occupants of the area were involved in an intensive plant-gathering economy, perhaps even cultivating chenopods and amaranths. They were thus "preadapted" or predisposed to accept plant husbandry, and there was even some evidence of settled living at some San Pedro stage sites, albeit without direct evidence of maize agriculture. Nevertheless, he argued, it was not until more drought-tolerant cultivars appeared or techniques of irrigation agriculture were developed that agriculture became important in the lower elevations of the Southwest. Settled village life did not appear until near the time of Christ.

Dick (1965) posited much the same scenario as Haury, and later explanatory models such as those of Whalen (1973) and Woodbury and Zubrow (1979) were in essential agreement with Haury's perception.

The Initial Appearance of Agriculture

Michael Berry (1982, 1985) reviewed the age of maize in the Southwest in the early 1980s and demonstrated that the previously accepted dates of 2000 B.C. or older for the first appearance of maize were not supported by a critical evaluation of the archaeological evidence. Poor excavation methodology, dubious association of cultigens with dated sample materials, dates on wood or charcoal rather than the cultigens themselves, and dates produced by the obsolete and often inaccurate solid carbon method all combined to give an erroneous impression of the antiquity of maize. Berry (1985) concluded that 500 B.C., or at most 750 B.C., were more reasonable dates for the initial appearance of maize.

Berry's review coincided with the development of the AMS (accelerating mass spectrometry) radiocarbon dating technology. One of the first AMS facilities was the University of Arizona–National Science Foundation laboratory, which targeted the direct dating of cultigens as a research priority. Renewed field research, most notably the University of Michigan's reinvestigation of Bat Cave in 1981 and 1983 (Wills 1988a), supplied new samples of cultigens from carefully controlled excavations at this pivotal site. Maize cob fragments or kernels from several other sites scattered across the Southwest, both known and newly sampled, were also dated. Soil flotation provided recovery of carbonized maize from open sites in southeastern Arizona such as Tumamoc Hill (P. Fish and others 1986), Matty Canyon and Milagro (B. Huckell 1988), the Cortaro Fan Site (Roth 1989), as well as from the Chaco Canyon area (Simmons 1986). At present, these directly dated cultigens demonstrate that maize and squash certainly had reached the Southwest sometime between 1500 B.C. and 1000 B.C., and there are a few assays that suggest the possibility of even greater antiquity, perhaps back to 2000 B.C. (Smiley and Parry 1990). Beans appear to have arrived a few centuries later than maize and squash, perhaps around 500 B.C. As more cultigens are recovered and dated from new sites, these intervals may change, but it is clear that agriculture appeared in the Southwest at least by the beginning of the first millennium B.C.

The Spread of Agriculture

During the last two decades, several archaeologists have proposed explanatory models for the process by which agricultural production strategies reached the Southwest from its center of domestication in Mesoamerica. One general class of models proposes that crop plants and the technical knowledge needed for their cultivation and use spread across a base of preexisting hunter-gatherer populations. A second class of models posits the immigration and spread of populations already in command of agriculture into the Southwest, replacing or displacing existing foraging groups. A third model, based on morphological and ecological changes in maize and the development of cultivation practices, has recently been suggested as a partially independent alternative to the other two (Matson 1991).

Models of the first general class are the lineal descendants of Haury's 1962 formulations. Ford (1981) refined and updated Haury's model, portraying the spread of what he termed the "Upper Sonoran Agricultural Complex" (maize, squash, bottle gourd, and common bean) into the higher regions of the Southwest (above 2,000 m or 6,500 feet) among nomadic hunter-gatherers. These crops did not serve as dietary staples because of their low productivity and the conflicting demands of mobility as required by hunting and gathering with farming. The value of cultivated crops was that they produced localized, high density patches of edible resources that were predictable in time and space. Further, cultivation created disturbed habitats (actively used and abandoned fields) favored by valued wild annual plants, thereby creating even greater concentrations of resources (Ford 1984).

Building on Ford's ideas, Minnis (1985a, 1992) asserted that what he termed "casual" agriculture might be readily integrated into a hunter-gatherer economy at a low level without causing any dramatic changes in the basic subsistence-settlement system. As long as the goal of food production was to supplement rather than replace hunting and gathering, the labor demands associated with agriculture might not interfere with the demands of higher mobility associated with foraging. Agriculture would thus enhance overall economic security without detracting from the primary subsistence pursuits. The Western Apache, in Minnis' view, were an excellent historic analog of such a strategy. Why hunter-gatherers should adopt agriculture at all was further considered by Minnis, who suggested that either necessity or opportunism might be involved. Increased population density, reduced access to resources, or climatic changes or fluctuations might dictate the adoption of agriculture to offset reduced resource availability. Opportunistic adoption of agriculture might occur simply because cultivation could enhance economic security with little additional investment of labor. Minnis added that these stress-based and opportunistic models were not mutually exclusive.

Several archaeologists (Hard 1986; Hunter-Anderson 1986; MacNeish 1992; Wills 1988a, 1988b, 1990) have suggested that Southwestern foragers adopted agriculture to offset loss of access to wild resources caused by increased population during the late preceramic period. Hard (1986) observed that the times at which some level of dependence on agriculture became important should be a function of variation in the natural productivity of particular biotic communities in different parts of the Southwest. Specifically, he suggested that under conditions of population growth, earlier adoption of agriculture by foragers should occur in those environments where the potential to intensify hunting and gathering was low. Wills (1988a) cited increasing environmental uncertainty caused by pressure on the resource base by growing regional populations as a factor that dictated the adoption of agriculture to enhance resource predictability. The addition of cultivation would create resources with a yield highly predictable in time and space and amenable to storage. This might in turn foster the establishment of short-term settlements with domestic structures and storage features in areas where access to and monitoring of the development of wild resources would be enhanced. Knowledge of locales where the largest harvests of wild resources could be obtained would, under conditions of environmental uncertainty, enhance a population's ability to obtain sufficient food from gathering and hunting. Suzanne and Paul Fish and John Madsen (1990, 1992) have suggested that in southern Arizona the high productivity of the Sonoran Desertscrub and other easily accessible biotic communities may have promoted the establishment of sedentary or semisedentary communities of hunter-gatherers prior to the arrival of agriculture. These communities may have existed in certain locales with easy access to a few critical resources such as grasses and mesquite. Mobility, then, would have been limited to simple biseasonal moves, or perhaps none at all. They posit that such communities would be in a much better position to accept agriculture and its associated labor demands because they were already sedentary or nearly so.

The second class of models invokes the arrival and spread of agriculture in the Southwest with immigrant populations already involved in farming. The roots of these models are more specifically archaeological than the models of the first class; that is, they are developed from empirical observations of the archaeological record. The arrival of agriculture with immigrants has been advocated most recently by Michael and Claudia Berry (M. Berry 1982; Berry and Berry 1986). Observing a dramatic change in material culture from the Chiricahua stage to the San Pedro stage, the Berrys suggest that this change marks the arrival of immigrants bringing maize agriculture with them. Environmental conditions of the time, specifically the "Fairbank Drought" identified by Antevs (1955) at the San Pedro stage type site, forced these immigrants into more mesic upland environments and encouraged agricultural production. With climatic amelioration, the lower elevation environments became more habitable and agricultural populations then dispersed to many different parts of the Southwest.

I have applied this model to southeastern Arizona and have suggested that improving conditions along permanent rivers and streams of this area fostered the spread of agriculture into the region (B. Huckell 1990, 1992a). Recent investigations at Sayles' Fairbank Site, as well as excavations at the site of Milagro (Huckell and Huckell 1984; B. Huckell 1990), reaffirm the distinctive character of San Pedro material culture, suggest apparent connections to the south (such as fired clay human figurines, shell jewelry, and bell-shaped storage pits), and document extended site occupational intensity and duration. Small domestic structures and bell-shaped storage pits are prominent features at these sites. Further, maize macrofossils are surprisingly abundant in these sites, a condition consistent with site locations adjacent to prime arable land and one that suggests substantial economic reliance on agricultural production. If the initial appearance of agriculture in southeastern Arizona occurs as a well-developed part of the subsistence economy in the context of large, intensively occupied sites, immigration of populations practicing a mixed farming-foraging economy must be considered as a viable possible explanation of its arrival. Unfortunately, the paucity of comparable information from northern Mexico and a limited understanding of the cultural situation in the Southwestern region immediately prior to the appearance of these San Pedro settlements make this class of models difficult to empirically verify.

As a final observation, it may be that both models are applicable across the Southwestern region as a whole, depending on the particular area and period of time being addressed. Thus, the adoption of agriculture by indigenous foraging populations may have occurred in one place, and the northward spread of populations already practicing agriculture may have occurred in another (B. Huckell 1990; Smiley and Parry 1990).

R. G. Matson (1991) has advanced what he calls a maize evolutionary model as an alternative to models of the first two classes. It is based on the evolutionary history of maize; on the morphology and ecology of the maize cultivar Chapalote, putatively the earliest maize found in the Southwest; and on changes in cultivation practices across space and time. The earliest maize agriculture, according to Matson, was floodwater farming of Chapalote in the southern Basin-and-Range province at approximately 1000 B.C. With the development of cultivars more tolerant of colder, shorter growing seasons, floodwater farming appeared on the Colorado Plateau by 500 B.C. with the Basketmaker II culture. With the development of maize cultivars better adapted to extreme drought stress and colder, still briefer growing seasons, dry farming cultivation practices reached the northern part of the Plateau by A.D. 200 to 400. Matson stated that his model could prove viable regardless of which of the other two classes of models may eventually prove correct. One element of Matson's model, the importance of genetic change in maize as a means of understanding its spread across the Southwest, echoes earlier models (Haury 1962; Dick 1965) that specified the increased productive capacity of maize over time.

In summary, the mode by which the adoption and spread of agriculture occurred in the Southwest remains the subject of discussion and modelling efforts. It was a complex process, and depending on the particular part of the Southwest and the time period under discussion, both of the first two classes of models may accurately portray that process. Changes in maize cultivars and the range of variation, identity, and relationships of early Southwestern maize remain topics in need of research. The need to better understand cultural and natural conditions immediately prior to the initial appearance of agriculture, both in the American Southwest and in the Mexican Northwest, seems an obvious priority for future research.

The Impact of Agriculture

There are two schools of thought, again in disagreement with one another, concerning what socioeconomic impact the adoption of agriculture may have had on late preceramic Southwestern populations. One view is that agriculture played a useful but minor role for several centuries if not longer, until the rise of early ceramic period villages after the second century A.D. The second position is that agriculture produced rapid, substantial changes in late preceramic subsistence and settlement.

The former position has a long history, extending back to the Haury model. Based on the apparent lack of change in material culture and settlement following the initial appearance of maize in the Mogollon highland sites such as Bat Cave, Tularosa Cave, and the Cienega Creek Site (Point of Pines area), Haury reasoned that preceramic groups failed to integrate agriculture into their economies to any significant degree (Haury 1962). In searching for a reason, Haury turned to the botanical reconstructions of early maize, which portrayed the grain as primitive and incapable of producing significant yields (Mangelsdorf and Smith 1949). Only with the subsequent introduction of maize cultivars with greater productive capabilities did "village life" appear in the Southwest. Dick (1965), Woodbury and Zubrow (1979),

Ford (1981), Simmons (1986), and Minnis (1985a, 1992) have all agreed with Haury's assessment. Minnis, in fact, characterized the arrival of agriculture in the Southwest as a "monumental nonevent with little *immediate impact* on native human populations" (Minnis 1985a: 310, emphasis in the original). Maize and other cultigens simply served to augment hunting and gathering, enhancing economic security in some way but not creating excessive labor demands because agriculture was practiced on a "casual" basis. Crop failure was not catastrophic because primary economic dependence remained on foraging.

The second position is that agriculture was rapidly integrated into a prominent position in the economy of late preceramic Southwestern societies (Berry and Berry 1986; B. Huckell 1990; Smiley and Parry 1990; Wills and Huckell 1994). This view is derived from more recent research at some of the "classic" sites and newly investigated ones from various parts of the Southwest. One area that figures prominently in the development of this view is the southern portion of the Southwest, where maize macrofossils are abundant in sites of the San Pedro stage type (P. Fish and others 1986; Elson and Doelle 1987; Huckell and Huckell 1988; B. Huckell 1990). These sites are among the earliest in the Southwest with evidence for agriculture, and the levels of abundance of maize macrofossils often exceed the levels observed at younger Hohokam sites. Further, these settlements show profound differences in occupational intensity and permanence from any known sites dating to the preceding centuries. This increase in residential stability implies a decrease in residential mobility, or a reorganization of the type of mobility used to obtain wild resources, or both.

Smiley and Parry (1990) reviewed the dating of early agriculture across the Southwest, and noted that maize seems to have appeared at nearly the same time from the southern through the northern Southwest. In addition, they, too, observed significant change in the appearance, contents, and organization of Southwestern settlements at that time. Wills (1988a), reviewing Bat Cave, Tularosa Cave, and other late preceramic sites in the Mogollon Highlands, has pointed out that these sites in fact show either a change in the nature of occupation with the appearance of agriculture or reflect a pattern of greatly intensified use of these upland environments. Among the changes are the greater numbers of late preceramic components in that area, the appearance of storage pits, the abundance of evidence for cultigens, and the much higher densities of artifacts. The apparently coeval shift implies that agriculture was perceived as filling a critical need in the subsistence economy, perhaps providing buffering from the effects of climatically induced variation in the production of wild resources (B. Huckell 1990).

There has been little direct evidence of exactly how important agriculture initially was to these late preceramic societies, but coprolites and stable carbon isotope information on skeletons from Cedar Mesa, southeastern Utah, suggest a level of dependence on maize during the late Basketmaker II period that was only slightly less than that in the succeeding ceramic period (Matson and Chisholm 1991).

It has also been suggested (B. Huckell 1990; Wills 1988a; Wills and Huckell 1994) that the adoption of agriculture may have enhanced the effectiveness of hunting and gathering. The addition of cultigens may have allowed extended occupation in the upland parts of the region, in turn permitting more intensive utilization of wild plant and animal resources there (Wills 1988a). The inclusion of cultigens in the diet could facilitate overwintering in a residential location, reducing the need to forage and remain mobile during that season. The storability of maize and other cultigens would facilitate their use in overwintering in any part of the Southwest. In turn, this storage technology may have been extended to certain wild plant products, enhancing the efficiency of their use by extending the period of their availability and encouraging their collection in greater quantities.

Agriculture was embraced to varying degrees by late preceramic peoples across the Southwest. Its impact likely varied according to the ecological conditions in specific regions and to the perception by late preceramic societies of its usefulness to them (Hard 1986; Roth 1989, 1992; Smiley and Parry 1990; Wills and Huckell 1994).

These views on various issues in the transition to agriculture in the Southwest provide a coherent context for assessing the late preceramic settlements in the Cienega Valley. Clearly we are still struggling to adjust both theoretically based and empirically driven models to a rapidly growing and changing data base. These issues are addressed further in Chapter 8.

LATE PRECERAMIC CULTURAL SYSTEMATICS

The present taxonomy applied to the Archaic period, particularly to that portion of it after approximately 3500 B.P., has two major drawbacks. First, it no longer adequately represents our current knowledge of the subsistence economies of late preceramic groups, and second, it is perpetuating inaccurate perceptions of time-space relationships across the Southwest as a whole. If the functions of cultural systematics are to help organize perceptions of prehistoric cultural development and foster communication among scholars, some modifications are needed to accommodate the information that has accumulated during the past decade.

For some years it has been evident that the Cochise culture model in its original (Sayles and Antevs 1941) and revised (Sayles 1983) forms does not adequately portray the preceramic prehistory of southern Arizona and other parts of the Southwest (B. Huckell 1984a; Berry and Berry 1986; Wills 1988a). As a consequence and in recognition of material culture similarities across the Southwest, the terms "Archaic" or "Southwestern Archaic" have largely supplanted the term "Cochise culture." A three-part Early–Middle–Late Archaic nomenclature has been widely use in southern Arizona (B. Huckell 1984a). Other proposed systems of division for the Archaic period include that of the Berrys (1986; Period I, Period II, and Period III) and of Matson (1991; Earliest, Early, Middle, Late, Latest). "Archaic," as Cordell (1984) has noted, is used not only to refer to the post-Paleoindian to early ceramic time period (about 8,500 to 1,800 years ago), but also to identify a basic economic pattern or ecological adaptation consisting of broad-spectrum hunting and gathering. This dual usage, when coupled with other subregional systems of cultural taxonomy, leads to inconsistent use of the same terms for different periods of time across the Southwest and is particularly difficult with respect to the late part of the Archaic period.

Since the mid 1980s, "Late Archaic" has largely replaced "San Pedro stage Cochise" in southeastern Arizona and elsewhere. This usage has resulted in an unanticipated quandary, however, as more evidence of the presence and importance of agriculture has come to light from sites of this age in the southern Southwest. Moreover, "Late Archaic" on the Colorado Plateau and other parts of the northern Southwest commonly refers to the latest part of the preagricultural, preceramic record (Matson 1991); "Basketmaker II," of course, has long been used to characterize the earliest agricultural complex of the preceramic period in that region. Increasing evidence of the contemporaneity of the "Late Archaic" in southeastern Arizona with Basketmaker II on the Colorado Plateau further exacerbates this problem.

Continued use of "Late Archaic" to designate preceramic sites with evidence of agriculture is certainly confusing with respect to ecology. Not only does it conflict with an increasing body of evidence concerning the importance of agriculture (Huckell and Huckell 1988; B. Huckell 1990; Wills 1988a), but it is counterproductive to have "Archaic" used in two different senses within the Southwest as a whole.

To rectify these conceptual and terminological problems, I propose the reintroduction of an element of culture systematics first put forward more than 40 years ago: the Early Agricultural period (Woodbury 1993: 223; Paul Sydney Martin and Rinaldo 1951). This term was part of a comprehensive scheme for the designation of Southwestern cultural horizons that was conceived by Harold Colton, Fred Wendorf, and Ned Danson and presented to the 1953 Pecos Conference for consideration as a system encompassing the entire Southwestern region. Woodbury (1993) characterized the six-part system as ambitious and innovative, but noted that the response of conferees to it was apathy. Although the merits of the system as a whole are debatable, the Early Agricultural period provides a simple, effective solution to the Late Archaic problem with only slight modifications from the original definition.

As formulated by Colton, Wendorf, and Danson, the Early Agricultural period spanned an interval between 2500 B.C. and A.D. 500, and included Basketmaker II, Chiricahua and San Pedro Cochise, San Jose, and the Concho complex. The age range and associated cultural entities were clearly based heavily on what was then known of early agriculture from Bat Cave. Adjusting this definition to better fit current knowledge, I suggest that it be viewed as spanning the period of time from the initial appearance of agriculture between 1500 B.C. or 1200 B.C. to A.D. 200, and including San Pedro Cochise, Basketmaker II, and En Medio Oshara. Use of the label "Early Agricultural" to designate the final part of the preceramic period is appropriate, for it is with the arrival of agricultural production strategies that significant changes are observed in material culture, settlement occupational intensity, and patterns of land use. Adoption of the Early Agricultural period does not necessitate the abandonment of subregional systematics,

for as Irwin-Williams (1967) noted, taxonomies usually serve both regional (integrative) and more local (isolative) needs. The principal advantages of the Early Agricultural period as a taxonomic level are two: recognition of unifying temporal and cultural relationships across the Southwest, and more accurate characterization of the economic adaptations of this part of the late preceramic period.

In southern Arizona the Archaic period may be redefined as the preagricultural part of the preceramic period, equivalent with the former Early and Middle Archaic periods. It is beyond the scope of this report to consider how the Archaic period might be reconfigured, but one aspect of it may be to use the term "Late Archaic" for those preceramic groups that did not adopt agriculture.

For the remainder of this monograph, Early Agricultural period is used to designate the final portion of the preceramic prehistory of the Southwest. In addition, two phases of the Early Agricultural period are used to subdivide the period in southeastern Arizona: the San Pedro phase, representing the early part of the period, and the Cienega phase, encompassing the later part. Both terms were used previously by Matson in 1991, but not explicity defined, and I suggested this basic division some years earlier (B. Huckell 1984a). These phases are differentiated on the basis of artifact assemblages, architecture, and time. The San Pedro phase includes the patterns recognized by Sayles (1941, 1945, 1983) in his definition of the San Pedro stage of the Cochise culture and amplified by recent excavations (B Huckell 1990). The Cienega phase is based on information obtained from the Matty Canyon sites described herein, from AZ EE:2:30 and EE:2:137, and from recently investigated sites in the Tucson Basin (Mabry and Clark 1994). The San Pedro phase spans the interval from approximately 1500–1200 B.C. to 500 B.C., and the Cienega phase dates from 500 B.C. to A.D. 200. Specific definitions for each phase and consideration of other issues involved with the Early Agricultural period are presented in Chapter 8.

CHAPTER TWO

The Modern Environment of the Cienega Creek Basin

One of the most picturesque parts of southeastern Arizona is the Cienega Creek Basin. The broad, high valley contains an almost pure grassland, parts of which give the appearance of misplaced portions of the High Plains. Perhaps this land is so striking because it is located between the shrub-dominated desert grassland and desertscrub communities that fill the adjacent valleys of the Santa Cruz and San Pedro rivers to the west and east of it, respectively (Fig. 1.1). The basin is drained by Cienega Creek, which is today ephemeral in its upper reaches but perennial for the lower two-thirds to three-fourths of its length. This stream, the surrounding grassland, and nearby mountain ranges are the principal attractions responsible for human settlement of the basin from prehistoric times onward.

Eddy (1958; Eddy and Cooley 1983) has provided detailed descriptions of the environmental setting of the Cienega Valley. His treatment is briefly recapitulated to provide a general sense of the landscape, climate, and resources that surround the buried sites in Matty Canyon. This basin is also known as the Empire Valley, named after a huge nineteenth-century ranch that covered nearly all of it, and it was referred to as the Stock Valley in the 1880s and 1890s (Eddy 1958: 2). Following Eddy (1958), Cienega Valley and Cienega Creek Basin are used interchangeably in this volume.

PHYSIOGRAPHY OF THE CIENEGA CREEK BASIN

Like other basins in southern Arizona, the Cienega Valley is a north-south trending basin bordered by high mountain ranges (Fig. 1.2). It is thus a typical part of the Basin-and-Range Physiographic Province or, as Gehlbach (1981) has described it, a land of mountain islands and desert seas. This structural basin is demarcated on the west by the Santa Rita and Empire mountains, on the east by the Whetstone Mountains and Mustang Hills, and on the south by the Canelo Hills. The small Empire Mountain range defines the northwestern end of the basin; aligned on a northeast-southwest axis, it constricts the valley and forces Cienega Creek through a zone of limestone hills and terraces known as The Narrows. The mountain ranges are bordered by well-defined pediments and terraces, most of them constructed of coarse alluvium deposited by ephemeral drainages tributary to Cienega Creek. Nearer the axis of the valley are lower terraces formed on alluvium deposited by Cienega Creek. This piedmont has been dissected by ephemeral streams into a complex landscape of ridges and valleys.

The Santa Rita Mountains contain rocks of various kinds and ages, including Paleozoic sedimentary rocks, Mesozoic and Tertiary granite, Mesozoic volcanics and sediments, and some Precambrian granite. The Empire Mountains exhibit much the same composition, but the Whetstone Mountains and Mustang Hills on the east side of the basin are predominantly made up of Paleozoic sediments. The northern slopes of the Canelo Hills consist of Paleozoic sedimentary deposits and Mesozoic volcanic and sedimentary rocks. This diversity of rock types comprises numerous materials suitable for the manufacture of flaked and ground stone tools, including chert, chalcedony, silicified sediments, granite, porphyritic igneous rock, and vesicular basalt.

The Cienega Creek Basin is the product of block-faulting and igneous activity that occurred in three general episodes, beginning with the Laramide Orogeny that was initiated some 75 to 80 million years ago and ended about 50 million years ago. A second period of intense tectonism and volcanic activity known as the Mid-Tertiary Orogeny occurred between approximately 30 million years ago and 20 million years ago. It was followed by the Basin-and-Range Orogeny some 15 million years ago to 8 million years ago (Nations and Stump 1981). These events produced the classic basin-and-range topography, consisting of horst and graben faults in which two blocks rose in relation to a third, which dropped to create a basin. This process, coupled with subsequent erosion of the surrounding mountains and accompanying deposition in the valley during the Pliocene and Pleistocene, created a broad valley measuring some 26 km (16 miles) in length and up to 20 km (12.4 miles) in width. The surrounding mountains today reach elevations of 1,615 m (5,300 feet) in the Empire range, up to 2,340 m (7,680 feet) in the Whetstones, and as high as 2,880 m (9,450 feet) in the Santa Rita range.

Cienega Creek is the principal stream in the Cienega Valley, but not the only one; both Babocomari Creek and Sonoita Creek have their headwaters just inside the valley. Babocomari Creek, an eastward-flowing tributary of the San Pedro River, has captured most of the area between the Mustang Hills and Canelo Hills at the southeast end of the valley (Fig. 1.2). Sonoita Creek has its headwaters at the southwestern end of the valley and takes most of the runoff from the south end of the Santa Ritas westward to join the Santa Cruz River (Fig. 1.2). Cienega Creek rises at the northern edge of the Canelo Hills and the southeastern end of the Santa Rita Mountains, and flows northward. Along its course, it is joined by ephemeral drainages from the east side of the Santa Rita Mountains and the west side of the Whetstones; Matty Canyon is one of a series of such tributaries draining the west-central part of the Whetstones. As it leaves the Cienega Valley, Cienega Creek receives the flow of another tributary known as Mescal Arroyo and becomes Pantano Wash. Pantano Wash is itself a tributary of the Rillito, which eventually joins the Santa Cruz River at Tucson. The highest elevation of the sources of Cienega Creek is 1,676 m (5,500 feet) in the Canelo Hills; where it becomes Pantano Wash its elevation is approximately 1,097 m (3,600 feet).

Along the lower half of its course today, and formerly over much more of its length, Cienega Creek is characterized by large areas of slowly flowing or ponded water surrounded by dense vegetation. To the Spanish and Mexican settlers of southern Arizona these were the *cienegas* that gave the valley its name. *Cienega* refers to lushly vegetated, riparian marshlands often found along stream courses; typically these are groundwater supported, leading some to suggest that the origin of the term was from *cien aguas*, literally a hundred waters or springs (Hendrickson and Minckley 1984). Unfortunately, many of these wetlands have been destroyed by the widespread arroyo cutting that began about a century ago. Today they are greatly reduced in numbers and extent, both in the Cienega Creek Basin and elsewhere in the Southwest, and those that survive

have often done so only with the aid of dams (Hendrickson and Minckley 1984). The steep-walled arroyos that have replaced the cienegas often show in profile the distinctive, highly organic sediments that accumulated in those former marshes.

The soils developed in the Cienega Creek Basin consist primarily of torrifluvents on the floodplains of Cienega Creek and its tributaries. These are typically moderately fine-grained deposits with entisols developed on them. The older, dissected alluvium of the piedmont slopes that border the floodplains exhibit haplargids or calciustols, ancient soils with strong argillic and calcic horizons. The floodplain entisols have good agricultural potential, but the older soils do not (Hendricks 1985).

CLIMATE

The Cienega Creek Basin enjoys a climate slightly wetter and cooler than that in the adjacent Santa Cruz and San Pedro valleys. Although recording stations in the basin are few, a record of precipitation made near the southeastern head of the valley at the small community of Elgin (Fig. 2.1; elevation 1,494 m or 4,900 feet) reveals an annual average of 35.5 cm (13.96 inches) for the 30-year period from 1941 to 1970 (Sellers and Hill 1974). H. V. Smith (1956) reported a mean annual precipitation of 36.75 cm (14.47 inches) for the period from 1912 to 1953 for this same station.

Precipitation in southeastern Arizona is strongly biseasonal, with distinct summer and winter rainy seasons separated by spring and fall droughts. Of the average annual total, 62.5 percent, or 22.2 cm (8.73 inches), arrives in the summer rainy season during the months of July, August, and September. Convective thunderstorms, fueled with moisture from the Gulf of Mexico and Gulf of California, produce the summer precipitation, often in the form of localized downpours. Significantly, this rainy season coincides closely with the growing season for New World cultigens. Eddy and Cooley (1983, Table 1.1) report an average growing season of 164 days at Elgin, spanning the period between June 5 and October 1 in most years. Winter precipitation takes the form of frontal systems moving eastward from the Pacific Ocean; an average of 13.0 cm (5.1 inches) of this precipitation falls as snow.

The area of the Matty Canyon-Cienega Creek confluence lies some 200 m (700 feet) lower than Elgin. Although there are no direct observations of climatic conditions available from this locale, it is undoubtedly slightly warmer, with a growing season a bit longer than that at Elgin. Annual precipitation is likely some-

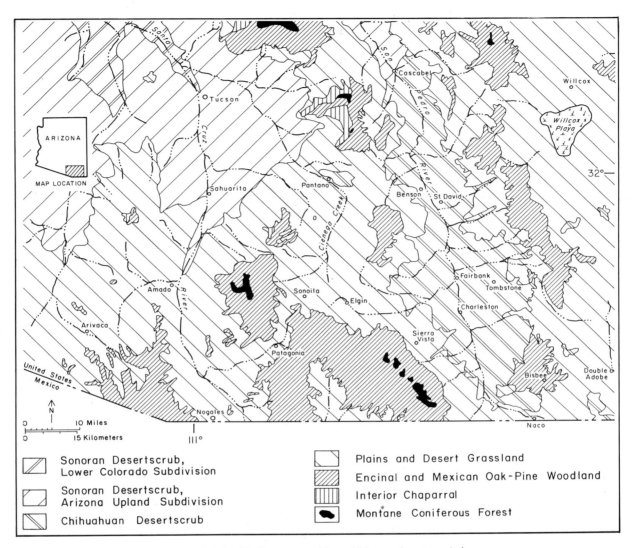

Figure 2.1. Major biotic communities within southeastern Arizona.
(Adapted from B. Huckell 1990 and Brown and Lowe 1981.)

what less, although probably still in excess of 30 cm (11.8 inches) in an average year. As is true of arid lands everywhere, however, the annual average has a large standard deviation.

VEGETATION

The Cienega Creek Basin and the mountain ranges that border it support several distinct biotic communities, defined primarily on the basis of distinctive suites of plants (Fig. 2.1). In ascending elevational order from the axis of the valley, these include the riparian communities along the drainages, the semidesert grassland, the oak woodland, and the pine forest. Brown (1982a) provides specific descriptions of the composition of the

communities, and Paul Schultz Martin (1983a, Fig. 1.4) illustrates their elevational zonation across Cienega Valley.

Riparian Communities and Historic Change

The composition of the present vegetation of Cienega Valley is the product of the last hundred years of human land use practices, particularly as they impacted the riparian plant communities along the now-entrenched drainage system of the area. In common with other valleys of southeastern Arizona, the pre-1880 configuration of the Cienega Valley provides a stark contrast to its modern appearance (Hastings and Turner 1965; Eddy and Cooley 1983; Hendrickson and Minckley 1984; Bahre

Figure 2.2. A portion of a cienega along Cienega Creek, approximately 0.7 km (0.4 mile) south of the Cienega Ranch at an elevation of 1,310 m (4,300 feet). Cattail dominates the ponded water, and cottonwoods and willows grow at the margins of the cienega. View is to the northwest. (ASM photograph by Lisa W. Huckell, 1994.)

1991). Based on nineteenth-century observations by ranchers, immigrants, and military personnel, it was formerly a broad, grassy valley with a shallow, perennial stream along its axis. The stream flowed slowly through an ill-defined channel, broken by frequent patches of essentially ponded water surrounded by lush vegetation, the cienegas that gave the valley its name (Fig. 2.2). Around their margins, the cienegas supported large deciduous trees dominated by willow (*Salix* spp.) and cottonwood (*Populus fremontii*), with some ash (*Fraxinus velutina*), black walnut (*Juglans major*), and mesquite (*Prosopis velutina*), and large quantities of aquatic plants such as cattails (*Typha* sp.), rushes (*Juncus* spp.), and sedges (*Scirpus*, *Eleocharis*, and *Cyperus*). A few such cienegas are extant to this day in the valley, but the erosional regime initiated in the latter part of the nineteenth century eliminated many of them (Hendrickson and Minckley 1984, Figs. 12 and 13; in Table 1 the authors list common cienega plants). That such communities have long characterized this valley is

evident in the stratigraphic record exposed in the present day arroyos, as discussed in Chapter 3 and by Eddy and Cooley (1983: 37–50).

By 1890, as part of a virtually pan-Southwestern event, Cienega Creek began to trench its channel. The causes for this have been investigated and discussed by a number of researchers, most of whom suggested that some combination of natural climatic or geomorphic processes and cultural practices initiated arroyo cutting (Bryan 1925; Hastings and Turner 1965; Cooke and Reeves 1976; Dobyns 1981; Bahre 1991). However, the most recent treatment (Bahre 1991) of the issue makes a strong case that changes in land use practices associated with the Euro-American settlement of the region were the principal factors in this dramatic change in the landscape. In southeastern Arizona, such changes included the introduction of hundreds of thousands of head of livestock onto the valley grasslands, the creation of irrigation systems and roads, firewood and timber harvesting, mining, and fire suppression.

Figure 2.3. Overview of the confluence of Matty Canyon and Cienega Creek, looking west across the broad, mesquite-covered floodplain of Matty Canyon toward the cottonwoods, willows, and mesquites lining the channel of Cienega Creek. The creek is visible (*upper center*) as a narrow band at the foot of the piedmont slopes. Elevation of the Cienega Creek floodplain here is approximately 1,305 m (4,280 feet). (ASM photograph by Lisa W. Huckell, 1994.)

In the Cienega Valley, two large ranches were established in the early 1870s, the Empire Ranch and the Sanford (later Cienega) Ranch. The headquarters of the Sanford Ranch was at the junction of Matty Canyon and Cienega Creek, and its pastures supported cattle and some sheep. Approximately 9 km (5.6 miles) to the south was the Empire Ranch headquarters. By the late 1880s, owner Walter Vail had expanded the Empire Ranch by buying out other ranch holdings, large and small, that of Don Alonzo Sanford included. Vail controlled most of the valley and raised cattle and horses. In addition, he purchased and operated the Total Wreck Mine, located in the northeastern portion of the Empire Mountains. A terrible drought occurred between 1891 and 1893, during which the grasslands were stripped to the roots by livestock. Heavy summer rains in succeeding years fell on a comparatively barren landscape. Runoff concentration, and attendant increases in stream power and gradient, contributed to the inception of the entrenchment. The shallow channels and cienegas of the Cienega Valley were replaced by deep, narrow arroyos.

At the same time, a mesquite "invasion" of the valley bottoms and flanks began. Though mesquite is a long-time resident of the area (Eddy and Cooley 1983, Table 2.1), its numbers have increased dramatically in the last century (Fig. 2.3), probably through seed dispersal by livestock. Hastings and Turner (1965: 109–182) documented this process in southeastern Arizona through the use of repeat photography. Thick mesquite *bosques* (forests) now populate the former floodplain of Cienega Creek and its ephemeral tributaries. Dense stands of tall sacaton grass (*Sporobolus wrightii*) formerly covered much of the floodplain and still exist in small patches in the vicinity of Matty Canyon and its confluence with Cienega Creek. Elsewhere the grass has been replaced by scrub mesquite and annuals of the Compositae, Amaranthaceae, or other families.

Today, a hike down the Cienega Creek or the lower portion of Matty Canyon reveals a channel lined with cottonwood, willow, hackberry (*Celtis reticulata*), mesquite, and walnut trees (Fig. 2.4), with such other plants as seep willow (*Baccharis glutinosa*), cockle bur

Figure 2.4. Cottonwood and willow gallery forest along Cienega Creek 4 km (0.25 mile) south of the Matty Canyon sites at an elevation of approximately 1,317 m (4,320 feet). View is to the southeast, with the southern end of the Whetstone Mountains in the background. (ASM photograph by Bruce B. Huckell, 1994.)

(*Xanthium strumarium*), sunflowers (*Helianthus* sp.), rushes, and sedges. Minckley and Brown (1982) classify this community as Sonoran Riparian Deciduous Forest. Upstream of the emergent water table and areas of active flow, scattered mesquites and desert willows (*Chilopsis linearis*) may be seen, along with rabbit brush (*Chrysothamnus nauseosus*).

Grassland Communities

For most of its length, Cienega Creek flows northward through what has been variously described as a plains grassland (Lowe 1964; Bahre 1991) or Semidesert Grassland (Paul Schultz Martin 1963, 1983a; Brown 1982b). In the southern half of the valley it is nearly a pure grassland, but in the lower half of the valley shrubs and trees are abundantly interspersed with grass. Paul Schultz Martin (1983b, Table 1.2) lists the common types of grass found in the valley; various species of grama (*Bouteloua*) are dominant. The most common trees and shrubs that occur with the grasses are mesquite and burro weed (*Isocoma* spp.).

As one ascends the terraces and pediments flanking the stream, representatives of other plant communities are encountered within the grassland. Proceeding up Matty Canyon, bear grass (*Nolina microcarpa*), agave (*Agave palmeri*), sandpaper bush (*Mortonia scabrella*), tar bush (*Flourensia cernua*), white thorn acacia (*Acacia constricta*), and juniper (*Juniperus monosperma*) appear. The agaves, tar bush, white thorn, and sandpaper bush are present primarily because of the limestone-derived soils along Matty Canyon. Growing in the vicinity are yucca (*Yucca elata* and *Y. baccata*), cholla (*Opuntia* spp.), prickly pear (*Opuntia* spp.), and ocotillo (*Fouquieria splendens*). The foregrounds of the photographs in Figures 2.3 and 2.4 show some of these plants.

On reaching the higher north-facing slopes of the major tributary washes extending toward the basin from

Figure 2.5. Lower margin of the oak woodland on the north-facing slope of Oak Tree Canyon, 9.6 km (6 miles) west of Cienega Creek at an elevation of 1,585 m (5,200 feet). View is to the east, across the grassland with scattered oaks on the opposite slope and the Whetstone Mountains in the distance. (ASM photograph by Lisa W. Huckell, 1994.)

the Santa Rita and Empire mountains, Emory oak (*Quercus emoryi*) trees appear within 3 km to 4 km (1.9 to 2.5 miles) to the west of the Matty Canyon-Cienega Creek confluence. An extensive mosaic of oaks and grasses, dictated by slope exposure and edaphic factors, covers much of the ridge-and-valley topography of the piedmont between Cienega Creek and the mountains that border it (Fig. 2.5).

Oak Woodland Community

The actual *encinal*, or oak woodland, is part of the Madrean Evergreen Woodland (Brown 1982c), and it occupies most of the east-facing slopes of the Santa Rita Mountains at elevations above 1,600 m (5,200 feet). To the east, on the west-facing slopes of the Whetstones, it begins at a slightly higher elevation. Emory oak, blue oak (*Quercus oblongifolia*), and Arizona oak (*Quercus arizonica*) occur on ridge slopes and along the floors of the canyons. Scattered through the oaks are junipers (*J. monosperma* and *J. deppeana*), mesquite, and border

piñon pine (*Pinus discolor*), together with such shrubs as gray thorn (*Zizyphus obtusifolia*), silktassel (*Garrya wrightii*), buckthorn (*Ceanothus greggii*), mimosa (*Mimosa* spp.), sotol (*Dasylirion wheeleri*), bear grass, and yucca. Agaves also occur in some abundance. In general, this community is relatively open, but achieves greater densities of trees on north-facing slopes (Fig. 2.5) and along canyon bottoms.

Conifer Forest Community

In the higher elevations of the Santa Rita Mountains above the *encinal* is the Madrean Montane Conifer Forest (Pase and Brown 1982). The lower portion of it is dominated by ponderosa pine (*Pinus ponderosa*), but with increasing elevation Douglas fir (*Pseudotsuga menziesii*), white pine (*Pinus reflexa*), silver leaf oak (*Quercus hypoleucoides*), and other trees appear. This community occupies a small area of the range above an elevation of approximately 2,061 m (6,700 feet; see Fig. 2.1).

ANIMALS OF THE CIENEGA CREEK BASIN

As would be expected, Cienega Valley and the surrounding mountains are inhabited by a rich and varied fauna. No detailed list is presented here, but it is useful to briefly note the potentially economically significant species present here today and in the past.

Both cottontail rabbits (*Sylvilagus* sp.) and jackrabbits (*Lepus* sp.) range from the center of the valley well up into the surrounding mountains. The grasslands, particularly south of the Matty Canyon–Cienega Creek confluence, contain one of the few populations of antelope (*Antilocapra americana*) in southern Arizona. Mule deer (*Odocoileus hemionus*) generally are more common along the lower elevations of the valley; white-tailed deer (*O. virginianus*) are more numerous in the higher elevation oak woodland community. Javelina (*Tayassu tajacu*) are frequently encountered along the washes from the floor of the valley up into the surrounding mountains. Predators include coyotes (*Canis latrans*), kit fox (*Vulpes macrotis*) and gray fox (*Urocyon cinereoargenteus*), bobcat (*Lynx rufus*), and rarely, in the mountains, mountain lion (*Felis concolor*). Badgers (*Taxidea taxus*) and skunks (*Mephitis* spp.) round out the list of smaller predators.

Three other species of large mammals may formerly have been residents of the Cienega Valley. Archaeological contexts have revealed the remains of bighorn sheep (*Ovis canadensis*), bison (*Bison bison*), and, possibly, elk (*Cervus canadensis*). Bighorn sheep have been identified from AZ EE:2:30 ASM (Chapter 6; Eddy 1958) and from younger Hohokam contexts (Glass 1984) in the nearby foothills of the Santa Rita Mountains. Eddy (1958) also tentatively identified elk bones from AZ EE:2:30. Immediately southeast of the valley, along Babocomari Creek, Di Peso (1951) discovered bison bones in Classic period deposits. Bison would be logical members of the grassland community, and both bighorn and elk may have inhabited the surrounding mountains.

LOCAL ENVIRONMENT OF THE MATTY CANYON SITES

It was the post-1900 entrenchment that created the deeply eroded arroyo we know today as Matty Canyon. This ephemeral wash drains the western slopes of the Whetstone Mountains and has trenched its channel in response to the downcutting of Cienega Creek. It enters the floodplain of Cienega Creek at an elevation of approximately 1,280 m (4,200 feet), and flows in a sub-

parallel course for nearly 1.6 km (1 mile) before it joins Cienega Creek (Fig. 1.2). For most of that distance it is confined to a 5–m to 6–m deep, 20–m to 30–m wide channel. In an attempt to stop the progress of headward erosion, a cement block masonry spillway was constructed approximately 500 m upstream of the site of AZ EE:2:30 sometime in the late 1960s or early 1970s. Above the spillway, Matty Wash is only 1.5 m to 2.0 m deep.

Although actually an ephemeral stream, water flowed almost year round in the canyon in 1983 because of two factors. First, in the lower 1.5 km of Matty Canyon the water table is intersected by the floor of the 5–m deep channel, producing a continuous, low volume, sluggish flow. Second, along the east edge of the Cienega Creek floodplain a 10–m deep canal was excavated in the early 1970s, diverting a significant portion of the flow of Cienega Creek to facilitate irrigation of its broad eastern floodplain in this area (Fig. 1.2). The canal was cut through into Matty Canyon, joining it approximately 100 m downstream of the masonry spillway. This canal was no longer in use for irrigation by 1983, but continued to divert much of the Cienega Creek flow into Matty Canyon. The net effects were to keep the portion of Matty Canyon on the Cienega Creek floodplain a semipermanent stream, flowing during all but the driest months of the year, and to markedly increase the rate of both vertical and lateral erosion of its channel. The increased erosion since about 1970 has helped to more fully expose AZ EE:2:30 and other buried late preceramic sites within the canyon. Since the Bureau of Land Management acquired the Empire-Cienega area in 1988, they have attempted to restore the flow of Cienega Creek to its natural channel.

Today's environmental conditions within Matty Canyon are generally similar to those along Cienega Creek immediately to the west. The lower 1.5 km (0.9 mile) reach of Matty Canyon has a shallow perennial stream of variable width, the product of effluent groundwater flow. Occasional bank collapse may block the stream in certain areas, creating shallow, temporary pools. Major floods periodically reposition and modify these pools and the stream course. Point bar terraces, located on the inside of meander bends within the entrenched channel, contain cottonwood, willow, ash, walnut, and mesquite trees in addition to grass, scattered shrubs, and various spring and summer annuals. The active channel floor consists of sand and cobble to boulder gravel bars prone to rearrangement during flood events. Sedges, rushes, watercress (*Rorippa nasturtium-aquaticum*), and other aquatic and semiaquatic plants line the flowing stream.

As described in Chapter 3, the site of Los Ojitos (AZ EE:2:137 ASM) is located at the point where the perennial flow begins, under the shade of several tall cottonwood and willow trees. The channel here makes a sharp bend to the northeast (shown in Fig. 1.2), and in 1983 the site was only exposed at the base of the 5.5-m high vertical bank on the outside of the bend. In 1957, the channel was not sufficiently deep to reveal the buried cultural deposit, so Frank Eddy had no opportunity to observe it. The tremendous flood in October of 1983 reburied this exposure under as much as 1 m of sediments, and today the cultural deposit cannot be seen below a growing thicket of young willow and cottonwood trees.

AZ EE:2:30 is approximately 300 m upstream of the perennially flowing lower reach of Matty Canyon and is located at a meander bend at which the channel turns fairly sharply to the north. Over the eight or more decades of the current erosional regime, the deepening channel of the wash has migrated to the southwest as this meander has progressed downstream. The result is that the west side of the active channel, along the outside of the meander, flows against a 7-m high vertical bank. The east side of the channel is bordered by a much lower, 1-m to 1.5-m high bank that slopes upward gradually for a distance of some 35 m to 55 m before reaching a 2.5-m high vertical bank that marks the edge of the entrenched channel. Fortuitously, this means that much of the site on the inside of the meander bend is accessible for excavation, being covered by as little as 0.25 m of sand and gravel.

In 1983 this low erosional terrace supported a xeric, dense growth of mesquite trees and shrubs, desert willow, rabbit brush, mimosa, amaranth, prickly poppy, and cockle bur, along with a lone walnut tree. The channel, still prone to frequently high-magnitude floods coursing down the old irrigation canal, consisted largely of sand and cobble to large boulder gravel barren of vegetation. As this description is being written, ten years later, the flow of Cienega Creek has been largely restored to its proper course, and the channel of Matty Canyon in the site area is thickly lined with young, 3-m to 4-m high cottonwood and willow trees. The documented changes in Matty Canyon during the last 35 years show that this arroyo, like others in southeastern Arizona, is a dynamic part of the landscape.

THE LAND AND HUMAN SUBSISTENCE

The Cienega Valley affords a relatively diverse and certainly productive environment for human subsistence.

It is today a modified terrain, the product of Euro-American patterns of land use as played out against the variable climatic conditions characteristic of arid and semiarid environments. Despite the changes that have occurred during the past 125 years, the basic qualities that attracted prehistoric settlement here can still be recognized.

The most striking feature of this valley is the presence within a small area of three major plant communities: riparian, grassland, and oak woodland. A portion of a fourth community, the conifer forest, is only a few kilometers away, and the Sonoran desertscrub was accessible to the northwest within one day of travel. This diversity is engendered by the basin-and-range physiography, which creates diversity through the vertical "stacking" of communities along an elevational gradient (Paul Schultz Martin 1963: 9–13).

The attractiveness of this situation for prehistoric people was twofold. First, a wide range of resources available at different times of the year was present within a relatively small, accessible area. Both perennial and annual plant species grow in all three of the major communities and include plants available for harvest and consumption as greens, fruits, or seeds during the middle to late spring and during the summer and fall. Mesquite pods, chenopod greens and seeds, cattail pollen and rhizomes, and agave, yucca, bear grass, and sotol flower stalk buds occur primarily in the riparian and semidesert grassland communities during the middle to late spring, and the agaves, yuccas, bear grass, and sotol extend into the oak woodland. The summer and fall seasons provide acorns and walnuts; chenopod, amaranth, purslane, and horse purslane greens and seeds; caryopses (seeds) from several species of grass; juniper berries; wild grapes; and mesquite pods again. The semidesert grassland and oak woodlands are at their most productive during this part of the year. This list of potentially economically significant plants in Cienega Valley is not exhaustive, but does show the relative abundance of plant resources here. Animals such as deer, antelope, rabbits, and possibly bighorn and even bison may have roamed the confines of the valley. They could have been hunted year-round, but the large mammals would have been in better condition and fatter during the summer and fall than during the winter and particularly the spring.

The second attraction of the Cienega Creek Basin for human foragers was that these resources could be easily accessed, without making long-distance trips. From the riparian community where the Matty Canyon sites are located, the oak woodland community is no more than

8 km (5 miles) away and 300 m (1,000 feet) higher. To reach it, one passes through the semidesert grassland. Such a distance could conceivably be covered in a single, day-long foraging trip, or the resources of the oak woodland could be collected over a day or two from a temporary gathering camp. If, as the archaeological evidence suggests, the Matty Canyon sites represent long-term occupations, the ease of access of these other plant communities would have been an important advantage in resolving the problem of the spatial and temporal discontinuities in resource availability.

Arable land is another important resource of the Cienega Valley, for as is shown, agriculture is an important part of the late preceramic subsistence strategy of these people. The alluvial record indicates that since about 4,000 years ago, the floodplain of Cienega Creek has been steadily aggrading. Paul Schultz Martin (1963) and Schoenwetter (1960) have reported that maize was being grown on the floodplain during the last 2,500 years or more, as the floodplain of the creek grew in both width and depth. Essentially modern climatic conditions, which were established by at least 3,000 to 4,000 years ago, are certainly adequate for crop production. The area also contains the always critical resources of permanent water, wood for construction and fuel, and stone of sufficient quality for the manufacture of flaked and ground stone tools. Matty Canyon and the Cienega Creek Basin are not a second Garden of Eden, but they do offer a combination of resource diversity, abundance, and accessibiliity that is evident in few other parts of southeastern Arizona. With such a resource base, the foundations for long-term residency were in place by some 3,000 years ago.

CHAPTER THREE

Archaeology of the Early Agricultural Period in Matty Canyon

Serendipity, so often the friend of the archaeologist, provided an unsought opportunity for scientists to return to the Cienega Valley 25 years after Frank Eddy's investigations. In 1980, severe flooding from heavy, localized, summer thundershowers caused major channel scouring and bank collapse in Matty Canyon. Two years later, John Donaldson, the lessee of the Empire Ranch, reported to Emil Haury at the University of Arizona that a human burial was eroding out of a bank in Matty Canyon. Haury and a group of Arizona State Museum archaeologists visited the locality with Donaldson in late 1982 and determined that the burial, largely lost to the wash, was probably of Sedentary Hohokam age. In order to examine the burial, however, it was necessary to stand on a low erosional bench at the base of the 5-m high vertical bank; that bench was composed of fire-cracked rock, artifacts, and bone in a dark gray, highly organic matrix. The attention of the party quickly focused on this cultural deposit, which extended for a considerable distance both upstream and downstream of the position of the younger burial.

Detailed examination of the much lower, 1.5-m high east bank of the wash revealed another burial, this one nearly complete and positioned within the older cultural deposit. The surrounding area contained abundant flaked stone artifacts and fire-cracked rocks but no potsherds, indicating that this deposit might well be of preceramic age. Because continued episodes of flooding would have gradually destroyed the burial and the exposed deposit, plans were made to conduct a small-scale excavation to sample the deposit and to assess its extent, age, and composition. The locality was assigned a number in the Arizona State Museum site survey system, in the belief that it was a new site. After investigations had begun in the late spring of 1983, William J. Robinson, who was then Director of the Laboratory of Tree-Ring Research at the University of Arizona and who had worked with Frank Eddy in 1957, convinced us that this locus was in fact site AZ EE:2:30 (ASM). The intervening years had changed the appearance of the site by deepening the channel of Matty Canyon by about 1 m, resulting in a much more extensive exposure of the buried site. In honor of its "rediscoverer," it was named the Donaldson Site; its location is shown in Figure 3.1.

In the course of establishing a grid on the Donaldson Site in May of 1983, an exploratory walk downstream revealed another, compositionally identical, buried cultural deposit. It was located at the base of a 5.5-m high vertical bank, opposite an area where a series of small springs appeared in the floor of the channel to create a permanent flow of water. Careful examination of the exposed deposit strongly suggested that it, too, was of preceramic age. Even more surprising, a burial was also eroding out of this deposit, and plans were expanded to include some investigation of this locality. The presence of the springs suggested a name for the site: Los Ojitos ("the little springs," in Spanish). It was assigned site number AZ EE:2:137 ASM (Fig. 3.1.).

Exploration of both sites in a timely fashion was crucial, if the significant evidence they contained of the preceramic period was to be preserved. Permission to excavate was granted by the ANAMAX Mining Company, owner of the Empire Ranch at that time. Six weeks in May and June of 1983 were devoted to an investigation of the two sites.

STRATIGRAPHIC CONTEXT

The alluvial units exposed along Matty Canyon and Cienega Creek were studied in detail by Cooley (Eddy 1958, Appendix A; Eddy and Cooley 1983: 6–9, 31–42). A brief description is included here to review the geological setting of the sites. Figure 3.2 (*top*) presents a stratigraphic profile of a portion of the Donaldson Site (AZ EE:2:30) and Figure 3.2 (*bottom*) a profile of Los Ojitos (AZ EE:2:137).

Unit 100

The cultural deposits at both sites rest on an eroded alluvial unit of calcified clayey silt to fine sand that grades into a cobble to boulder gravel in some areas.

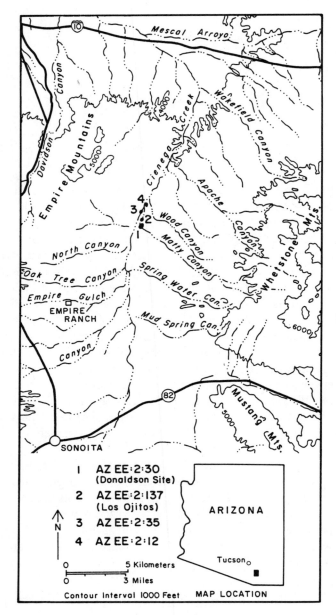

Figure 3.1. Locations of the Donaldson Site and Los Ojitos in Matty Canyon, southeastern Arizona.

The southwestern portion of the Donaldson Site is one such area, and here the gravel is well cemented by calcium carbonate. Cooley (1958; Eddy and Cooley 1983: 6–7) designated this as Unit 100 and described it as stream-laid sand and gravel of Pleistocene age (Fig. 3.3). A paleosol is discernible on the finer-grained portions of this unit, marked by a reddish brown argillic horizon with Stage 1 carbonate development (Machette 1985). The surface of this unit slopes upward to the east, and as one proceeds in that direction the paleosol

shows more intensive development. It is on this surface that the prehistoric settlements were placed. Although generally the surface of Unit 100 appears to be devoid of much topographic relief, the cultural deposit at the west edge of the Donaldson Site exhibits a slightly steeper slope to the west than does the rest of the site. Perhaps the settlement was positioned on top of a low erosional terrace that had developed on Unit 100. The steeper slope may represent an erosional scarp that forms the riser of the terrace. It was unclear whether or not Los Ojitos rested on a similar feature.

Units 5–7

Along Cienega Creek, Eddy and Cooley (1983) identified three alluvial deposits that signaled the initial depositional events after the erosion of and soil development on Unit 100. The first of these, Unit 7, was described as a sand to silty sand with angular inclusions that was exposed in only a few areas. At least one isolated stone artifact was present in this unit at AZ EE:2:12 (Eddy 1958, Figs. 12, 14a). The unit was not dated, but was probably of San Pedro stage age or earlier. Eddy and Cooley (Eddy 1958: 113) hypothesized that Unit 7 was "an accumulation of residual-colluvial sediments occurring along the sides of Cienega Valley," in contrast to the fluvially deposited units above it. The Unit 7 colluvium was observed to intertongue with Units 3, 4, 5, and 6 along the margins of the valley, thus confirming this depositional origin.

Overlying Unit 7 was the much more extensive Unit 6 (Fig. 3.3), a mud or clay to silty clay deposited in cienegas; apparently it was devoid of artifacts. In part overlying and in part interfingering with Unit 6 was Unit 5, a fluvial deposit of sand and silty sand with occasional indications of bedding and cross bedding in channels. As noted in Chapter 1, AZ EE:2:35 was contained within Unit 5. Radiocarbon dates from that site suggest that this deposit is approximately 2,600 to 3,000 years old. Unit 5 intergrades upward (and perhaps laterally) with Unit 4.

Cultural Deposits

The cultural deposits were not given separate stratigraphic unit designations by Cooley, but they are easily distinguished as depositional events. Both sites appear as dark gray clayey sand units varying from 0.25 m to 1.00 m (average, approximately 0.40 m) in thickness and containing abundant artifacts, fire-cracked rock fragments, animal bones, and charcoal lumps and flecks.

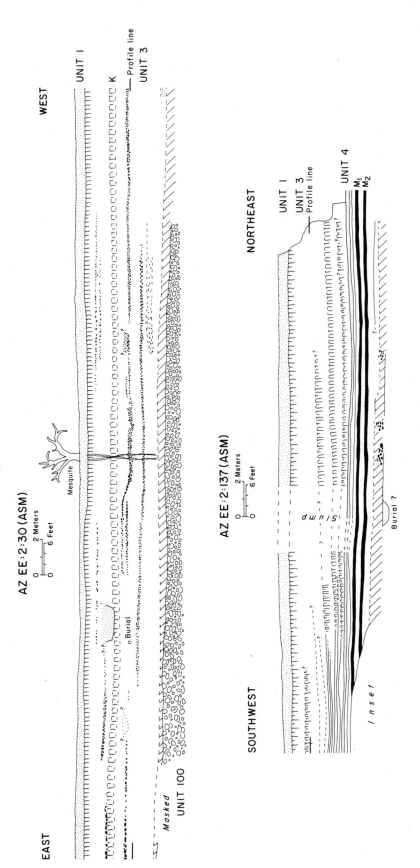

Figure 3.2. Stratigraphic profile of the left bank of Matty Wash at the Donaldson Site (*top*) and at Los Ojitos (*bottom*). Hatchured unit is the cultural deposit.

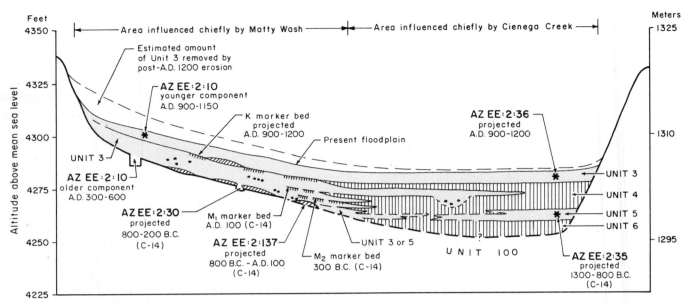

Figure 3.3. Schematic east-west cross section through the Cienega Creek floodplain in the area of the Matty Canyon confluence. (Modified and reproduced with permission of the Arizona Board of Regents from Eddy and Cooley 1983, Fig. 1.6.)

The deposits are slightly calcareous and are well indurated in comparison with the younger, overlying units. These cultural midden deposits rest unconformably on Unit 100, and many of the pit features were excavated into Unit 100. As use of the term "midden" implies, this deposit is thought to be principally of cultural origin. More detailed information on midden composition is presented below.

As part of the 1983 research, the cultural deposits at both sites were dated by radiocarbon. Table 3.1 presents the dates obtained from the Donaldson Site and from Los Ojitos both in terms of radiocarbon years before present and as calibrated to the Christian calendar. The two dates from Los Ojitos were AMS (accelerator) assays from the undifferentiated cultural deposit, one on

wood charcoal and one on maize. Both are in close agreement with one another. The large standard deviations of these two dates reflect the level of precision being achieved by the Arizona accelerator during its developmental phase in the early 1980s. The four dates from the Donaldson Site include two conventional dates on wood charcoal samples from a roasting pit (Feature 15) and a hearth in a pit structure (Feature 11), and two AMS dates on maize from other pit features. Three of the four dates are in close agreement (A–4200, A–4201, and AA–13125), but the fourth date is slightly younger and barely overlaps with the other three. As discussed below, based on stratigraphic evidence Los Ojitos should be slightly older than the Donaldson Site, but radiocarbon dating does not support this relationship.

Table 3.1. Radiocarbon Dates from the 1983 Investigations at the Donaldson Site and Los Ojitos

Site	Feature	Lab. Number	Sample	Age in years B.P.	Calibrated Date* 1 sigma	2 sigma
Donaldson	11	A-4200	Wood charcoal	2400 ± 90	750–390 B.C.	790–210 B.C.
	15	A-4201	Wood charcoal	2380 ± 90	750–380 B.C.	790–210 B.C.
	4	AA-13124	Maize	2320 ± 55	400–260 B.C.	500–210 B.C.
	19	AA-13125	Maize	2505 ± 55	790–410 B.C.	800–410 B.C.
Los Ojitos		A-3501	Wood charcoal	2270 ± 200	750–50 B.C.	810 B.C. – A.D. 130
		A-3500	Maize	2170 ± 170	390 B.C. – A.D. 1	750 B.C. – A.D. 130

* University of Washington Quaternary Isotope Laboratory Radiocarbon Calibration Program CALIB 3.0.3 (Stuiver and Reimer 1993). Calibrations for dates with standard deviations greater than 50 years have been rounded to the nearest 10 years.

Unit 4

Conformably overlying the cultural deposits at both sites are 4 m or more of silts, sands, gravels, buried soils, and, at Los Ojitos, peat beds. The peat beds at Los Ojitos are probably part of Unit 4, as defined by Eddy and Cooley (1983: 8). This unit consists primarily of silty clay cienega deposits. At Los Ojitos, the cultural deposit is overlain by 0.50 m of fine sand and silt, and on top of that rests the first of two peat deposits (Fig. 3.2, *bottom*). The lower peat is approximately 0.30 m thick, strongly bedded, and can be split along bedding planes to reveal poorly preserved, carbon residues of leaves, twigs, and seeds. It actually consists of two peats separated by a 0.10-m thick bed of light gray fine sandy silt. The lower peat is overlain by a 0.40-m to 0.50-m thick unit of banded silts and sands, above which is the upper peat. This peat is structurally similar to the lower bed and is about the same in thickness. These two peat deposits appear to correlate with what Eddy and Cooley (1983, Fig. 5.1) labeled, respectively, the M_2 and M_1 marker beds.

Radiocarbon assays were obtained from these beds by Eddy (1958, Table 8; Eddy and Cooley 1983, Table 3.1) and by Paul Schultz Martin and others (1961, Table 6; B. Huckell 1983, Table C.1). Table 3.2 presents only dates obtained through use of the CO_2 gas method; solid carbon dates are not considered because of their demonstrated tendency to be less accurate. In this particular case, the solid carbon dates reported by Eddy were in the 2700–3000 B.P. range, several centuries older than the dates obtained by the CO_2 method (Eddy and Cooley 1983, Table 3.1, A88a, b, and av).

Although the dates given in Table 3.2 are not precise, they are consistent and are in reasonable accordance with the observed stratigraphic relationships between the two deposits.

Three dates from the M_2 bed (Sh–5565, Sh–5389, and A–92) clearly overlap with the two AMS dates obtained from the cultural deposit at Los Ojitos, despite the fact that the M_2 peat is more than a half-meter above the cultural deposit. During August of 1983, summer floods cleared sufficient talus from the banks of Matty Canyon to permit the tracing of the M_2 bed and its associated soil facies from Los Ojitos upstream to the Donaldson Site, where it interbedded with the west edge of the cultural deposit. It was this discovery that suggested that Los Ojitos should be older than the Donaldson Site on stratigraphic grounds.

Unit 3

Above the peat deposits at Los Ojitos, and resting directly on top of the cultural deposit at the Donaldson Site, is a 3-m to 4-m thick complex alluvium designated Unit 3 (Fig. 3.3) by Eddy and Cooley. Three distinct deposits were assigned to Unit 3: channel deposits of bedded sand and gravel, massive sandy silt, and dark gray silts probably representing buried organic paleosols. These paleosols often achieved considerable horizontal extent and several served as stratigraphic marker beds. Some, if not all, of these paleosols were thought to be lateral extensions of Unit 4 cienegas. Unit 3 is in part coeval with Unit 4; it represents fluvially laid, overbank deposits accumulating away from the center of the valley at the same time as the repeated cycle of

Table 3.2. Radiocarbon Dates from the M_1 and M_2 Marker Beds in Matty Canyon

Unit	Lab. Number	Sample	Age in years B.P.	Calibrated date* 1 sigma	Calibrated date* 2 sigma
M_1	Sh-5664a	Peat	1940 ± 170	160 B.C. – A.D. 320	380 B.C. – A.D. 530
	Sh-5664b	Humates	1760 ± 190	A.D. 40–540	170 B.C. – A.D. 660
	Sh-5664av	Average of a + b	1860 ± 130	A.D. 30–340	170 B.C. – A.D. 530
	Sh-5358	Peat	1850 ± 150	A.D. 1–380	200 B.C. – A.D. 540
	A-88 bis	Peat	2010 ± 150	200 B.C. – A.D. 210	390 B.C. – A.D. 380
M_2	Sh-5565	Peat	2470 ± 200	810–260 B.C.	1050–50 B.C.
	Sh-5389	Peat	2150 ± 140	380 B.C. – A.D. 20	480 B.C. – A.D. 130
	A-92	Peat	2220 ± 150	400–50 B.C.	760 B.C. – A.D. 110
	A-196	Peat	2190 ± 100	380–60 B.C.	400 B.C. – A.D. 50

NOTE. Dates do not include the solid carbon assays from these deposits reported by Eddy (1958).

Sources: Eddy and Cooley 1983, Table 3.1; B. Huckell 1983, Table C.1.

* University of Washington Quaternary Isotope Laboratory Radiocarbon Calibration Program CALIB 3.0.3 (Stuiver and Reimer 1993). Calibrations for dates with standard deviations greater than 50 years have been rounded to the nearest 10 years.

cienega formation and destruction was occurring along Cienega Creek (Eddy and Cooley 1983, Fig. 2.16). Within the typical Unit 3 matrix of silty sand are discontinuous, interbedded channel deposits of gravel pebbles and small cobbles in a sand matrix, weakly developed paleosols, and occasional concentrations of ceramic period artifacts and features. These various deposits are evident in the profiles of the two sites (Fig. 3.2). At the Donaldson Site, the sand and gravel deposits are probably minor channel braids of Matty Wash, which swung back and forth across the site as Unit 3 floodplain sediments aggraded.

One cultural occupation zone appears at the Donaldson Site some 1.5 m to 2.0 m above the preceramic midden (Fig. 3.2, *top*). In age it apparently dates to the Hohokam Sedentary period (A.D. 900 to 1150), based on the presence of Rincon Red-on-brown painted pottery. It may represent the margin of a settlement largely destroyed during the late nineteenth- to early twentieth-century incision of Matty Canyon or an area of short-term occupation. The burial discovered by Donaldson's nephew in 1982 was part of this occupational horizon. This cultural deposit may correlate with a weak paleosol, the K marker bed of Eddy and Cooley (1983, Fig. 1.6). If so, it suggests that the floodplain may have been occupied briefly in the Hohokam Rincon phase during a short hiatus in deposition.

At Los Ojitos (Fig. 3.2, *bottom*), immediately overlying the peat, there is a series of as many as eight, highly organic bands of dark brown clay that appear to have been formed in shallow channels or declivities of limited horizontal extent. These clay beds give way laterally to weakly developed soils, some of which can only be traced for a few meters. These beds and soils are separated by reddish-brown sandy silt. It seems probable that the clay beds were deposited in sloughs or abandoned channel meanders of Cienega Creek.

Unit 2

At certain places in Matty Canyon and Cienega Creek, within 1.5 m to 2.0 m of the surface of the historic floodplain, Eddy and Cooley (1983) observed an ill-defined channel filled with coarse pebble-cobble gravel. They suggested that this channel represented a major but short cut-and-fill episode for the whole valley that resulted in the removal of a large part of Unit 3 (Eddy and Cooley 1983: 9). An event of such magnitude is not represented in the stratigraphy at either the Donaldson or Los Ojitos sites, although at the Donaldson Site there is a 10-cm thick band of pebble gravel

near the top of Unit 3 (Fig. 3.2, *top*). Approximately 0.75 m to 1.0 m above the gravel band is a prominent soil zone; the same highly organic soil is present at Los Ojitos (Fig. 3.2, *bottom*). The channel fill and the soil were assigned to the Sanford Formation, as Unit 2 was named. The soil was forming on the floodplain during the late nineteenth century, prior to the onset of erosion, and it reaches thicknesses of 0.60 m.

Unit 1

Lying unconformably on the Unit 2 soil is Unit 1, an unconsolidated sand to silty sand that at both sites measures between 0.25 m to 0.75 m in thickness. It represents the flushing of sand onto the floodplain from the adjacent piedmont slopes at the beginning of the modern cycle of erosion and is the last depositional unit before entrenchment began (Eddy and Cooley 1983: 9). The inception of channel cutting is believed to date around A.D. 1900, based on interviews conducted by Eddy (1958: 24–25) with long-term valley residents. It terminated approximately 2,500 to 3,000 years of nearly continuous alluviation in this area of Cienega Creek Basin.

ARCHAEOLOGICAL INVESTIGATIONS IN 1983

Because of the nature of the exposures at the Donaldson Site and Los Ojitos, excavations at both were necessarily limited. At the Donaldson Site (AZ EE:2:30), the cultural deposit was exposed on both sides of the wash channel, although the principal exposure was on the right bank as one faces downstream. Because of the frequent bends made by the Matty Canyon arroyo, the geological terms "right" and "left" are used to designate banks. The left bank is always on the left as one faces downstream, but may in some places be the south bank and in other places the west bank as the channel meanders.

To provide provenience control at the Donaldson Site, a system of 2–m grid squares was constructed over the narrow area of exposed deposit, and squares or parts of squares were selected for investigation on a judgmental, nonrandom basis. A total of 48 square meters of the exposed deposit was excavated during a four-week period of May and June of 1983. The left arroyo bank was profile mapped over a distance of approximately 46 m (Fig. 3.2, *top*). Additionally, three backhoe trenches were excavated into the low terrace on the right side of the wash channel to trace the extent of the site in that direction. At the beginning of October in

Figure 3.4. Excavations in progress at the Donaldson Site; view is downstream. People in the center are examining Feature 11. (ASM photograph by Helga Teiwes.)

1983, a tremendously powerful tropical storm hit southeastern Arizona and caused massive flooding and erosion in Matty Canyon. This dramatic event revealed additional features and burials, and a few of them were investigated over the course of that month. Figure 3.4 illustrates part of the site area during excavation in June, 1983. Figure 3.5 shows the locations of the excavations and the backhoe trenches, and indicates the positions of the arroyo banks and exposures of the midden before the October flood.

Downstream at Los Ojitos (AZ EE:2:137 ASM), less than 9 square meters could be excavated. Here the cultural deposit was exposed only as a steeply sloping bed at the base of a curving, 5.5-m high section of the left bank. Work was limited to excavating judgmentally selected, 1-m wide sections of the cultural deposit inward as a vertical face until the back of the excavation was coincident with the vertical arroyo bank. Horizontal and vertical provenience control was maintained through the use of a 35-m long level line installed to facilitate profile mapping of the site (Fig. 3.2, *bottom*). To make

excavation possible, the stream flow had to be kept away from the base of the bank, a feat accomplished by creating a dam of sand and gravel reinforced with mud and digging a bypass channel from the pond that formed behind the dam to carry away the accumulating water.

At the Donaldson Site, 2-m grid squares were the standard sample units, although excavations actually proceeded by quarters within each 2-m square. One-meter-wide squares, defined in reference to the stratigraphic profile mapping level line, were used at Los Ojitos. Within the cultural deposits at both sites, arbitrary 10-cm levels were dug, each in reference to a vertical datum plane. The cultural deposits were designated Stratum 1, and the 10-cm levels were numbered sequentially from the top to the base of the deposit. The fill of features at both sites was designated Stratum 10 and was also excavated in 10-cm levels. Most features were excavated independently of the grid system as naturally defined provenience units, but the grid proveniences were maintained during the excavation of large features such as structures.

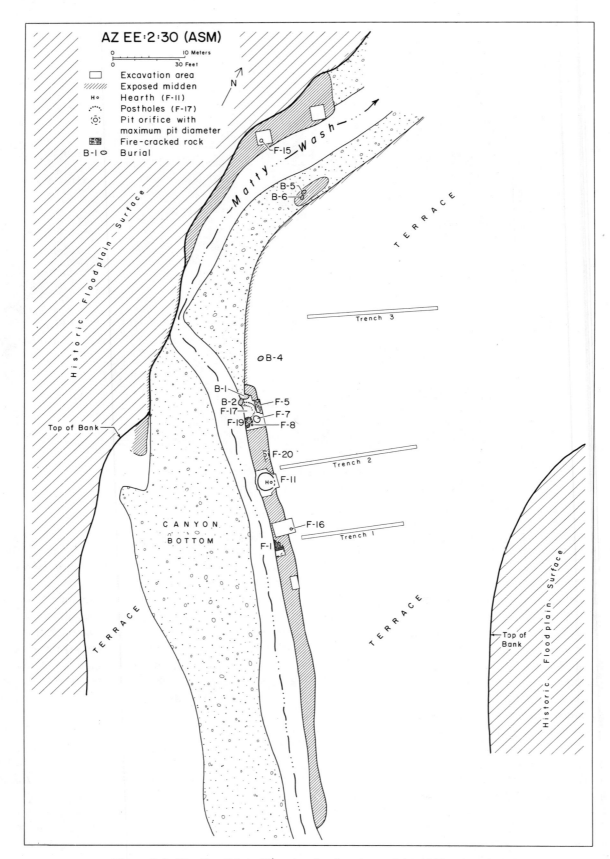

Figure 3.5. The Donaldson Site, showing locations of the 1983 excavations.

Table 3.3. Material Composition of the Cultural Deposit at the Donaldson Site (AZ EE:2:30 ASM)

Grid or Feature	Average thickness of deposit (m)	Debitage N	%	Flaked stone tools N	%	Ground stone tools N	%	Animal bone N	%	Fire-cracked rock N	%
N98E110	0.52	618	(67.1)	14	(1.5)	1	(0.1)	141	(15.3)	147	(16.0)
N98E116	0.29	391	(67.5)	11	(1.9)			30	(5.2)	147	(25.4)
N100E116	0.46	567	(62.7)	16	(1.8)	2	(0.2)	75	(8.3)	244	(27.0)
N116E56	0.27	1083	(67.1)	35	(2.2)	4	(0.3)	151	(9.3)	340	(21.1)
Feature 11	0.40	644	(74.2)	12	(1.4)	4	(0.5)	78	(9.0)	130	(14.9)

NOTE: Grids are 2–m by 2–m squares except N98E116, a 1–m by 2–m unit. All levels are combined. Feature 11 is a pit structure.

When moist, the midden deposit at the Donaldson Site could be easily moved with trowels or shovels, but when dry, railroad picks were necessary. All excavated earth was passed through ¼–inch mesh screens at both sites, but the dry portion of the cultural deposit at the Donaldson Site often had to be broken apart with pick mattock handles to get it through the screen. The opposite problem was faced at Los Ojitos, because the cultural deposit was saturated from the underlying water table. It was necessary to screen wash the excavated earth; fortunately an abundant supply of surface water was available from the pond behind the dam. All excavated sediments were dumped on a ¼–inch mesh screen stacked on top of a 1/16–inch mesh screen and flushed with water until only artifacts, charcoal, bone, and carbonized archaeobotanical materials remained. When discovered, features were excavated as naturally bound provenience units but within the system of arbitrary grids and levels. Features were abundant at both sites, so much of the effort was devoted to their exploration.

The limited extent of excavations at both sites clearly makes it difficult to produce a detailed treatment of the attributes of either site. Nonetheless, even this limited work produced some valuable glimpses into the composition of these settlements, both in terms of the cultural deposit or midden constituents and the types of features and artifacts that occurred in them.

THE DONALDSON SITE

Excavations at the Donaldson Site began along the exposed midden on the low, right bank of the wash and extended across the channel to a 3–m to 4–m wide bench at the base of the left bank that contained intact cultural deposits. The main excavation area on the right bank is shown plainly in Figure 3.4, and the secondary area on the left bank is barely visible in the background at the left center of the photograph.

The Cultural Deposit

It is appropriate to begin a description of the Donaldson Site (Fig. 3.5) with an examination of its thick, dark gray midden, which is exposed for a horizontal distance of approximately 140 m along the right bank of Matty Canyon arroyo. One of the primary goals was to obtain a detailed understanding of the midden's composition. Such a discrete deposit undoubtedly was formed by the accumulation of inorganic sediments and artifacts, organically enriched by the addition of carbonized wood charcoal and ash, and the decomposition of plant remains and other organic products. However, the development of a deposit that averages 0.40 m in thickness also clearly involves the elements of time and intensity of occupation. One measure of the intensity of occupation is the identification and enumeration of the constituents of the cultural deposit.

To examine the midden at the Donaldson Site, five categories of material were tabulated: flaked stone debitage; flaked stone implements; ground stone implements; animal bone; and fire-cracked rocks. Table 3.3 shows the composition of the midden using these classes of material for four grid squares and Feature 11, a completely excavated pit structure. These four grid squares were chosen because they represented the full horizontal extent of the investigations, and the feature was selected because it contained a relatively large quantity of postoccupational fill. The midden yielded large quantities of artifacts, modified rocks, and animal bones in a consistent composition, with the relative quantities of the material classes remaining similar from one provenience unit to the next. From the grid squares alone, an average of 197 artifacts (excluding animal bone and fire-cracked rocks) was recovered from each square meter of the midden. The range in artifact density was from 145 specimens to 282 specimens per square meter of midden.

Table 3.4. Attributes of Features Excavated at the Donaldson Site in 1983

Feature	Location	Type	Length (m)	Width (m)	Depth (m)	Plan shape	Pieces of rock (N)	Flaked stone	Ground stone	Bone
1	Surface, N½ of N98E110	Rock cluster	1.45	1.30		Ovoid	364	+		+
2	Base of S1, L2, N½ of N98E98–100	Rock cluster	2.75	1.60		Irregular	400*	+	+	+
3	Base of S1, L2, N½ of N98E116	Rock cluster	1.45‡	0.85‡		Irregular	62‡	+	+	+
4	Base of S1, L4, NE¼ of N100E116	Pit, small	0.38	0.35	0.06	Subcircular		+		
5	Base of S1, L5, SE¼ of N100E98	Rock cluster	2.50*	0.75‡		Irregular?	54‡	+		+
6	Base of S1, L5, SE¼ of N98E98	Rock cluster	1.85	0.55		Irregular	58	+	+	+
7	Base of S1, L4, SW¼ of N100E100	Pit, straight-sided	1.48	1.78‡	0.40	Ovoid	112‡	+	+	+
8	Base of S1, L5, NE¼ of N98E100	Pit, small	0.55	0.52	0.24	Circular	4	+		+
9	Base of S1, L2, NE¼ of N108E58	Pit, small	0.26	0.24	0.07	Circular		+		+
10	Base of S1, L2, NW¼ of N98E110	Pit, small	0.38	0.38	0.04	Circular		+		+
11	Base of S1, L2, N98–N100E108–110	Structure								
12	Deleted (not a feature)									
13	Base of S1, L2, SW¼ of N100E100	Rock cluster	0.40	0.30		Irregular	20	+		+
14	Base of S1, L3, E½ of N108E58	Rock cluster	1.75‡	1.20‡		?	228‡	+	+	+
15	Base of S1, L6, N108E58	Pit, roasting	0.80	0.60	0.35	Ovoid	137	+	+	+
16	Base of S1, L1, NW¼ of N98E120	Pit, small	0.50*	0.44	0.10	Ovoid		+		
17	Base of S1, L7, N98–100E96–100	Structure								
18	NE corner of Feature 11, under floor	Pit (not excavated)								
19	E½ of Feature 17, through floor	Pit	1.65	1.70‡	0.20	Irregular	292	+	+	+
20	Base of S1, L3, SW¼ of N100E106	Pit, bell-shaped	0.90	0.90	0.45	Circular	56	+		+
21	Base of S1, L3, N100E102–106	Structure (not excavated)								

+ Present; * Estimated; ‡ Incompletely exposed. Location S1, L2 = Stratum 1, Level 2

How long a period of accumulation is represented by the midden? Unfortunately, there are only four radiocarbon dates from the Donaldson Site (Table 3.1), and it is difficult to ascertain how accurately they portray the period of time during which it was occupied. Taking the most conservative view, the maximum and minimum values of the dates calibrated at 2 sigma suggest that the occupation might have covered nearly 600 years, from about 800 B.C. to 200 B.C. However, this interval is probably too long, and a span of 200 or 300 years may be more realistic. Certainly the close correspondence of three of the four dates (A-4200, A-4201, and AA-13125), which come from three widely separated features, suggests that the occupation may have been shorter and more intensive.

Within the midden, and also at its base extending into the culturally sterile substrate (Unit 100), 26 cultural features were uncovered, including two domestic structures, six human burials, seven rock clusters, nine pits, and one rock-filled roasting pit (Table 3.4).

Structures

Two domestic structures, Features 11 and 17, were encountered by chance in the sample of selected 2–m grid squares. Neither had been exposed or was obvious in profile in the wash bank, and those particular squares were not chosen with the knowledge that architecture lay beneath the surface of the cultural deposit. What remained of both structures was completely excavated. In addition, two features, probably representing structures, were identified in profile but not excavated. One was discovered in the northwest wall of Trench 3 (Fig. 3.5); it had a maximum length of approximately 4.0 m and a depth of 0.40 m. The second structure appeared in profile after the right bank of the stream had been eroded back by approximately 2 m during the October 1983 flood. It measured about 2.8 m in length by at least 0.20 m in depth; it was assigned a feature number (21) but was not excavated. This structure was located approximately 1 m southeast of Feature 17, one of the two excavated structures, and slightly more than 3 m northwest of Feature 11, the other excavated structure.

Feature 11

The structure located in the south-central part of the site had been excavated approximately 0.33 m into the sterile reddish brown alluvium (Unit 100) underlying the cultural deposit. Feature 11 (Figs. 3.6, 3.7) was

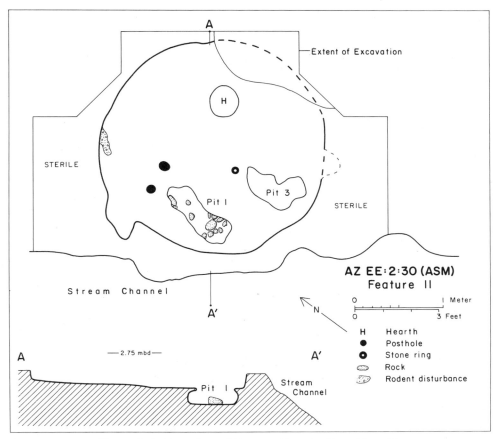

Figure 3.6. Plan view of Feature 11 at the Donaldson Site.

Figure 3.7. Feature 11 after excavation, showing the large hearth in the upper center of the floor. (ASM photograph by Bruce B. Huckell.)

[37]

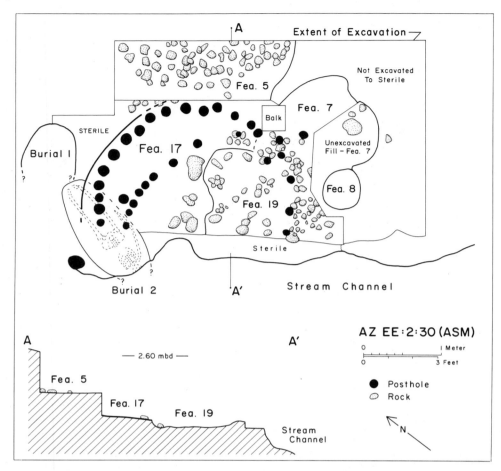

Figure 3.8. Plan view of Feature 17 and related features.

subcircular in plan with a mean diameter of 2.46 m. The floor was the unplastered bottom of the prehistoric excavation, and the floor features consisted of a hearth, two holes, possibly for posts, and three amorphous pits. The pits contained fire-cracked rocks and appeared to predate the structure; all had been packed with a mixture of sterile reddish brown sandy clay and dark gray, culturally enriched sediments. The east edge of the floor was truncated by a large pit; time did not permit its exploration. The hearth, located near the east edge of the floor, was 0.35 m in diameter and 0.10 m deep, an unplastered pit with large amounts of charcoal. A single burned branch segment from it yielded a radiocarbon date of 2400 ± 90 B.P. (calibrated at one sigma to 750–390 B.C., A–4200). The two holes, Floor Pits 2 and 4 (Fig. 3.6), were near one another in the west-central part of the structure and were probably postholes; both were approximately 0.10 m in diameter, one being 0.20 m deep and the other merely 0.05 m deep. The only floor contact artifact was a perforated stone ring (Fig. 3.6).

Feature 17

Slightly less than half of a second structure was uncovered about 10 m northwest of Feature 11 (Fig. 3.5). Feature 17 (Fig. 3.8) consisted of a subcircular remnant of floor truncated by Matty Wash on the southwest and intruded on the south by Feature 19, an amorphous, shallow depression with an abundance of fire-cracked rock. A maize cupule from the fill of Feature 19 was dated to 2505 ± 55 B.P. (calibrated at one sigma to 790–410 B.C., AA–13125; Table 3.1).

The floor of Feature 17 was an unplastered surface excavated approximately 0.30 m to 0.40 m into the sterile reddish brown substrate (Unit 100) and was ringed by postholes. It is estimated that its original diameter was approximately 2.70 m; a second, inner ring of eight postholes was the only floor feature (Fig. 3.8). Because of the disturbance caused by the intrusive feature and stream erosion, it was not possible to determine whether the inner ring of postholes was associated with the outer ring or represented a younger or older structure that

Table 3.5. Attributes of the Preceramic Inhumations from Matty Canyon

Burial	Position	Completeness	Sex	Age	Placement	Head	Orientation
Donaldson Site							
1	Flexed	Nearly complete	Male	40+	On back	To Northeast	Northeast-southwest
2	Extended	Missing cranium	Female	35+	On back	To South	North-south
4	Flexed	Nearly complete	Male	40+	On back	To Southeast	Northwest-southeast
5	Flexed	Lower limbs	Male?	Adult	Unknown	Unknown	Unknown
6	Flexed	Lower torso	Female?	Adult	On right side	To Northwest	Northwest-southeast

NOTE: Burial 3 was a partial Hohokam interment in Unit 3 overlying the preceramic deposit.

Burial	Position	Completeness	Sex	Age	Placement	Head	Orientation
Los Ojitos							
1	Flexed	Nearly complete	Female?	25–35	On left side	To west	East-west
2	Flexed	Complete	Female	20–25	On left side	To west	East-west
6	Flexed	Missing lower limbs	Female?	25–30	On left side	To west	East-west
7	Flexed	Lower limbs only	Uncertain	13–16	On right side	To east?	East-west?
8	Flexed	Nearly complete	Female	18–20	On left side	To west	East-west
9	Flexed?	Cranium, upper torso	Female	25–30	On right side	To north	North-south
4–1	Secondary	Nearly complete?	Female	45+			
4–2	Secondary	Nearly complete?	Male	40+			
4–3	Secondary	Nearly complete?	Male	30–40			
4–4	Secondary	Nearly complete?	Male	30–40			

NOTE: Burials 4–1 through 4–4 are from a secondary multiple burial, Feature 4.

utilized the same floor surface. The outer ring contained 19 identifiable postholes, four of which were connected by a shallow groove. These four partially overlay an extended burial (Burial 2), over which the structure had been constructed (Fig. 3.8). The postholes averaged 0.15 m in diameter, and were from 0.10 m to 0.22 m deep, spaced at approximately 0.10 m intervals. The inner ring of postholes was slightly smaller in diameter and the holes were less regularly spaced. Subsequent cultural disturbance and the recent erosion of Matty Wash have combined to leave an incomplete record of this second structure.

Discussion

Both structures were circular in plan and constructed in shallow pits. Based on the presence of postholes in Feature 17, the partial structure, the walls were probably of pole and brush construction, perhaps covered with grass thatch. No evidence of wall or roof plaster was observed, but because neither structure burned, this does not necessarily mean that they were unplastered. Feature 11, the complete structure, had a single, large hearth positioned away from the center of the floor, but in neither structure was there evidence of an entryway. Little can be deduced from the two structures observed in profile except that the one in Trench 3 appeared to be larger in size (4 m as exposed) than the excavated ones.

Burials

Eight human burials were reported by Eddy in 1958, nearly all of them in Test 2. They were in pits, but most were described as being fragmentary and difficult to remove from the highly compacted midden sediments. Four of the better preserved burials were in flexed positions on their sides (3) or back (1); no accompanying offerings were recognized. The burial of a domestic dog, also without offerings, was recorded in the 1955 excavation of Test 1.

Six more human interments were discovered at the Donaldson Site: three were excavated in late 1982 and early 1983, and three more were exposed by the October 1983 flood and excavated shortly thereafter. Of this total, five were in direct association with the late preceramic cultural deposit, and one (Burial 3) was positioned more than a meter above it in the younger Hohokam occupational horizon. Table 3.5 summarizes the basic attributes of the preceramic burials and their locations are shown in Figure 3.5.

Flexed Burials

Four of the five preceramic burials (1, 4, 5, and 6) were in flexed positions. Burials 1 and 4 were interred in supine positions, Burial 6 on its right side, and the placement of fragmentary Burial 5 was not discerned.

Burial 1 was in a shallow pit immediately to the west of and 0.25 m above the floor of Feature 17, the partial structure. The oval pit containing the body measured approximately 1.10 m long (incomplete due to erosion), 0.75 m wide, and 0.40 m deep. This interment was an adult male, lying in a tightly flexed, knees-on-the-chest, supine position. It was complete except for the feet and distal portions of the lower leg bones, which had been removed by erosion in Matty Wash. The left arm, bent slightly at the elbow, lay across the chest with the left hand touching the right shoulder. The right arm was tightly flexed at the elbow with the right hand resting on the left wrist. The axis of the body was oriented northeast-southwest, head to the northeast, and there was no evidence of offerings.

Burial 4 was exposed by the flood of early October, 1983, approximately 6 m north of Burial 1 (Fig. 3.5). In this case, the body was covered by a large basin metate placed almost directly on top of it. The adult male was resting in an oval pit measuring 0.85 m long, 0.68 m wide, and 0.35 m deep. The body was tightly flexed in a supine position, although the legs were to the left of the chest. The right arm was slightly bent at the elbow, with the right hand resting on the lower abdominal region; the left arm was sharply bent at the elbow and the left hand was found 15 cm from the left shoulder. The axis of the body was oriented northwest-southeast, head to the southeast, and, except for the metate and one large unmodified slab of rock, there were no associated offerings.

Burial 5, located approximately 15 m north of Burial 4, had been exposed and almost completely removed by the October 1983 flood. Excavation revealed a small amount of postcranial material (lower limbs), representing the tightly flexed burial of an adult, possibly male.

Burial 6, 0.40 m east of Burial 5, was also exposed by the October 1983 flood. The cranium was lost in the flood, as was much of the upper portion of the pectoral girdle. Remaining were the legs, a portion of the pelvis, several ribs, and elbow sections of both arms. The body was in a tightly flexed position, lying on its right side, and oriented northwest-southeast with the head to the northwest. The arms were bent sharply at the elbows, indicating that the hands probably extended upward to the head. The oval pit in which it lay was also incomplete, but was approximately 0.95 m long, 0.70 m wide, and at least 0.20 m deep. Both the fragmentariness and poor preservation of the remains limited identification, but the bones seemed to represent an adult, possibly female. Again, no nonperishable offerings were present with the interment.

Extended Burial

A single extended interment of an adult female, Burial 2, was discovered in a shallow, narrow, elongated pit below the floor of the partial structure (Feature 17; Fig. 3.8). It also partly underlay Burial 1, although the bottom of the burial pit was 0.44 m deeper than the base of the pit that contained Burial 1. This interment was complete except for the cranium and left arm, which had been removed by Matty Wash. The pit was in excess of 1.5 m long, 0.65 m wide, and its base lay only 0.17 m below the floor of Feature 17. The body was in an extended, supine position, and no accompanying offerings were present. The long axis of the body was aligned north-south with the head to the south. The burial was revealed only when the postholes associated with Feature 17 were excavated; the right knee was encountered at the bottom of one of the postholes. Feature 17 had been built on top of Burial 2, and probably some of the burial pit fill was removed during its construction.

Hohokam Burial

Burial 3 was originally located by the Donaldson family on the left bank of Matty Wash. It was positioned approximately 1.30 m above the late preceramic cultural deposit (Fig. 3.2, *top*), and it consisted only of a partial cranium and the left clavicle, scapula, and humerus of an adult of uncertain sex. It, too, lacked associated offerings. Burial position could not be determined.

Discussion

Several human burials have been unearthed in preceramic sites in the Cienega Valley during the years of sporadic archaeological investigation there. Frank Eddy (1958: 52-53; Eddy and Cooley 1983: 22–23) encountered eight, poorly preserved inhumations in the course of his work at AZ EE:2:30. All had been placed in pits, and three were in flexed positions on their sides. No offerings were present with these burials. Seven of them were together in one relatively restricted area against what was at the time the left bank of the wash (Fig. 1.3), six of them within a space 3.5 m long by 1 m wide. This area was probably within 10 m of Burials 1 and 2 from the 1983 excavations.

Emil Haury informed me that in the mid-1920s he and a few other students with Byron Cummings investigated several burials exposed in Cienega Creek. The interments were some 3.5 m below the floodplain surface, and they lacked offerings. Although no associated cultural horizon was in evidence, scattered basin metates and manos nearby in the channel of Cienega Creek strongly hinted that the burials were preceramic.

The late preceramic Pantano Site (AZ EE:2:50 ASM), located 17 km (10.6 miles) north of Matty Canyon on Pantano Wash and only 1.5 km (0.9 mile) below the confluence of Cienega Creek and Mescal Arroyo where Pantano Wash begins (Fig. 1.2), has yielded two burials (Hemmings and others 1968). One was in a tightly flexed position on its left side in a pit within a well-developed midden deposit that had a horizontal extent of 150 m. Like Burial 4 at the Donaldson Site, this young adult male was covered with parts of two large metates and at least two cobbles. The other burial, excavated in 1964, was that of an infant, with a few additional elements from an adolescent. Two radiocarbon dates on wood charcoal from that site are 1780 ± 100 B.P. (calibrated at one sigma to A.D. 130–410, A–885) and 1660 ± 60 B.P. (calibrated at one sigma to A.D. 260–530, A–886). I observed two other burials at this site in 1977 and recorded but did not excavate them. One was tightly flexed in a supine position and the other was in a seated position with the legs drawn up toward the chest.

Preceramic burials are uncommon in southeastern Arizona, and the Cienega Valley sites contain the largest cluster thus far known to archaeologists. Sayles (1983: 129) reported San Pedro stage burials from two sites in the San Pedro Valley; both are unpublished. Three additional preceramic burials have been reported from San Pedro Valley sites, two by Turner (1969) and one by McWilliams (1971). In the Santa Cruz Valley, 5 burials, presumably preceramic, were excavated from the Brickyard Site, and as many as 50 others were apparently destroyed by modern quarrying, according to Terah Smiley (B. Huckell 1984b: 140). No offerings were with the Brickyard Site burials; they were either flexed or in seated positions. Near Picacho, along the Santa Cruz River, excavations at Coffee Camp yielded two burials assigned to the late preceramic period, one flexed and one semiflexed (Dongoske 1993).

From this small sample, it appears that flexed interment was the predominant mode of treatment of the dead during the Early Agricultural period, with some extended and seated burials. It is unclear what circumstances dictated position. Cremations recovered from the Cienega Creek Site at Point of Pines (Haury 1957) and from Coffee Camp (Dongoske 1993) indicate further variation in burial practices.

Rock Clusters

Seven concentrations or "piles" of fire-cracked rocks were encountered in the course of the work at the Donaldson Site. Not all were exposed completely, and as noted in Table 3.4, their attributes are in some cases based on only the portions that were exposed within the excavated grid squares. Those that were investigated varied from small concentrations less than 1 m in maximum dimension and containing approximately 20 fire-cracked rocks up to large piles 2.75 m in maximum dimension and containing nearly 400 fire-cracked rocks. None of these clusters occurred in pits; all appeared to have been placed on level surfaces. It is suspected that most of the rock clusters resulted from the cleaning out of roasting pits after the food was cooked. Four of the larger, denser rock clusters contained relatively abundant amounts of charcoal, some flaked stone, and animal bone fragments; four had broken ground stone implements within them. Fire-cracked rocks represent one of the most common constituents of the midden deposit (Table 3.3), although most often they occur as isolated, dissociated pieces.

Eddy (1958: 37–38; Eddy and Cooley 1983: 17–18) reported five of these features, which he termed "surface hearths." He speculated that these concentrations were places where rocks were heated before being transferred to cooking pits.

Pits

The nine excavated pits varied in size and morphology: small (5), large straight-sided (1), irregular (1), bell-shaped (1), and rock-filled (1). Their attributes are presented in Table 3.4.

Small pits

Features 4, 8, 9, 10, and 16 were discerned as dark, circular concentrations of charcoal lumps or flecks and ash. In diameter they typically ranged from 0.26 m to 0.55 m, and excavation revealed shallow, basin-shaped pits less than 0.25 m deep. With one exception, these features occurred within the midden, excavated not into sterile sediments but completely contained within the cultural deposit. Commonly they contained only a few flakes or small numbers of animal bone fragments. These features may represent small pits used for a variety of cooking or heating tasks; the hearth in the Feature 11 structure is morphologically similar. They were probably constructed on an as-needed basis, and seem to be abundant at the site. A carbonized maize cupule from Feature 4 yielded a date of 2320 ± 55 B.P. (calibrated at one sigma to 400–260 B.C., AA–13124; Table 3.1).

Straight-sided Pit

Feature 7, the only straight-sided pit, was irregularly oval in plan; it measured 1.48 m long by 1.78 m wide and about 0.40 m deep. Because only a portion of it was excavated into sterile sediments, its exact configuration is unknown. Slightly more than half of its fill was removed, yielding large quantities of fire-cracked rocks, flaked and ground stone tools, and animal bone, suggesting that it had been filled with trash. Eddy (1958) reported seven straight-sided pits, and he postulated different uses for them (see *Discussion* below).

Irregular Pit

Part of a large, amorphous pit (Feature 19) was exposed in the area of Feature 17, the partial structure. A portion of Feature 19 had been eroded away by Matty Wash. What remained of it was a scatter of nearly 300 fire-cracked rocks and unmodified cobbles in a pit excavated 0.20 m through the southeastern half of the structure floor. It may be clearly seen in Figure 3.8. Also present in this pit were substantial quantities of charcoal, bone, and flaked and ground stone artifacts. No evidence of burning was noted on the floor or sides of the pit, and its original purpose is unknown. It was impossible to determine from what level in the deposit this pit may have originated, but it must predate Feature 6, a rock cluster that was approximately 0.15 m above the uppermost rocks of Feature 19. An AMS date of 2505 ± 55 B.P. (calibrated at one sigma to 790–410 B.C., AA–13125; Table 3.1) was obtained from a carbonized maize cupule from the feature.

Bell-Shaped Pit

The one bell-shaped pit (Feature 20) was revealed in section by the October 1983 floods and was located in the right arroyo bank immediately south of an unexcavated structure (Feature 21). Excavation revealed that about 80 percent of the pit remained intact (Fig. 3.9). It measured approximately 0.45 m in depth, had a maximum basal diameter of 0.90 m, and an orifice diameter of 0.28 m. Its fill was rich in charcoal and carbonized plant remains, including fire-cracked rock, flaked stone debitage and tools, and animal bone, suggesting it was

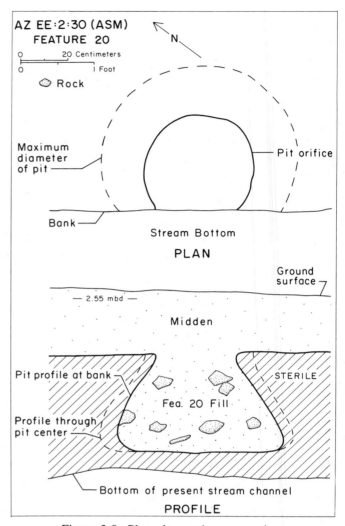

Figure 3.9. Plan view and cross section of Feature 20, a bell-shaped pit.

trash-filled. Eddy (1958: 31, Table 1; Eddy and Cooley 1983: 17) uncovered eight such pits, which he termed "undercut;" most of them were larger than Feature 20. Suggested functions of these pits are discussed below.

Roasting Pit

Feature 15, a rock-filled roasting pit, measured 0.80 m by 0.60 m and was 0.35 m deep. In cross section the pit had a deep hemispherical shape with nearly straight sides and a rounded bottom. In addition to 137 fire-cracked rocks, the pit yielded a large quantity of charcoal, flaked and ground stone artifacts, and a small amount of bone; at the bottom were three large, thermally fractured cobbles. A single charcoal lump from the base of the pit yielded a date of 2380 ± 90 B.P.

(calibrated at one sigma to 750–380 B.C., A– 4201; Table 3.1). One of the larger clusters of fire-cracked rocks (Feature 14) was immediately adjacent to this pit and perhaps it represents material cleaned out from Feature 15 or another similar pit nearby. Feature 15 probably served as a small roasting pit.

Discussion

Considering the relatively small area (48 square meters) excavated in 1983, the discovery of so many features is surprising; this abundance reflects the complexity of the cultural deposit. Eddy (1958) made a similar observation when he encountered high densities of features in his excavations (Fig. 1.3). Moreover, the intrusion of one feature on another as the deposit grew in thickness was noted by Eddy, particularly in reference to his Test 1 and Test 2 areas. This same complexity of superposition as it was encountered in one area during the 1983 investigations in shown in Figures 3.10 through 3.13. The four photographs were taken as excavation proceeded, and they document repeated episodes of fire-cracked rock dumping, pit excavation, and trash disposal within the fill of a structure, which was itself built over a burial. The thickness of the cultural deposit in this area reached 1 m. No other late preceramic sites thus far excavated in southeastern Arizona exhibit this degree of feature density and superposition.

Function is apparent for some of the various pit features, but more obscure for others. Eddy devoted some thought to possible functions served by the pits he excavated, based primarily on their contents and secondarily on their morphology. He recognized three morphological types (Eddy 1958: 31–32, Table 1; Eddy and Cooley 1983: 17–18): bell-shaped pits, or "undercut" in his terminology (8); straight-sided pits (7); and flare-rimmed pits (4). Eddy (1958: 33–36) identified five pits (four bell-shaped and one straight-sided) that he believed were probably used as earthen cooking ovens, based on the presence of abundant charcoal in the lower third of the pit fill, animal bones, and fire-cracked rocks. At least one of the straight-sided pits and three of the flare-rimmed pits may have been primarily for storage or burial, because charcoal was not common in their fills. However, he also noted that many pits had been put to secondary uses, including trash disposal and graves for the deceased (Eddy 1958, Table 1).

In my opinion, it is likely that most of the bell-shaped pits originally served storage needs. Such pits are common at other late preceramic sites in southeastern Arizona. Sayles (1941) reported bell-shaped pits from the San Pedro stage type site at Fairbank on the San Pedro River and suggested they were used for either storage or cooking. They have been found at Bat Cave (Wills 1988a: 105) and in many other late preceramic sites all over the Southwest, including Chaco Canyon (Simmons 1986), Durango (Morris and Burgh 1954), Kayenta (Guernsey and Kidder 1921), Black Mesa (Leonard and others 1983: 123–154), and Tucson (Huckell and Huckell 1984). Further, they are common in the central and eastern United States in archaeological sites (De-Boer 1988) and have been described from Early Formative sites in Mesoamerica as well (Winter 1976).

Historically, bell-shaped pits are recorded as being used for storage among the Western Apache (Buskirk 1986), Navajo (Hill 1938: 42-43, Fig. 6a), and Missouri River tribes (Wilson 1987). Their design, featuring a comparatively small opening and increasing diameter with depth, offers both a large capacity and a small, fairly easily sealed orifice, making them excellent storage features. However, they are also known to have relatively short use lives, and at a settlement like the Donaldson Site, they would have made convenient places to dispose of rubbish when they were no longer used for storage.

The possible functions of other types of pits at the Donaldson Site have been briefly mentioned. Halbirt and others (1993) have explored the possible functions of pits at the late preceramic site of Coffee Camp, located approximately 20 km southwest of Picacho, Arizona. Excavations there produced a sample of 333 pit features, not including domestic structures or burials. Halbirt and others (1993) searched the ethnographic literature to document the types and morphologies of pit features used for cooking or heating (thermal pits) and storage, processing, tool caching, and other functions not involving fire (nonthermal pits). After developing a set of expectations for the kinds of functions likely to have been served by pits, they examined 214 pits from Coffee Camp. Using pit surface area and depth, as well as contents, they identified three classes of thermal pits (open fires in shallow pits, pit ovens, and miscellaneous ash pits and fire-affected rock concentrations). Considerable overlap in size and morphology was observed between the first two types. The nonthermal pits were divided into eight types based on surface area and depth, and secondarily on artifactual contents. The types included postholes, basket rests, cache pits, three varieties of storage pits, two varieties of processing pits, and a miscellaneous grouping. Their success in identifying feature function was limited, primarily because of the absence of a clear separation of pit size and a lack of

Figure 3.10. Feature 2, a rock cluster, after exposure. Datum stake is on the pedestal near the center of the excavation area; arrow indicates grid north. (ASM photograph by Bruce B. Huckell.)

Figure 3.11. Features 5 and 6, rock clusters discovered after Feature 2 was removed, and Feature 7, a pit under excavation to the right. (ASM photograph by Bruce B. Huckell.)

Figure 3.12. Feature 17, a partial pit structure, and other features adjacent to it. Feature 5 is still in place north of and above Feature 17. (ASM photograph by Bruce B. Huckell.)

Figure 3.13. Feature 17 and related features after final excavation. Compare with Figure 3.8. (ASM photograph by Bruce B. Huckell.)

Figure 3.14. Excavations in progress at Los Ojitos; view is west across Matty Wash. The cultural deposit is at the base of the vertical bank. (ASM photograph by Bruce B. Huckell.)

confidence in the relationship between the artifacts recovered from the pits and the functions those pits may have served originally. They concluded that inferring pit function is difficult, but that studying archaeobotanical remains might offer more insightful results. Unfortunately, the cultural and noncultural processes responsible for filling the pits may limit the confidence that can be placed in this approach also (L. Huckell, Chapter 5).

In summary, the Donaldson Site pit features probably encompass a variety of specific functions, including those involving use of fire or heat and those that do not. Attempts to build more specific inferences using pit contents are liable to be compromised by the uncertainty surrounding the linkage between the original function of a pit and the assemblage of remains it contained when excavated. This problem is compounded at a settlement such as the Donaldson Site, where long-term occupation is strongly indicated.

LOS OJITOS

The two weeks of work accomplished at Los Ojitos revealed a cultural deposit essentially identical to that at the Donaldson Site. As exposed during work in June of 1983 (Figs. 3.14, 3.15), the deposit had a horizontal extent of 26 m on the left bank of the arroyo. It had been truncated on the north by a former channel meander of the Matty Wash arroyo; what had not been removed by erosion may have been buried beneath a younger inset terrace. Its extent to the south was masked by a considerable accumulation of talus from the collapse of the arroyo bank in that area. Because it was protected by another inset terrace, floodwaters seldom reached that area to carry away the accumulations of talus sediments. However, summer floods during August of 1983 removed much of this loose talus upstream of the area in which we worked, revealing a continuous cultural deposit covering an estimated 65 m to 70 m on a north-south axis. Scarcely five weeks later, the October 1983 flood buried the entire exposure under 0.50 m to 2.0 m of sand and silt. Ten years after that flood, the site area is characterized by a thick growth of young cottonwood and willow trees, seep willow, annuals, grasses, and aquatic plants. The available information suggests that Los Ojitos was an unusually extensive preceramic deposit, similar to the Donaldson Site.

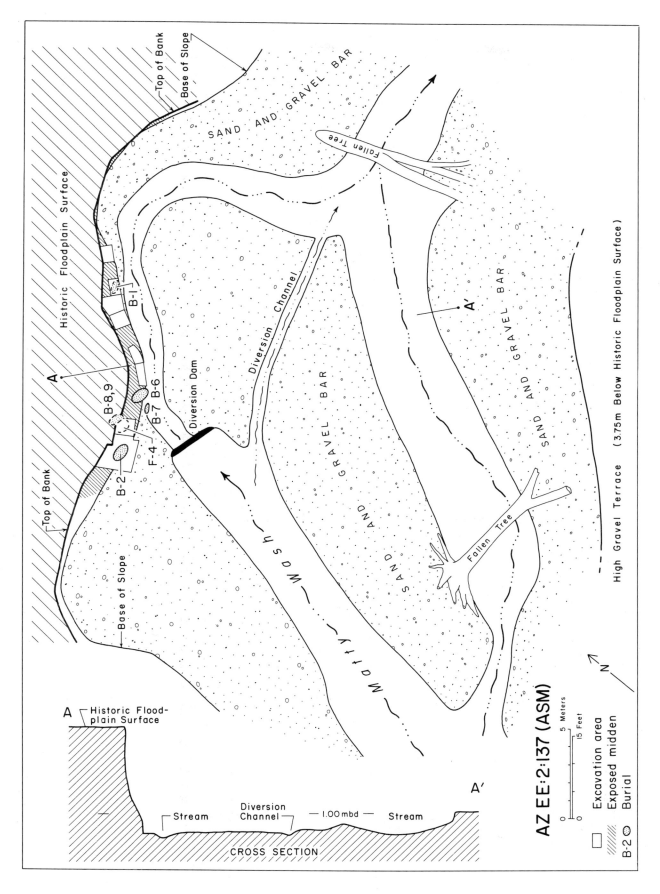

Figure 3.15. Los Ojitos, showing the locations of the 1983 excavations. F–4 is the multiple burial.

Table 3.6. Material Composition of the Cultural Deposit at Los Ojitos (AZ EE:2:137 ASM)

Grid	Average thickness of deposit (m)	Debitage N	%	Flaked stone tools N	%	Ground stone tools N	%	Animal bone N	%	Fire-cracked rock N	%
W4	0.50	773	(82.3)	9	(1.0)	1	(0.1)	110	(11.7)	46*	(4.9)
E5	0.30	459		10				42		NR	
E2	0.60	608	(78.8)	12	(1.6)	2	(0.3)	84	(10.9)	66*	(8.5)
E1	0.60	468	(76.7)	15	(2.5)			58	(9.5)	69*	(11.3)

NOTE: Percentages of artifact classes are not calculated for Grid E5, because quantities of fire-cracked rock were not recorded.
* Quantities of fire-cracked rock in the lowest level were not recorded; these amounts are fewer than the actual number excavated.

The cultural exposure at Los Ojitos ranged in thickness from approximately 0.30 m to 0.90 m, and, like its counterpart at the Donaldson Site, it contained abundant pieces of fire-cracked rocks, flaked and ground stone artifacts, animal bone, and much ash and charcoal. The brief explorations there were limited to excavating 1–m-wide, judgmentally selected, sloping sections of the deposit inward toward the vertical plane of the arroyo bank. Six individual inhumations, one multiple inhumation, and four rock cluster features were uncovered. Figure 3.14 shows the part of the site that was excavated and Figure 3.15 presents a map of the area investigated and the extent of exposure in June of 1983.

The Cultural Deposit

Materials from four of the 1–m grid squares excavated at Los Ojitos were analyzed in order to compare the composition of the cultural deposit to that of the Donaldson Site (Table 3.6). Interpretation of these compilations must be tempered with two cautions. One, as can be seen from the outlines of the excavation areas in Figure 3.15, none of the grid squares at Los Ojitos is actually a 1–m by 1–m square because of the uneven exposure of the deposit, which sloped outward from top to bottom. Usually the upper level of a grid was much smaller in actual area than the bottom level, so the quantities in the table reflect different volumes of the cultural deposit. Two, because the excavators of Los Ojitos were predominantly new crew members who were less familiar with established procedures, the recording of fire-cracked rock was inconsistent. As reflected in the table, all four of the grids selected for analysis are lacking certain information for fire-cracked rock, so the percentages for the various constituents of the deposit are skewed or, in one case, not calculable. Despite these drawbacks, comparing Table 3.6 with Table 3.3 does show that, in general, similar relative

proportions of debitage, flaked stone tools, ground stone tools, animal bone, and fire-cracked rock are evident at both sites. If the fire-cracked rocks had all been counted, the percentages would be nearly equal.

The quantities recorded indicate that the middens at the two sites are composed of the same constituents in similar relative amounts and that the Los Ojitos deposit also contains a high density of cultural material. The inference is clear that the Los Ojitos deposit accumulated at a settlement where the prehistoric occupation was similar in its intensity and perhaps duration to that of the Donaldson Site. Unlike the Donaldson Site, features at Los Ojitos were limited to burials and rock clusters. The lack of other types of features probably results from the limited space available for investigation and the place within the site at which the arroyo had created the exposure.

Burials

When Los Ojitos was first discovered, a single interment (Burial 1) was in the process of being exposed by Matty Canyon Wash. Excavations initiated at judgmentally selected locations along the bank face quickly revealed a second individual burial and a multiple burial (Fig. 3.15, F–4). During the course of the summer, four more inhumations were exposed by flooding and subjected to complete or partial excavation. By the time the October 1983 flood buried the site, portions of ten individuals had been recovered from six single inhumations and one multiple secondary burial.

Flexed Burials

The six single burials discovered at Los Ojitos were flexed inhumations (Table 3.5).

Burial 1 was the nearly complete interment of an adult, probably female; no discernible grave pit could be detected. The body had been placed on its left side in a flexed position with the arms tightly bent and the hands folded under the chin. The left leg was much closer to the chest than was the right leg. Orientation of the body was on an east-west axis, head to the west. No apparent offerings accompanied the burial.

Burial 2 was that of an adult female, in an irregular pit that measured 1.55 m long by 0.90 m wide and that extended at least 0.15 m into the underlying Unit 100 sediments. The body was on its left side in a tightly flexed position. The long axis of the body was east-west, with the head to the west. The arms were sharply bent at the elbows and the hands were extended along the sides of the head. A complete projectile point was on top of the right side ribs; whether it represented an offering or an incidental inclusion in the grave fill could not be ascertained.

Burial 6 was exposed by the summer rains and was probably an adult female. The innominates, the lower left leg, and the entire right leg were lost to the wash. Like Burials 1 and 2, it was tightly flexed, lying on the left side. The long axis of the body was aligned east-west, head to the west, arms bent, with the hands extended along the sides of the face. The grave measured approximately 1.10 m long by 0.60 m wide, and extended 0.35 m into Unit 100. No accompanying offerings were in evidence.

Only 0.25 m south of Burial 6 was part of another interment, Burial 7. All that remained were the lower legs, which revealed that the body had been placed on its right side in a flexed position. The long axis of the body was east-west, with the head to the east. It is likely that this was the burial of an adolescent; no offerings were discovered.

Burial 8, an adult female, was also exposed by the summer floods. The cranium, mandible, thoracic vertebrae, and right arm were missing, and no obvious pit limits were identified except on the north. The body was tightly flexed and lying on the left side. The long axis of the body was east-west aligned, with the head to the west. Traces of red ocher were found on some of the elements, but there were no apparent offerings.

Directly beneath Burial 8 was Burial 9, which consisted of the upper torso of another flexed burial. Time and the water table prevented proper exploration of this burial, and only days after its discovery in late September, the October 1983 flood removed the remainder of it. However, the cranium was collected, which indicated that the burial was that of an adult female. The body was clearly oriented north-south and lay on its right side. No offerings were observed. The bones of Burial 8 were nearly touching those of Burial 9, so it is possible that excavation of the grave for Burial 8 partially exposed Burial 9.

Multiple Secondary Burial

The discovery of a secondary burial containing the remains of at least four persons was unexpected. It was located in the same area as the majority of the individual inhumations and initially appeared to contain the remains of three people, based on the presence of three skulls protruding through the top of an impressive mass of long bones. With the exception of occasional articulated elements, the bones appeared to have been tightly stacked or piled as individual elements in a small, ovoid pit. The entire mass covered an area approximately 0.80 m northwest-southeast by 0.60 m northeast-southwest. By the time this multiple secondary burial was completely defined, the summer rainy season was beginning. We did not try to excavate each element in the field; instead, the entire mass was jacketed in burlap and plaster and removed. When excavated in the laboratory, a fourth skull was discovered, along with a few elements of other individuals. Examination of all of the remains in the multiple burial indicated the presence of three adults, along with portions of the upper torso of a fourth adult and three elements apparently of two children less than two years old (not listed in Table 3.5). This multiple inhumation may represent the reburial of bones from separate individual inhumations, perhaps disturbed by the construction of one or more large pit features somewhere within the settlement. No associated artifacts were present.

Discussion

The single burials from Los Ojitos show some consistent patterns in the treatment of the dead. All were placed in flexed positions, four on their left sides and two on their right sides. They were oriented with the long axis of the body east-west, except one that was oriented north-south. The four bodies lying on their left sides all had the head to the west; one positioned on the right side had the head to the east, the other to the north. Another notable aspect of body placement involved the position of the hands. In three cases the hands were pulled up to the head, and in two of these the hands partly covered the face; in a fourth they were folded beneath the chin. Assuming that the projectile point found above Burial 2 was an unintentional inclusion in the dirt used to fill the grave, nonperishable offerings were lacking in all burials.

The interments appeared to be in a sort of cemetery. All, including the multiple secondary burial, were located in a small area measuring about 10 m along the bank face, and five were present in an area measuring 4 m across. One (Burial 8) had been placed directly on top of another (Burial 9). This density is similar to that observed by Eddy (1958) in his Test 2 area at the Donaldson Site.

With the exception of the multiple burial, the interments at Los Ojitos are similar to those recorded at the Donaldson Site both in 1957 and 1983. Eddy (1958: 53; Eddy and Cooley 1983: 22) reported a similar positioning of the hands along the face in one of the burials he excavated. It is likely that the tight clusterings of the burials at Los Ojitos and at the Donaldson Site (Eddy's Test 2, Fig. 1.2) represent discrete cemetery areas within the overall space covered by the settlements.

Rock Clusters

The only nonburial features encountered at Los Ojitos were four rock clusters, Features 1, 2, 3, and 5. As at the Donaldson Site, they consisted of discrete concentrations of a few dozen to a few hundred fire-cracked rocks resting on a former surface within the cultural deposit. None was exposed in its entirety by the excavation. Occasionally mixed in with the rocks were flaked stone artifacts, pieces of animal bone, and charcoal, probably representing material that had been cleaned out of roasting pits.

Discussion

The excavations at Los Ojitos have provided a small, nonrepresentative sample of cultural features from what must be a large, complex settlement. Yet, at the same time, the work has presented an unparalleled look at the skeletal remains and burial customs of this time period. The 10 individuals represented among the seven burials offer one of the first opportunities to study the physical characteristics of these late preceramic inhabitants of southeastern Arizona (Chapter 7). Despite being buried beneath the tremendous weight of 5.5 m of overlying sediments, the bones were in excellent condition. This high quality preservation resulted in part from the location of Los Ojitos, which is nearer the active channel of Cienega Creek than is the Donaldson Site. The cultural material at Los Ojitos was buried rapidly as the floodplain deposits accumulated. The localized high water table ensured that the deposit stayed wet, or at least moist, during the last 2,200 or more years, enhancing preservation. As discussed by Lisa Huckell in Chapter 5, these same conditions created excellent preservation for the macrobotanical remains as well. Thus, this tantalizingly small sample proved to be an extremely informative one.

The temporal relationship of Los Ojitos to the Donaldson Site is complicated. Two radiocarbon dates were obtained from samples collected in the general cultural deposit at Los Ojitos (Table 3.1). At one sigma they are calibrated to 750–50 B.C. (A–3501) and 390 B.C. to A.D. 1 (A–3500). This wood charcoal and a carbonized maize cob fragment were dated shortly after the NSF-Arizona AMS Facility was built. Their standard deviations are relatively large but do overlap at one standard deviation. These dates suggest that Los Ojitos is younger than the Donaldson Site, by perhaps 200 years or so, conflicting with the observed stratigraphic relationship between the two sites.

Some 0.75 m above the Los Ojitos cultural deposit is a peat deposit, the M_2 marker bed of Eddy and Cooley (1983). In the summer of 1983, careful tracing of the M_2 marker bed upstream from Los Ojitos revealed that it gradually became a buried organic paleosol that interdigitated with the distal end of the Donaldson Site midden. The stratigraphic information, therefore, suggests that Los Ojitos is the *older* of the two settlements. The M_2 marker bed itself has been subjected to radiocarbon dating (Table 3.2). With the exception of one date (Sh–5565), the assays are in close agreement with one another and with the two dates from the cultural deposit beneath the peat. One wonders whether soluble organic acids from the decomposing plant remains that ultimately became the peat might have leached downward and been absorbed by the charcoal and carbonized plant remains in the cultural deposit. If not completely removed during pretreatment, this addition of younger organic carbon might produce dates that are slightly too young. The dating of two fractions of another sample of "carbonaceous earth" from the Cienega Valley (B. Huckell 1983, Table C.1) showed the existence of just such a problem: the solid or residue fraction dated 2140 ± 60 B.P. (calibrated at one sigma to 350–50 B.C., A–227a), whereas the soluble fraction dated 1790 ± 400 B.P. (calibrated at one sigma to 350 B.C. to A.D. 650, A–227b). For now, I prefer to accept the stratigraphic evidence that Los Ojitos is the older of the two sites.

CHAPTER FOUR

Artifact Assemblages from the Donaldson Site and Los Ojitos

The 1983 excavations at the Donaldson Site, like the investigations of Frank Eddy 25 years earlier, provided an impressively diverse and rich assemblage of artifacts. In addition to the simple utilitarian flaked stone, ground stone, and bone tools one would expect from a late preceramic site, there were also some surprising ground stone artifacts of more elaborate form, as well as a few pieces of marine shell jewelry. The limited scope of the work at Los Ojitos naturally resulted in the recovery of a smaller, less varied sample of artifacts from that site. Still, when combined, the samples from these two sites offer a good characterization of the kinds of artifacts that may be considered representative of the Cienega phase.

THE DONALDSON SITE

The four weeks of excavation at the Donaldson Site produced a remarkable quantity of artifacts. A basic descriptive analysis of this material was made to determine the range of morphological variation present in the stone, bone, and shell assemblages. The analysis involved examining all the ground stone and flaked stone tools from the site, but analyzing only a small sample of the debitage. The few bone and shell artifacts were all studied.

Both the flaked and ground stone tools were sorted by morphological type following a basic formal classification system. All identifiable flaked stone implements were extracted from the field bags of flaked stone to segregate the tools from the debitage. Four grid proveniences (N98E110, N98E116, N116E56, N100E116) and the fill of the complete pit structure, Feature 11, were arbitrarily selected for a study of debitage. This process involved a simple sorting and counting by material type; no systematic attempt was made to investigate other attributes of the debitage. Because they were numerically fewer, ground stone implements from all proveniences were classified as to form, condition, and material type, and all pieces of worked bone and marine shell were identified as to form and taxon. To aid in broadening this descriptive treatment, several specific and general comparisons with artifacts from other sites and cultures are included.

Flaked Stone Tools

Excavations at the Donaldson Site produced 299 flaked stone specimens that were classified as implements. Of this number, 126 (42.1%) are bifacially flaked; 117 (39.1%) are unifacially retouched; 40 (13.4%) are flakes utilized without intentional retouch; and 16 (5.4%) are hammerstones. Within each of these major groups of implements, various formal categories were recognized. Table 4.1 presents tool frequencies, and Table 4.2 itemizes the raw materials used for each group of implements.

Bifacially Flaked Tools

Five classes of bifacially flaked implements were identified in the assemblage: projectile points, bifaces, drills, wedges, and partially bifacially retouched flake tools (Table 4.1).

Projectile Points

Forty-six projectile points, representing more than one-third of all bifacially flaked tools, were recovered. Aside from unclassifiable tip, midsection, and other fragments, four styles of points were recognized. The first style is a distinctive, deeply corner-notched point (Fig. 4.1*a–i*). This style has been christened Cienega, in recognition of its characteristic form and its association with the Cienega phase of the Early Agricultural period in the Cienega Valley of southeastern Arizona (B. Huckell 1988). It is clearly the dominant style at the Donaldson Site: 27 points or 77.1 percent of the classified projectile points. Only three of these points are complete, but the Cienega style is readily recognized from fragments. When not badly damaged, these points usually display small, expanding "stems" or hafting

Table 4.1. Flaked Stone Tools from the Donaldson Site

	Number	Total	Percent
Bifacially Flaked Tools		126	42.1
Projectile points		46	36.5
Cienega points	27		
San Pedro points	3		
Cortaro points	3		
Trimmed flakes	2		
Unclassified fragments	11		
Bifaces		44	34.9
Leaf-shaped	5		
Triangular	3		
Incipient, ovoid	11		
End fragments	9		
Unclassified small fragments	16		
Retouched flake tools		10	7.9
Incipiently modified	8		
Edge trimmed, pointed	2		
Drill, expanded base		1	0.8
Wedges		25	19.8
Unifacially Retouched Tools		117	39.1
Scrapers		39	33.3
Ovoid, steep	11		
Side, single-edge	13		
double-edge	2		
End, single-edge	6		
Nosed	4		
Convergent, double-edge	3		
Notched flakes		14	12.0
Single notch	6		
Multiple notches	8		
Projections		14	12.0
Large	9		
Small (gravers)	5		
Planes		3	2.6
Denticulated flakes		13	11.1
Large	8		
Micro	5		
Finely flaked tools		5	4.3
Flakes with irregular retouch		9	7.7
Miscellaneous fragments		20	17.0
Utilized Flakes		40	13.4
Polished	12		
Damaged	23		
Polished and damaged	5		
Hammerstones		16	5.4
Reused core or flaked	15		
Cobble	1		
Total		299	

elements created by deep corner notches driven at a diagonal to the long axis of the point, long sharp blade tangs, and a triangular to slightly incurvate blade that is occasionally serrated (Fig. 4.1*b*). The size of Cienega points suggests that they were intended for use on atlatl darts and were shaped and finished primarily by pressure flaking. With only three exceptions, chert, chalcedony, or other fine-grained siliceous materials were chosen for their manufacture (Table 4.2). Unfortunately, or perhaps intentionally, these points have a structural weakness at the top of the notches where the stem is narrowest. This attribute seems to have facilitated frequent snap breaks, resulting in the recovery of 11 basal stem fragments (Fig. 4.1*h, i*) and, less frequently, essentially complete blade portions of the points (Fig. 4.1*f, g*). Even these small stem fragments are sufficiently diagnostic to permit their recognition as portions of Cienega points.

The narrow, triangular to bulbous stem created by diagonally directed corner notches distinguishes the Cienega point style from the San Pedro point style. Measurement of maximum stem width (the widest part of the stem) and minimum stem width (width of the stem at the top of the notches) for the Donaldson Site Cienega points produced mean values of 11.59 ± 2.52 mm (n = 17) and 7.45 ± 1.33 mm (n = 20), respectively. Measurement of a sample of San Pedro points from the site of Milagro in the eastern Tucson Basin (Huckell and Huckell 1984; B. Huckell 1990) yielded a mean maximum stem width of 22.17 mm ± 2.32 mm (n = 15) and a mean minimum stem width of 15.99 ± 2.56 mm (n = 21). In neither of these two attributes do the styles overlap at two standard deviations, suggesting that they are useful in distinguishing the two styles. Not only are the notches on San Pedro points shallower than on Cienega points, they tend to be broader and without the diagonal angle to the long axis of the point.

The Donaldson Site is not the first locality to yield this point style, although it is the first habitation site in which it is clearly isolated within a distinct cultural and temporal framework. Similar points were discovered at Jemez Cave (Alexander and Reiter 1935, Fig. 5, Type 3b), at the Cienega Creek Site at Point of Pines (Haury 1957, Fig. 17*m–w*), in Tularosa and Cordova caves (Paul Sydney Martin and others 1952, Fig. 45*e–h* and Fig. 70, Type B–1), possibly at Bat Cave (Dick 1965, Fig. 30*j, k*), at Ventana Cave (Haury 1950, Fig. 65*a–c*), and from sites in the Avra Valley west of Tucson (Downum and others 1986, Fig. 4.5*i–l*). Johnson (1960, Fig. 17*n, o*) illustrated two Cienega points from among his 45 "deep corner notched" points at the La Playa Site in northwestern Sonora. Cienega points were recovered from the Split Ridge Site (AZ EE:2:103 ASM) in the

Table 4.2. Raw Material Composition of Flaked Stone Tools from the Donaldson Site

Tools	Metasediment N	%	Quartzite N	%	Silicified limestone N	%	Chert N	%	Chalcedony N	%	Jasper N	%	Quartz N	%	Rhyolite N	%	Obsidian N	%	Limestone N	%	Total
Projectile Points																					
Cienega	1	3.7	1	3.7	1	3.7	10	37.0	11	40.8	3	11.1									27
San Pedro	1	33.3	1	33.3	1	33.3									1	33.3					3
Cortaro							2	66.7	1	33.3											3
Trimmed flakes	1	50.0							1	50.0											2
Fragments			2	18.2			3	27.2	5	45.5					1	9.1					11
Bifaces																					
Leaf-shaped			2	40.0			2	40.0	1	20.0											5
Triangular	1	33.3			1	33.3			1	33.3											3
Incipient	5	45.5			4	36.3	1	9.1											1	9.1	11
Fragments	3	12.0	3	12.0	2	8.0	10	40.0	3	12.0	1	4.0					2	8.0	1	4.0	25
Retouched flakes	3	30.0	3	30.0	2	20.0			1	10.0									1	10.0	10
Drill	1	100.0																			1
Wedges	3	12.0					6	24.0	9	36.0	4	16.0	3	12.0							25
Scrapers																					
Ovoid	2	18.2	4	36.3	5	45.5															11
Side	5	33.3	7	46.6	1	6.7			1	6.7			1	6.7							15
End	4	66.6	1	16.7	1	16.7															6
Nosed	1	25.0	2	50.0	1	25.0															4
Convergent	2	66.7			1	33.3															3
Notched flakes	8	57.2	3	21.4	2	14.3									1	7.1					14
Projections	3	21.4	4	28.6	3	21.4	2	14.3	2	14.3											14
Planes	1	33.3	1	33.3	1	33.3															3
Denticulates																					
Large	5	62.5	2	25.0	1	12.5															8
Micro	1	20.0							3	60.0	1	20.0									5
Finely flaked tools	1	20.0	1	20.0	1	20.0	1	20.0	1	20.0											5
Flakes with																					
irregular retouch	4	44.4	5	55.6																	9
Misc. fragments	10	50.0	2	10.0	3	15.0	1	5.0	3	15.0	1	5.0									20
Utilized flakes	17	42.5	16	40.0	7	17.5															40
Hammerstones	7	43.7	6	37.5	1	6.3													2	12.5	16
Total	89	29.8	66	22.1	39	13.0	38	12.7	43	14.4	10	3.3	4	1.3	3	1.0	2	0.7	5	1.7	299

Figure 4.1. Projectile points and fragments from the Donaldson Site: *a–i*, Cienega style; *j*, *k*, San Pedro style. Length of *a* is 52 mm. (ASM photograph by Helga Teiwes.)

Rosemont area of the Santa Rita Mountains some 15 km (about 10 miles) west of the Donaldson Site (B. Huckell 1984a, Fig. 5.23*b–e*). Interestingly, the two projectile points illustrated by Eddy (1958, Fig. 10*c*, *d*; Eddy and Cooley 1983, Fig. 2.12*c*, *d*) from his work at the Donaldson Site are not easily classified to style but are not Cienega points. However, a nearly complete point from Pit 12 that he sketched in his field notes (the point was subsequently lost) is clearly of this style.

The San Pedro point style is represented by only three specimens. Named by Sayles (1941, Plate 16*c*, *d*), San Pedro points are distributed widely across the southern portions of Arizona and New Mexico and south well into Sonora (Sayles 1983: 125–131). Two of the specimens from the Donaldson Site are large basal fragments made on relatively coarse-grained materials (Fig. 4.1*j*, *k*). This style has long been equated with the late preceramic period in the southern Southwest, but it now appears that it may slightly predate the Cienega point (B. Huckell 1984a: 169–197, 208; Huckell and Huckell 1984).

Three triangular points with concave bases, all badly damaged and reworked, are representative of a recently named projectile point style known as Cortaro. Cortaro points, although common in southern Arizona, have yet

to be securely dated and associated with a particular cultural manifestation. Present evidence indicates an age of either "late Middle Archaic or Late Archaic" (Tagg and Huckell 1984: 88–89, Fig. 2.20*g–n*). They appear to be limited to the southern part of the Southwest, occurring principally in southern Arizona and southwestern New Mexico (Roth and Huckell 1992).

Two complete points are best described as trimmed flakes. Both are made on thin flakes that have been unifacially or partly bifacially trimmed along their margins to produce small, triangular-bladed, square-stemmed forms. Neither appears to be the product of an experienced stone-working artisan, but they vaguely resemble the Cienega points in form.

Eleven specimens are of sufficient size and character to be classified as fragments of projectile points, but they retain no features identifiable as a particular style. Six are tip fragments, four are midsection fragments, and one is probably a basal corner fragment.

Bifaces

The 44 bifaces were separated from projectile points by characteristics of shape, manufacturing technique, regularity of form, and completeness. Two types of

Figure 4.2. Flaked stone tools from the Donaldson Site: *a–e*, bifaces; *f*, drill; *g, h*, small projections (gravers); *i, j*, small denticulated flakes. Length of *e* is 62 mm. (ASM photograph by Helga Teiwes.)

finished bifaces were recognized: leaf-shaped and triangular. The five leaf-shaped examples are simple, convex-sided forms with rounded bases (Fig. 4.2*c–e*) measuring up to 62 mm in length. They typically display percussion flake scars, but occasionally have what appear to be pressure flake scars along one or both margins. Triangular bifaces (Fig. 4.2*a, b*) have straight to slightly convex sides and a flat base. Both percussion and pressure flake scars are apparent on the three specimens of this type, and in general they are smaller (approximately 40 mm long) and better thinned than most of the leaf-shaped bifaces. The triangular forms may have been designed to serve as hafted knives, and the leaf-shaped forms may have been either hand-held knives or perhaps preforms abandoned at an advanced stage of reduction. Both types of bifaces are made of fine-grained to medium-grained metamorphic materials or of fine-grained siliceous materials (Table 4.2).

Eleven other specimens were classified as incipient bifaces (Table 4.2). These were usually flakes displaying varying amounts of bifacial percussion flaking that apparently were discarded after initial attempts at reduction proved ineffective, caused breakage, or revealed flaws. Their shapes are varied, but generally elongated ovoid in outline. With one exception, all are of metamorphic, medium-grained materials.

There were 25 small end fragments and edge and midsection pieces of bifaces that remained unclassified because of their tiny size. These categories probably contain pieces from leaf-shaped, triangular, and incipient bifaces and perhaps projectile points.

An additional 10 specimens were classified as partly bifacially retouched implements. These are flakes that display a single bifacially retouched edge or margin, and, like the incipient bifaces, are made of metamorphic materials. The functions that they may have served are unclear, but it is possible that they are simply bifaces that were abandoned early in the reduction process.

Eddy (1958, Fig. 10*a, b*; Eddy and Cooley 1983, Fig. 2.12*a, b*) recovered a few bifaces of both the leaf-shaped and triangular form at the site. Similar bifaces are common at other late preceramic sites in southern Arizona, including several San Pedro stage sites (Sayles 1941, table accompanying Plate 16), the Split Ridge Site (B. Huckell 1984a, Fig. 5.23*k–p*), and Ventana Cave (Haury 1950, Figs. 52*e–i*, 53*a–h*, 54, 56*a–f*).

Figure 4.3. Wedges from the Donaldson Site. (ASM photograph by Ken Matesich.)

Drill

A single, expanded base drill with a long but broken bit was made from a flake of metasediment (Fig. 4.2*f*). It displays a carefully pressure-flaked, strongly biconvex bit with prominent wear polish. Although lacking the tip of the bit, this specimen measures 40 mm long by 9.5 mm wide and 6.5 mm thick.

Haury (1950, Fig. 67*j*) recovered similar drills from preceramic deposits in Ventana Cave. He identified them as a "large flange" type, the most common drill form in those deposits (Haury 1950, Table 12).

Wedges

An unusual component of the Donaldson Site assemblage consists of 25 bifacially flaked or spalled wedges (Fig. 4.3). These distinctive small tools are characterized by crushed or battered margins on opposing sides, and flat, broad flake scars on both surfaces that often extend from one edge to the other. Occasional "flakes" or spalls may break the piece transversely as well, producing fragments that display portions of both flaked faces of the specimen. The typical wedge from this site resembles a small biface fragment, 10 mm to 50 mm in maximum dimension (averaging 15 mm to 30 mm), but is distinguished by the battered, crushed edges and long, sheetlike flake scars. Some thicker examples might be classified as small, bipolar cores, but their small sizes make it difficult to believe that useful flakes were being removed from them. It is noteworthy that 22 of the 25 wedges are of fine-grained chert, chalcedony, jasper, and quartz; most of the other bifaces (excluding projectile points) are made of medium-grained metamorphic rocks (Table 4.2). Perhaps these finer grained rocks fractured more readily, producing sharper margins and flatter faces.

Tixier (1963) has termed these "piéces esquillées" and proposed that they served as wedges for splitting wood or bone (see also LeBlanc 1992). They have been recognized in such diverse contexts as Hohokam sites in the Santa Rita Mountains (Rozen 1984: 489, 492, Fig. 5.19*a–l*), preceramic sites in Panama (Ranere 1975: 190–192), and Paleoindian sites in Maine (Lothrop and Gramly 1982). A question has been raised whether or not these artifacts may simply be small, bipolar cores (Shott 1989). This notion is feasible when such pieces are recovered from later, ceramic period sites, because the reduction of small, rounded pieces of material by bipolar percussion is an efficient means of producing small, flat flakes that can be pressure flaked into arrow points. At the Donaldson Site, however, large dart points were the only projectile form, and there were no other tools made on small flakes that could have come from these bipolar specimens. The inference, then, is that they served as wedges rather than cores. Experimental research (Ranere 1975) has shown that small wedges of cryptocrystalline material such as these can be used to split wood.

Unifacially Retouched Tools

Of the total flaked stone tool assemblage at the Donaldson Site, 117 specimens (39.1%) are characterized by working edges composed of unifacially directed retouch flakes. Seven general classes are defined; four of these have from two to five subclasses each: scrapers, notched flakes, projections, planes, denticulated flakes, finely flaked tools, and flakes with irregular retouch. A miscellaneous category contains 20 fragments (Table 4.1). In contrast to the bifacially flaked tools, the unifaces are made predominantly on pieces of medium-grained metamorphic rock (Table 4.2).

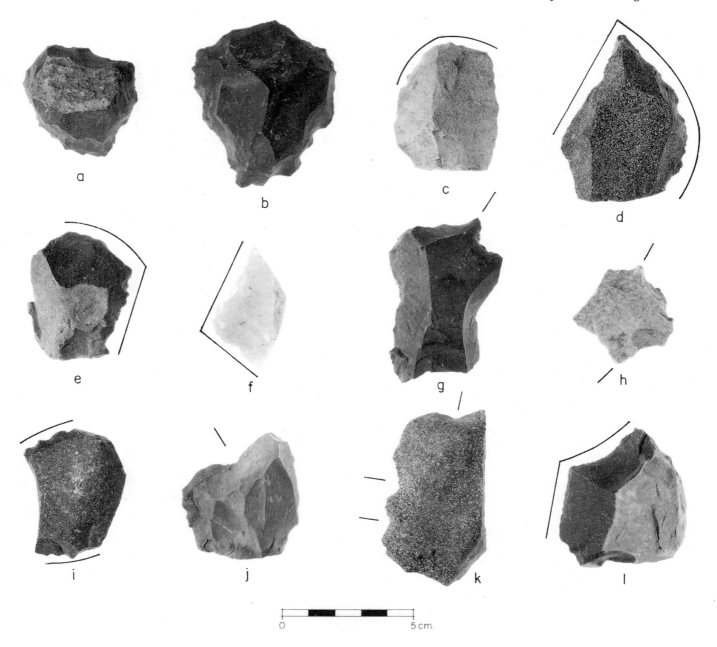

Figure 4.4. Unifacially retouched tools from the Donaldson Site: *a–f*, scrapers; *g*, *h*, projections; *i*, denticulated flake; *j*, *k*, notched flakes; *l*, finely flaked tool. Lines indicate working edges. (ASM photograph by Ken Matesich.)

Scrapers

The 39 scrapers, 33.3 percent of the unifacially retouched tools, have working edges of varying length and configuration composed of continuous unifacial retouch. They are separated into five subclasses based on morphology and position of retouch: ovoid scrapers, single-edge and double-edge side scrapers, single-edge end scrapers, "nosed" end scrapers, and double-edge

convergent scrapers. With rare exceptions, they are made on flakes of medium-grained to coarse-grained metamorphic rock (Table 4.2).

Ovoid Scrapers. Eleven ovoid scrapers are characterized by essentially continuous retouch around their perimeters, usually creating an irregular working edge and a domed appearance on the exterior surface of the tool (Fig. 4.4*a*, *b*). They range in maximum dimension from approximately 45 mm to 75 mm and in thickness from about 20 mm to 30 mm.

Side Scrapers. Single-edge side scrapers with the retouch located on the lateral margin of a flake or on the long side of a chunk are the most common type of scraper, with 13 examples. Steep, continuous retouch along one margin typifies these specimens (Fig. 4.4*e*, *f*), and, as is evident on the ovoid scrapers, this retouch is often irregular. Maximum dimensions of the single-edge side scrapers range from approximately 35 mm to 60 mm. The two double-edge side scrapers are identical to the single-edge scrapers except they have working edges on both lateral margins.

Single-edge End Scrapers. The six single-edge end scrapers each have a working edge constructed on the distal end of a flake (Fig. 4.4*c*). These specimens range in maximum dimension from 35 mm to 85 mm and usually bear relatively evenly retouched working edges composed of flake scars less than 10 mm in length.

"Nosed" End Scrapers. Four "nosed" scrapers resemble the end scrapers, but their convex working edges are confined to only a small, projecting portion of the margin of a flake or chunk. This restricted working area produced a noselike appearance in plan view.

Double-edge Convergent Scrapers. Three double-edge convergent scrapers are similar to the single-edge and double-edge scrapers noted above, but they display two lateral working edges that converge at a single point at the distal end of the flake (Fig. 4.4*d*).

Scrapers were the most abundant class of flaked tools recovered from the Donaldson Site by Eddy (1958, Table 4, Fig. 10*g–i*, *k*, *n*; Eddy and Cooley 1983, Fig. 2.12*g–i*, *k*, *n*), and he, too, observed considerable formal diversity in this group of implements. Haury (1950: 212–236) has shown how great the range in scraper forms was for Ventana Cave during the 8,000 to 10,000 years that shelter was occupied. At other late preceramic sites in southeastern Arizona, scrapers are usually among the most common retouched implements (Sayles 1941, table accompanying Plate 16).

Notched Flakes

Fourteen notched flakes (12% of the unifacially retouched implements), have concave working edges created by single, large retouch flakes or, less frequently, by multiple small retouch flakes (Fig. 4.4*j*, *k*).

Six single-notched flakes and eight flakes with multiple notches were identified. Flakes or chunks measuring from 45 mm to 75 mm in maximum dimension were preferred for the manufacture of these implements. The notches are positioned at almost any point on the perimeter of the flake, and, if multiple, may occur side-by-side (Fig. 4.4*k*) or widely separated. All are made of medium-grained metamorphic or igneous materials (Table 4.2).

Notched flakes have not been consistently classified into a separate tool category by other workers, so it is difficult to ascertain how common they may be at other late preceramic sites. Both types of notched flakes were present at the late preceramic Split Ridge Site in the Rosemont area of the Santa Rita Mountains, where they numbered nearly 11 percent of the unifacially retouched implements (B. Huckell 1984a, Table 5.18).

Projections

Tools were classified as projections when the purpose of retouching appeared to be the creation of a short, broad point on the margin of a flake. Fourteen such implements (12% of the unifacially retouched tools) were noted. Typically projections were produced by the creation of two closely spaced notches along the margin of a metamorphic rock flake; the portion of the margin between the notches was intentionally left as the projection and often was enhanced by the removal of smaller retouch flakes. Nine of the projections are made on large (35 mm to 70 mm) flakes (Fig. 4.4*g*, *h*), and the other five are made on flakes less than 25 mm in maximum dimension (Fig. 4.2*g*, *h*). The projections on the large specimens range from 6 mm to 10 mm long and on the small ones are less than 4 mm long. The latter could be termed gravers and the former are basically larger examples of the same thing. They do not appear to have been drills, based on the lack of wear on the margins of their projecting tips, but their function is uncertain. Most of these implements are made of medium-grained metamorphic materials, although three of the five small projections and one of the large ones are of chert or chalcedony.

Except for small "gravers," projections, like notched flakes, have not been categorized as a type of tool until recently. Rozen (1984: 486, Fig. 5.16) first recognized them at Hohokam sites in the Santa Rita Mountains and noted that they might encompass what others classified as gravers or perforators. The smaller projections have often been identified from preceramic sites as gravers and chisel gravers (Haury 1950, Fig. 42).

Planes

Three large pieces of metamorphic material bear unifacial retouch, producing "scraper planes." They are slightly larger than the scrapers, measuring from 60 mm to 80 mm in maximum dimension and are two to four times thicker than the flakes used for scraper manufacture. Usually a single, steep, slightly convex working edge was created.

Eddy (1958: 44–45, Fig. 10*l*; Eddy and Cooley 1983, Fig. 2.12*l*) recovered a dozen of these tools from his work at the Donaldson Site. Haury (1950, Table 14, Fig. 28) recorded them in large numbers at Ventana Cave, particularly in the preceramic levels, and Sayles (1941, table accompanying Plate 16) recovered what he termed "plano-convex axes" in large numbers from San Pedro stage sites. These tools may be either choppers or planes, or both.

Denticulated Flakes

Although the general regularity and quality of the unifacial retouch on most of the tools is poor, there are 13 specimens (11.1% of the unifacially retouched tools) that bear an intentionally denticulate retouch on their margins; they are separated into large and small varieties. The large denticulated flakes (8) exhibit a coarse, irregularly denticulate retouch (Fig. 4.4*i*). The retouch on these implements consists of deeply struck, consistently spaced, notching blows, leaving a series of toothlike projections. Usually only a single margin or portion of a margin bears such retouch, and in maximum dimension the metamorphic rock flakes treated in this fashion range from 35 mm to 70 mm. Their function is uncertain, but they may have been effective at tasks involving the shredding of soft plant materials. The separation of agave fiber from softer, surrounding leaf tissue is one possibility.

Five small flakes, four of them of fine-grained siliceous materials, bear finely (micro) denticulated working edges (Fig. 4.2*i*, *j*). The largest of these flakes is 30 mm long and the smallest is 15 mm long; each bears a fine, denticulate retouch along one lateral margin. In all cases, pressure flaking has been used to create the working edge. These may be simply diminutive versions of larger, more coarsely denticulated flakes.

Flaked tools of similar morphology were recognized at Hohokam sites in the Rosemont area of the Santa Rita Mountains by Rozen (1984: 462, Fig. 5.2), who classified them as flakes with continuous, marginal, extensive retouch.

Finely Flaked Tools

Five implements display well-formed working edges produced by a finer, more regular unifacial retouch than the large irregular type seen on the tools discussed above. This retouch typically consists of a series of flake scars less than 2 mm in length that creates a straight, even working edge on flakes of sedimentary or metamorphic material less than 40 mm in maximum dimension (Fig. 4.4*l*). Haury (1950: 236–238, Fig. 41) identified similar tools from Ventana Cave as "flake knives," although he restricted use of the term to thin-edged flakes. Eddy (1958) reported, but did not describe in detail, 268 "flake knives"; some may be examples of finely flaked tools.

Flakes with Irregular Retouch

Nine flakes exhibit what is most easily described as irregular or unpatterned unifacial retouch. This retouch usually consists of two or three flake scars that are removed in a series, but they do not create a working edge that is easily classified with any of the preceding tool classes. Considering the generally poor quality of most of the unifacially retouched implements, it is possible that these specimens represent either unsuccessful attempts to produce certain types of tools, or they are less extensively retouched examples of other tools. In terms of size and material, they are similar to the implements made on larger flakes or chunks described above.

Fragments of Unifacially Retouched Tools

Twenty unifacially retouched implements are represented only by fragments. In all cases they have been broken in such a way as to make their assignment to any particular formal tool class questionable. They are typically made on flakes or chunks of medium-grained metamorphic material.

Utilized Flakes

In addition to the retouched tools, 40 unretouched flakes with evidence of wear (13.4% of the flaked stone implement assemblage) were recognized. They include 12 specimens showing smoothed or polished margins, 23 with edges damaged by crushing or spalling, and 5 with both damage and polish. Such damage is interpreted to be the result of prehistoric use of the flake for cutting or scraping tasks. Flakes with obviously recent edge damage, probably produced during the excavation process, are not included in this category.

Table 4.3. Raw Material Composition of Debitage from the Donaldson Site

Material	Grid N98E110 N	%	Grid N98E116* N	%	Grid N100E116 N	%	Grid N116E56 N	%	Feature 11 Pit structure N	%	Total N	%
Metasediment	214	34.6	140	35.8	208	36.7	367	34.0	149	23.1	1078	32.6
Quartzite	131	21.2	28	7.2	60	10.6	173	16.0	100	15.5	492	14.9
Silicified limestone	138	22.3	122	31.2	132	23.3	243	22.4	250	38.8	885	26.8
Chert	74	12.0	64	16.3	67	11.8	119	11.0	90	13.9	414	12.5
Chalcedony	42	6.8	8	2.1	40	7.0	131	12.1	19	3.0	240	7.3
Jasper	4	0.7	7	1.8	6	1.0	12	1.1	1	0.2	30	0.9
Quartz	3	0.5			2	0.4	1	0.1	8	1.2	14	0.4
Obsidian							2	0.1			2	0.1
Basalt					5	0.9	1	0.1			6	0.2
Rhyolite					4	0.7	2	0.1	1	0.2	7	0.2
Unknown metamorphic			15	3.8	24	4.2	13	1.2	7	1.1	59	1.8
Limestone	12	1.9	7	1.8	19	3.4	19	1.8	19	3.0	76	2.3
Total	618	18.7	391	11.8	567	17.2	1083	32.8	644	19.5	3303	

* Grid = 1 m by 2 m.

These flakes are of fine-grained to medium-grained metamorphic rock, including quartzite, metasediment, and silicified limestone (Table 4.2). These unretouched tools range from 35 mm to 100 mm in maximum dimension, averaging approximately 60 mm to 63 mm. Their working edges are typically slightly convex or straight and rarely concave. Edge angles were not specifically measured, but probably average between 30 and 40 degrees with a range of from 10 to 80 degrees. No microwear analysis was attempted, so the functions to which these tools were put remain unknown.

Eddy (1958: 47) mentioned that there were 268 "flake knives and scrapers" in the Donaldson Site assemblage that seemed to have acquired finely flaked edges from use rather than from intentional retouch. It is likely that some of these were utilized flakes, but their abundance implies that this category must include types of retouched tools as well.

Hammerstones

Of the 16 hammerstones (5.4% of the flaked stone tools), 15 are of the flaked or reused core variety, identified by their flaked surfaces. Materials represented are metasediment, quartzite, limestone, and silicified limestone (Table 4.2). Prominences and ridges on these artifacts display the usual diagnostic battering. In addition, however, three bear short, linear gouge marks on a flat surface (from use as anvils?), two display heavily ground or smoothed facets on an edge or surface, and one retains traces of red ocher on parts of its surface. A single unmodified cobble hammerstone is included in the assemblage. The hammerstones range

from 62 mm to 112 mm in maximum dimension and average approximately 78 mm.

Hammerstones are common at late preceramic sites in southern Arizona. Sayles (1941, table accompanying Plate 16) found them at several of his San Pedro stage sites, and Eddy (1958, Fig. 10m; Eddy and Cooley 1983, Fig. 2.12m) recovered several from the Donaldson Site. Haury (1950, Table 20) documented them throughout the preceramic deposits at Ventana Cave.

Debitage

A total of 3,303 pieces of unmodified debitage was examined during the brief analysis of three 2-m by 2-m and one 1-m by 2-m grid squares and Feature 11, a pit structure. Debitage and cores make up 62.7 percent to 74.2 percent of the total number of artifacts, including flaked and ground stone, fire-cracked rocks, and bone (Table 3.3), from each of the five provenience units, although only 23 cores were recovered in these sample grids. The cores are described separately below.

No attempt was made to conduct a detailed analysis of the debitage; it was counted and classified as to material type (Table 4.3). Nonspecific metamorphosed sedimentary rock (metasediment) represents nearly one-third (32.6%) of the total sample, followed by silicified limestone (26.8%), quartzite (14.9%), chert (12.5%), and chalcedony (7.3%). Igneous rocks are poorly represented; together obsidian, basalt, and rhyolite make up less than one percent of the total. With the exception of obsidian and other volcanics, and perhaps some of the fine-grained siliceous rocks, virtually all the materials can be procured from the modern bedload of

Matty Canyon and Cienega Creek or from the older terrace and pediment surfaces bordering them. The bulk of the debitage appears to be the product of hard-hammer flake production from cores. Mixed in with these flakes are numerous pieces bearing the characteristics of soft-hammer biface thinning flakes, including faceted striking platforms with lipping and grinding.

In the analyzed sample, debitage consistently represents between 96 and 98 percent of the flaked stone. Apparently a substantial amount of stone tool manufacture occurred at the settlement, perhaps related in part to the abundant lithic material in close proximity.

Eddy (1958) did not describe or discuss the unmodified flakes he recovered from the Donaldson Site.

Cores

The four grids and the Feature 11 pit structure included in the analytical sample produced 23 cores, but the sorting of all excavated material increased the total to 49 cores. They were classified by form (based on striking platform characteristics; B. Huckell 1973: 189–190) and sorted by material type. In terms of form, there are 8 single-platform cores, 3 double-platform cores, 7 bifacial cores, 14 globular cores, and 9 unclassifiable fragments. Also present are two cores with apparently intentionally constructed projections, two tested pieces of material, and four cores that cannot be accommodated in any of the other categories. More than half the cores are of quartzite (13) and metasediment (14), followed in quantity by silicified limestone, limestone, chert, and chalcedony. This distribution generally reflects the relative abundance of the various materials observed in the debitage, except that there is a higher percentage of limestone cores than flakes.

Ground Stone Artifacts

The following paragraphs (pp. 61–67) on the ground stone artifacts are quoted from a manuscript by Emil W. Haury written in 1987. The manuscript is on file in the Haury papers of the Arizona State Museum Archives.

Stone artifacts shaped by intentional pecking and grinding occurred sparingly in the Donaldson Site assemblage, as compared to those tools shaped through use and by percussion and pressure flaking. The ratio is about four to one, a somewhat puzzling difference considering the apparently sedentary nature of the community and the convincing evidence of maize agriculture. The total ground stone sample numbers only 69 specimens. Further, the tools altered by the work done with

them, such as grinding stones, outnumber by a factor of roughly five those that have been carefully shaped for a designated purpose, as, for example, the stone rings. The contrast in the two classes of lithic products is so great in form and finish that questions are raised about their traditional histories, as is touched on later.

For the most part, tool stone was gathered directly as cobbles of varied materials from the slopes and terraces of the Cienega Valley or from the stream bed of Matty Canyon. These materials are ultimately traceable to the mountains ringing the valley. Quartzite, metasandstone, and sandstone were preferred for milling stones, the last being in the minority. Limestone, locally abundant in nature, had limited use as flattened and edge-ground pebbles. Dense porphyritic rocks and the porous scoriaceous basalt were used for "specialty" artifacts, such as discoidals, trays, and rings. Scoria was the only clearly imported material among ground stone artifacts, for there is no evidence of basic lava-producing vulcanism within the confines of the Cienega Valley.

Table 4.4 enumerates the total yield of ground stone artifacts, together with pertinent descriptive data. Many specimens in most categories are highly fragmented by thermal processes because, as tools broke or outlived their usefulness, the stone was recycled as hearth material, the abundance of which in the site has been noted (Table 3.3). The following observations and inferences are drawn as a quick way of understanding the cultural and other values we see in the ground stone sample.

Ground Stone Milling Equipment

The typology of the grinding stone implements matches the assemblage already described in detail by Eddy (1958: 39–42; Eddy and Cooley 1983: 18–22) from the Donaldson Site and by Sayles (1941: 24–25; 1983: 125–131) from other late preceramic sites in southeastern Arizona. Knowledge of the milling stone complex at this moment in prehistory is crucial for understanding the trend in shaping those tools. Stone tool manufacturing was about to undergo an abrupt change, as witnessed by the contrasting lithic products of the Pioneer period Hohokam. The food processing stones remained remarkably uniform, exhibiting only a few minor diagnostic features for a long time, some 8,000 years (Fig. 4.5). Although the flat-surfaced nether stone was still much in use, the deep basin metate, first observed in Chiricahua stage deposits, was also present (Fig. 4.6a). Curiously, one mano in the collection (Fig. 4.5f) has longitudinal striations and was suitable for use in the single basin metate (Fig. 4.6a).

Table 4.4. Ground Stone Artifacts from the Donaldson Site

Grinding Stones		*51*
Nether (metate)		
Whole		
Basin (Fig. 4.6*a*): stream boulder, quartzite, no shaping; 56 cm by 30 cm by 15 cm; placed right-side-up over Burial 4		1
Flat surface: stream cobble, quartzite, no shaping; 31 cm by 22 cm by 5.5 cm		1
Fragments		
Trough (Fig. 4.6*b*): quartzite, no external shaping; grinding surface concave both axes		1
Flat surface (Fig. 4.6*c*)		2
Handstones		
Whole		
Rubbing (Fig. 4.5*a*): quartzite pebbles, uniface and biface		2
Manos		
Uniface (Fig. 4.5*b, c*)		2
Biface (Fig. 4.5*d–f*): quartzite stream cobbles; slight to extensive marginal trimming; grinding face sharpened by denting; average size 12 cm by 9 cm by 4 cm		4
Fragments: quartzite 33, sandstone 4, granite 1		
Uniface		14
Biface, certain: parallel grinding faces 9, wedge-shaped 11, biconvex 4		24
Ground Stone Disks, Shaped Pebbles (Fig. 4.12*a, b*)		*6*
Flat limestone stream pebbles, brought to circular or ellipsoidal form by edge-chipping, face and edge grinding; diameter range 4.6 cm to 6.2 cm, average thickness 1.2 cm; use unknown		
Rod (Fig. 4.12*c*)		*1*
Slate, squared, slightly tapered; fragmentary		
Rings		*7*
Whole (Fig. 4.7*a*): scoria; precisely finished, biconical perforation with minimum diameter of 3.1 cm; maximum diameter of object 9.1 cm, thickness 3.2 cm; located on floor of Feature 11 pit structure		1
Fragments (Fig. 4.7*b, c*): quartzite 3, sandstone 2, scoria 1; broken after perforation 4; broken during perforation 2 (Fig. 4.7*d*); diameter range 8 cm to 13 cm; use unknown, restricted size range suggests similar function for these objects		6
Discoidal (Fig. 4.10)		*1*
Porphyry; diameter 14 cm, thickness 8.2 cm; weight 2,960 g; fine surface finish; edge slightly convex curving strongly to meet faces; one face centrally dented with suggestion of same on opposite face; no obvious abrasion as from use; possibly a "chunkee" stone		
Trays		*2*
Whole (Fig. 4.8): metasandstone; 17.3 cm by 15.2 cm by 6.3 cm, depth 3.5 cm; rim dimension uniform; floor smooth; shows no obvious wear scars; red hematite stain visible on one outer convex edge		1
Fragment (Fig. 4.9): scoria; original size estimated to have been about 20 cm by 12 cm; ends slightly concave, sides weakly convex; corner projection bifurcated horizontally; underside carries wide lines, shallow bas-relief; tray floor finely finished but no striations visible; use as a plant (chili) grinder has been suggested		1
Perforated Stone (Fig. 4.11)		*1*
Discovered in 1954 among stream cobbles in site area; porphyry; diameter 22 cm, thickness 10 cm, weight 8.4 kg; perforation biconical exhibiting polish in narrowest part of throat (diameter 2.5 cm); larger face slightly concave, smaller face weakly convex and heavily polished, exhibiting faint radial striae; tapered edge uniformly scarred with pecking marks creating sharply defined margins with finish on faces; use unknown		
Total		69

NOTE. Compiled by Emil W. Haury.

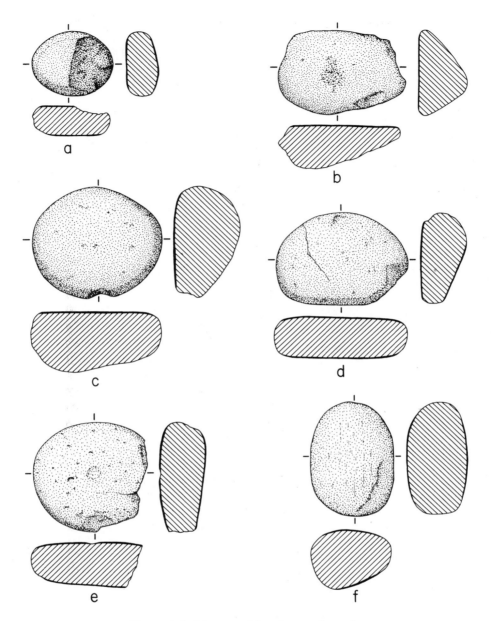

Figure 4.5. Manos and handstones from the
Donaldson Site. Width of *d* is 13.2 cm.

The Donaldson Site collection contains one fragment of a metate of the trough type (Fig. 4.6*b*), suggesting that a fundamental change in grinding behavior was beginning to take place. That change was the shift from an unconfined to a confined grinding stroke, determined by the fact that the mano filled the width of the grinding surface and rode between the side walls of the trough. The basin metate permitted curving and variable stroke directions. A matching mano type, suitable for use in the troughed nether stone, was not found.

The well-formed trough metate exhibiting meticulous external shaping, as well as care for internal symmetry, is an established artifact type in the earliest Hohokam phase, the Vahki (Haury 1976: 200–201). It was considered part of an introduced milling complex and not as an evolution out of the preceramic Archaic (Cochise) grinding tool complex. [However, in 1989 a complete one-end-open trough metate was recovered from a bell-shaped pit at the Fairbank Site, showing that the form does have antiquity. BBH]

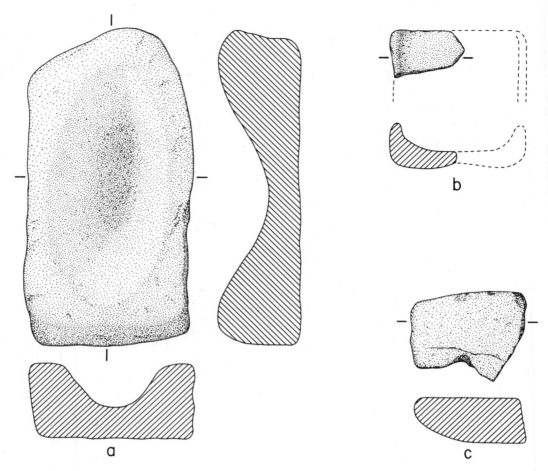

Figure 4.6. Whole metate and metate fragments from the Donaldson Site. Length of *a* is 56 cm.

Rings, Trays, and Discoidals

Particular interest centers on the rings, trays, and discoidals (Figs. 4.7–4.11). They exhibit a much higher mastery of stone working than one sees in roughly contemporary collections from other areas, with the exception of the Cienega Site in the Point of Pines area (Haury 1957). The repetitive evidence of their presence removes the possibility of accidental intrusions into the cultural debris from later overlying cultural materials and allows us to view them as true elements in the stone tool assemblage. The nature of these artifacts, and because they have no known prototypes or analogs in local Archaic sites, prompts questions as to origins and relationships.

Despite our inability to identify the uses to which these objects were put, and whether personal property or not, they suggest activities that go beyond the basic tasks related to survival. The dimensional symmetry and finish achieved in the stone rings (Fig. 4.7) and discoi-

dals (Figs. 4.10, 4.11), and the bas-relief decoration on the scoria tray (Fig. 4.9), speak of both aesthetic values and pride in workmanship unique to the time and place.

Stone rings, not uncommon elements in site collections of southern Arizona, were thought to be late in the time scale, A.D. 1000 or later. Three Pioneer period associations at Snaketown, one derived from Vahki phase contexts, were viewed with skepticism (Haury 1976: 290), but now the Donaldson Site specimens (Fig. 4.7) remove any doubt of their early presence. Interestingly, the late preceramic specimens are more expertly fashioned than the later Hohokam rings, with smaller perforations relative to the diameter, flatter faces, and no evidence of edge or pulley-grooving. Although the evidence clearly shows that stone rings do occur in sites without pottery, it remains to be demonstrated that the element is truly of prepottery age in southern Arizona. This uncertainty introduces the question as to whether or not the Donaldson Site rings were made locally or were acquired from neighbors, a prob-

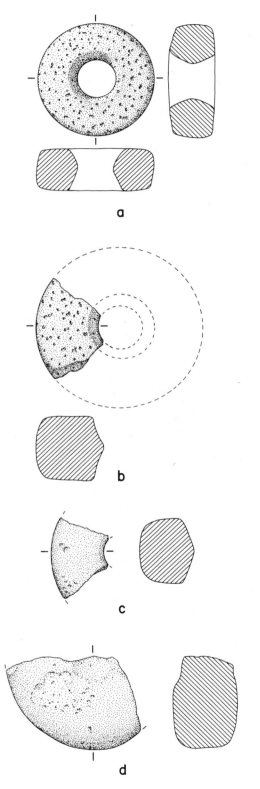

Figure 4.8. Complete stone tray or vessel from the Donaldson Site. Length is 17.3 cm.

Figure 4.7. Perforated stone rings (*a–c*) and a ring preform probably broken during manufacturing (*d*) from the Donaldson Site. Maximum diameter of *a* is 9.1 cm.

lem not now resolvable. The apparent absence of rings of equal quality of workmanship in pottery-producing sites supports the notion that they were locally produced, although the idea may have been borrowed.

Stone trays, as do rings, frequently appear in collections from northern Mexico and southern Arizona sites. What the Donaldson Site tells us is that they, too, have a long history in the region. Hollowing out cobbles was practiced as early as Chiricahua stage times (Sayles 1941, Fig. 11), and a petal-shaped tray was unearthed in the Cienega Creek Site near Point of Pines (Haury 1957: 19) with a prepottery cremation of about the same age as the Matty Canyon examples. One of the Donaldson Site specimens is a comparatively plain, four-sided, subsquare tray made from a cobble of metasandstone (Fig. 4.8). It was collected from the Donaldson Site by a nephew of John Donaldson after our excavations; he

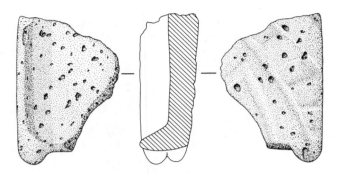

Figure 4.9. Fragment of stone tray with bas-relief carved design from the Donaldson Site. Length of fragment is 10.8 cm.

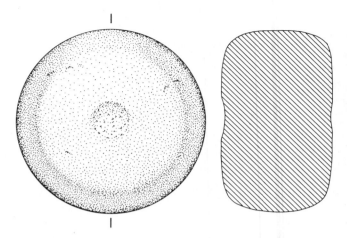

Figure 4.10. Unperforated stone discoidal from the Donaldson Site. Diameter is 14 cm.

found it in situ on the left bank of the wash in the cultural midden in November of 1983. The second specimen is a fragment of a much more elaborately carved tray. The paired concavoconvex sides of the fragmentary tray, further accentuated by corner projections (Fig. 4.9), give the vessel a shape uniqueness that enhances comparison to similar specimens from other times and places. Particular interest attaches to this fragmentary specimen because of its bas-relief decoration on the underside. This expression of "fine art" is not recorded in earlier or even in contemporary Archaic assemblages. The pattern of simple, geometric linear construction with a prominent ladderlike band is too incomplete to speculate what the rest of it was, but the sculpturing itself and the style of the pattern remind one of Mesoamerican bas-relief treatments. I cannot escape the feeling, because it was made of a nonlocal material and because of the style of its decoration, that this specimen may not be indigenous to the site.

The discoidal and the large perforated discoidal (Figs. 4.10, 4.11) we assume to be a part of the Donaldson Site lithic complex; their craftsmanship further testifies to the stone-working ability of the settlement's occupants. The dimpled but unperforated discoidal was recovered from the bottom of a pit exposed on the right bank of Matty Wash west of our excavations, near where Burials 5 and 6 were exposed later by the 1983 floods. The large perforated discoidal was collected in 1954 from the bedload of Matty Wash near the Donaldson Site, and we presume that it came from the midden.

Other small ground stone items merit attention. Six round to ellipsoidal disks of limestone, roughly shaped by chipping and grinding (Fig. 4.12*a, b*), were recovered from the midden. In size and shape they resemble the chipped stone disks reported by Sayles (1941, Plate 16*e*; 1983, Fig. 10.4*m, n*) and by Cattanach (1966, Fig.

Figure 4.11. Large perforated stone discoidal from the Donaldson Site. Diameter is 22 cm.

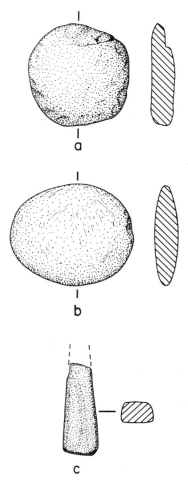

Figure 4.12. Ground stone disks (*a*, *b*) and fragment of a ground slate rod (*c*) from the Donaldson Site. Maximum dimension of *a* is 5.5 cm.

3*r*) from San Pedro stage sites and disks obtained by Eddy from the Donaldson Site (Eddy 1958, Fig. 10*f*, *j*; Eddy and Cooley 1983, Fig. 2.12*f*, *j*). The final specimen is a fragment of what appears to be a slate rod (Fig. 4.12*c*), perhaps originally tapered in form like an awl. It is rectangular in cross section rather than oval, and it resembles specimens from Snaketown (Gladwin and others 1937, Plate 83). [End of section written by Emil W. Haury.]

Discussion

The ground stone assemblage from the Donaldson Site contains an unprecedented mixture of the kinds of utilitarian implements commonly unearthed at late preceramic sites, with several unusual items whose functions remain problematical. The 1983 work produced few complete manos or metates; most specimens were fragments thermally fractured from use in roasting pits. There is nothing particularly remarkable about them, except for the narrow, deep basin metate that was discovered on top of Burial 4. It would have required the use of a cobble mano much like the one noted by Haury for its unusual wear pattern (Fig. 4.5*f*).

Perforated stone rings are well represented at the Donaldson Site; the 1983 work yielded one complete example and six fragments, and Eddy recorded two (Eddy 1958, Table 2). As described above by Haury, they are of excellent workmanship, if somewhat baffling in terms of function. Their perforations are evenly biconical, their edges square, and their faces flat, demonstrating considerable care in manufacture. It is possible that they were weights for digging sticks, or formed the heads of wooden-handled stone clubs, or they may have been used to shell maize kernels from the cob. Similar rings have been reported from other late preceramic sites. One came from the Pantano Site (AZ EE:2:50; Hemmings and others 1968) just north of the Donaldson Site (Fig. 1.2). Others have been reported from the Coffee Camp Site near Picacho (Montero and Henderson 1993: 268), from the La Playa Site in northwestern Sonora (Johnson 1960: 138, Fig. 24*e*), and from the Santa Cruz Bend Site in the Tucson area (Mabry and Clark 1994).

The large, perforated discoidal (Fig. 4.11) has no known counterparts, and its function is a mystery. A great deal of effort went into creating it and forming the extremely regular, biconical perforation through its 10-cm thickness. Unlike the smaller stone rings, its edges are not square but taper from one face to the other. The functions suggested above for the stone rings do not seem particularly appropriate for this 8.4 kg specimen.

Also enigmatic is the large unperforated stone discoidal (Fig. 4.10). Like the large perforated discoidal, it is made of porphyritic igneous rock that required considerable effort to peck and then grind to its extremely precise, round, flat-faced shape. The small dimples, one on each face, suggest that it, too, was going to be perforated, or that it served some function that required a small depression. It is not uncommon to find manos in preceramic sites of varying ages that bear similar pecked depressions (Sayles 1983: 70, Fig. 6.20). Such pits may have aided in the splitting or cracking of nuts (B. Huckell 1984a, Fig. 5.12). However, it seems unlikely that such effort in shaping as that shown by the Donaldson Site specimen would have gone into a simple utilitarian object designed to serve such a mundane function. Similar specimens have been recovered from sites in the midwestern United States, where they are sometimes called "chunkee" stones. Although the name derives from a game, the actual use served by the stones remains obscure.

The stone vessels or trays illustrated in Figures 4.8 and 4.9 are also rare in late preceramic contexts. One of the two from the Donaldson Site is an unembellished form, although considerable effort was invested in creating its thin, high side walls. The vesicular basalt fragment with the bas-relief design on its underside shows equal care in manufacture but greater effort at decorative elaboration. From the Sonoran site of La Playa, Johnson (1960: 120–121, Fig. 22c) recovered five fragmentary rectangular stone vessels, three with short corner projections like the one Donaldson Site specimen. Since Haury described these vessels, two more have been unearthed at the late preceramic site of Coffee Camp (Montero and Henderson 1993, Fig. 11.7). One of these is oval in form and plain; the other is of rectangular form with a short, broad handle at one end and is made of vesicular basalt. Neither one is decorated like the Donaldson specimen.

The small, casually made limestone disks are relatively abundant for such a small lithic sample. They are of generally similar size (46 mm to 62 mm in diameter), and it is tempting to speculate that they served as counters or markers in some sort of game. They may be functionally identical to the chipped stone disks from other late preceramic sites noted by Haury. The slate rod fragment remains unique.

Shell Artifacts

Five shell items were recovered from the Donaldson Site, four from undifferentiated midden fill. The fifth, a bracelet fragment, came from the backdirt at the southern end of backhoe Trench 1 (Fig. 3.5), but it is highly probable that its association with the late preceramic cultural deposit is valid.

Two *Olivella* beads were created by breaking off their spires and lightly grinding the broken edges; both have varying portions of the body chipped or broken away and appear well worn. The *Glycymeris* bracelet band fragment is thin and well made. It would not be out of place in a Hohokam assemblage. A small *Laevicardium* valve fragment retains a portion of a bliconically drilled hole and has a well-polished exterior. It is uncertain what form the shell object may have had originally, although the presence of the hole suggests that it was a pendant. A set of small fragments represents a single piece of nacreous shell, possibly the fresh water clam *Anodonta*, with no evidence of modification.

Eddy's work at the site produced no shell artifacts, and shell jewelry is not common at late preceramic sites. At the 2,800 to 2,900 year-old site of Milagro (B. Huckell 1990) in the Tucson Basin, *Olivella* shell beads and square cut beads or pendants of a nacreous marine shell, probably *Pinctada*, were unearthed. A necklace composed of more than 900 such quadrilateral beads was associated with a cremation at the late preceramic Coffee Camp site (L. Huckell 1993, Fig. 13.2), and other pieces of worked shell and a round shell disc bead came from that site. Recent excavation at a Tucson area site yielded numerous pieces of shell jewelry, representing several different taxa (Mabry and Clark 1994).

Bone Artifacts

Of the 16 pieces of worked bone recovered from the Donaldson Site, 12 are complete or fragmentary awls. The two complete awls include a splinter (120 mm long) from an artiodactyl limb element and a split artiodactyl humerus or femur (143 mm long). Among the ten fragmentary tools are two proximal ends of awls, six medial segments, and two tip fragments. With the exception of one made on a mule deer (*Odocoileus hemionus*) ulna, the rest are too fragmentary to identify beyond noting that they are from large mammal bones, probably representing deer, antelope, or bighorn sheep.

Only one of the remaining four pieces of worked bone is sufficiently complete for identification. It is a short (24 mm long by 2 mm wide), thin splinter whose ends have been carefully ground to points; although lacking a hole, it most closely resembles a needle. The other three pieces of bone are small fragments that exhibit scratches, striae, and polish on their surfaces but are too tiny to provide any clue to their original form.

The 1957 excavations at the Donaldson Site produced several bone implements, including one complete awl, an unspecified number of awl fragments, a complete bone tube, and a bone cylindrical object. Antler flint-knapping tools, including tine pressure flakers and a fragment of a hammer, were also recorded (Eddy 1958, Fig. 11; Eddy and Cooley 1983, Fig. 2.13).

LOS OJITOS

Excavations at Los Ojitos were limited to digging 1-m wide sample squares of the cultural deposit at the base of the 5.5-m high vertical left bank of Matty Canyon (Figs. 3.14, 3.15). The nature of the exposure and the amount of effort devoted to uncovering the several burials discovered in this small area limited the size of the artifact assemblage recovered from this work. Even so, the assemblage shows important similarities to the one described from the Donaldson Site with respect to patterns of raw material use and implement morphology; some differences are also apparent.

For the purpose of this monograph, an arbitrary sample consisting of four of the excavated squares was selected for artifact analysis. The same analytical approach described previously for the Donaldson Site was used for Los Ojitos. The selected squares (E1, E2, E5, W4) were chosen for the relatively large numbers of artifacts they had yielded and for their spatial distribution across the excavated area. The kinds and quantities of artifacts, animal bone, and fire-cracked rocks that they contained are enumerated in Table 3.6. Combined, the four grids produced over 2,300 flaked stone artifacts but only five pieces of ground stone. In the following brief description of this assemblage, comparisons to artifacts from other sites are only made for forms that are unique to Los Ojitos or are not discussed above for the assemblage at the Donaldson Site.

Flaked Stone Tools

The analyzed sample contains 49 specimens classified as flaked stone tools. Of these, 16 (32.7%) are bifacially flaked, 20 (40.8%) are unifacially retouched, 10 (20.4%) are utilized flakes, and 3 (6.1%) are hammerstones. The various subclasses under each of these major categories are reported in Table 4.5; Table 4.6 presents the frequencies of raw materials for each class of tools.

Bifacially Flaked Tools

Three classes of bifacially flaked implements were identified: projectile points, bifaces, and wedges.

Of the four projectile points recovered, one is a good example of a Cienega point with a serrated blade (Fig. 4.13d) and one is a typical San Pedro point (Fig.4.13a). Both points display breakage produced by hard use. The other two specimens are unclassifiable midsection fragments. The Cienega point is made of chalcedony and the San Pedro point of chert; one of the two fragments is chalcedony and the other is jasper.

In addition to the Cienega and San Pedro points, Figure 4.13 illustrates points recovered from other grids or features within the excavations that reveal more of the range of projectile point forms at Los Ojitos. The point in Figure 4.13c may possibly be San Pedro style, but the typological affinities of the other two specimens

Table 4.5. Flaked Stone Tools from Los Ojitos

	Number	Total	Percent
Bifacially Flaked Tools		16	32.7
Projectile points	4		25.0
Cienega point	1		
San Pedro point	1		
Unclassified fragments	2		
Bifaces	9		56.3
Triangular	2		
Incipient, ovoid	2		
End fragments	3		
Unclassified small fragments	2		
Wedges	3		18.7
Unifacially Retouched Tools		20	40.8
Scrapers	10		50.0
Ovoid, steep	3		
Side, single-edge	5		
double-edge	1		
End, single-edge	1		
Notched flakes	2		10.0
Single notch	2		
Projections	4		20.0
Large	3		
Small (graver)	1		
Denticulated flake	1		5.0
Micro	1		
Finely flaked tool	1		5.0
Miscellaneous fragments	2		10.0
Utilized Flakes		10	20.4
Polished*	4		
Damaged	6		
Hammerstones		3	6.1
Reused core or flaked	3		
Total		49	

* Includes 1 utilized core fragment.

(Fig. 4.13b and e) are more obscure. One (Fig. 4.13e) resembles a point from the Donaldson Site illustrated by Eddy (1958, Fig. 10d; Eddy and Cooley 1983, Fig. 2.12d). The other one (Fig. 4.13b) looks like a cross between the San Pedro and Cienega styles in terms of notch form and size. One heavily damaged point, possibly of the Cortaro style, is not illustrated.

Two large basal fragments of triangular bifaces represent the only apparently finished bifaces among the nine bifaces in the analyzed sample. They are judged to be finished because their shapes are symmetrical and their margins are evenly finished. The other bifaces include two incipient bifaces, three end fragments, and two fragments too small to classify as to form. All of them appear to have been broken or aborted in manu-

Table 4.6. Raw Material Composition of Flaked Stone Tools at Los Ojitos

	Metasediment	Quartzite	Silicified limestone	Chert	Chalcedony	Jasper	Total
Projectile points							
Cienega					1		1
San Pedro				1			1
Fragments					1	1	2
Bifaces							
Triangular		1			1		2
Incipient	2						2
Fragments	2	1	1	1			5
Wedges						3	3
Scrapers							
Ovoid	3						3
Side	4	2					6
End	1						1
Notched flakes				1	1		2
Projections	2	1				1	4
Micro denticulate			1				1
Finely flaked tool				1			1
Utilized flakes	7	2	1				10
Hammerstones	2	1					3
Misc. fragments			2				2
Total	23	8	5	4	5	4	49
Percent	*46.9*	*16.3*	*10.2*	*8.2*	*10.2*	*8.2*	

facture, because of marked formal asymmetry and flake scars displaying prominent negative bulbs of percussion. Seven of the bifaces are made of medium-grained metamorphic materials, and the other two are chert and chalcedony (Table 4.6).

Three wedges, all of jasper, were identified in the analyzed sample. Only one is complete; the other two are small wedge fragments less than 15 mm in maximum dimension that apparently split off during use.

Unifacially Retouched Implements

As indicated in Table 4.5, scrapers, notched flakes, projections, a denticulate, and a finely flaked tool are present in the sample of 20 unifaces. Scrapers comprise half of these tools and include three ovoid scrapers, six side scrapers (all but one of the single-edge type), and one end scraper. All are made of medium-grained metamorphic materials (Table 4.6), and, like their counterparts at the Donaldson Site, most display irregularly retouched working edges.

The other unifacially retouched tools include four projections, two notched flakes, one denticulate, one finely flaked tool, and two unclassifiable fragments. Of the four projections, three are of the large variety described above for the Donaldson Site, one of which is a core fragment with two small projections created by retouch. The fourth is a small projection or graver.

Figure 4.13. Projectile points from Los Ojitos: *a*, San Pedro style; *b*, *e*, style uncertain; *c*, possibly San Pedro style; *d*, Cienega style. (ASM photograph by Ken Matesich.)

Table 4.7. Raw Material Composition of Debitage from Los Ojitos

Material	Grid W4		Grid E5		Grid E2		Grid E1*		Total	
	N	%	N	%	N	%	N	%	N	%
Metasediment	262	33.9	112	24.4	251	41.3	179	38.2	804	34.8
Quartzite	107	13.8	45	9.8	68	11.2	42	9.0	262	11.4
Silicified limestone	100	12.9	37	8.1	67	11.0	76	16.2	280	12.1
Chert	167	21.6	110	24.0	113	18.6	89	19.0	479	20.8
Chalcedony	91	11.8	110	24.0	66	10.9	48	10.3	315	13.7
Jasper	14	1.8	14	3.0	11	1.8	2	0.4	41	1.8
Quartz	2	0.3	5	1.1			1	0.2	8	0.3
Basalt			1	0.2			8	1.7	9	0.4
Rhyolite	2	0.3	2	0.4	4	0.7	6	1.3	14	0.6
Unknown metamorphic	18	2.3	17	3.7	21	3.4	12	2.6	68	2.9
Limestone	10	1.3	6	1.3	7	1.1	5	1.1	28	1.2
Total	773	33.5	459	19.9	608	26.3	468	20.3	2,308	

* Includes material from Feature 2, a cluster of fire-cracked rocks.

Both notched flakes are on flakes of fine-grained material, and both were made by detaching several small flakes to create the concave working edge. The single denticulate is of the "microdenticulate" variety and is made on a lateral margin of a 32-mm long flake of silicified limestone. The finely flaked tool is made on a small (20 mm long) chert flake.

Utilized Flakes

The 10 utilized flakes consist of nine flakes and one utilized core fragment. The core fragment and three of the flakes bear evidence of use in the form of polish along one margin, and the other six flakes bear edge damage. All the utilized flakes are of medium-grained materials, predominantly metasediment (Table 4.6). In general, these implements conform to those described from the Donaldson Site. Working edges are convex or straight and typically are fairly acute, regardless of the type of wear they exhibit.

Hammerstones

The three hammerstones in the sample are of the flaked variety, and all measure approximately 80 mm in maximum dimension. One is of quartzite and the other two are of metasediment.

Debitage

Debitage amounts to 97.4 percent of the flaked stone artifacts from the four sample squares and consists of 2,308 complete and fragmentary flakes, including shatter fragments. This is a remarkably large quantity, considering that so small a sample from the site was analyzed. As was the case with the Donaldson Site, the debitage from Los Ojitos was simply sorted by material type; the results are presented in Table 4.7.

Slightly more than one-third of the debitage is metasediment, followed in descending order of abundance by chert (20.8%), chalcedony (13.7%), silicified limestone (12.1%), and quartzite (11.4%). Other materials such as jasper, quartz, basalt, rhyolite, limestone, and unknown metamorphic rock each equal 3 percent or less of the total.

As at the Donaldson Site, the Los Ojitos debitage appears to consist of a mixture of flakes produced by hard-hammer core reduction and soft-hammer biface manufacture, with the former clearly predominating. Further, the impression gained from analyzing the debitage is that the flakes from Los Ojitos are smaller on average than those from the Donaldson Site. Some of this perceived difference may derive from the fact that the Los Ojitos sample comes from a small area of the site, where perhaps secondary refuse from the cleanup of tool manufacturing areas was finally deposited. By contrast, the sample of debitage analyzed from the Donaldson Site comes from several different areas of the settlement. Although certainly it also represents secondary trash deposits for the most part, the Donaldson Site sample may include areas that were not places where high density secondary trash resulting from intensive tool manufacture was dumped. It is noteworthy that chert and chalcedony are more abundant at Los Ojitos than at the Donaldson Site, and nearly all the debitage of these materials at Los Ojitos is quite small in size. It is also possible, considering the tendency for chert and chalcedony to be used preferentially for projectile point manufacture, that much of the small debitage at Los Ojitos was derived from point or biface manufacture. Detailed study of debitage striking platform attributes would help to assess this possibility. However, as noted below, the relative abundance of chert and chalcedony cores from the analyzed Los Ojitos sample certainly suggests that these materials were also serving for flake production.

Cores

The 10 cores in the analyzed sample encompass a fairly diverse suite of forms. Globular cores, multiple platform cores, bifacial cores, and tested pieces are all represented by two specimens each. One single-platform core and one core fragment complete the sample. Four cores are of chert, three of quartzite, two of chalcedony, and one is metasediment. The higher percentages of chert and chalcedony cores reflect the greater relative abundance of debitage of these two materials than is present at the Donaldson Site.

Ground Stone Artifacts

Notably few pieces of ground stone were recovered from Los Ojitos; the analyzed sample is limited to three fragmentary specimens of utilitarian ground stone and two pieces of stone jewelry. The implements include two mano fragments and a portion of a metate. Manos are represented by roughly half of an oval, unifacial, granite mano and a small spall from the grinding face of a quartzite mano. A small sandstone fragment derived from the grinding surface of a metate was found; nothing can be said of the form of the metate from this small specimen. Perusal of the few other pieces of ground stone artifacts recovered from other excavation units at Los Ojitos revealed only nondescript fragments.

A pendant and a bead were recovered from the sample squares. The pendant is rectangular in general form, is made on a tabular piece of purplish brown siltstone, and was subsequently spalled on one end and most of one face by burning. A biconically drilled hole is positioned at the unspalled end. In its present condition, the pendant measures 23.5 mm long, 14.5 mm wide, and 3.0 mm thick. The bead is a slightly modified segment of a fossil crinoid stem, perhaps ultimately derived from the fossiliferous Paleozoic limestones that ring the Cienega Basin. It is thin and wedge-shaped, with what is probably a natural central perforation that may have been enhanced by breaking or reaming so that the naturally circular crinoid stem fragment served as a bead.

The Los Ojitos pendant is similar in form to one illustrated by Eddy (1958, Fig. 10e; Eddy and Cooley 1983, Fig. 2.12e) from his investigations at the Donaldson Site, except that Eddy's specimen is not perforated. Eddy also mentioned two other pieces of thin, tabular stone (material not identified) that had been ground into trapezoidal shapes. Although stone pendants have not been reported from other preceramic sites in southeastern Arizona, they are known from Basketmaker II sites in northeastern Arizona. Kidder and Guernsey (1919, Fig. 74) illustrate three such pendants, including a rectangular one closely similar in shape and size to the Los Ojitos specimen. Guernsey (1931, Plate 17h) also reported a stone pendant from White Dog Cave. These four pendants do not show much attention to symmetrical shaping, an attribute they share with the Los Ojitos pendant.

DISCUSSION

In most respects, the analyzed artifact assemblage from Los Ojitos is like the one from the Donaldson Site. The similarities are especially strong for the flaked stone implement assemblages. At Los Ojitos, tools comprise 2.1 percent of the assemblage, at the Donaldson Site 2.6 percent. The basic composition of the flaked stone implement assemblages differs primarily in the relative frequencies of bifacially flaked tools (32.7% of the Los Ojitos assemblage, 42.1% of the Donaldson Site assemblage) and utilized flakes (20.4% at Los Ojitos, 13.4% at the Donaldson Site). Some of these differences may be a function of the small sample size from Los Ojitos, or a product of the relatively small area of Los Ojitos that was investigated, or both. Regardless, both assemblages show considerable diversity in implement form and in general can be described as unspecialized in their composition. They suggest that a wide range of tasks involving flaked stone implements occurred at both settlements; nothing about either assemblage implies any specialization in settlement function. The debitage and cores demonstrate that tool manufacture was an important activity at both places as well, and that the artisans focused their manufacturing efforts on raw materials that could be obtained in reasonably close proximity to the settlements.

It is also noteworthy that the unifacially retouched implements from both sites are relatively poorly made. There is little formal standardization and working edges tend to be irregular, as shown in Figure 4.4. In morphological terms, they more closely resemble later Hohokam implements (Rozen 1984) than earlier Archaic ones (B. Huckell 1984a). Nevertheless, the projectile points and many of the bifaces reflect considerable refinement in terms of both form and manufacturing skill. In general, the two assemblages are more expedient in character than assemblages recovered from Early and Middle Archaic hunter-gatherer sites in the nearby Rosemont area of the Santa Rita Mountains (B. Huckell 1984a). Probably partly because of the extended nature of occupation at the two settlements and because of the local availability of raw material, the occupants of the Matty Canyon settlements found it unnecessary to rely on a strategy of implement manufacture and use that emphasized the curation of formal tools and the conservation of raw material.

The projectile points from the two sites show some typological differences that may be time-dependent. Cienega points are without question the dominant style at the Donaldson Site, but the small sample from Los Ojitos suggests that San Pedro points and Cienega points are present in similar quantities. Also, there is some suggestion that specimens of intermediate character between the two styles are present at Los Ojitos. Such a situation might be expected if, as described in Chapter 3, the stratigraphic relationships between the two sites are accepted as demonstrating that Los Ojitos is older than the Donaldson Site. It could be hypothesized that the Cienega style was in the process of devel-

opment at the time Los Ojitos was occupied, and that it had almost completely replaced the San Pedro style by the time the Donaldson Site was settled.

Considering the small sample of ground stone artifacts from Los Ojitos, comparisons with the Donaldson Site are not especially meaningful. However, the pendant from Los Ojitos does appear comparable to specimens excavated by Eddy at the Donaldson Site. The stone artifact assemblages from both sites would certainly repay more intensive analysis than has been possible here.

The artifacts recovered from the Donaldson Site (including Frank Eddy's investigations) and from Los Ojitos serve as a first approximation of the material inventory of the Cienega phase of the Early Agricultural period. As introduced in Chapter 1, the Cienega phase constitutes the final segment of the preceramic period, spanning an interval between about 500 B.C. and A.D. 200. It can be recognized by the first appearance of certain types of artifacts like the Cienega point and by an elaboration of the ground stone assemblage.

The inventory of material culture that is diagnostic of the Cienega phase continues to expand as this intriguing and highly important cultural transition period receives heightened investigation from archaeologists in southern Arizona. Chapter 8 describes our current understanding of the distinctive content of the Cienega phase and discusses the basis for its separation from the San Pedro stage.

CHAPTER FIVE

Farming and Foraging in the Cienega Valley
Early Agricultural Period Paleoethnobotany

Lisa W. Huckell

In 1983, Arizona State Museum personnel conducted archaeological investigations at two Early Agricultural period sites. The Donaldson Site (AZ EE:2:30 ASM) and Los Ojitos (AZ EE:2:137 ASM) are located about 56 km (35 miles) southeast of Tucson along Matty Canyon, a major tributary of Cienega Creek. The two sites, which are separated by a distance of approximately 200 m (656 feet), are characterized by the presence of a conspicuous, thick, dark gray, highly organic midden of cultural origin. As fieldwork began at the Donaldson Site, it was immediately apparent that this stratum contained an abundance of exceptionally well-preserved plant macrofossils, many of which were easily visible with the unaided eye. The inventory of plant remains recognized during fieldwork included a maize shank, a maize grain or kernel, more than 100 maize cobs, some large leguminous seeds, and several walnut shell fragments. This impressive list suggested that these sites would provide unprecedented information on the nature of late preceramic subsistence practices in southeastern Arizona.

This chapter describes the analysis of the 14 flotation samples taken from the two sites. The three samples from Los Ojitos were taken exclusively from the cultural deposit. The 11 samples from the Donaldson Site came from two pit structures and seven pit features; they yielded an array of plants that exceeded the optimism generated by the field observations. Initial results have identified 29 genera from a total of 23 families, with one other family represented by unidentified seeds (Tables 5.1–5.4). Of the entire assemblage, maize is the only cultivated plant positively identified, although squash may be present as well. The rest of the assemblage represents economically significant wild plant resources or components of the flora surrounding the sites.

METHODS

Selection of flotation samples at the Donaldson Site was based primarily on the integrity of feature fill and was limited to pits and structure floors. Rock clusters were excluded because of the high probability that they represented roasting pit clean-out episodes in which the material removed was left exposed on the then current occupation surface.

Flotation samples were processed using the method described by Bohrer and Adams (1977: 37). After the volume was measured, each sample was passed through a fine screen into a water bath. Readily visible macrofossils were removed from the screen, and all remaining dirt was added to the water. The sediment was gently agitated to free the buoyant macrofossils, and the liquid was then decanted through a 0.5 mm mesh screen. The heavy fraction was not saved.

As recounted in Chapter 3, only limited excavations were conducted at Los Ojitos, and most of the work focused on selected 1-m wide grid squares. They were dug in arbitrary 10-cm levels, a procedure followed at the Donaldson Site, but because the cultural deposit at Los Ojitos was saturated, the soil had to be screen washed to recover artifacts, bones, and other materials. A ¼-inch mesh screen was stacked on top of a $\frac{1}{16}$-inch mesh screen; excavated sediments from the cultural deposit were piled into the ¼-inch mesh screen and then flushed with water taken by bucket from the active flow in Matty Canyon. Material remaining in the ¼-inch mesh screen was hand picked, resulting in the recovery of numerous maize cob fragments and other plant macrofossils. The contents of the $\frac{1}{16}$-inch mesh screen were dumped onto newspaper to dry. When thoroughly dried, this material was bagged as "concentrate," essentially a partially processed flotation sample.

Because all of the concentrate from Los Ojitos could not be analyzed at this time, I examined a small subsample of alternating levels from one grid square, W4. Bags of concentrate from three of five levels (designated Levels 1, 3, and 5) were chosen and refloated using the bucket method described previously. This procedure separated the remaining macrobotanical material from the fine sand, silt, and clay that had accumulated in the $\frac{1}{16}$-inch mesh screen. These samples represent the undifferentiated cultural deposit or midden, not features.

Table 5.1. Plant Remains from the Donaldson Site (AZ EE:2:30 ASM)

Gramineae spp.		Aizoaceae	
Zea mays L.	Maize, corn	*Mollugo verticillata* L.	Carpetweed, Indian chickweed
Sporobolus spp.	Dropseed	*Trianthema portulacastrum* L.	Horse purslane
cf. *Bromus/Agropyron*	Brome/Wheatgrass	Cactaceae	
Cyperaceae spp.	Sedges	*Carnegiea gigantea* (Engelm.)	Saguaro
cf. *Scirpus* sp.	Bulrush	Britt. & Rose	
Agavaceae		*Opuntia* sp.	Prickly pear
Agave sp.	Agave, century plant	Anacardiaceae	
Yucca elata Engelm.	Palmilla, soaptree yucca	*Rhus* sp.	Sumac
Yucca baccata Torr.	Banana yucca	Labiatae	
Juncaceae		*Salvia* sp.	Sage
Juncus sp.	Rushes	Convolvulaceae	
Cupressaceae		*Ipomoea* sp.	Morning glory
Juniperus deppeana Steud.	Alligator juniper	Zygophyllaceae	
Chenopodiaceae		*Kallstroemia* sp.	Kallstroemia
Chenopodium spp.	Lamb's quarters, quelites	Compositae spp.	
Atriplex cf. *elegans* (Moq.)	Wheelscale saltbush	*Ambrosia* sp.	Ragweed, bursage
D. Dietr.		cf. *Viguiera* sp.	Golden eye
Amaranthaceae		Euphorbiaceae	
Amaranthus sp.	Amaranth, bledo	*Euphorbia* sp.	Spurge
Polygonaceae		Fagaceae	
cf. *Rumex* sp.	Dock, sorrel	*Quercus emoryi* Torr.	Emory oak
cf. *Rumex/Polygonum*	Dock/Knotweed, smartweed	Juglandaceae	
Cucurbitaceae		*Juglans major* (Torr.) Heller	Arizona walnut
Cucurbita sp.	Squash or wild gourd	Leguminosae	
Solanaceae		*Prosopis* sp.	Mesquite
cf. *Physalis/Solanum*	Ground cherry/Nightshade	Malvaceae sp.	
Portulacaceae			
Portulaca sp.	Purslane, verdolaga		

Further, because they represent screen-washed concentrate rather than midden sediments bagged directly in the field, statistical measures of taxonomic abundance cannot be applied to them, so direct comparisons with the Donaldson Site assemblage are difficult. Still, the analysis of these three samples provides, at the very least, baseline information concerning the presence and relative abundance of many taxa. The plants with very small-sized seeds are likely to be underrepresented, for their seeds could have been lost through the $\frac{1}{16}$-inch mesh screen.

When completely dry, all samples were put through a graduated series of geological screens that divided them into five size classes: Class 1, greater than 4.75 mm; Class 2, between 2.0 mm and 4.75 mm; Class 3, between 1.0 mm and 2.0 mm; Class 4, between 0.495 mm and 1.0 mm; and Class 5, 0.495 mm or less. This strategy enhances the ease and reliability of microscopic sorting and is useful when subsampling is required.

A binocular stereozoom microscope with a magnification range of 10X to 70X, equipped with an ocular micrometer for measuring specimens, was used for sort-ing. All carbonized seeds, stems, fruits, thorns, and other recognizable plant parts were retrieved for identification. Incomplete specimens and fragments bearing distinctive or potentially diagnostic features were also set aside in the hope that with more time some portion of them could be successfully identified. This group consisted primarily of fragmentary seed coats, endosperm, cotyledons, and badly distorted incomplete seeds and caryopses, and it constituted the bulk of the "Unknown" category. All seeds were measured with the hilum or seed attachment scar oriented down, so that length may not always correspond with the long axis of the seed. Small quantities of wood charcoal were present in most of the samples, but were not analyzed as part of this study.

To assess the nature and degree of disturbance experienced by the sampled features at the Donaldson Site, counts were made for microvertebrate bones, mollusks, fecal pellets, and insect parts (Table 5.3). Modern contaminants introduced into the Los Ojitos samples by the stream water used in the processing technique compromised the value of these observations,

Table 5.2. Carbonized Plant Remains Recovered from the Donaldson Site, AZ EE:2:30 ASM
Number counted and (estimated number) in each sample

Plant	Feature: Level, Field No.: Volume (ml):	4, Pit L1, 4–2 3260	7, Pit L6, 7–10 3780	8, Pit L5, 8–1 4260	9, Pit L1, 9–1 1560	11, Hearth L7, 11–75 2960	15, Pit L8, 15–17 3900
Zea, cob fragment		3					
Zea, cob shank							1
Zea, cupule		512	265	146	468	12	153
(Estimated)						(114)	
Zea, kernel		3	4	8	12		7
Zea, embryo							
Zea, glume		69		23			11
Cyperaceae, achene		6	5	2	2		2
(Estimated)			(8)	(9)	(8)		(8)
Cyperaceae, kernel				1			
(Estimated)				(4)			
Agave, heart				1			1
Agave, tooth				1			1
Yucca elata					1		
Yucca baccata							
Sporobolus		1					
(Estimated)		(6)					
cf. Bromus/Agropyron							
(Estimated)							
Gramineae, caryopsis		4	8	6			2
(Estimated)		(9)	(256)	(229)			(120)
Juncus, seed			1				
(Estimated)			(32)				
Chenopodiaceae, seed		20	13	11	2	1	15
(Estimated)			(44)	(47)	(8)	(84)	(108)
Amaranthaceae, seed		1	1		2		1
(Estimated)			(4)		(8)		(7)
Cheno-ams, seed		13			1	1	3
(Estimated)		(24)			(4)	(10)	(127)
Portulaca, seed				3	1		
(Estimated)				(13)	(4)		
Mollugo, seed			1				
(Estimated)			(32)				
Trianthema, seed		7		8			2
(Estimated)		(23)		(24)			
cf. Rumex, achene			9				
Prosopis, seed			1				
(Estimated)							
cf. Prosopis, seed				1			
(Estimated)				(4)			
Carnegiea, seed			1				
Opuntia, seed							
Opuntia, embryo							
(Estimated)							
Atriplex, fruit							
cf. Viguiera, achene				1			1
(Estimated)				(4)			(7)
Euphorbia, seed		1					
Quercus, nut shell		5	27	49	1	2	32
(Estimated)				(117)			
Malvaceae, seed				1			
Juglans, nut shell							
Rhus, endocarp							1
Leguminosae, seed			1				
Leguminosae, pod base							
(Estimated)							
Columnar-celled seed coat frag.		104	21	63	4	5	20
(Estimated)		(358)		(203)			
Unknown		31	47	30	50	1	57
(Estimated)		(48)	(53)	(47)	(53)		(165)
TOTAL		780	405	355	544	22	310
(Estimated)		(1088)	(758)	(881)	(571)	(216)	(771)

Table 5.2. Carbonized Plant Remains Recovered from the Donaldson Site, AZ EE:2:30 ASM (continued)
Number counted and (estimated number) in sample

Plant	Feature: 15, Pit Level, Field No.: L9, 15–21 Volume (ml): 4400	17, Structure L9, 17–11 2920	19a, Pit L9, 19–1 3600	19b, Pit L9, 19–1 3780	20, Pit 20–3 2000	(Estimated total in sample)	TOTAL 36,420
Zea, cob fragment		3			1		7
Zea, cob shank							1
Zea, cupule	73	140	208	241	95		2313
(Estimated)					(104)	(2424)	
Zea, kernel	5	2	5	6	1		53
Zea, embryo					1		1
Zea, glume	21			11	3		138
Cyperaceae, achene	4	2	7	2	1		33
(Estimated)			(15)	(8)		(69)	
Cyperaceae, kernel	2	3					6
(Estimated)						(9)	
Agave, heart	2						4
Agave, tooth	1						3
Yucca elata							1
Yucca baccata					2		2
Sporobolus		1			43		45
(Estimated)		(35)			(608)	(649)	
cf. Bromus/Agropyon	1	1					2
(Estimated)	(13)					(14)	
Gramineae, caryopsis	1	4	3	2	15		45
(Estimated)	(156)	(38)	(4)	(14)	(210)	(1036)	
Juncus, seed	1			1			3
(Estimated)	(156)		(40)			(228)	
Chenopodiaceae, seed	28	64	17	12			183
(Estimated)	(358)	(200)	(74)	(133)		(1076)	
Amaranthaceae, seed			2	1			8
(Estimated)			(4)	(7)		(31)	
Cheno-ams, seed			3	5	9		35
(Estimated)			(6)	(84)	(133)	(388)	
Portulaca, seed	3	4		1			12
(Estimated)	(40)			(7)		(68)	
Mollugo, seed							1
(Estimated)						(32)	
Trianthema, seed	6	2	2	4			31
(Estimated)			(3)	(10)		(70)	
cf. Rumex, achene	1						10
Prosopis, seed	4		2				7
(Estimated)	(17)					(20)	
cf. Prosopis, seed		3			4		8
(Estimated)						(11)	
Carnegiea, seed							1
Opuntia, seed	1						1
Opuntia, embryo	2						2
(Estimated)	(26)					(26)	
Atriplex, fruit		3					3
cf. Viguiera, achene	1						3
(Estimated)	(13)					(24)	
Euphorbia, seed							1
Quercus, nut shell	11	27	41	46			241
(Estimated)						(309)	
Malvaceae, seed		1	1				3
Juglans, nut shell	2		1				3
Rhus, endocarp							1
Leguminosae, seed	1				1		3
Leguminosae, pod base	1						1
(Estimated)	(13)					(13)	
Columnar-celled seed coat frag.	27	18	9	17	497		785
(Estimated)	(210)				(1361)	(2226)	
Unknown	46	31	28	13	180		514
(Estimated)	(380)	(65)	(109)	(25)	(240)	(1186)	
TOTAL	245	309	328	363	853		4514
(Estimated)	(1512)	(547)	(520)	(611)	(2670)	(10,145)	

Table 5.3. Noncarbonized Remains Recovered from the Donaldson Site, AZ EE:2:30 ASM
Number counted and (estimated number) in each sample

Feature: Level, Field No.: Volume (ml):	4, Pit L1, 4–2 3260	7, Pit L6, 7–10 3780	8, Pit L5, 8–1 4260	9, Pit L1, 9–1 1560	11, Hearth L7, 11–75 2960	15, Pit L8, 15–17 3900
Snails	24	10	10	9	3	13
(Estimated)	(29)	(16)	(19)	(21)	(86)	(156)
Bones	11	20	9	1	1	7
(Estimated)		(24)	(74)			(66)
Fecal pellets	17	12	22	1	3	30
(Estimated)	(66)	(77)	(352)		(31)	(691)
Insect parts	1	1	2			
(Estimated)			(5)			

→

so counts were made only for microvertebrate bones and snails (*see* Table 5.4).

For each sample, Size Classes 1, 2, and 3 were completely examined. Size Class 4 was completely sorted when its bulk was small; otherwise, it was randomly subsampled. Size Class 5, which was invariably the most time-consuming fraction, was consistently subsampled. For those size classes that were subsampled, estimates of the total number of each taxon present were calculated based on the numbers present in the subsample. Although they were recorded separately, specimens for which more than one-half was present were combined with specimens less than one-half complete in the compilation of the summary data tables.

Identifications were made using various sources that included manuals and floras (A. Martin and Barkley 1961; Mason 1957; Berggren 1969) and comparative collections maintained by the University of Arizona in the Herbarium and Tumamoc Hill Desert Laboratory and by me. The taxonomy used here follows Kearney and Peebles (1960), except for the grasses, which follow Allred (1993). Table 5.1 lists the plants recovered. Some of the entries are preceded by the letters "cf.," indicating "compare." These identifications are probable, not absolute. They represent the best match among an incomplete pool of candidates, with other possibilities requiring investigation before a confident identification can be made. Because it signifies a lower level of

Table 5.4. Carbonized Plant Remains and Noncarbonized Remains from Grid W4, Los Ojitos

Plant	Level 1 Counted	Level 1 (Est.)	Level 3 Counted	Level 3 (Est.)	Level 5 Counted	Level 5 (Est.)	Total	(Est.)
Zea, rachis	8		46	(56)	23		77	(87)
Zea, cupule	1230	(1232)	1229	(1972)	751	(1149)	3210	(4353)
Zea, glume	216		262	(461)	128	(226)	606	(903)
Zea, kernel	26		103	(126)	50	(64)	179	(216)
Zea, embryo	4		6		1		11	
Cucurbita, rind			2		3	(6)	5	(8)
Prosopis, pod	1		2				3	
Prosopis, seed	45		51	(61)	21	(29)	117	(135)
Quercus, shell	84		87	(157)	64	(106)	235	(347)
Columnar-celled seed coat fragment	164	(171)	144	(293)	105	(187)	413	(651)
Opuntia	2		8	(9)	3	(5)	13	(16)
Juglans, shell	3		12		5		20	
Juniperus	9		12	(18)	6	(9)	27	(36)
Chenopodium	10		2	(7)	1		13	(18)
Cheno-ams	5		2	(7)			7	(12)
Atriplex, fruit	1		1	(3)	1	(2)	3	(6)
cf. *Bromus/Agropyon*	32		18	(39)	1	(2)	51	(73)
Gramineae	3		2	(5)			5	(8)
cf. *Rumex*	7		135	(195)	26	(39)	168	(241)
cf. *Rumex/Polygonum*			1	(2)	1	(2)	2	(4)

→

Table 5.3. Noncarbonized Remains Recovered from the Donaldson Site, AZ EE:2:30 ASM (*continued*)
Number counted and (estimated number) in sample

Feature: Level, Field No.: Volume (ml):	15, Pit L9, 15–21 4400	17, Structure L9, 17–11 2920	19a, Pit L9, 19–1 3600	19b, Pit L9, 19–1 3780	20, Pit 20–3 2000	(Estimated total in sample)	TOTAL 36,420
Snails	6	3	3	2	7		90
(Estimated)	(161)		(4)	(15)	(11)	(521)	
Bones	6	22	4	12	6		99
(Estimated)	(30)		(6)	(36)	(14)	(285)	
Fecal pellets	8	26	16	7	2		144
(Estimated)	(534)	(196)	(261)	(195)	(29)	(2433)	
Insect parts		2	3	4			12
(Estimated)			(44)	(16)		(69)	

identification confidence, it must not be omitted when referring to any of the taxa so designated.

RESULTS

The flotation samples from the Matty Canyon sites are remarkable in several ways. The richness of the samples has been noted. Rarely do open sites, particularly those in excess of 2,000 years in age, offer the quantity, taxonomic diversity, and excellent state of preservation that characterize these macrofossil assemblages. The Donaldson Site samples are also remarkably free of evidence of bioturbation. The destructive results of rodent, root, and insect activity are well-known to every excavator. However, these samples contained minuscule amounts of rootlets, modest quantities of mollusks and small animal bones, and relatively low numbers of fecal pellets, most of which were termite. Insect exoskeletal fragments were also infrequent; their near-absence from the site correlates with the total absence of modern, uncarbonized seeds in the feature fills.

Analysis results for the Donaldson Site are presented in Tables 5.2 and 5.3; Table 5.4 summarizes the results for Los Ojitos. Actual and estimated quantities are presented for each category. The column and row totals for estimated quantities are achieved by recalculating the total number counted but substituting the estimated figure for the actual figure each time it is available.

Table 5.4. Carbonized Plant Remains and Noncarbonized Remains from Los Ojitos (*continued*)

Plant	Level 1 Counted	(Est.)	Level 3 Counted	(Est.)	Level 5 Counted	(Est.)	Total	(Est.)
Cyperaceae	2		1	(3)	1	(2)	4	(7)
Ambrosia, involucre	1						1	
cf. *Physalis/Solanum*	1						1	
cf. Solanaceae	1						1	
Trianthema	1		3	(6)			4	(7)
Kallstroemia	1						1	
Agave, tooth	1		1	(2)			2	(3)
cf. *Yucca*	1		3				4	
Salvia			1	(2)			1	(2)
Carnegiea			1	(2)			1	(2)
Rhus					1		1	
Ipomoea					1		1	
Malvaceae			1	(2)			1	(2)
Unknown	541	(547)	411	(766)	232	(360)	1184	(1673)
Total	2400	(2415)	2547	(4219)	1425	(2220)	6372	(8854)
Snails	4		17	(34)	3	(6)	24	(44)
Bones	6		10	(17)	8	(10)	24	(33)
Bones, burned	1		2	(3)	3		6	(7)
Total	11		29	(54)	14	(19)	54	(84)

NOTE. All items are seeds unless otherwise specified; parenthetical figure is estimated number in sample.

Gramineae

Both sites produced significant quantities of grass caryopses or seeds that belong to several species. Many of the specimens had been badly distorted and damaged by exposure to intense heat and had suffered postdepositional damage as well. These conditions, coupled with the paucity of published information on caryopsis morphology and the absence of a comprehensive modern reference collection, precluded specific identification of most of the grains. However, three categories of grasses were isolated based on their distinctive morphology: *Zea mays*, *Sporobolus*, and cf. *Bromus/Agropyron*.

Wild grass seeds have been an important food for many Southwestern aboriginal groups (Doebley 1984). Cool season grasses that mature in late spring and early summer were a vital source of calories that became available at a time when stored food supplies were nearly depleted or exhausted and the new season's crop of wild foods was still largely unavailable (Bohrer 1975). Warm season grasses that ripen in late summer and early fall offered grain that could be collected and stored in quantity. The integration of maize into a subsistence economy based on gathering provided a way in which people could play a direct role in food production, thereby actively enhancing the probability that adequate quantities of food would be available for immediate consumption as well as for long-term storage.

Zea
(Maize)

Maize remains recovered from the flotation samples at both sites include more than 70 cob or rachis fragments, more than 5,000 dissociated cupules, more than 200 kernels and kernel fragments, and a shank (Tables 5.2, 5.4). Most of the maize kernels are incomplete, consisting mainly of the cap or apical portion of the kernel. Shapes of the more complete grains are highly variable, a situation greatly influenced by extreme heat distortion, suggesting that the kernels burned after being removed from the cob. The grains are small; one nearly complete kernel that lacks an embryo, from Feature 7 at the Donaldson Site, measures 5.0 mm in height, 6.1 mm in width, and has a minimum thickness of 5.0 mm. It is broadly trapezoidal in shape, but it is impossible to be certain if this reflects the original appearance. Endosperm textures visible in the broken grain interiors are also variable, with indications that both flinty and floury types may be present.

The single shank was obtained from Feature 15 at the Donaldson Site, a roasting pit. It is small, measuring 5.0 mm in length, 3.2 mm in width, and 1.7 mm in thickness. It appears to be complete, although it is difficult to be certain because of heat damage. It has an elliptical cross section and bears three to four closely spaced nodes, each of which provided leaf sheaths that formed the husk.

In addition to the rachis fragments and cupules recovered from the flotation samples, more than 50 cob fragments were obtained from both sites during the fieldwork. Because of this unexpected cob windfall, no additional analysis beyond raw counts has been made on the flotation-derived cupules and rachis fragments. A brief summary of maize from the sites, based on my continuing study of the cobs, is provided.

All the cobs from both sites are fragmentary. Most measure between 7.0 mm and 20.0 mm in length and are less than 10.5 mm in maximum width. Width dimensions are rachis widths rather than cob widths, as the lower glumes are either missing or consist of basal remnants. The figures represent maximum width, as many of the specimens have elliptical rather than round cross sections. A single, nearly complete cob from Los Ojitos has a length of 42.0 mm and a width of 9.0 mm. An estimated complete length for the specimen would be approximately 50 mm. It is slightly tapered at the base and gradually tapered toward the tip. The cross section is elliptical.

Certain attributes of corn cobs are useful in the comparison of maize populations (Cutler 1966; Bird and Bird 1980). Among the more important are kernel row number and the dimensions of the cupule, the lignified pocket in the cob that subtends a pair of grains and is arranged in vertical files along the axis. Of the 13 cobs from the Donaldson Site examined thus far, 10 are complete enough to obtain the row number. Figure 5.1 shows the emerging pattern of high row number dominance, a pattern well established for Los Ojitos (Fig. 5.2), where the analysis of just over half the cob fragments indicates that 12-rowed and 14-rowed cobs represent almost two-thirds of the assemblage.

The cupules from the Matty Canyon cobs exhibit a range of shapes, including trapezoidal, arch-shaped, triangular, and subrectangular. Further, all have well-developed lateral margins known as rachis flaps or cupule wings. Cupule measurements for both sites are presented in Table 5.5 and were obtained by measuring the cupules on several cob fragments from Los Ojitos and the Donaldson Site. Mean cupule height and width, as well as the standard deviations and ranges for each, are presented for cobs from both sites. All measurements were made to the nearest tenth of a millimeter. Note

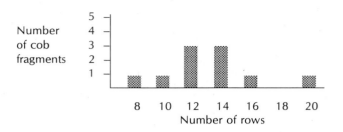

Figure 5.1. Distribution of maize cob row number at the Donaldson Site.

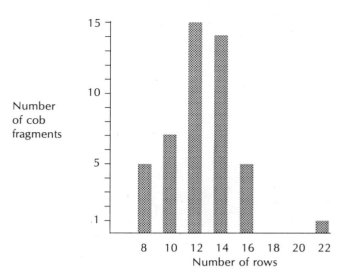

Figure 5.2. Distribution of maize cob row number at Los Ojitos.

that although cupules are treated as independent units for each measurement, in fact cupules occurring on the same cob fragment are not truly independent of one another. However, in order to obtain as large a population of measured cupules as possible from the sites, this lack of independence of measurements was accepted. Moreover, measuring all sufficiently intact cupules increased the probability that all parts of cobs, not just cupules at the midsection, would be represented.

At Los Ojitos, as few as one cupule to as many as 52 cupules were measured on the cob fragments; at the Donaldson Site the range was from 2 to 22 cupules per cob fragment. Fragmentation and abrasion rendered many of the cupules on these cob fragments unfit for accurate measurements. For comparative purposes, Table 5.5 also includes similar data from three other Early Agricultural period sites in southeastern Arizona (Huckell and Huckell 1984; P. Fish and others 1986;

Miksicek 1987), pre-Chapalote and Chapalote from El Riego Cave in the Tehuacán Valley in Mexico (Alvarez del Castillo and Briffard 1978 cited in Miksicek 1987), and a modern population of Chapalote that I experimentally carbonized (obtained from Native Seeds/SEARCH, an organization based in Tucson dedicated to traditional crop conservation). The Tehuacán cobs are uncarbonized and their measurements were modified by Miksicek who subtracted a 20 percent shrinkage factor.

The figures obtained for the two Matty Canyon sites reveal a pattern of small cupules with moderately rec-

Table 5.5. Comparison of Selected Maize Populations

Site	Cobs N	Cupules N Height	Cupules N Width	Row Number Mean	Row Number (Range)	Cupule Height Mean	Cupule Height SD	Cupule Height (Range)	Cupule Width Mean	Cupule Width SD	Cupule Width (Range)	Cupule W:H Ratio Mean	Sources
Donaldson	10	101	102	13.2	(8–20)	1.72	0.36	(1.1–3.2)	2.56	0.63	(1.7–4.2)	1.49	A
Los Ojitos	46	336	338	12.5	(8–22)	1.67	0.34	(0.9–3.1)	2.93	0.71	(0.9–5.2)	1.75	A
Milagro	5	28	28	10.8	(8–14)	1.73	0.38	(1.0–2.4)	2.86	0.64	(1.7–4.0)	1.65	A
Tumamoc Hill		13	13		(10–14)	2.60		(1.8–3.6)	3.80		(2.7–6.1)	1.46	B, C
Mission Road		13	13	12.7	(10–16)	2.60		(1.4–3.4)	2.90		(2.1–4.0)	1.12	C
El Riego Cave, pre-Chapalote*	22			11.5	(8–16)	2.60		(1.1–3.2)	3.80		(2.4–4.8)	1.46	D
El Riego Cave, Chapalote*	20			13.1	(8–16)	2.30		(1.5–2.7)	4.60		(3.2–6.4)	2.00	D
Chapalote, modern carbonized	10	50	50	11.6	(10–14)	1.23	0.25	(1.0–1.6)	4.01	0.77	(3.4–4.5)	3.26	A

* Uncarbonized, 20% shrinkage factor subtracted

NOTE: SD = Standard Deviation

Sources: A, Lisa Huckell, unpublished notes; B, Paul Fish and others 1986; C, Miksicek 1987; D, Alvarez del Castillo and Briffard 1978 cited in Miksicek 1987

tangular shapes. With an average height of 1.72 mm and an average width of 2.56 mm, the Donaldson Site cupules tend to be half again as wide as they are high. Cupules from Los Ojitos are slightly more broad, with a mean width of 2.93 mm and a mean height of 1.67 mm. This shape is reflected in the mean cupule width/height ratios given for both. As used by Galinat (1970), this ratio represents the degree of rectangularity present, with increasingly higher values from that of 1.0, a square, indicating progressively greater rectangularity. Similar moderately rectangular values are calculated for the other southeastern Arizona sites.

The width and height figures also indicate a high degree of intrasite variability within the cob populations, as reflected in the standard deviations and ranges. To what degree this phenotypic variability is affected by factors such as environment or the effects of carbonization is impossible to determine. However, there is considerable intersite consistency between the Matty Canyon sites and the Milagro Site.

Attempts to assess the significance of the similarities and differences shown in Table 5.5 must be made with caution, for the actual degree of comparability is uncertain. Factors to be considered include idiosyncratic variability in recording by investigators, differential size and composition of the maize sample (cobs versus dissociated cupules), chronometric ages of the populations, paucity of data on environmental conditions under which each population was grown and any resulting morphological effects, and problems associated with attempts to use shrinkage compensation factors to achieve comparability of burned and unburned cob populations.

Despite these problems, the information from southeastern Arizona does show an overall pattern of small cupules that tend to have widths that are less than twice the height, a characteristic of early maize. Continuous selection by people for desirable features such as larger kernel size, coupled with heterosis among different maize populations and later infusions of new germplasm, resulted in cupule changes that included increasing width and decreasing height, creating the broad, vertically compressed cupules that characterize more recent maize races (Galinat 1985, Fig. 86). The adjusted figures for pre-Chapalote from El Riego Cave fit within the observed pattern. The trend through time toward larger cobs with fewer rows and broader cupules has been described by Cutler (1966).

Using row number and mean cupule width, the cob samples from the two sites can be plotted graphically (Fig. 5.3). In comparing that distribution pattern with patterns obtained from various archaeological sites and

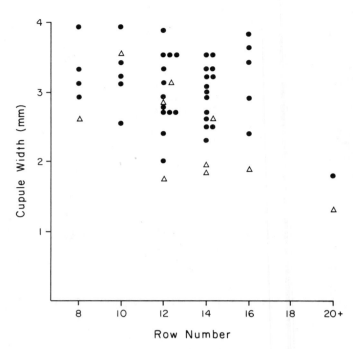

Figure 5.3. Cob fragments from Los Ojitos (•) and the Donaldson Site (△) plotted by row number and mean cupule width. Figures are uncorrected for shrinkage caused by carbonization.

extant Southwestern cultures (Brooks and others 1962, Fig. 6; Cutler 1966, Figs. 4, 7, 11, 12), it is apparent that the Matty Canyon maize population is distinctive. The predominance of 12-row and 14-row cobs and the small average cupule size in this assemblage are noteworthy. These two attributes are considered to be characteristic of "primitive" or early maize (Cutler 1966). The cupule dimensions for the early maize from Milagro, Donaldson, and Los Ojitos are similar to those available for early "pre-Chapalote" maize from El Riego Cave, but differ substantially from the El Riego Chapalote and modern Chapalote. These metric values suggest that significant morphological differences exist in cupule size and shape, although the underlying factors responsible for these differences are unclear at present.

For more than 40 years, the race to which early prehistoric maize from Mexico and the Southwest has been assigned is Chapalote, and until recently it has been considered to be one of four ancient races of Mexico (Wellhausen and others 1952: 54–58; Galinat 1985: 268; Wills 1988a: 127; Matson 1991: 209–216). Found today only along the coastal plain of northwest Mexico, Chapalote is a popcorn characterized by slender tapered cobs bearing 10 to 14 rows of brown flinty kernels (Benz 1986: 216–219). Recent studies by Doebley (1990), Doebley and others (1983, 1985), and Benz

(1986) have provided new information that strongly suggests that Chapalote is not an ancient race, and that other options for the progenitors of the prehistoric and historic maizes found in the Southwest should be considered. The answers may lie with promising new genetic studies that will, in conjunction with AMS direct dating of maize, enable us to determine the relationships between prehistoric maize populations.

Sporobolus
(Dropseed)

The Donaldson Site yielded 45 caryopses that may be assigned to the genus *Sporobolus*. None are documented at Los Ojitos, which may result from a size bias because of the recovery method employed and the small sample size exclusively derived from a midden context. Two species appear to be represented: sand dropseed [*S. cryptandrus* (Torr.) Gray], and Sacaton (*S. wrightii* Munroe). Today these species are common floral components of the mesic floodplains of the semidesert grassland that covers much of the Cienega Valley. Maturing in the late summer and fall, dropseed produces tiny seeds that seldom exceed 1.0 mm in length. The small size is offset by the abundant quantities produced. The seeds also disarticulate easily from the lemma and palea, the chaffy bracts that enclose each grain, a desirable feature that greatly facilitates the process of cleaning the grain. The ethnographic record attests to the importance of *Sporobolus* species in historic Southwestern aboriginal economies (Doebley 1984, Table 1, 59–60).

cf. *Bromus/Agropyron*
(cf. Brome/Wheatgrass)

Quantities of a large, distinctive caryopsis were obtained from both sites, with the majority coming from Los Ojitos. The grains are elongated, with straight sides and slightly contracting apices and bases; the largest complete specimen measures 5.3 mm in length, 1.3 mm in width, and 1.0 mm in thickness. Transverse cross sections tend to be either C-shaped, because of the presence of a lengthwise furrow, or elliptical, with a narrow, shallow channel or crease running the length of one face.

Other surface features include embryos that are quite small and rounded apices that offer no remaining evidence for the presence of a brush. Lemmas and paleas are gone, perhaps removed by parching. Efforts to identify the caryopses were hampered by the lack of a good collection of grains, but comparison with the limited seeds and published information available suggests that the grains may belong to two genera of the Pooideae subfamily, *Bromus* and *Agropyron*. The elongated grains of brome are characterized by a longitudinal furrow that creates a C- or U-shaped cross section. Wheatgrass is a member of the Triticeae tribe (Allred 1993: 6), many of whose members such as wheat, oats, and barley are known for producing large, creased grains. The archaeological assemblage includes considerable morphological variability and will require additional study before identifications may be assigned with confidence. Both of the genera suggested as possibilities here have been exploited as food resources by historic groups in the Southwest (Doebley 1984, Table 1).

Cyperaceae
(Sedges)

Sedge macrofossils were obtained from both sites. The large Donaldson Site sample includes three distinctive achene types. The first type is represented by 13 specimens. It is obovoid in shape, has a plano-convex cross section and bears a distinctive style base remnant at the apical end. The exterior surface is smooth with many fine vertical striations. The seed coat is thick and largely composed of radially oriented, long mechanical or palisade cells. The largest achene is 2.2 mm long, 1.6 mm wide, and 0.8 mm thick. Los Ojitos yielded three achenes of this type.

The second type encompasses a range of shapes, including ovoid, ellipsoid, and rhomboid. Most of the 18 specimens have an elliptical cross section. The exterior surface is smooth with many fine vertical striations. Seed coat thickness appears to be much thinner than that of the first type. The largest of the 18 specimens has a length of 2.2 mm, a width of 1.4 mm, and a thickness of 0.9 mm.

The third achene type is represented by two specimens, both of which are damaged. They differ from the other two types in having a strongly trigonous cross section. Measurements could not be taken on these fragments.

Attempts to identify these three types have been unsuccessful because of the lack of readily available comprehensive comparative material. Initial efforts indicate that the first type compares well with *Scirpus*, the bulrush or tule, and the other two may be members of the large and phenotypically variable genus *Carex* or sedge (Mason 1957; A. Martin and Barkley 1961: 138; Berggren 1969).

The Cyperaceae, or sedge family, contains grasslike genera that grow primarily in wetland areas. Sedges have provided Native Americans with raw materials for baskets and utilitarian items (tough stems), medicine (roots), and food (tender young lower stems and tubers), but it is the bulrush that has been most widely used for food (seeds, young stem bases, pollen) and for raw material (stems) to produce boats, baskets, mats, and bedding (Coville 1897: 92; Chamberlin 1911: 365, 381; Merrill 1970; Gunther 1973: 22; N. Turner 1978: 68; Rogers 1980: 23). The seeds have been recovered from coprolites from Great Basin Archaic levels in Danger Cave and Hogup Cave in Utah (Fry 1976), suggesting that the starchy achenes have a long history of exploitation for food.

Pollen profiles from Matty Canyon and nearby Cienega Creek (Paul Schultz Martin 1963, Figs. 17 and 18) show the recurring presence of Cyperaceae pollen, which suggests the repeated development of cienega (marsh) areas. The substantial Cyperaceae component present in the basal portion of the Matty Canyon sequence means that marshy conditions probably prevailed at the time of the Early Agricultural period occupation. It is likely that cyperaceous plants were easily obtained either near the Donaldson Site settlement or close by in the surrounding valley. The presence of the achenes in all but one of the 14 flotation samples suggests that they were readily available and could have constituted an important wild plant food resource.

Agavaceae

Agave

Four tiny fragments of agave heart tissue and three marginal teeth from the edges of leaves were recorded in Features 8 and 15 at the Donaldson Site. Two marginal teeth were recovered from Levels 1 and 3 at Los Ojitos. The tissue fragments are small; the largest measures 7.8 mm long, 4.3 mm wide, and 3.1 mm thick. The amorphous lumps are distinguished by the presence of distinctive flat, elongated styloid crystals. No fibers are present. Of the five teeth, two are basal fragments and the remaining three are complete or nearly so. Dimensions for the largest are 3.1 mm in length, 1.6 mm in width, and 0.3 mm in thickness. All have strongly compressed elliptical cross sections and bear some resemblance to rose thorns.

Agave has long provided food, drink, fibers, soap, and other valuable products to those people sharing its territory (Castetter, Bell, and Grove 1938; Gentry 1982: 3–24). The sweet, nutritious food called mescal is ob-

tained by pit-roasting the heart of the plant and it has been a vitally important resource for many Southwestern Indian groups. Archaeological evidence for its exploitation by several prehistoric cultures, in the form of roasting pits, has been recorded throughout the plant's range. Recent work in the Tucson Basin indicates that the plant was being grown in massive numbers by the Hohokam, probably for the large scale production of mescal and the extraction of the long, strong leaf fibers for cordage and textiles (S. Fish and others 1985; S. Fish, P. Fish, and J. Madsen 1992).

The antiquity of mescal consumption has been established by Callen (1967) in his study of coprolites from cave sites in the Tehuacán Valley of Mexico, where mescal or maguey remains consistently appear from 6500 B.C. to A.D. 1500. Although the chronology developed for these sites may be substantially condensed through the redating of maize and other plant macrofossils by AMS dating (Long and others 1989), the sequence still demonstrates consistent reliance on this plant food through time. The small sample recovered from the Matty Canyon sites represents the first and earliest documented occurrence of mescal in a preceramic context in southeastern Arizona.

The inhabitants of both settlements had ready access to wild agaves. Three species, *Agave palmeri* Engelm., *A. parryi* Engelm., and *A. schottii* Engelm., grow in the oak grasslands of the Santa Rita Mountains to the west (McLaughlin and Van Asdall 1977; Lowe 1981), and *A. palmeri* appears on the rocky slopes of Matty Canyon just 3.2 km (less than 2 miles) up canyon from the Donaldson Site. *A. schottii* is too small and bitter for consumption, but the large Palmer and Parry agaves have been widely used because of their low content or lack of bitter glycosides (Gentry 1982: 206–207, 447, 539). The plants are collected in late spring or early summer when emergent flower stalk buds signal that the stored sugar content is at its highest level. Preparation involves the removal of the formidably armed leaves, leaving the round, lettuce-size heart or *cabeza* ("head," in Spanish). The hearts are placed in pits lined with hot rocks and coals, covered with earth, and allowed to steam for one to three days. The juicy cooked product is sweet and strongly flavored, tasting somewhat like molasses (Castetter and others 1938: 28–30, 37–57; Buskirk 1986: 169–172). It can be pounded into sheets or sun-dried and stored for later use, and it keeps for as long as several years.

The small teeth are identical to those along leaf base margins; they were undoubtedly introduced into the settlements on the leaf base portions remaining on the hearts after the leaves had been trimmed off. Their presence offers no insight into whether the hearts were roasted onsite or elsewhere. The ethnographic record indicates that contact with the raw cabezas often resulted in uncomfortable skin reactions to the calcium oxalate present in the plants (Buskirk 1986: 170), making preparation at the collecting site a better strategy for minimizing contact with raw plants. Calcium oxalate is neutralized by heat. The small heart fragments may be losses incurred while cooking, as mescal was often added to foods to sweeten them (Castetter and others 1938).

Yucca

Evidence for the presence of two species of yucca was found at the Donaldson Site. One complete seed and one fragment of the thick seeds characteristic of indehiscent, fleshy-fruited, broad-leafed yuccas were obtained from Feature 20, a pit. Although split in half lengthwise, the complete seed is 7.6 mm in height, 8.5 mm in width, and 4.3 mm in thickness. Four fragments of what is probably the same kind of yucca were recovered at Los Ojitos, but their small size precludes more than a tentative identification of cf. *Yucca*. Based on modern distributions, the seeds belong to either the banana yucca (*Y. baccata* Torr.) or hoary yucca (*Y. schottii* Engelm.).

A seed fragment of a second yucca species came from Feature 9, another pit at the Donaldson Site. The specimen displays the broad marginal wing and rugose surface texturing found on the seeds of *Y. elata* Engelm., the palmilla or soaptree yucca, one of the indehiscent, dry-fruited, narrow-leafed species.

Like agaves, yuccas have furnished a variety of important materials and products to Sonoran desert dwellers, with virtually all parts of the plant utilized. Leaf fibers were made into basketry, cordage, sandals, and textiles; stalks were converted into fire drill hearths and ritual objects; roots were used for hair brushes and as a source of soap; and the hearts, flower petals, fruits, and seeds were consumed as food (Bell and Castetter 1941). The presence of the seeds at the two sites most likely reflects the use of the fruits and seeds for food. In the case of the fleshy species, the ethnographic record indicates that the fruits were eagerly sought, with those of the sweet banana yucca the most popular. The fruit pulp of the latter was often processed in bulk into a dried paste that could be stored for long periods. The dry palmilla fruits are inedible when mature, but may be eaten when young. The seeds could be ground into meal.

All three of these species would have been available to Matty Canyon residents. Today *Y. elata* and *Y. baccata* grow upstream from the sites in Matty Canyon as components of the desert grassland. *Y. schottii* is restricted to higher elevations and inhabits the oak woodlands along the foothills of the eastern slope of the Santa Rita Mountains. The fruits become available in late summer and early fall.

Juncus
(Rush)

Three seeds identified as *Juncus*, or rush, came from Feature 7 (1), Feature 15 (1), and Feature 19 (1) at the Donaldson Site. These numbers are undoubtedly deceptively low, as the tiny seeds were obtained from the small subsamples taken from Size Class 5. The estimated total in the samples is 228.

Two specimens are badly damaged; the basal third is missing in almost identical fashion in both. The third seed is complete, but distorted. The seeds appear to have been ellipsoidal in shape, with round cross sections. The length of the whole specimen is 0.7 mm and the diameter is 0.4 mm. The exterior surface is finely reticulate, with the vertical elements consisting of closely spaced, conspicuous ribs.

There is little evidence to suggest what role, if any, rushes played in the Early Agricultural period economy. The ethnographic record indicates that the tough stems have been used for basketry and cordage (Bean and Saubel 1972: 80–81; Gunther 1973: 23), the young shoots and rootstocks may have been eaten (Gunther 1973: 23), and the plant has been used ceremonially because of its close association with water (Whiting 1939: 70). The tiny seeds were collected for food by the Owens Valley Paiute, but in general they do not appear to have been a popular resource (Ebeling 1986: 144). The archaeological specimens may have been inadvertently introduced into the settlement in ripe capsules incidentally included in collections of desired vegetal material.

Rushes are present in the Cienega Valley today and occur in small numbers along the margins of active drainages. Seeds are produced from late summer into early fall.

Juniperus
(Juniper)

Seed and seed fragments of juniper were obtained from all three levels at Los Ojitos. Of the 27 items identified, four were complete seeds. They exhibit a wide range of shapes; the largest has an angular tear-drop shape and is 5.0 mm long, 3.5 mm wide, and 3.2 mm thick. The size, exterior seed morphology, and extremely thick seed walls that thin dramatically at the apex indicate that the seeds are those of *J. deppeana* Steud., alligator juniper.

The resinous female cones or berries of virtually all species of junipers have been used throughout the Southwest for food and as a seasoning (Castetter 1935: 31–32), although some are more valued than others. Alligator juniper is often mentioned as one of the best because of the sweet flavor the fruits develop when ripe (Vestal 1952: 12; Kirk 1975: 19, 21). Other useful products may be obtained from the tree, including ornaments (beads, bracelets, and necklaces made from the bony seeds); wood for fuel, construction, and tools; shredded bark for many utilitarian purposes; and foliage for ritual and medicinal needs (Vestal 1952: 11–12; Buskirk 1986: 187–188). Juniper was readily available to people living along Cienega Creek, as one-seed juniper [*J. monosperma* (Engelm.) Sarg.] would have been scattered through the surrounding grasslands and would have been more concentrated up Matty Canyon along north-facing slopes with increasing elevation. Alligator juniper grows in the oak woodland and begins to appear at roughly 1,373 m (4,500 feet) elevation (Kearney and Peebles 1960: 59). In order to obtain materials from this species, gatherers would have had to travel several kilometers either west to the Santa Rita Mountains or east to the Whetstone Mountains (Fig. 1.2). The fruits may be found in late fall through winter.

Chenopodiaceae-Amaranthaceae (Cheno-ams)

Seeds of both the chenopod and amaranth families were recovered from the Donaldson Site; Los Ojitos yielded seeds of the Chenopodiaceae. Many species in these families produce tiny, lenticular seeds that are structurally similar and can be difficult to distinguish, particularly after experiencing severe morphological changes induced by carbonization. The most serious of these conditions is seed coat loss, which leaves behind the nondiagnostic embryo-encircled perisperm. Because of their greatly similar growth habits, seasonality, environmental parameters, and aboriginal preparation methods, it is not critical that the two families be distinguished in order to achieve an accurate interpretation of their role in the local economy. As a matter of convenience, they are lumped together and referred to as "Cheno-ams."

At least three species of chenopods are represented in the assemblages from both sites. One is a *C. berlandieri* type with a strongly alveolate testa, the second has a faintly alveolate testa, and the third has a smooth, finely striate testa. All are small in size, not exceeding 1.0 mm in diameter. Other types may be present as well. The amaranth seeds exhibit considerably less variability and may be members of a single species. The seeds are obovate in outline and have a biconvex cross section. A prominent rim is present. The largest of the three complete specimens is 1.0 mm long, 1.0 mm wide, and 0.6 mm thick. The specimens compare well with *Amaranthus palmeri* Wats., Palmer amaranth. No evidence was found for the presence of domesticated species of either family.

Annual chenopods and amaranths have offered desert dwellers two important food resources: seeds and greens. The small seeds are produced in prodigious quantities and are easily harvested in the summer and fall. The young, tender plants can be prepared as potherbs from early spring into the fall. Both foods are nutritious, supplying vital amino acids, vitamins, and minerals to the diet (Meals for Millions/Freedom From Hunger Foundation 1980; National Research Council 1984). Until relatively recently, the plants were exploited by many contemporary Southwestern groups (Castetter 1935: 15–17, 21–23). Although evidence for the consumption of greens is usually lacking in the archaeobotanical record, the seeds appear as common components of macrofossil inventories ranging in age from the Archaic through the ceramic periods (Fry 1976, Table 9; Gasser 1982, Table 1; Huckell and Huckell 1984, Table 7; L. Huckell 1986, Table 12.4).

Amaranths and chenopods prefer disturbed, open soils such as those occurring along roadsides, in arroyos, along ditch banks, and in agricultural and pasture lands (Parker 1972). In the Cienega Valley, Palmer amaranth grows on the banks of active drainages. Patches of herbaceous chenopod species have appeared in the immediate vicinity of the Donaldson Site on newly cleared, low, open sandy point bar deposits; but they have been quickly replaced by young cottonwood (*Populus*) saplings and shrubs such as rabbit brush (*Chrysothamnus*) and burrobush (*Hymenoclea*). Pollen profiles compiled by Paul Schultz Martin (1963, Figs. 17, 18) for Cienega Creek and Matty Canyon indicate that cheno-ams have been a constant feature of the local vegetation during the last 2,200 years or more. The archaeological seeds may represent the harvesting of wild stands located in naturally disturbed areas or they may have come from plants that were tolerated or encouraged around the village or agricultural fields because of their recognized food value.

Atriplex
(Saltbush)

Fruits of a small, weedy saltbush were obtained from both sites. The fruits have been considerably damaged, losing most of the delicate margins of the bracts, which makes specific identification difficult. They are irregularly round to rectangular in shape with lenticular cross sections; some still bear the remnants of three prominent vertical ridges on each face. Measurements for the largest incomplete specimen are 1.6 mm long, 1.35 mm wide, and 0.85 mm thick. They compare most favorably to *Atriplex elegans* (Moq.) D. Dietr., a common herbaceous annual that grows in disturbed and highly alkaline soils. The prominent ridges on some of the archaeological specimens match patterns exhibited by var. *thornberi* Jones, which is distinguished by the presence of vertical crests on the bracts.

Like other chenopods, saltbush has edible seeds, although their utility can be compromised by high labor investments needed to extract the edible seeds from the bracts of some species. As the common name suggests, the herbage has a high salt content and has been used to season roasted and boiled foods (Ebeling 1986: 424, 479–481). *A. elegans* is listed as one of these seasoning species (Kearney and Peebles 1960: 258). An annual, it is available in the summer months, setting seed in late summer and the fall (Parker 1972: 94).

cf. *Rumex* and cf. *Rumex/Polygonum*

Distinctive achenes or seeds belonging to the Polygonaceae or buckwheat family were obtained from both sites. The bulk of the material was retrieved from Los Ojitos, which yielded 170 specimens. Most of the seeds have experienced considerable swelling from heat exposure, and pericarp and seed coat loss is high, revealing an abundance of starchy endosperm. The largest specimen is 2.8 mm long, 2.6 mm wide, and 2.5 mm thick.

The seeds are characterized by a trigonous shape with a broad base and contracting, pointed apex. The transverse cross section shape is a highly inflated triangle. The closest matches are dock (*Rumex*) and smartweed or knotweed (*Polygonum*). The diagnostic feature used to separate the often morphologically similar seeds of these two genera is embryo location, with the dock embryo running up the middle of one side, whereas the knotweed embryo runs up one of the three corners (A.

Martin and Barkley 1961: 147). Incomplete specimens reveal that the embryos are not adnate to the wall but are more centrally located in the endosperm. The limited comparative material presently available did not provide an identical match, but the embryo orientation of the archaeological specimens more closely approximates that of *Rumex*, to which they are therefore tentatively assigned. Two nearly complete achenes with intact pericarps that do not permit an interior view are tentatively classified as cf. *Rumex/Polygonum*. They may simply be better preserved examples of the cf. *Rumex* achenes.

Docks and smartweeds are herbaceous genera. They occur in disturbed habitats such as roadsides and fields, but tend to favor mesic habitats and are often found around ditches and along, and in some cases within, streams and lakes. Many in the modern flora are naturalized weedy species, several of which, such as curly dock (*Rumex crispus* L.), have been integrated into historic traditional subsistence and ethnomedicinal systems (Castetter 1935: 50; Vestal 1952: 23–24). Species of both genera have been exploited for their edible leaves, leaf petioles, roots and seeds (Castetter 1935: 50; Kirk 1975: 53–54, 56; Ebeling 1986: 37, 220, 222, 423, 477–478) and as sources of medicine and fish poison (Vestal 1952: 23–24; Ebeling 1986: 751). Several species are known to be rich in toxic secondary compounds such as tannin and oxalic acid, the negative effects of which can be mitigated by boiling or roasting prior to consumption. The starchy seeds have been widely used; the domesticated grain buckwheat (*Fagopyrum esculentum* Moench) is in this family. The seeds recovered from both sites were most likely obtained from locally available riparian species, with seasonal availability potentially ranging from the fall through the spring, depending on the species involved.

Cucurbita
(Squash or Wild Gourd)

Levels 3 and 5 at Los Ojitos produced five pieces of the pericarp or rind of a member of the squash family. The fragments are quite small; the largest measures 5.6 mm in length, 2.6 mm in width, and 0.5 mm in thickness (maximum thickness recorded for all pieces is 0.5 mm). The tabular fragments have a smooth exterior surface from which the epidermis has been lost. Two distinctive layers are visible in the cross section, with the upper hypodermal layer composed of several rows of dense, compacted cells followed by a thicker layer consisting of large, isodiametric cells. Comparison with available rind samples indicates that the fragments are not bottle gourd (*Lagenaria siceraria* Standl.), but are either squash or wild gourd (*Cucurbita*). Species differentiation of carbonized rind based on rind features is extremely difficult because of considerable phenotypic variability among cucurbit species and the morphological changes that take place as a result of carbonization (R. Ford 1986: 15); the small size of the Los Ojitos specimens also increases the risk of erroneous identifications. Supporting evidence from other, more diagnostic parts of the fruits such as seeds and peduncles or fruit stems is lacking. As a result, the identification must be left at the genus level.

It is possible that the fragments are pieces of wild gourd rind (*Cucurbita* spp.). At least two species grow in the environs of Cienega Creek today: buffalo gourd (*C. foetidissima* H.B.K.) and finger-leaved gourd (*C. digitata* Gray). Parts of the buffalo gourd have been used in a variety of ways: the dried thin rind for containers, the seeds and fruits for food, and the large roots and fruits with their high saponin content for soap (Ebeling 1986: 329, 527–528). The fruits are available in late summer and early fall.

The other possibility is that the fragments are squash (*Cucurbita pepo* L.), which has been found in Early Agricultural period contexts elsewhere in the Southwest, appearing along with the earliest maize. The same type of squash was widely grown throughout the Southwest until A.D. 900, when other varieties appeared (Cutler and Whitaker 1961, Table 2; R. Ford 1981: 14). The fresh fruits provided edible oil-rich seeds and flavorful flesh, and when dried, the sturdy shells were used as containers. The absence thus far of evidence for the presence of this important cultigen in Early Agricultural period sites in southeastern Arizona may be attributed to a combination of factors: the small number of sites of this age investigated to date, sampling bias, and the notoriously poor preservation qualities of cucurbit remains in open sites. The remarkable environment at the Matty Canyon sites may have finally provided the first bits of proof for the presence of this important member of the triad forming the crop complex of maize, squash, and beans that should have been in place by this time in this part of the Southwest as well.

cf. *Physalis/Solanum*
(cf. Groundcherry/
Nightshade)

A single complete seed of the Solanaceae or nightshade family was recovered from Level 1 at Los Ojitos.

It is circular in outline with a strongly compressed ellipsoidal cross section. The hilum is located on the margin; there is no associated beak or notch. Despite damage to one face and erosion of the other, traces of distinctive testa sculpture of wavy muri are visible. The seed is 1.5 mm in length, 1.6 mm in width, and 0.5 mm in thickness. It compares well with both *Physalis* and *Solanum*, genera that are often difficult to distinguish (A. Martin and Barkley 1961: 196).

Groundcherries are low-growing herbs that produce sweet, many-seeded berries enclosed in a papery husk formed by the calyx. The berries of all species are edible, with some more sweet than others (Kirk 1975: 74). They may be eaten both raw or cooked, and can be dried for future use (Ebeling 1986: 434, 524). They grow in a variety of habitats, but are commonly found in disturbed ground such as along roadsides and fields. Because of the berries produced, the plants have often been tolerated or encouraged by Native American traditional farmers (Castetter 1935: 39–40; Ebeling 1986: 524). Direct evidence for their use has been reported in Basketmaker III and Pueblo III coprolites from sites in the Mesa Verde area (Stiger 1979). Nightshade is a large genus that includes both poisonous and edible species (Kearney and Peebles 1960: 756; Kirk 1975: 241). The plants also frequent various habitats, but are often located in disturbed soils and mesic environments. Among the edible products available are starchy tubers, greens from the leaves, and berries (Castetter 1935: 51; Ebeling 1986: 56, 254, 328, 525). Species of both of these genera should have been locally available to the people living along Cienega Creek. Fruits are available in the summer and fall.

Portulaca
(Purslane)

Four pits and a pit structure at the Donaldson Site yielded a total of 12 purslane seeds (Table 5.2). The distinctly tuberculate, apostrophe-shaped seeds average 0.65 mm in length, 0.68 mm in width, and 0.4 mm in thickness. Purslane is a weedy, herbaceous genus that prefers disturbed soils. The succulent, tart plants are available during the summer and fall, and can be consumed raw or cooked as greens. The tiny seeds are also edible, and, like the plant itself, they have been exploited by many cultures (Castetter 1935; Meals For Millions/Freedom From Hunger Foundation 1980; Ebeling 1986: 485, 647). The seeds are frequently recovered from Hohokam sites (Gasser 1982, Table 1; L. Huckell 1986, Table 12.4).

Aizoaceae

Mollugo
(Carpetweed)

A single carpetweed seed was recovered from Feature 7 at the Donaldson Site. The tiny, comma-shaped seed has been badly damaged by heat, which has caused the loss of the encircling embryo. The incomplete specimen is 0.45 mm in length, 0.50 mm in width, and 0.40 mm in thickness.

Carpetweed is an annual herb that grows in disturbed soil. It can be used as a potherb from mid-summer into the fall. It is often found in Hohokam archaeobotanical assemblages (Gasser 1982, Table 1).

Trianthema
(Horse Purslane)

Seven Donaldson Site samples yielded a total of 31 horse purslane seeds (Table 5.2). Mean measurements for the small, apostrophe-shaped seeds are 1.41 mm in length, 1.56 mm in width, and 0.82 mm in thickness.

Like its relative, carpetweed, horse purslane grows in disturbed soils where the fleshy plant can be collected for preparation as a potherb from late spring to late fall (Curtin 1984: 64). The frequency with which the seeds appear in Hohokam sites suggests that the plant was extensively utilized (Gasser 1982, Table 1; L. Huckell 1986, Table 12.4).

Cactaceae

Carnegiea
(Saguaro)

Single saguaro seeds were recovered from both sites. The largest of the intact seeds measures 2.05 mm in length, 1.30 mm in width, and 1.15 mm in thickness.

The importance of the saguaro cactus to Sonoran Desert people has been extensively documented (Castetter and Underhill 1935; Crosswhite 1980; Ebeling 1986). It has provided foods, beverages, and raw materials for construction and tool manufacture. The sweet red fruits ripen in early summer, at which time they are often gathered in large quantities for processing into jam, syrup, wine, and dried pulp. The oily seeds are harvested and dried for later consumption.

Saguaros are extremely rare in the vicinity of Matty Canyon, a result of edaphic and elevational constraints on the plant's growth (Steenbergh and Lowe 1977).

Temperature is the major controlling variable in the northern range of this cold–intolerant, semitropical plant. It generally thrives at elevations below 915 m (3,500 feet), although it has been reported as high as 1,373 m (4,500 feet) and, on at least one occasion, at 1,556 m (5,100 feet; Kearney and Peebles 1960). The closest saguaros to the Donaldson Site are probably those to the west in the Rosemont area of the Santa Rita Mountains, where a rare, disjunct individual occasionally is seen. The plants occur in some quantity 16 to 18 km (10 to 11 miles) to the north along the south-facing slopes of Davidson Canyon. O'odham collecting expeditions often traveled great distances to reach preferred or family-owned saguaro stands. These seeds may represent a similar investment of time and labor to procure a prized food or reflect a chance encounter by a village inhabitant with an isolated local plant.

Opuntia
(Prickly Pear)

Surprisingly little evidence was recovered for the use of prickly pear and cholla. Feature 15 at the Donaldson Site produced a seed fragment and two embryo fragments that may well be from the same seed. Of the 13 specimens recovered from Los Ojitos, 8 are complete seeds. All of the seeds and fragments bear a distinctive, well-developed corky rim, which indicates that the seeds are prickly pear. Cholla seeds (Benson 1982: 50) usually have a narrow, more inconspicuous rim.

Prickly pear has been widely exploited throughout the Southwest for its edible leaves or pads, buds, succulent fruits, and seeds (Castetter 1935: 35–37; Kirk 1975: 50, 52; Curtin 1984: 61; Ebeling 1986: 382). The antiquity of the consumption of the fruits and seeds has been documented by means of coprolite evidence from Utah and Colorado (Fry 1976, Tables 8–11; Stiger 1979, Table 1). Fruits and seeds become available during the summer months. The modest quantity of seeds recovered may simply reflect sampling bias or preservation bias resulting from widespread consumption of raw fruit, or it may indicate that the cacti were less readily available than current distributions would suggest. Both cholla and prickly pear species are present in the Cienega Valley today, but modern distributions and densities have been greatly altered by cattle grazing, which promotes the spread and extensive colonization by prickly pear and cholla species of heavily grazed grasslands (Humphrey 1958: 39). Cactus fruits may have been a long-distance commodity that was obtained from the foothills of the Santa Rita and Whetstone mountains.

Rhus
(Sumac)

Single sumac endocarps or seeds were recovered from both sites. Distorted from heat exposure, the seeds are irregularly reniform in shape, with elliptical cross sections. The smooth seed coats are broken by multiple small fissures in the thick palisade layer. The Donaldson Site specimen is the largest, measuring 3.2 mm in height, 4.0 mm in width and 2.1 mm in thickness.

Sumacs have proven to be valuable resources for western desert dwellers, producing food, beverages, basketry materials, and dyes (Kirk 1975: 116, 270; Ebeling 1986: 126, 243, 307, 324, 502–504). Most of the species produce small red or orange drupes that are covered with hairs, the noteworthy exception being poison ivy (*R. radicans* L.). Gathered for food by several aboriginal groups, the fruits have been widely used to prepare refreshing drinks by steeping in water to release a tart, lemon flavor. The most popular species for this purpose was *R. trilobata* Nutt., known as skunkbush. It has also been a preferred material of prehistoric and historic Native American basketmakers because of its pliable stems (Bohrer 1983). Skunkbush inhabits the foothills of the Santa Rita Mountains, where it grows in canyons at the upper reaches of the semi-desert grassland among oaks and junipers. It is joined there by evergreen sumac, *R. choriophylla* Woot. & Standl. Both would be available in the Whetstone Mountains as well. Fruits ripen in late summer and the fall. The small size of the archaeological seeds suggests that they may be little leaf sumac (*Rhus microphylla* Engelm.), but they also fit within the small end of the size range of the larger skunkbush and evergreen sumac. Little leaf sumac is a large shrub to small tree that is scattered through the semidesert grassland. It would have been the most accessible sumac for the villagers; a very large individual grows today on the eastern margin of the Donaldson Site.

Salvia
(Sage)

A single nutlet or seed belonging to the genus *Salvia* was obtained from Level 2 at Los Ojitos. It has sustained heavy damage, but the distinctive hilum area has remained intact. The slightly obovate seed is 2.0 mm high and 1.2 mm wide; loss of one side precluded a thickness measurement. The seeds from several sage species have been gathered by many Southwestern peoples for the production of seed meal and a beverage based on the production of mucilage by seeds immersed in water (Kirk 1975: 85; Ebeling 1986: 388–389). Locally available species are generally herbaceous and favor mesic environments. They produce large numbers of seeds that can be gathered in quantity when plant densities are high. The seeds of some species are available in the late spring and early summer; others may be collected through the summer months and into early fall.

Ipomoea
(Morning Glory)

A single morning glory seed was obtained from Level 3 at Los Ojitos. Although seriously damaged, the overall configuration remains intact. The sectoroid seed is 3.2 mm long, 2.0 mm wide, and 2.2 mm thick. The intact basal hilum is elliptical, with the orientation paralleling the long axis of the seed, the diagnostic feature that distinguishes this genus from *Convolvulus*, which has a perpendicularly oriented hilum (A. Martin and Barkley 1961: 192).

Morning glories have long been appreciated and extensively cultivated for the colorful flowers they produce. Economically, the most well-known member of the genus is the edible sweet potato (*I. batatas* Lam.), but members of this genus as well as others in the Convolvulaceae have become increasingly known as sources of toxic compounds that have been used by traditional societies as well as Western science as sources of medicinal drugs. At least one species, *I. violacea*, shares with some other family members a narcotic, hallucinogenic compound that was commonly used as a divination aid by the Aztecs. Recent research has revealed that the distribution of this property among the family's genera is considerably more extensive than expected (Schultes 1976: 128–136). The presence of a single seed at Los Ojitos can hardly be construed as evidence of the use of morning glory as a hallucinogen, although a medicinal use is certainly a reasonable possibility. As members of the desert grassland flora, several species grow locally in the Cienega Valley (Kearney and Peebles 1960: 676–678). Time did not permit a search for information as to chemical constituents present in any of these wild species.

Kallstroemia

A single nutlet of kallstroemia was obtained from Level 1 at Los Ojitos. Sectoroid in shape, it is complete, measuring 2.7 mm in length, 1.6 mm in width, and 1.2 mm in thickness. The dorsal tuberculate sculpture has been eroded to the point that a species determination cannot be made. The plants are summer annuals that produce showy flowers; all four species occur in southeastern Arizona where they favor plains and mesas (Kearney and Peebles 1960: 492). The achenes rarely appear in the archaeobotanical record, and ethnobotanical sources offer no clues as to possible uses of the plants.

Compositae

Ambrosia
(Ragweed)

Level 1 at Los Ojitos yielded a single complete disseminule of a ragweed (*Ambrosia*). The achenes are enclosed within the fused involucral bracts, which form a hard case or bur that bears protuberances or spines that often effectively aid in dissemination. The specimen is 2.5 mm long, 1.7 mm wide, and 1.5 mm thick; it bears no obvious evidence for the presence of spines on the irregularly protuberant exterior, although this may be masked by surface erosion that has occurred.

Ambrosia, which now includes the genus *Franseria* (Lehr 1978: 150–151), is a widely distributed herbaceous annual, with preferred habitats of disturbed ground and mesic settings such as washes, springs, and streams. Few ethnobotanical uses are recorded for members of this genus. The roots of one species have been gathered for food (Castetter and Bell 1942: 60); their allergenic capabilities are well-known. Several species of ragweed would have been locally available to residents of the Cienega Valley. Considering the tendency toward bur formation, it is possible that the involucre was inadvertently introduced into the cultural deposit.

cf. *Viguiera*
(Golden Eye)

The three achenes from the composite or sunflower family came from Feature 15 (2) and from Feature 8 (1) at the Donaldson Site. The smooth, obovate specimens have a finely ribbed exterior surface and a biconvex cross section. Mean dimensions are 1.57 mm in length, 0.75 mm in width, and 0.48 mm in thickness. The specimens compare well with achenes of golden eye, *Viguiera annua* (Jones) Blake, an annual herb that grows on hills, plains, and in river bottoms. Achenes are produced in the summer and fall (Kearney and Peebles 1960: 902).

There are no readily available sources that document aboriginal exploitation of the small achenes for food. It is possible that other plant parts were used. Among the Tarahumara, the leaves of two *Viguiera* species are eaten, and the root of a shrubby species has been used by the Seri to prepare a contraceptive tea (Felger and Moser 1985: 286; Ebeling 1986: 759). It is also possible that the achenes are inadvertent introductions into the midden deposits.

Euphorbia
(Spurge)

A single seed belonging to the spurge family came from Feature 4. The ellipsoidal seed is embellished with regularly spaced, intersecting, vertical and horizontal ridges and has a round cross section. It is 0.93 mm long and 0.60 mm in diameter. It compares well with seeds of several species of spurge (*Euphorbia*), a large, widely distributed genus; many of its species are weedy herbs that prefer disturbed, open soils.

Members of this genus and family often contain an acrid, toxic latex that effectively discourages predation by herbivores. The secondary compounds present in this latex as well as the roots, seeds, and entire plant result in several species being used in traditional and commercial medicines as well as in industrial products (Kearney and Peebles 1960: 501, 511; Bean and Saubel 1972: 73–74; Curtin 1984: 99–100). The presence of a single seed in the archaeological assemblage suggests that it probably came from the local weed flora, although the possibility exists that it reflects the prehistoric medicinal use of the plant.

Quercus
(Oak)

Nearly 500 tiny fragments of acorn shell or pericarp were identified in the assemblages. They were present in every sampled provenience except Feature 20 at the Donaldson Site. The fragments never exceed 3.5 mm in length or width and range in thickness from 0.45 mm to 1.2 mm. Exterior surfaces are smooth to finely striate, depending on the amount of deterioration experienced. Most of the fragments are general wall pieces, although a few come from the rim encircling the distinctive basal scar area.

Acorns have been used extensively by many cultures for food (Castetter 1935; Gallagher 1977). The calorie-rich nuts contain high levels of carbohydrates and fats (Heizer and Elsasser 1980, Table 4) and could be collected in large quantities for storage. Several species contain objectionable levels of bitter tannin, which resulted in the development of leaching techniques that effectively removed the toxic ingredient. Other acorns are sweet and do not require treatment prior to consumption. The shelled nuts could be eaten raw or parched, but were primarily prepared by grinding into meal that was used in soups, stews, mush, and bread.

Acorns would have been readily available in quantity to village residents. At least four species of oak are present in the foothills of the Santa Rita Mountains to the west of the Donaldson Site (McLaughlin and Van Asdall 1977): Arizona oak (*Quercus arizonica* Sarg.), Emory oak (*Q. emoryi* Torr.), Mexican blue oak (*Q. oblongifolia* Torr.), and Palmer oak (*Q. palmeri* Engelm.). Emory oak and Mexican blue oak were gathered in July by the O'odham (Castetter and Underhill 1935), who also traded blue oak acorns to the Pima (Russell 1908). No mention is made in the ethnographic record of leaching by aboriginal groups in Arizona, suggesting that sweet acorns were highly preferred for food (Gifford 1971: 240; Gallagher 1977).

Several fragments of the apical cap scar area of the pericarp were recovered from both sites. Comparison with modern samples of the four available oaks indicates that the consistently small diameters observed match the small size that characterizes Emory oak, suggesting that gathering parties left the villages to collect the sweet acorns in the higher elevation oak woodland and returned with the unshelled nuts.

Acorns were stored in a variety of forms, including whole unshelled and shelled nuts and as meal (Gallagher 1977). The nearly ubiquitous presence of the tiny shell fragments in all but one of the flotation samples must mean that acorns were being brought back to the villages for processing or for storage in their shells rather than being processed at the place of collection. The appeal of these acorns still exists today. People still gather them in the Santa Rita Mountains in July, and they are occasionally sold in markets in Tucson.

Juglans
(Native Walnut)

Walnut shell fragments were present in the macrofossil inventories of both sites. The largest is 6.3 mm long, 4.0 mm wide, and 1.3 mm thick. The exterior surface is smooth and bears a narrow groove or channel identical to grooves forming the network of fissures that cover shells of the thick–walled globose nuts. The other specimens exhibit smooth or grooved exterior surfaces and still bear traces of the elaborate interior shell sculpture that effectively encloses the cotyledons or nutmeats.

Walnuts were often used for food by prehistoric peoples (Ebeling 1986: 475, 500). The 2.5–cm to 4.0–cm diameter nuts contain modest quantities of nutmeats, but their sweet, oil-rich taste seems to justify the high labor investment required to extract them. Even today, when the ripe nuts fall from the trees in late June and July, family gathering parties may be encountered in the mountains around Tucson. The shells have also been used to make a dye for basketry (Bryan and Young 1940; Bean and Saubel 1972: 24).

Carbonized walnut shell fragments were recovered from a late preceramic context at the Split Ridge Site (AZ EE:2:103 ASM), which is located in the Rosemont area of the Santa Rita Mountains (L. Huckell 1984: 268). The phreatophytic walnut occurs along washes and drainages throughout the state. A young tree has become established on the Donaldson Site and others grow nearby in the foothills and valley floor, an indication of the ease with which the nuts could have been obtained.

Leguminosae Seeds
(Legumes)

The Donaldson Site yielded three seeds assignable to the legume family: Feature 7 (1), Feature 15 (1), and Feature 20 (1). The specimen from Feature 7 is an ellipsoidal cotyledon with the radicle still attached at a diagonal angle to the long axis. No vestiges of the seed coat or hilum area remain. It is 2.70 mm long, 2.75 mm wide, and 1.30 mm thick. The second seed is oblong, with an elliptical cross section. The smooth seed coat has been badly damaged but parts of it are intact. What appears to be a small, inconspicuous hilum is located in the middle of one long axis. The seed is 1.4 mm long, 1.9 mm wide, and 1.1 mm thick.

The poor condition of the specimens and the extensive legume flora present in southeastern Arizona precluded more specific identifications. Based on the bent embryo structure and the overall oblong shape, all three can be placed in the Papilionoideae or bean subfamily (A. Martin 1946: 630). This is the largest of the three legume subfamilies, and it encompasses many genera, including beans (*Phaseolus*), ironwood (*Olneya*), locoweed (*Astragalus, Oxytropis*), deer vetch (*Lotus*), vetch (*Vicia*), and clover (*Trifolium*). Whether the seeds represent weedy inclusions in the cultural deposits or plants economically significant in prehistory is impossible to determine.

The third seed, from Feature 20, is ovoid in shape and has a compressed elliptical cross section. It is 7.8 mm long, 5.9 mm wide, and 3.2 mm thick. Both cotyledons are still intact, but most of the seed coat has been lost. The few remaining, highly fractured vestiges reveal a thick testa composed of palisade cells that is similar to the testa in mesquite and palo verde (*Cercidium* spp.) seeds. The hilum is missing. Existing features suggest the placement of a straight radicle just off-center along one of the short sides of the seed, a characteristic indicating that the seed belongs to one of the two legume subfamilies, Mimosoideae or Caesalpinioideae. Unfortunately, the destruction of the seed coat has obliterated a major diagnostic feature, the pleurogram, a horseshoe-shaped line that appears on both seed faces of some caesalpinioid genera and a majority of mimosoid genera (Gunn 1981). The size, overall seed shape, and seed coat structure compare best with blue palo verde, which belongs to the Caesalpinioideae and lacks a pleurogram, but this is a very tentative identification.

Legume Pod Base

A fragment of a leguminous pod was recovered from Feature 15 at the Donaldson Site. It consists of the calyx base, a small portion of the attached pedicel, and remnants of the exocarp and mesocarp. The specimen is 1.6 mm long, has a maximum width of 1.1 mm, and is 1.3 mm thick. Among the major representatives of known economically significant wild legumes in the area, the conspicuous, discoidal calyx base compares most closely with Jerusalem thorn (*Parkinsonia aculeata* L.) and blue palo verde (*Cercidium floridum* Benth.). Continuing controversy regarding the indigenous or introduced origin of the few populations of Jerusalem thorn found in southern Arizona, as well as the plant's disputed palatability to animals and humans (Nabhan and others 1979: 177), indicate that these beans were probably not an important resource, if they were available at all.

In the case of the blue palo verde, the ethnographic record documents the plant's use by several aboriginal groups (Russell 1908; Castetter and Underhill 1935; Castetter and Bell 1951; Kelly 1977; Felger and Moser 1985). The trees supplied a variety of edible products, including tender green pods, sweet immature seeds, nectar-rich flowers, and large, fully developed seeds. Of these, the mature seeds were the most significant, for they were often an important source of meal. The parched seeds were either eaten whole or ground into meal for immediate use in mush or for storage. Although not present in the Matty Canyon area, the seeds and pods could be obtained from trees growing along washes and on floodplains at elevations primarily below 1,100 m (3,500 feet; Kearney and Peebles 1960). The blue palo verde is found at some distance from the Donaldson Site on the west side of the Santa Rita Mountains in the Sycamore Canyon area (Lowe 1981).

Identification possibilities for the pod base have not yet been exhausted. Additional areas that merit consideration include the extensive local wild legume flora, and the possibility that it may be a domestic bean. Common beans (*Phaseolus vulgaris* L.) have been recovered from Early Agricultural period contexts in several sites in the Mogollon highlands (R. Ford 1981; Wills 1988a). Beans from Bat Cave and Tularosa Cave recently yielded radiocarbon dates of 2140 ± 110 B.P. (A-4184) and 2470 ± 250 B.P. (A-4179), respectively (Wills 1988a, Table 18). Common beans were probably grown near the Donaldson settlement as well.

Prosopis and cf. *Prosopis*
(Mesquite)

Modest evidence for the use of mesquite came from both sites. The remains from the Donaldson Site consist almost entirely of badly distorted seed fragments, whereas the Los Ojitos material includes 13 complete seeds, more than 100 seed fragments, and three tiny pieces of the pod mesocarp.

The importance of mesquite to Southwestern aboriginal subsistence economies has been described in detail by Bell and Castetter (1937). The primary product sought is the pod, which contains a mesocarp with a high sugar content. The small, protein-rich seeds are also edible. The pods are usually processed by pounding in a mortar, which pulverizes the mesocarp and frees it from the seeds and the bony endocarps that enclose them. Winnowing separates the meal from unwanted constituents, from which the seeds may be extracted and used or simply discarded with the rest. The beans appear in mid summer and sometimes, in lesser quantities, in the fall. Large amounts can be collected and stored, a strategy employed by several societies whose members built large basket granaries on rooftops and platforms to contain the beans (Russell 1908, Fig. 4; Bell and Castetter 1937: 21–30). Large cakes of processed meal were also prepared and stored (L. Huckell 1987).

Mesquite is a phreatophyte found along washes and watercourses that often forms large stands or *bosques* along river floodplains. It is also dispersed through the desert grasslands and on mountain bajada slopes. Mesquite densities have increased during the historic period as a result of fire suppression and livestock activity in the grasslands, and mesquite populations are becoming considerably more abundant (Humphrey 1958; Bahre 1991: 179–180). Based on early descriptions of the river valleys of southern Arizona, mesquite should have been easily procured by residents of the Matty Canyon villages (Humphrey 1958: 9–33).

Malvaceae
(Mallow Family)

Both sites yielded seeds belonging to the mallow family. One of the comma-shaped, sectoroid seeds is still partially encased by the papery carpel. The carpel bears a series of transverse ridges across the dorsal or abaxial surface that are similar to those on cheeseweed (*Malva parviflora* L.), an introduced spring and summer annual that frequents disturbed ground. The largest specimen measures 1.7 mm in length, 1.8 mm in width, and 1.4 mm in thickness and has a triangular cross section. The seed has a heat-induced, inflated appearance, and has longitudinal splits in the seed coat. It is impossible to determine whether the two seeds represent the same species because the surface of the first specimen is effectively concealed. The lack of modern contaminants in the midden and the carbonized state of the seeds means they are probably not cheeseweed.

Possible uses of malvaceous plants are reported in the ethnographic literature, which indicates that in the Southwest and northern Mexico many members of this family have been used as potherbs and especially as medicinal herbs (K. Ford 1975; Ebeling 1986).

Columnar-celled Seed
Coat Fragments

More than 1,000 tiny fragments of a distinctive thick-walled seed coat were recorded, with pieces occurring in every sample analyzed. The angular, irregularly fractured pieces are characterized by a smooth exterior surface and a thick underlying layer of long, vertically oriented, anticlinal palisade cells that provide the seed coat with considerable mechanical strength. Thicknesses range from 0.15 mm to 0.20 mm. The largest fragment is 3.6 mm in length, but most seldom exceed 2.0 mm in length or width.

Similar fragments have been reported from other archaeobotanical assemblages (Huckell and Huckell

1984; L. Huckell 1987), where they also tend to be ubiquitous in feature fills, suggesting that they represent a commonly exploited, important food. Attempts to identify them by means of seed coat topography using scanning electron microscopy (L. Huckell 1987) failed; the few features visible on large-seeded legume species were often shared among genera and were largely destroyed by heat. Research on this problem is ongoing, with members of the legume, squash, soapberry, and other families under consideration.

DISCUSSION

More than 10,000 macrofossils were obtained from the 14 flotation samples taken from Los Ojitos and the Donaldson Site. The extraordinary richness of the samples is exemplified by the Donaldson assemblage, which produced an average of 124 macrofossils per liter. The estimated number is even more impressive, with 279 items per liter.

Several methods may be used for quantitative comparison and interpretation of the results from the Donaldson Site. The low number of samples from Los Ojitos, their recovery from different levels of the same grid square, and the absence of soil volume measurements limit their use in quantitative evaluations. The focus here, therefore, is on the Donaldson Site material. One method that is relatively free of the biases that affect these kinds of data is the presence value, a relative measure in which the importance of a taxon is measured by the number of samples in which it occurs (Hubbard 1980). Expressed as a percentage, higher figures are interpreted as indicating greater usage of that plant. Presence values for the Donaldson Site taxa are given in Table 5.6. Three taxa, maize, cheno-ams, and columnar-celled seed coat fragments, are ubiquitous, occurring in all seven features, and acorn shells and Cyperaceae were recorded in all but one sample. Grass caryopses were present in 78 percent of the samples. Their presence in nearly all features sampled suggests that these plants played a major role in the economy of the settlement.

The remaining taxa occurred in considerably fewer features, the majority of which were pits. The two pit structures probably represent sampling bias and do not constitute a reliable representation of this class of feature. The extramural pits were more susceptible to the introduction of plant parts that were inadvertently carbonized, and plant remains may have been incorporated into pits by trash fill from the midden. Many of the species were weeds but were economically useful,

Table 5.6. Presence Values for Taxa from Features at the Donaldson Site

Plant	Pits N = 7 %	Structures N = 2 %	Total N = 9 %
Zea	100	100	100
Cheno-ams	100	100	100
Columnar-celled seed coat fragments	100	100	100
Cyperaceae	100	50	89
Quercus	86	100	89
Gramineae	86	50	78
Portulaca	57	50	56
Trianthema	57	50	56
Prosopis	43		33
cf. Prosopis	71	50	67
Juncus	43		33
cf. Viguiera	43		33
Leguminosae	43		33
Agave	29		22
Juglans	29		22
cf. Rumex	29		22
Malvaceae	29		22
Carnegiea	14		11
Euphorbiaceae	14		11
Legume pod base	14		11
Mollugo	14		11
Opuntia	14		11
Rhus	14		11
Yucca elata	14		11
Yucca baccata		50	11
Atriplex		50	11

NOTE: Gramineae includes all grasses. Cheno-ams includes all *Chenopodium*, amaranths, and undifferentiated cheno-ams.

and others, like agave thorns, walnut shells, and legume pod bases were waste products that would have been discarded as trash. The evidence supports the observation that features were filled with secondary trash. Ironically, what is needed to help assess the feature contents more accurately is one or more samples from the general cultural deposit at the Donaldson Site, which was the only context sampled at Los Ojitos.

A second method of quantitative comparison is an index of the relative abundance of each plant. It is obtained by dividing the counts for each taxon by the sample volume or total number of liters of soil processed (Gasser 1987). This index can be used as an additional source of evidence for determining possible feature functions. The relative abundance index is expressed as parts per liter (ppl) and Table 5.7 summarizes selected plants by individual feature. Calculations were made using both the actual number of macrofossils

recovered and the estimated totals (Table 5.2). These figures are intended to convey a relative, general idea of the abundance of a given plant.

In preparing similar indices for Hohokam assemblages, Gasser (1987) has discovered that the abundance measure is commonly less than 1.00 ppl. Larger values, particularly those of 5.00 ppl or greater, are significantly different from the norm and may reflect feature function. However, the absence of an established norm for Early Agricultural plant inventories makes it impossible to knowledgeably compare Hohokam and preceramic results. This is even more true for a situation like the Donaldson Site, in which the preservation must be considered exceptional. Values for the selected nine plants range from a low of 0.27 ppl for *Prosopis* to a high of 307.69 ppl for maize. The most impressive values are those for maize, which, with one exception, are all in double or triple digits. A sample from the hearth of the Feature 11 pit structure has a conspicuously low value of 4.05 ppl, but, correspondingly, in three out of four categories, Feature 11 has the lowest ppl figures present and the fourth category figure is second from the lowest. The small volume of the hearth sample and the probably frequent cleanings of the hearth that would eliminate the accumulation of residue may be factors in these low values. The consistent presence of maize in all features may result from the use of cobs for pit and hearth fuel, from the casual disposal of cobs in still-smoldering pits, or from the steady incorporation of discarded cobs into the actively developing midden that ultimately filled the features. The high number of cheno–ams in Feature 17 may reflect a spill of the tiny seeds during parching or their disposal after being accidentally burned.

Efforts to elucidate insights into feature function from the botanical remains are hampered by the small site sample size and the inadequate pit type sample, in which only one type, small pits, is represented by multiple features (Table 3.4). Table 5.8 presents a summary of the ppl index by feature class and for the site as a whole. The data support the contention that most of the investigated features were probably filled with secondary trash as the same space was recycled for other uses through time. Features 7, 15, 19, and 20 contained fire-cracked rock, flaked and ground stone, bone, and charcoal in quantities that point toward trash filling (see Chapter 3). Features 11, 17, and 19 were unburned, suggesting that carbonized material within them had to have been added following their abandonment. The three small cooking pits (Features 4, 8, and 9) that were sampled may have a better chance at maintaining some

Table 5.7. Parts-per-liter Values by Feature for Selected Taxa at the Donaldson Site

Feature: Taxon / Liters:	4 Pit 3.26	7 Pit 3.78	8 Pit 4.26	9 Pit 1.56	15 Pit 8.30	19 Pit 7.38	20 Pit 2.00	11 Structure 2.96	17 Structure 2.92
Zea	180.06	71.16	41.55	307.69	32.65	63.82		4.05	49.66
(Estimated)							(55.00)	(38.51)	
Cheno-ams	10.43	3.70	2.82	3.21	6.02	5.42	4.50	0.68	21.92
(Estimated)	(23.26)	(12.70)	11.03)	(12.82)	(77.12)	(41.73)	(66.50)	(31.76)	(68.49)
Columnar-celled seed coat fragment	31.90	5.56	14.79	2.56	5.66	3.52	248.50	1.69	6.16
(Estimated)	(109.82)		(47.65)		(27.71)		(680.50)		
Cyperaceae	1.84	1.32	0.70	1.23	0.96	1.22	0.50		1.71
(Estimated)		(2.12)	(3.05)	(5.13)	(1.69)	(3.12)			
Quercus	1.53	7.14	11.50	0.64	5.18	11.79		0.68	9.25
(Estimated)			(27.47)						
Gramineae	1.53	2.12	1.41		0.48	0.68	29.00		2.06
(Estimated)	(4.60)	(67.73)	(53.76)		(34.82)	(2.44)	(409.00)		(25.34)
Trianthema	2.15		1.88		0.96	0.81			0.69
(Estimated)	(7.06)		(5.33)			(1.76)			
Agave				0.47	0.60				
Prosopis		0.27			0.40	0.27			
(Estimated)					(2.05)				

Table 5.8. Parts-per-liter Values for Pits and Pit Structures at the Donaldson Site

Taxon	Pits (30.54 L) N	(Est.)	ppl	(Est.)	Pit structures (5.88 L) N	(Est.)	ppl	(Est.)	Total (36.42 L) N	(Est.)	ppl	(Est.)
Zea	2356	(2365)	77.14	(77.44)	157	(259)	26.70	(44.05)	2513	(2624)	69.00	(72.05)
Cheno-ams	160	(1201)	5.24	(39.33)	66	(294)	11.22	(50.00)	226	(1495)	6.21	(41.05)
Columnar-celled seed-coat frag.	763	(2203)	24.98	(73.35)	23		3.91		785	(2226)	21.55	(61.12)
Cyperaceae	34	(73)	1.15	(2.39)	5		0.85		39		1.07	(2.14)
Quercus	212	(280)	6.94	(9.17)	29		4.93		241		6.62	(8.48)
Gramineae	86	(1624)	2.82	(53.18)	6	(74)	1.02	(12.59)	92	(1698)	2.53	(46.62)
Portulaca	8	(64)	0.26	(2.10)	4		0.68		12	(68)	0.33	(1.87)
Trianthema	29	(68)	0.95	(2.23)	2		0.34		31	(70)	0.85	(1.92)
cf. *Rumex*	10		0.33						10		0.28	
Prosopis	7	(20)	0.23	(0.66)					7	(20)	0.19	(0.55)
Agave	7		0.23						7		0.19	
Juncus	3	(228)	0.10	(7.47)					3	(228)	0.08	(6.26)
cf. *Viguiera*	3	(24)	0.10	(0.79)					3	(24)	0.08	(0.66)
Juglans	3		0.10						3		0.08	
Opuntia	3	(27)	0.10	(0.88)					3	(27)	0.08	(0.74)
Leguminosae	3		0.10						3		0.08	
Malvaceae	2		0.07		1		0.17		3		0.08	
Yucca baccata	2		0.07						2		0.06	
Yucca elata	1		0.03						1		0.03	
Rhus	1		0.03						1		0.03	
Carnegiea	1		0.03						1		0.03	
Euphorbia	1		0.03						1		0.03	
Legume pod base	1	(13)	0.03	(0.43)					1	(13)	0.03	(0.36)
Mollugo	1	(32)	0.03	(1.05)					1	(32)	0.03	(0.88)
Atriplex					3		0.51		3		0.08	

NOTE: Parenthetical figure is estimated number in sample.

intact contents; the high maize values may reflect the use of the ideally suited cobs for small-sized pit fuel. However, the associated appearance in those samples of a consistently diverse array of macrofossils, including unequivocal refuse such as seed coat and nut shell fragments, also points toward mixed trash fill.

Despite the likelihood that the features contain secondary trash, their contents still serve to ably demonstrate the character of the subsistence strategy employed by residents of the settlement. The remarkable plant inventory confirms a system of maize agriculture combined with gathering of wild resources, some of which may have been obtained at some distance from the Matty Canyon settlements.

Prehistoric residents in Matty Canyon were optimally situated to take advantage of a number of different plant communities that were easily reached and offered diverse potential food resources. In his study of Archaic sites excavated in the Rosemont area of the Santa Rita Mountains, Bruce Huckell (1984a) examined the availability of food resources for mobile hunter-gatherers who used Rosemont as a base camp. A circle with a diameter of 50 km (31 miles) drawn around Rosemont included six distinctive biotic communities (B. Huckell 1984a, Fig. 2.3), each of which would have offered a different suite of potential plant and animal foods. A similar catchment area can be applied to the Donaldson Site as well, for it is located roughly 24 km (14 miles) southeast of Rosemont. Acorn shells, alligator juniper, and perhaps sumac indicate use of the upland zone, and one Rosemont site, Split Ridge (AZ EE:2:103 ASM), is roughly coeval with the Donaldson Site (B. Huckell 1984a: 80–88, 163–175). The saguaro seeds and possibly the palo verde seeds may reflect foraging trips to lower elevation desertscrub communities.

Our inventory of similar sites with which to compare is still small for southeastern Arizona, and of those, most are represented by a meager flotation record. An exception to this is Milagro, a San Pedro phase site located in the eastern Tucson Basin (Huckell and Huckell 1984; Huckell and others 1994). Like the Matty Canyon sites, Milagro is also situated optimally to exploit abundant water from active streams and springs, with a fertile floodplain ideal for agricultural activities

and a variety of biotic communities offering a diverse array of plant and animal resources. The archaeobotanical record reflects the same eclectic foraging pattern, with upland species (juniper, oak, manzanita, possibly agave), desertscrub species (cacti, grasses, annuals), and riparian/mesic species (mesquite, sage, walnut, Cyperaceae) indicative of collecting activity across a broad geographical area (L. Huckell 1994, Table 4.1). Maize is the only cultivated plant recovered from the site; it also occurs in almost all features investigated to date, reflecting the same extraordinary ubiquity evident at the Matty Canyon sites. Maize agriculture is clearly integral to the local economy. Again, the conclusion to be drawn is that these people enjoyed similar benefits by effectively integrating both foraging and farming. Recently discovered Cienega phase sites along the Santa Cruz River (Mabry and others 1995) will offer additional opportunities to investigate the nature of this adaptation in a different setting, that of the valley floor, with settlements located at greater distances from upland biotic communities.

The modest quantities of flotation samples analyzed from the Matty Canyon sites have provided the most extensive record of subsistence obtained thus far from a site dating to the Early Agricultural period in southern Arizona. In addition to overwhelming evidence for the successful production of maize in impressive quantities, fragments of what may be a second cultigen, squash, have also been recovered. Based on contemporaneous records elsewhere in the Southwest, it is highly likely that squash and beans were grown at the villages; a larger sample from other parts of the sites might provide conclusive evidence.

We have obtained an unprecedented view of the subsistence base of the preceramic occupants of Matty Canyon, which encompassed a range of choices that offered greater variety and higher nutrition levels than many reconstructed prehistoric diets. Although we are almost certainly missing a significant part of the archaeobotanical record because of sampling and preservation biases, it is clear that an effective mixture of crop production and wild food collecting was maintained by these people, who resided in an optimal area in which to successfully blend these economic strategies.

CHAPTER SIX

Faunal Remains from the Donaldson Site

The 1983 investigations at the Donaldson Site produced substantial numbers of animal bones, as did Eddy's excavations in 1957 (Eddy and Cooley 1983, Table 2.2). A sample consisting of all vertebrate remains from four grid squares (N98 E110, N98 E116, N110 E116, and N116 E56) and from the fill and floor of one pit structure (Feature 11) was selected for examination. To learn more about late preceramic patterns of animal use and to increase the sample size, the remainder of the collection was scanned for identifiable elements. This sample, augmented by the identifiable remains from the rest of the site, numbered 575 individual pieces of bone, more than 81 percent of which was unidentifiable scrap. The extensive use of ¼-inch mesh screens during the 1983 investigations promoted the recovery of more fragmentary bone and smaller fauna than had been previously obtained from the site.

From each provenience unit, all bone was segregated into two groups. The first group included elements lacking diagnostic features. It almost exclusively consisted of diaphyseal fragments of limb elements, but also contained rib fragments, pieces of dermal bone, and cancellous tissue. All unidentifiable scrap was sorted into size categories and counted: small (rabbit- or rodent-size animals), medium (dog-size animals), and large (deer-size animals). Because in some cases a fragment could not be easily assigned to one of these three classes, two intermediate classes, small-to-medium and medium-to-large, were added. The number of elements that showed evidence of burning was recorded by size category.

Elements or large parts of elements that retained sufficient features to permit more precise identification formed the second group. Identifications were made with the help of comparative specimens from the National Park Service faunal collection housed at the Arizona State Museum Zooarchaeological Laboratory. Christine R. Szuter, Amadea M. Rea, and Jennifer G. Strand aided in the identification process. Each bone was identified to element and side, portion, completeness of fusion, burning, and whether or not it exhibited weathering.

FAUNAL IDENTIFICATIONS

Table 6.1 lists the animals identified from the Donaldson Site and presents the NISP (number of identified specimens) from both the 1983 and the 1955–1957 investigations. With few exceptions, these two samples are similar, although the 1983 excavations yielded some additional rare taxa.

Artiodactyla

Three genera of artiodactyls were identified: *Odocoileus* (including *O. hemionus*, mule deer), *Ovis canadensis* (bighorn sheep), and *Antilocapra americana* (pronghorn antelope). *Odocoileus* was by far the most common; the other two were represented by fewer than five elements each. In addition, several fragmentary or nondiagnostic elements could be classified only as representing some member of the Artiodactyla. Table 6.2 presents information on the kinds and quantities of elements identified for the artiodactyls. With the exception of teeth, the carpals-tarsals, and some phalanges, all the bones are fragmentary.

Odocoileus

Of the 24 elements assigned to the genus *Odocoileus*, only 5 could be specifically identified as *O. hemionus*, the mule deer. The most common elements that were attributed to this genus were from the lower limbs. Phalanges, metapodials, podials, and distal tibiae and radii make up this part of the assemblage (67% of the 24 total). Also recovered were isolated teeth, mandibular and maxillary fragments, one proximal scapula, and one proximal rib. Conspicuously missing were the large, proximal limb elements such as the humerus or femur.

Eddy's faunal assemblage (Table 6.1) was also dominated by deer, although he recovered both *Odocoileus hemionus* (55 elements) and *O. virginianus*, the white-tailed deer (9 elements). An additional 15 specimens

Table 6.1. Faunal Remains from the Donaldson Site

Scientific name	Common name	1983 (Huckell)	1955– 1957 (Eddy)
Aves			
Gruidae	Cranes	1	
Ardeidae	Herons, bitterns		
Ardea	Heron	1	
Passeriformes	Perching birds	1	
Mimidae	Mockingbirds, thrashers	1	
Thraupidae <u>or</u>	Tanagers		
Fringillidae	Grosbeaks, finches, sparrows, buntings	1	
Testudinata	Turtles, tortoises	2	
Bufonidae	Toads		
Bufo Woodhouseii	Woodhouse's toad	3	
Leporidae	Rabbits, hares		
Lepus sp.	Jackrabbit	27	24
Lepus californicus	Black-tailed jackrabbit	2	1
Lepus alleni	Antelope jackrabbit	1	
Sylvilagus sp.	Cottontail rabbit	18	2
Rodentia	Rodents		1
Cricetinae	New World mice, rats	2	
Sigmodon sp.	Cotton rat	2	
Thomomys cf. *bottae*	Botta's pocket gopher	2	1
Carnivora			
Felidae			
Lynx rufus	Bobcat	4	
Canidae	Dogs, foxes		
Canis sp.	Coyote, wolf, dog	5	
Canis latrans	Coyote		2
Canis familiaris	Domestic dog*		1
Urocyon cinereoargenteus	Gray fox	1	
Artiodactyla	Even-toed ungulates	10	
?*Cervus* sp.	Elk		4
Odocoileus sp.	Deer	19	15
Odocoileus hemionus	Mule deer	5	55
Odocoileus virginianus	White-tailed deer		9
Antilocapridae	Pronghorn		
Antilocapra americana	Pronghorn antelope	1	31
Bovidae	Cattle, sheep		
Ovis canadensis	Bighorn sheep	3	3
Total		108	153

* Articulated skeleton
Sources: Huckell, this volume; Eddy, Eddy and Cooley 1983

were attributable only to the generic level (Eddy 1958, Table 11). Specific element identifications were not provided by Eddy, and it is not possible to compare patterns of element frequencies between the two samples.

Mule deer are commonly encountered along Cienega Creek or Matty Canyon today. Although a few white-tailed deer also inhabit the valley, they are more abundant in the oak woodland of the surrounding mountains.

Ovis canadensis

A vertebra, a metapodial, and a phalanx were identified as the bighorn sheep, *Ovis canadensis*. All three elements came from different parts of the site, so probably more than one individual is represented.

Eddy (1958, Table 11) listed three elements as probably representing bighorn sheep. Bighorns today occur no closer to the Cienega Valley than the Santa Catalina Mountains north of Tucson, a distance of some 70 km (44 miles). However, a few bighorn bones were also recovered from three Hohokam sites in the northern Santa Rita Mountains some 15 km (9 miles) west of the Donaldson Site (Glass 1984). The presence of bighorn sheep at sites not far from one another but separated in time by more than a thousand years suggests the possibility that these animals may have once inhabited the Santa Ritas, Whetstones, or some of the other ranges bordering the Cienega Valley.

Antilocapra americana

Only one element, a metacarpal, was identified as antelope, but Eddy (1958, Table 11) recovered 31 bones assigned to this species. Antelope have long favored the Cienega Valley and its grasslands. Bones of *Tetrameryx*, the extinct four-pronged antelope, came from Pleistocene deposits in Papago Springs Cave in the northern Canelo Hills (Skinner 1942). Antelope remains have been found in Hohokam sites in the northern Santa Rita Mountains (Glass 1984).

Undifferentiated Artiodactyla

The 10 elements identified only to the order Artiodactyla were extremely fragmented or were portions not assignable to a taxonomic level below order. Based on the identified remains above, three families may be included: Cervidae, Bovidae, and Antilocapridae. The elements include fragments of teeth, a podial, proximal scapulae, and three pieces of antler. The antler might normally be attributed to deer, but Eddy (1958) recovered antler fragments questionably assigned to *Cervus* sp., the elk. Recognizing the possibility that elk may have been present in the fauna, the antler fragments are best assigned to the Cervidae.

Leporidae

Both jackrabbits (*Lepus* spp.) and cottontails (*Sylvilagus* sp.) were recognized among the faunal remains. Jackrabbits were roughly 1.5 times as common as cottontails. The elements assigned to these two genera are enumerated in Table 6.2.

Lepus

Bones of jackrabbits were recovered from throughout the midden; 30 elements were assigned to this genus. For the most part, it was not possible to accurately determine the species represented, because both the black-tailed (*L. californicus*) and antelope (*L. alleni*) jackrabbits are present within or near the Cienega Valley today. Perhaps more elements of the two species could be differentiated with a good comparative collection and, in some cases, with measurements (Gillespie 1989). Two elements, a complete radius and a complete calcaneus, were assigned to *L. californicus*, and Jennifer Strand saw a mandible that she believed to be *L. alleni* on the basis of its large size. Both jackrabbits thus appear to be present at the site.

Bones representing nearly all body parts of the jackrabbit were recorded (Table 6.2). Jackrabbits occupy the Cienega Valley today and range throughout the desertscrub, semidesert grassland, and oak woodland biotic communities. Eddy (1958, Table 11) reported 25 elements of jackrabbits and attributed one of those elements to *L. californicus*.

Sylvilagus

The 18 cottontail elements were classified only as *Sylvilagus*. Two species of cottontails, *S. floridanus* (the eastern cottontail) and *S. audobonii* (the desert cottontail), are present in southern Arizona and they are difficult, if not impossible, to separate osteologically. Cottontails occur in and near the Cienega Valley today. *S. floridanus* may be more abundant in the oak woodland biotic community, whereas *S. audobonii* may prefer desertscrub or semidesert grassland (Hoffmeister 1986).

Eddy (1958, Table 11) reported only two cottontail elements from his investigations. The 1983 sample includes portions of the limbs and cranium (Table 6.2) and is derived from all parts of the midden.

Table 6.2. Numbers of Elements (NISP) Identified for Large Mammals and Rabbits at the Donaldson Site
(1983 Sample)

	Odocoileus	Antilocapra	Ovis	Artiodactyla	Lepus	Sylvilagus
Skull	1			3*		
Mandible	1				2	4
Tooth fragment	3			3		
Vertebra			1	1		1
Rib	1					
Scapula	1			2		2
Humerus					3	3
Radius	1				1	1
Ulna	1				1	
Carpal						
Metacarpal	1	1				
Innominate					1	3
Femur					3	3
Tibia	2				6	
Tarsal				1	3	1
Metatarsal	1		1		2	
Phalanx	4			1	6	
Sternum					1	
Sacrum					1	
Metapodial	2					
Total	24	1	3	10	30	18

* Antler

Canidae

Canis sp.

Five elements, three from one feature and two from a grid square some 6 m away, were identified as *Canis* sp. The bones included a first phalanx, a distal metatarsal, a proximal femur, part of an innominate, and a proximal ulna. Because the specimens were so fragmentary, and because previous work by Eddy (1958) had produced both coyote and domestic dog, identifications were not made below the generic level. The bones may represent coyote (*C. latrans*), domestic dog (*C. familiaris*), the gray wolf (*C. lupus*), or all three.

Eddy (1958: 53) reported that the 1955 test excavations had produced a dog burial. In 1983 the late summer floods exposed what appeared to be another dog burial on the right bank of Matty Wash, but it was removed by the October 1983 flood before it could be excavated. The exposed remains were certainly those of a canid, and they were articulated.

Coyotes occupy the Cienega Valley and the surrounding mountains today, and formerly gray wolves roamed this habitat (Gehlbach 1981). Dogs, the only domesticated mammal present in North America prehistorically, are occasionally found in preceramic sites, often in the form of intentional burials. White Dog Cave, the Basketmaker II site in northeastern Arizona, was named for one such burial (Guernsey and Kidder 1921). Dogs do not seem to have been used for food, but their fur was used in weaving by the Basketmakers. The occurrence of at least one dog burial at the Donaldson Site suggests that the Cienega phase dogs may have been accorded similar treatment.

Urocyon

The gray fox, *Urocyon cinereoargenteus*, was represented by a single axis vertebra. This small canid is at home in the desertscrub, semidesert grassland, or oak woodland biotic communities.

Rodentia

Of the five elements assigned to Rodentia, three could be referred to particular genera of rodents and two could not be identified beyond the subfamily level.

Sigmodon

The large cotton rat, *Sigmodon*, was represented by two elements, a left ramus and a right femur. Both bones came from the same grid square and probably represent the same individual. At present, three species of cotton rat live in or near the Cienega Valley (Hoffmeister 1986): *S. arizonae* (Arizona cotton rat), *S. fulviventer* (fulvous cotton rat), and *S. ochrognathus* (yellow-nosed cotton rat). It was not possible to distinguish among these species with the material on hand. Cotton rats prefer heavily grass-covered floodplains bordering active streams, but may range into more xeric desertscrub.

Thomomys

The pocket gopher is one of the most common burrowing rodents encountered along the rivers of southeastern Arizona. The Donaldson Site specimens, a complete ramus and a maxilla, have been identified as *Thomomys* cf. *bottae*, Botta's pocket gopher. However, *Thomomys umbrinus*, the southern pocket gopher, also ranges in this area and is difficult to separate from *T.*

bottae on osteological grounds. Eddy (1958, Table 11) reported one pocket gopher element from the Donaldson Site.

Cricetinae

The Cricetinae subfamily of the Muridae includes New World mice and rats. A complete humerus and a nearly complete left ramus were recovered from the same grid square and most likely are derived from the same animal, a mouse-size rodent. With a larger comparative collection, specific identification would be likely.

The recovery of rodents from the midden is not surprising, but raises the question of whether the remains postdate the occupation or represent food debris. The bones are not burned, and all exhibit only slight weathering. The rodent remains may represent animals that died in their burrows sometime after the settlement was abandoned, although the cotton rat (*Sigmodon*) is certainly large enough to have been considered edible.

Testudinata

From just above and within the fill of Feature 11, the complete pit structure, two turtle carapace fragments were unearthed. They may represent either land tortoise or true turtle, but the relative thinness of the carapace suggests that they are from a small turtle (*Kinosternon*, the mud turtle, or *Terrapene*, the box turtle) or a relatively young desert tortoise (*Gopherus*). With Cienega Creek nearby, more likely they are turtles.

Bufonidae

Toads are seldom found in archaeological sites, and the recovery of three elements of *Bufo woodhouseii* is unusual. Woodhouse's toad is a riparian species living principally along permanent and semipermanent streams in the eastern half of Arizona (Lowe 1964). A pair of scapulae, right and left, recovered in one grid square and a tibiofibula located in a distant feature imply that at least two individuals are represented. Because toads, too, are fossorial, it is possible that they are intrusive.

Aves

Five elements attributable to birds were recovered from the midden (Table 6.1). In 1988 Amadeo Rea identified one as representing a member of the Gruidae (crane family), another derived from the mimid (mock-

Table 6.3. Unidentifiable Bone Fragments by Size Class and Provenience from the Donaldson Site

Grid, Feature	Small		Small-Medium		Medium		Medium-Large		Large		Total	
N98 E110	14	(4)	18		7		11		76	(12)	126	(16)
N98 E116	6	(1)			1				18	(2)	25	(3)
N110 E116	3		4		2	(1)	8	(1)	48	(4)	65	(6)
N116 E56	27	(6)	4		2		5	(1)	87	(11)	125	(18)
Feature 11	17	(4)	2	(1)			74		33	(6)	126	(11)
Total	67	(15)	28	(1)	12	(1)	98	(2)	262	(35)	467	(54)

Quantity in parentheses is the number of burned fragments in the sample.

ingbird, thrasher family), and the other from another passerine bird. In 1995, while reexamining a few bones, Jennifer Strand recognized an element from *Ardea* sp., either a heron or egret, and another from the thraupid (tanager) family or fringillid (grosbeak, finch, sparrow, bunting) family. The presence of the *Ardea* and gruid bones is not surprising because of the localized abundance of open water. Tracks of the Great Blue Heron are common along Cienega Creek and the wet portions of Matty Canyon, and the birds themselves are sometimes seen. The riparian community is also home to numerous small passerine birds of various species.

FRAGMENTED REMAINS

As indicated in Table 6.3, of the 467 pieces of bone scrap recovered, the overwhelming majority (56.1%) came from large mammals. An additional 21 percent of the total was comprised of specimens assigned to the medium-to-large size class. Of these 98 pieces of scrap, 74 came from Feature 11 and 67 of those were from a subfloor pit and may represent the remains of a single animal. If those fragments are discounted, the relative abundance of large animal bone fragments is even greater. For all four grid squares, the large size class predominates, with the small animal size class equaling only 14.3 percent of the total. The small-to-medium size class (6.0%) and medium category (2.6%) contained few fragments. In retrospect, it is possible that use of the ¼-inch mesh screen biased the recovery of small animal bone fragments, for these could have slipped through the mesh.

The quantities of burned bone scrap were small, 11.6 percent of the 467 pieces. Within the individual size categories, burned fragments ranged from a low of 3.6 percent for the small-medium size class to a high of 22.4 percent for the small animal category. That the highest percentage should occur in the small animal cat-

egory is perhaps not surprising, for if the carcasses of these animals were occasionally roasted directly on the coals, their chances for burning would be greater. Of course, the occurrence of the bone in a midden riddled with roasting pit features and extensive areas of dumped fire-cracked rocks increased the probability that fortuitous, postconsumption burning of bones in the trash would be a likely event.

The quantities of bone scrap vary considerably among the four grid squares, although the relative abundance of each of the size classes tends to occur in the same order. Thus, although not completely homogeneous, the bone scrap scattered through the midden seems to be fairly well mixed and similar in the relative proportions of the particular size categories.

The sources of fragmentation are probably many. Small animal bones are commonly highly fragmented in archaeological sites, possibly as a result of processing the carcasses by pounding prior to cooking and consumption or breakage during butchering and disarticulation. Limb elements of large animals may have been intentionally smashed to remove the marrow or as part of the manufacturing process to convert certain elements into tools. Trampling, carnivore gnawing, other forms of incidental damage, and weathering processes must also have caused fragmentation.

ANIMAL PROCUREMENT AND UTILIZATION

The sample of faunal remains from the 1983 excavations differs in some specific aspects from that reported by Eddy (1958) from his investigations, but in terms of overall patterns there is general similarity between the two. Both samples show a predominance of large mammals, especially deer, but also include bighorn sheep and antelope. The 1983 sample contains few elements of bighorn (n = 3) or antelope (n = 1), and only one species of deer (*O. hemionus*) was positively identified. Eddy's sample produced a large number of antelope bones (n = 31), a similarly small number of what are probably bighorn bones (n = 3), but both *O. hemionus* and *O. virginianus*. Eddy also reported four questionable elements of elk, apparently antler fragments. Counting only identified elements, 35.5 percent (39 of 108 elements) of the 1983 sample consists of large mammals compared with 77.0 percent (117 of 153 elements) of the 1958 sample. Some of this difference is probably attributable to recovery technique. The 1983 sample was derived from sediments that were all passed through ¼-inch mesh screens, whereas it is uncertain how much screening occurred during the original work; thus the 1958 sample may be slightly skewed with an emphasis on large mammals. Although a large quantity of bone was recovered from the 1983 investigations, the portion of the sample that can be identified to a family level or lower totals fewer than 110 specimens. However, if Eddy's sample is combined with the one from 1983, a more complete picture of the representation of various large and small mammals is obtained, leading to a fuller understanding of the patterns of hunting.

With respect to those animals most likely to have served as food, in Table 6.1 the NISP (number of identified specimens) values are summarized for *Lepus* (55), *Sylvilagus* (20), *Odocoileus* (103), *Antilocapra* (32), *Ovis* (6), and ?*Cervus* (4). Other animals may have been eaten, but their contribution to the diet was probably less significant. In numerical terms alone, it is evident that the Donaldson Site hunters preferentially targeted large mammals; information from the bone scrap further supports this view. When body size is considered, the importance of large mammals becomes even more apparent. The mean live weight of a white-tailed deer is 45.36 kg, that of a mule deer is 68.04 kg, an antelope 47.63 kg, and a bighorn 71.22 kg (Glass 1984, Table A.13). By comparison, an adult black-tailed jackrabbit has a mean live weight of approximately 2.27 kg, and a cottontail registers approximately 0.95 kg. Although size is certainly not the only consideration for hunters, when available, a white-tailed deer will offer as much protein as 20 jackrabbits. The proportions of the various large and small mammals in the sample would be of interest; how many rabbits were being taken for each large mammal? Unfortunately, the minimum number of individuals represented for each taxon cannot be calculated for the combined sample, because Eddy's (1958) figures are presented simply as NISP. Considering the small size of the 1955–57 and 1983 samples relative to the entire site, MNI may not be particularly meaningful.

Utilization of the large mammal carcasses appears to have been intensive. The identified elements are typically those portions of the lower limbs that have no meat, accompanied by cranial and mandibular fragments. The likelihood is strong that the sizable quantities of unidentifiable large mammal bone scrap represent the marrow-bearing proximal limb elements. If so, the implication is that entire carcasses of deer (and presumably antelope and bighorn) were being brought to the settlement. Those portions of the carcass with little meat or marrow were discarded during butchering, and the large limb elements, once stripped of meat, were fractured to permit extraction of marrow. The crania, too, may have been broken open to obtain the brains, which could have been useful in tanning hides. It is important to remember, however, that domestic dogs were present at the settlement, and their gnawing of bones may also have produced some of the observed fragmentation.

It is not immediately clear to what uses the Donaldson Site inhabitants may have put the various types of birds recognized in the analysis. Large birds may have been consumed. Naturally, feathers from birds of all sizes could have served a number of functional and ritual purposes. Contemporary Basketmaker II populations in northern Arizona and southern Utah used feathers in various ways, including the fletching of atlatl darts, edging fur blankets, creating feather string, making hair ornaments and pendants, and adorning what are inferred to be ceremonial objects (Kidder and Guernsey 1919: 177, Plate 81, Figs. 83, 89*a*; Guernsey and Kidder 1921, Plate 18*a–b*, *d–g*, Plate 34*a–b*, Plate 39*b*; Kidder and Guernsey 1922: 82–85; Lockett and Hargrave 1953: 20; Hargrave 1970). A stuffed bird skin was recovered from White Dog Cave (Guernsey and Kidder 1921, Plate 39*a*).

COMPARISONS TO OTHER LATE PRECERAMIC ASSEMBLAGES

How does this sample compare to other Early Agricultural period faunal assemblages from southeastern Arizona? To date, unfortunately, no other sites of this age have produced good samples of faunal remains. Immediately west of the Donaldson Site in the Rosemont area of the Santa Rita Mountains, a small San Pedro and Cienega phase habitation site (AZ EE:2:103 ASM) yielded scattered bone fragments from what was probably a single deer (B. Huckell 1984a). From limited work at the Pantano Site, a large Cienega phase habitation site a short distance to the north (Fig. 1.2),

Hemmings and others (1968) reported three mule deer bones, four rabbit bones, one rodent bone, four large bird elements, and six small unidentifiable fragments.

Sayles' (1941) work at the San Pedro phase habitation site of Fairbank failed to produce animal bone, and my investigations there similarly lacked faunal remains (B. Huckell 1990); perhaps bone was not preserved in those deposits. Fewer than 20 pieces of bone were unearthed at Milagro, a San Pedro phase habitation site near Tucson (B. Huckell 1990; B. Huckell and others 1994), where two artiodactyl long bone shaft fragments, a *Lepus* tibia fragment, a *Sylvilagus* premaxilla, and several unidentifiable scraps of rodent- or rabbit-size animals recovered from the coarse fraction of flotation samples comprise the assemblage.

La Paloma (Dart 1986), a camp site in the foothills of the Santa Catalina Mountains, contained both preagricultural Archaic and San Pedro phase components. Christine Szuter (1986) reported that faunal remains believed to be associated with the San Pedro component consisted of 41 specimens, principally representing jackrabbit and cottontail; 6 fragments of unidentifiable large mammal bone were recovered also.

Another multicomponent preceramic camp site in the Sulphur Spring Valley that included a San Pedro occupation yielded a large quantity of bone, but it was not possible to separate the San Pedro-associated fauna from the earlier components. Ric Windmiller (1973, Table 2) reported that from feature contexts, small mammal bone fragments (including jackrabbit and cottontail) greatly outnumbered large mammal bone fragments.

Only Ventana Cave, far to the west, has produced a large sample of animal bone from a late preceramic context. Frank Bayham (1982) reanalyzed the assemblages from the preceramic and Hohokam levels of the midden and discovered that there was a strong trend through time toward increasing numbers of large mammals relative to rabbits. The San Pedro levels showed a greater abundance of large mammals than did the preagricultural levels, in which rabbits were the most abundant, but lesser quantities of large mammals than did the Hohokam levels. Bayham emphasized that, in part, this shift from rabbit-dominated to large mammal-dominated assemblages at Ventana Cave reflected a shift in the use of the cave from a base camp to a specialized resource procurement camp.

This information sheds little light on the Donaldson Site assemblage. Indications are that both deer and rabbits were taken by Early Agricultural period hunters, although the relative proportions of the two are not easily ascertained from any of these sites. It is evident, in terms of the abundance of large mammals, that Ventana Cave is more like the Matty Canyon settlements than are other sites, but after about 1000 B.C. Ventana Cave probably served only as a specialized site.

LARGE MAMMAL HUNTING AND EARLY AGRICULTURE

If comparisons to contemporary preceramic sites are less than satisfying, perhaps comparisons of the Donaldson Site to younger Hohokam sites are more informative. Rather than look at individual sites and their assemblages, more general comparisons can be made using data summaries. One by Christine Szuter and Frank Bayham (1989) is particularly useful because it not only summarizes information from numerous preceramic and Hohokam sites, but also provides ways of comparing assemblages. Szuter and Bayham (1989) discuss two indices that can be used to compare faunal assemblages among sites: the artiodactyl index and the lagomorph index. The artiodactyl index is calculated by dividing the NISP of artiodactyls by the combined total of lagomorphs and artiodactyls. For the Donaldson Site, a value of 0.66 is obtained. The lagomorph index is calculated by dividing the NISP of cottontails by the total NISP of all lagomorphs, producing a value of 0.27 for the Donaldson Site. As described previously, excavation techniques may have biased Eddy's sample toward larger animals, so these numbers probably underestimate the abundance of rabbits and other small animals. Two effects of this bias are an inflated artiodactyl index and, because cottontails are smaller than jackrabbits, a lower lagomorph index. Both should be borne in mind.

The 0.66 artiodactyl index fits at the upper end of the range of values (0.19–0.75) reported by Szuter and Bayham (1989, Fig. 8.6) for upland Hohokam sites. This is likely a function of the greater numbers of artiodactyls available in upland environments, and is perhaps even more affected by the availability of not just deer but also antelope and bighorn. However, simple availability is not the complete explanation; socioeconomic decision-making also played a role. There seems to have been a clear decision to pursue artiodactyls across a wide range of habitats. Both mule deer and white-tailed deer were represented in the Donaldson Site assemblages. Each has slightly different habitat preferences; white-tailed deer are more abundant in the oak woodland biotic community, and mule deer live in greater numbers in lower elevation semidesert grassland and desertscrub settings. Both were observed along

Cienega Creek during the course of the 1983 field season, so some overlap in their modern ranges exists. Antelope inhabit the grassland community, and bighorn sheep prefer rugged terrain in the mountains that supports chaparral or oak woodland. At the Donaldson Site, the relative abundance of these four species appears to be a function of distance and accessibility from the settlement. That is, mule deer (NISP = 60) are most abundant, followed by antelope (NISP = 32), white-tailed deer (NISP = 9), and bighorn (NISP = 6).

Analyzing a pair of large preclassic Hohokam sites in the Santa Rita Mountains about 10 to 15 km (6 to 9 miles) west of the Donaldson Site, Margaret Glass (1984) reported that the numbers of white-tailed deer exceeded mule deer. Both sites are either within or slightly below the present oak woodland, which would likely harbor white-tailed deer in greater numbers. This pattern may suggest that although white-tailed deer are smaller than mule deer, the occupants of more sedentary settlements may have taken whichever species was available nearest them. For the Donaldson Site hunters, that was apparently the mule deer; for the Rosemont residents it was the white-tailed deer. With respect to travel and search time, such decision-making seems appropriate. It also carries with it the implication that for the residents of both locales, much of the hunting was done near their villages.

The pattern of reliance on large mammal hunting by these Cienega phase farmer-foragers is consistent with a general trend toward increased reliance on large game by more sedentary populations involved with agriculture. Recent investigations of hunting patterns by prehistoric and recent farming societies (Bayham 1982; Speth and Scott 1989; Szuter and Bayham 1989) have shown that for the ceramic period throughout much of the Southwest, an increasing reliance on agriculture leads to an increasing focus on hunting large mammals. Speth and Scott (1989) have suggested that intensifying a commitment to agriculture, decreasing mobility, and perhaps changes in hunting techniques may be the factors responsible for an increasing reliance on large game. The depletion of animal populations in the areas nearest the villages, and a more stable resource base provided by agriculture, may permit hunters to concentrate their efforts on the procurement of large mammals. Despite the increased costs (search time, travel distance, transport) of this strategy, the payoff is greater in terms of protein, hides, sinew, and bone for tools. The Donaldson Site hunters also had the advantage of easy access to higher densities of large mammals within the Cienega Creek Basin, as well as to multiple species of large mammals in the area. It is not surprising that they took advantage of both the farming and hunting potential of the basin.

Rabbits, both jackrabbits and cottontails, are clearly an important part of the subsistence base, amounting to 45.0 percent of the identified fauna from the 1983 sample. Only 17.7 percent of Eddy's (1958) sample of animal bone was composed of leporids, although, as noted above, recovery techniques might have biased this figure. Rabbits have long been considered a mainstay of later Hohokam subsistence, usually dominating faunal assemblages from sites in the riverine basins of southern Arizona (Szuter and Bayham 1989). Typically, jackrabbit bones outnumber cottontail bones at most sites. For the Donaldson Site, a lagomorph index of 0.27 was calculated. This value suggests that jackrabbits were the more important of the two species, but there are several factors that may influence the interpretation of this number. Jackrabbits are larger and yield more meat, but cottontails are preferred by some groups for their sweeter taste. Often jackrabbits were hunted communally because of their tendency to aggregate, whereas cottontails were usually taken as single individuals by stalk hunting methods. Jackrabbits prefer more open habitats than cottontails and their populations increase in areas where either natural or cultural processes decrease the amount of vegetation. Large settlements, occupied for long spans of time, may thus exhibit larger numbers of jackrabbits than cottontails, although human prey choice and hunting practices (communal drives into nets) may also influence the abundance of jackrabbits. The complex interplay of environmental and cultural factors makes it difficult to interpret the relative abundance of the two species in the archaeological record. As a cautionary tale, it is instructive to note that use of Eddy's sample (25 jackrabbit elements and only 2 of cottontail) would show an almost complete dominance of jackrabbit, potentially leading to inferences of a degraded or open local habitat or perhaps a reliance on communal drive hunting of jackrabbits. The 1983 sample, where jackrabbits (n = 30) do not so strongly outnumber cottontails (n = 18), does not support such inferences.

The late preceramic occupants of the Donaldson Site were active hunters in an environment that offered them the opportunity to focus their procurement strategies on large mammals and, perhaps secondarily, on rabbits. Operating as well from what appears to have been a stable residential base supported at least in part by agriculture, they were able to take maximum advantage of that opportunity.

CHAPTER SEVEN

Bioarchaeology of the Donaldson Site and Los Ojitos

Penny Dufoe Minturn and Lorrie Lincoln-Babb

The human skeletal remains from the Donaldson Site and Los Ojitos represent one of the largest known late preceramic burial populations from southern Arizona or the Southwest. As such, they offer a rare opportunity to examine aspects of skeletal biology. The remains were studied to determine age, sex, stature, and the number of individuals represented in the collection, followed by detailed examinations of the pathologies and dentitions.

The skeletal material from these two sites had been cleaned and preserved shortly after excavation. Minturn used standard techniques for aging and sexing the material (Bass 1987; Bennett 1987; White 1991). Stature was determined using long bone lengths as reported by Genovese (1967). All skeletal material was examined under a strong light, and possible pathologies were studied with the aid of a 10X hand lens. Particular attention was directed toward assessing any pathological condition present in the material.

Information on dental pathologies was recorded by Lorrie Lincoln-Babb from the dentition of these individuals. Observations were made on each tooth present within the intact mandibles and maxillas and with the more fragmentary remains. The teeth of the individuals from Los Ojitos and the Donaldson Site at Matty Canyon were well preserved, but the mandibular and maxillary skeletal material from Los Ojitos was more complete, permitting a more detailed analysis of the dentition of those burials. All analyses were conducted at the Arizona State Museum.

THE DONALDSON SITE
(AZ EE:2:30 ASM)

Burial 1

The skeletal remains from Burial 1 indicate an adult male. The left femur head measures 46 mm in diameter, within the male range (Bass 1987); supraorbital ridges are large; the eye orbit is blunt; and the bone is generally robust. Tooth wear is extreme, indicating an age of more than 40 years (Lovejoy 1985). Muscle attachments are rugose, especially the deltoid tuberosity and the lateral epicondylar crest on the right humerus.

Tooth wear is extreme on the two molars and four premolars present with this individual. The cusps are completely worn off and only dentin is visible.

Additional skeletal material in Burial 1 includes fragments of two immature ribs and one immature vertebral body, probably from an individual aged 2 to 5 years.

Burial 2

Interred in Burial 2 was a small female, more than 35 years of age. The cranium was not recovered; it had been lost to erosion. The right femur head measures 36.8 mm in diameter and the right humeral biepicondylar width is 52.4 mm, both well within the female range (Bass 1987). In addition, the chin is rounded and the bones are extremely gracile. Tooth wear is extreme.

The fragmentary remains of the mandible contain only an extremely worn left third molar in place. Some abscessing is visible in the molar and premolar area of the left side. Loss of the first and second molars of that side appears to be postmortem. Molar loss on the right side appears to be antemortem as resorption of the tooth sockets has taken place.

Burial 3

A more recent, fragmentary Hohokam interment was designated Burial 3. It was not analyzed.

Burial 4

Skeletal remains in Burial 4 represent an adult male. The right femur head measures 46.4 mm in diameter, within the male range (Bass 1987). On the cranium, the

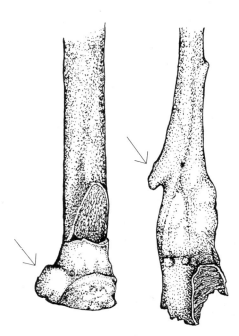

Figure 7.1. Extra bony growth on the right radius (*left*) and clavicle (*right*) from Burial 4 at the Donaldson Site.

mastoid processes are large, the eye orbits are blunt, and the supraorbital ridge is large. The mandible exhibits a square chin, and the gonial angle approximates 90 degrees. The bone is generally robust. Dental wear indicates an age of more than 40 years.

The proximal right radius exhibits moderate osteoarthritis, with extra bony growth and a rough anterior surface (Fig. 7.1, *left*). The right clavicle has a pronounced bony growth at the conoid tubercle, the attachment point for the conoid ligament that attaches to the coracoid process of the scapula and reinforces the joint between the two bones (Fig. 7.1, *right*). The right clavicle is also especially rugose at the attachment site of the deltoideus muscle. Both the left and right humerus have pronounced deltoid tuberosities. The left ulna exhibits a healed fracture just below the midpoint of the bone, but, curiously, the left radius shows no evidence of fracture.

There are no teeth remaining in place in the fragmentary remains of the mandible. The loose teeth of this individual are extremely worn and have noticeably short roots. Evidence of abscessing is present in the second molar region of the left side.

Burial 5

Most of the remains in Burial 5 apparently were removed by the October 1983 flood that exposed both

Burials 5 and 6. A femur head (side uncertain) measures an estimated 46 mm in diameter. The individual probably was a male adult of uncertain age. No dental material is present for this individual.

Burial 6

Burial 6 was also fragmentary. A right femur head measures approximately 42.7 mm in diameter, within the range of a female adult (Bass 1987). The right first metatarsal exhibits a small amount of arthritic lipping on the distal superior edge. There was no dental material.

LOS OJITOS
(AZ EE:2:137 ASM)

Burial 1

The skeletal remains in Burial 1 at Los Ojitos probably represent a female, 25 to 35 years of age. The individual is almost completely present and is excellently preserved. The skull reveals mixed results when examining it for sexual characteristics. The nuchal crest and mastoid processes are robust, and the gonial angle is close to 90 degrees, all of which are male traits. However, the supraorbital ridge and temporal crest are slight, and the forehead is vertical, all female traits. Skeletal measurements are indicative of a female. The left femur head measures 44.2 mm in diameter, and the femur length is 43.5 cm; left tibia length is 38 cm; left humerus epicondylar width is 51.8 mm, the right is 52 mm; the right humeral head measures 41 mm and is 32 cm long; left and right radius lengths are both 25 cm; and the right ulna measures 27.7 cm. The ratio of the lengths of the two main portions of the sternum (the gladiolus is 55 mm and the manubrium is 96.5 mm) is less than 2, indicating a female. Both the left and right humeri have septal apertures at the distal ends, a trait more prevalent in females than in males.

Stature estimate from the length of the long bones is approximately 164 cm or 64 inches (5'4").

This individual exhibits slight osteoarthritis of the second cervical vertebrae and moderate osteoarthritis in the lumbar region. The acromion of the left scapula is pathological in the area of articulation with the lateral clavicle. The lateral left clavicle is also slightly pathological, suggesting perhaps a healed shoulder dislocation. The central frontal bone displays a slight amount of porotic hyperostosis.

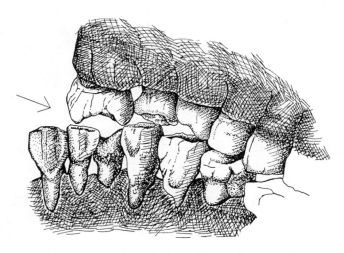

Figure 7.2. Lingual view of wear facet on the central incisors from Burial 1 at Los Ojitos.

All teeth are present for this individual. Dental wear is slight to intermediate, with the exception of the lower right second premolar (root stump), and caries are present on 7 of the 12 molars. There is no evidence of abscessing. A small amount of chipping is observable on the lingual side of the upper right second premolar and the upper right first molar. There is unusual wear on the lower right central incisor. The incisor sharply angles down from the distal to the mesial side, is more worn on the labial side, and protrudes slightly forward toward the labial. The incisal edge of the upper right central incisor is worn so that a small, smooth notch is present on the mesial side of center. When the teeth of the mandible and maxilla are positioned into occlusion, a small hole is observed between the incisal edges of these upper and lower incisors (Fig. 7.2).

Burial 2

The skeleton in Burial 2 represents a female aged 20 to 25 years. The left femur head measures 38 mm in diameter, well within the female range (Bass 1987). The chin is rounded, there is no development of the supra-orbital ridge, the mastoid processes are small, and the eye orbits are sharp. Left radius length is 21.4 cm; the right ulna measures 23.5 cm; the left ulna is 23.4 cm.

The distal anterior surface of the left tibia exhibits a healed greenstick fracture, 50 mm from the distal end of the bone.

All teeth are present with this individual except the lower right canine, which was lost postmortem. Dental wear is minimal and is slightly more pronounced on the

upper anterior dentition of the right side. There is no evidence of caries or abscessing. Chipping is observable on the upper first molar of both the right and left sides and on the upper second molar.

Burials 3, 4, 5

A multiple interment with not three but four individuals was originally assigned Burial numbers 3, 4, and 5. These remains are described below under Feature 4.

Burial 6

The skeletal remains in Burial 6 probably represent a female in her late 20s. The skull of this individual is somewhat robust, but the rest of the skeleton is gracile, the sacrum is flat, and measurements are within the female range. The right humerus head measures 38.8 mm in diameter, the right humerus length is 28.2 cm, and the biepicondylar width measures 55.9 mm. The left humerus head is 38.1 mm in diameter, the left humerus length is 28.3 cm, and the biepicondylar width is 57.4 mm. The right radius length is 22.5 cm, the left radius measures 23.0 cm, the right ulna measures 24.4 cm, and the left ulna is 24.8 cm long. The skull of this individual exhibits slight porotic hyperostosis along the sagittal and lambdoidal sutures. Auditory exostoses were present on both sides, nearly equal in size, approximately 5 mm in length (Figure 7.3).

The iliac crest is fused but not completely obliterated, and the first and second sacral vertebrae and fourth and fifth sacral vertebrae are not fused.

Eight teeth are missing, all of which appear to be postmortem loss except the lower left molar. The teeth of this individual are exceptionally robust in comparison to the other individuals of the Matty Canyon population. Dental wear is generally intermediate but is more pro-

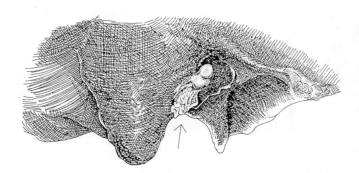

Figure 7.3. Auditory exostosis of the right side of Burial 6 at Los Ojitos.

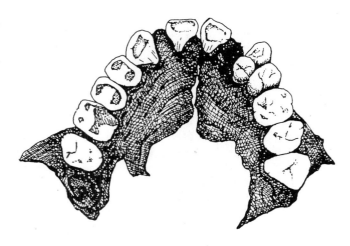

Figure 7.4. Crowding of the maxillary dentition of Burial 6 at Los Ojitos.

nounced on the right side. There the maxilla is asymmetrical; the right side is noticeably longer than the left. Malpositioning of the maxillary teeth on the left side may be due to this anomaly. The upper left canine is positioned in front of the upper left first and second premolars and there is some crowding of the upper left incisor (Fig. 7.4). This individual also had a palatal infection that was particularly severe on the right side. Enamel chipping is present on the upper right premolar. There is evidence of caries for four of the nine molars present. This individual may have had the protostylid trait, as the area affected by caries on three lower molars (between cusps 1 and 3) is where this trait occurs. In its most minimal expression, this trait appears as a buccal pit. This pit creates a location for the deposition of food and hence a susceptibility to caries, particularly if an individual has a sticky carbohydrate diet (Turner 1979). There is evidence of abscessing in the molar region of the left side.

Burial 7

The incomplete skeletal remains in Burial 7 indicate an adolescent aged 13 to 16 years, sex indeterminate. Only bones from the lower half of the skeleton are present; the remainder were carried away by the flood in the summer of 1983 that exposed this burial and Burial 8. Distal ends of the metatarsals are unfused, fibula ends are unfused, and the proximal femur and distal and proximal tibias are unfused. The calcaneus is fused. The diaphysis of the right fibula is 28.5 cm long, the right tibia diaphysis measures 30.1 cm long, and the left tibia diaphysis is 30.3 cm long. No dental material is present for this individual.

Burial 8

Burial 8 is that of a female aged 18 to 20 years. The small mastoid processes and no development of supraorbital ridges are both female traits. The right femur head measures 37.5 mm in diameter and the left femur head is 38.0 mm in diameter; the left humerus head is 33.8 mm in diameter. The crest of the left innominate is only partially fused, and the ischial tuberosity is unfused. The third molar is erupted.

Stature of the living individual, based on the lengths of the right and left femora (41 cm), was approximately 155 cm or 61 inches (5'1").

Healed and active porotic hyperostosis is present all along the sagittal suture, and on the frontal and occipital where they contact the sagittal. Partial sacralization of the fifth lumbar vertebra was noted. This individual exhibited squatting facets on the distal tibias. These small articular facets on the front of the lower tibias are most often attributed to the habit of squatting with the feet flat on the ground and the buttocks resting on the heels (Morse 1969).

Red pigment (ocher) was observed on several areas of the skeleton, including the head of the left humerus, the left metatarsals, the posterior surface of the left scapula, the anterior surface of the left innominate, and the left ulna. It is possible that more of the individual was covered with pigment at the time of original interment and that not all of it was preserved. The use of ocher in burials may have been for artistic or symbolic purposes, but medicinal use of ocher has been noted among the Gugadja of northwestern Australia (Peile 1979) and in the Near East and India in the thirteenth century (Levey and Al-Khaledy 1967). If the iron compounds in ocher promoted healing, as suggested by Wilcox (1911), it is possible that early people throughout the world may have been aware of it. The appearance of ocher in burials may represent an attempt to save the person's life, not just a preparation of the body after death.

All teeth are present for this individual except four that were lost postmortem. Dental wear is minimal. Evidence of caries only occurs at the crown-root junction of the upper left first molar. There is no evidence of abscessing.

Additional skeletal material in Burial 8 included a rib and thoracic neural arch of an infant, probably 2 to 3 years old. Additionally, a left ilium with an unfused iliac crest, first metacarpal, proximal epiphysis of the humerus, and left femur shaft probably represent an adolescent female. Some of the adolescent bone also was stained with red pigment, including the proximal epiphysis of the humerus and the posterior portion of the left ilium.

Burial 9

The female in Burial 9 was 25 to 30 years of age. Female traits are a rounded chin, sharp eye orbit, small mastoids, and a small supraorbital ridge. Only portions of the skull were recovered; the remainder of the burial was lost to the October 1983 flood before excavation was completed.

All teeth were present with this individual except five that apparently were lost postmortem. Dental wear is minimal. The lower left second molar and the upper right first molar exhibit evidence of caries. Abscessing appears in the lower left first molar region and behind the upper right third molar. There is some chipping to the lingual side of the upper right first molar. The maxillary right central incisor and left canine have visible evidence of enamel hypoplasia, with distinct horizontal grooves close to the cervical border (Fig. 7.5). Enamel hypoplasia has been determined to be an indicator of nutritional stress (Goodman and Rose 1991).

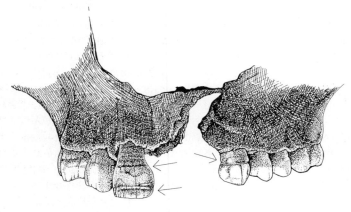

Figure 7.5. Enamel hypoplasia on the right central incisor and left canine of Burial 9 at Los Ojitos.

Feature 4, A Secondary Multiple Burial

Feature 4 is a multiple burial that includes the following remains: one female more than 45 years of age (Cranium and Mandible 1), one male more than 40 years of age (Cranium and Mandible 2), two males aged 30 to 40 years (Cranium and Mandible 3, Cranium and Mandible 4), and postcranial elements from these four individuals. In addition, there is skeletal material from a neonate, making a total of five individuals in this multiple interment.

Cranium and Mandible 1
(Female, 45 + years)

The chin is rounded, mastoid processes are small, and the gonial angle is more than 125 degrees, all female traits. Dental wear and loss is extreme. There is endocranial obliteration of the coronal, sagittal, and lambdoidal sutures; the coronal and sagittal sutures are closed and 50 to 70 percent are obliterated ectocranially.

The skull exhibits slight porotic hyperostosis along the sagittal suture and on the occipital at lambda (there is an inca bone at lambda). There is evidence of slight cribra orbitalia in the left eye orbit (the right orbit is missing). The right mandibular condyle and right temporomandibular joint are pathological, exhibiting porosity and extra bony growth. The left side appears slightly porous but with no extra bony growth; the right mandibular condyle measures 21.5 mm (medial to lateral) by 12 mm (posterior to anterior), the left measures 11.9 mm by 11.2 mm.

A small fragment of the maxilla is present with the left canine and premolars in situ. Dental wear is extreme. The mandible exhibits total socket resorption in the molar region and some resorption in the region of the two canines, indicating antemortem tooth loss. The lower central incisors were lost postmortem. The incisal edges of the two lower lateral incisors have more pronounced wear on the labial side. The roots of these incisors are very short, which may be attributed to genetic factors or root resorption or both. Root resorption is considered an age-related phenomenon (Burns and others 1976).

Cranium and Mandible 2
(Male, 40 + years)

The cranium has large supraorbital ridges, large mastoids, a square chin, and a gonial angle close to 90 degrees, all male traits. Dental wear is extreme. There is endocranial obliteration of the sagittal and lambdoidal sutures, ectocranial closure of the sagittal and partial closure of the lambdoidal sutures.

The maxilla of this individual is fragmented and only five of the anterior teeth remain, all with extreme dental wear. Evidence of caries is present for the upper left first premolar. There is chipping on the buccal side of the right canine. The mandible has five teeth missing, including the premolars and first molar of the left side and the two incisors of the right side. Dental wear is extreme and is more pronounced on the right side. The left third and second molars show less wear. The protostylid trait is not present on these molars.

Cranium and Mandible 3
(Male, 30 to 40 years)

A square chin and gonial angle close to 90 degrees indicate this is probably a male. Dental wear is intermediate to extreme; the sagittal and lambdoidal sutures are endocranially obliterated, and there is ectocranial closure of the coronal, sagittal, and lambdoidal sutures.

The right mandibular condyle and temporomandibular joint exhibit a slight amount of extra bony growth. An area of infection is present on the superior posterior portion of both the parietals.

There is one wormian bone in the right lambdoidal suture.

Only the upper right canine is present in the maxilla of this individual. Postmortem loss in the mandible includes the central incisors, the right lateral incisor, and the left second premolar. Antemortem loss occurred with the left first and second molars and the right second molar, based on socket resorption. There is evidence of abscessing in the molar region. The remaining teeth show intermediate to extreme dental wear. The enamel is chipped on the buccal side of the two right premolars.

Cranium and Mandible 4
(Male, 30 to 40 years)

Male traits on the skull are blunt eye orbits, large supraorbital ridges, and a large nuchal crest. Tooth wear is intermediate to extreme. The sagittal suture is closed ectocranially and obliterated endocranially.

The right and left mandibular condyles and temporomandibular joints are somewhat porous and the left condyle exhibits extra bony growth. The left condyle measures 23.5 mm (medial to lateral) by 15.5 mm (posterior to anterior), and the right measures 18.5 mm by 12.4 mm. The left mandibular ramus is slightly longer than the right, measuring 70 mm as compared to 66 mm. These bony differences between the sides of the mandible are reflected in differential wear of the teeth, with greater wear on the right side.

All maxillary teeth are present and dental wear is extreme on the right side. The incisors exhibit chipping of the enamel, as does the left canine. All teeth of the mandible remain and are extremely worn. The left lateral incisor is malpositioned; it is placed slightly posterior

to the canine of that side. The left third molar has a grade one (buccal pit) protostylid.

Postcranial Bone from Feature 4

It was not possible to separate the postcranial remains of the four individuals represented by the crania and mandibles described above. The following paragraphs briefly list the elements that were recovered from this secondary burial.

Upper limbs: 3 left and 4 right clavicles, 4 left and 2 right scapulae, 4 left and 3 right humeri, 3 left and 3 right radii, 3 left and 4 right ulnae, 5 carpals, 17 metacarpals, 10 manual phalanges.

Lower limbs: 3 left and 3 right femora, 3 left and 3 right tibiae, 3 left and 3 right fibulae, 1 left patella, 15 tarsals, 18 metatarsals, 6 pedal phalanges.

Trunk: hundreds of rib fragments, 14 cervical vertebrae, approximately 70 thoracic fragments, approximately 40 lumbar fragments, 2 sacrum fragments, 3 right innominates, plus many other small vertebral pieces.

Additional skeletal material in Feature 4 clearly did not pertain to the individuals represented by the crania and mandibles. It includes one left ilium (34 mm long), one right tibia diaphysis (72 mm long), one occipital fragment, and one vertebral spine that represent a late fetal or early newborn individual (8 lunar months to 0.5 years).

DISCUSSION OF PATHOLOGIES
(Penny Dufoe Minturn)

Nineteen individuals were in the burial assemblages from the Donaldson Site and Los Ojitos. The Donaldson Site contained two adult females, three adult males, and one child. At Los Ojitos there were six adult females, three adult males, two adolescents, one child, and one neonate. Some of these individuals were represented by only a few elements recovered along with more complete burials.

Bones of three individuals (15.8% of the assemblage) exhibited evidence of trauma. The 40-year-old male in Burial 4 at the Donaldson Site had a healed fracture of the left ulna. He also had a bony spicule on the right clavicle at the location of the conoid tubercle, perhaps indicating an injury to the clavicle and scapula area involving the conoid ligament. A female aged 25 to 35 years (Burial 1 at Los Ojitos) showed bone irregularities on the right clavicle and scapula in the area of articulation between the two bones; these characteristics indicate she may have had a shoulder dislocation. Another female, aged 20 to 25 years (Burial 2 at Los Ojitos), had a healed greenstick fracture of the lower left tibia.

It has been suggested that evidence of trauma is more frequent among hunters and gatherers than agriculturalists (Anderson 1965), with proportions of traumatic cases up to 80 percent (Pfeiffer 1977). There may have been more trauma in the individuals from Matty Canyon that was not detected because of missing bones or poor bone preservation. However, it seems doubtful that the percentage of individuals with trauma would approach 80 percent.

Cases of porotic hyperostosis or cribra orbitalia were recorded on the crania of four individuals, all from Los Ojitos, and all female. The amount of porotic hyperostosis in these individuals is slight, with the exception of Burial 8, a female 18 to 20 years of age in whom the amount was moderate.

Porotic hyperostosis results in a cortical bone thinning and a corresponding diploe hyperplasia that is evident on the external surfaces of the bone as small, porous openings. In mild cases, such as those observed in the Matty Canyon individuals, the only affected bone is the cranium.

The most common condition associated with porotic hyperostosis in human populations is iron deficiency anemia (El-Najjar and others 1976). In the American Southwest, this condition has been associated with maize-dependent groups. Maize is not in itself low in iron, but the phylates present in any maize inhibit the absorption of whatever iron is present (Ashworth and others 1973, cited in El-Najjar and others 1976). Subgroups most likely to develop iron deficiency anemia are young children, women of child-bearing age, and individuals with chronic bleeding (as might occur with intestinal parasite infection).

In the Matty Canyon group, only adult females were affected. At Los Ojitos, two females were free of the lesions, Burials 2 and 9. However, Burial 9 did exhibit enamel hypoplasia, another developmental defect attributed to insufficient diet (Goodman and Rose 1991). None of the five male crania showed porotic hyperostosis. There was no cranial material present for the children in this collection, and no observations could be made for this condition. Probably this group was experiencing at least a small amount of iron-deficiency anemia that manifested itself in porotic hyperostosis in the women of child-bearing age at these settlements.

At Los Ojitos, a female in her late 20s showed bilateral auditory exostoses (Burial 6). This bony growth in the ear canal has been linked to causes such as exploitation of marine and freshwater resources that require diving (Kennedy 1986), a long history of aural infection and drainage (DiBartolomeo 1979), and gout (Toynbee 1849 in DiBartolomeo 1979).

Hrdlička (1935, cited in Kennedy 1986) concluded that there is a hereditary predisposition to the development of ear exostoses, but that there must be an "exciting factor" for it to manifest itself. This factor can be anything mechanical or chemical that produces an irritation to the bony meatus. Burial 6 also exhibits dental crowding, an asymmetric maxillary arcade, and differential tooth wear. It is likely that the masticatory stress put on the temporomandibular joint because of the asymmetry of the maxilla would have been the "exciting factor" in this individual.

In conclusion, the collection of burials from Matty Canyon exhibits a range of age, sex, and pathologies normal for a prehistoric population. The low incidence of trauma and slight to moderate amount of porotic hyperostosis suggest a group at least partially dependent on agriculture for their diet.

DENTAL ANALYSES
(Lorrie Lincoln-Babb)

The assessment of certain pathologies of the teeth of a burial population provides useful information about the diet and general health of those people (Goodman and Rose 1991; Hawkey 1995; Schmucker 1985; Turner 1979; Turner and Cadien 1969). Measurements of the angle of wear on teeth and the type of wear also may indicate subsistence products and practices (Hinton 1981; Smith 1984). For the individuals of Matty Canyon, frequencies for caries, enamel hypoplasias, enamel chipping, and abscessing were recorded, and limited, but meaningful, observations were made on tooth wear.

Caries

Caries is a multifactorial disease and is defined here as a necrotic pit in the enamel or dentine. Consumption of sticky, processed carbohydrate foods significantly contributes to the development of caries, and a high frequency of caries in an individual may indicate a diet with more carbohydrate intake than protein. There were a number of carbohydrate-rich foods in the prehistoric Southwest, including maize, agave, yucca, mesquite, and acorns. Age of the individual and host resistance factors such as the nonimmunologic characteristics of the saliva may contribute as well to a high frequency of caries for an individual (Mandel 1976).

The teeth of the individuals from the Donaldson Site and Los Ojitos were observed for caries. The occurrence of this pathology at the Donaldson Site was rare, but there were more missing (antemortem and postmortem) teeth among these individuals than among those at Los Ojitos. Five primary inhumations (all females) from Los Ojitos were closely inspected for caries because their dentitions were intact and were less affected by extreme wear than were dentitions in the other burials, and almost all tooth loss was postmortem. There are 14 carious teeth among the 142 observed, a frequency of 9.9 percent. Turner (1979) wrote that the ranges of frequencies of carious teeth for three different economies may be proposed as: hunting and gathering groups, none to 5.30 percent; mixed economy groups, 0.44 to 10.30 percent; and agricultural groups, 2.30 to 26.90 percent.

The number of carious teeth (7) for Burial 1 is abnormally high in comparison to other individuals from Los Ojitos. Low host resistance, age, and differential intake of carbohydrates are factors that contribute to this pathology. The unusual wear pattern (task-related) observed for this individual may also be associated with the substantial amount of caries.

The high frequency of caries for this one individual may be out of the normal range for the group as a whole, and the population of Matty Canyon probably should be placed at the high end of the mixed economy range rather than within the agricultural range.

Enamel Hypoplasia

Only one individual of the Matty Canyon skeletal series, Burial 9 at Los Ojitos, exhibits clear evidence of enamel hypoplasia. Two teeth, the upper left canine and the upper right central incisor, have surficial hypoplastic grooves. According to their proximate distances from the cemento-enamel junction, these defects probably occurred between the ages of 3 and 6½ years. This developmental defect has been related to faulty nutrition, weaning stress, and to the health status of the individual (Brothwell 1963; Goodman and Rose 1991). Although this defect is not confined to any particular subsistence strategy, an increase in developmental enamel defects has been noted for prehistoric groups in transition from a mixed economy to a more agricultural one (Sciulli 1978; Goodman and others 1980).

Tooth Wear

An analysis of tooth wear was conducted by Bruce and Lisa Huckell (1988) on four of the Los Ojitos bur-

Table 7.1. Attributes of Dental Wear on Lower Right First Molars for Burials at Los Ojitos

Burial No.	Wear Stage	Angle in Degrees
1	4	7
2	5	10
8	4	7
9	5	9

Source: Huckell and Huckell 1988.

ials using the wear plane angle method developed by B. Holly Smith (1984). By measuring the wear angle on the molar teeth, Smith demonstrated that inferences may be drawn regarding the subsistence economy or type of food processing being practiced by a prehistoric group. She examined a series of skeletal populations from several areas of the world whose subsistence economy was known. Her results indicated that hunter-gatherer groups tend to have a relatively flat wear plane because their diet demands the mastication of tough, fibrous foods. An oblique wear plane of the molars results from mastication of more mechanically refined foods, suggesting an agricultural economy. Smith used bivariate regression (least squares) lines to model wear stage and wear angle of each population and to show the progression of increasing obliquity of wear with increasing stage of wear. This analysis showed a clear separation of hunter-gatherers and agriculturalists.

For the Los Ojitos burials, stage of wear was determined for each molar in the analysis according to diagrams provided by B. Holly Smith. Statistical analysis was used to assess the relationship of the wear plane to stage of wear. Burials 1, 2, 8, and 9 were chosen for this analysis based on their intact dentitions and relatively even amount of attrition to both sides of the mandibular and maxillary teeth. Observations were made on the lower right first molar (Table 7.1). The results from this analysis place the individuals of Los Ojitos within Smith's determined range for agriculturalists. The regression line calculated for the four burials (Fig. 7.6) is within the range of the agriculturalists studied by Holly Smith (1984, Fig. 5) and is distinct from that for the hunter-gatherers she examined.

Wear of the molars of other individuals not included in this analysis exhibited varying degrees of oblique wear plane, in addition to generally more extreme wear of the posterior dentition. This observation supports the notion that these two populations from Matty Canyon demonstrate a reliance on mechanically processed foods or a greater reliance on agricultural products than hunter-gatherers or both.

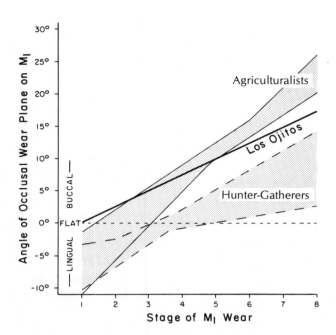

Figure 7.6. Least squares line of molar wear on the Los Ojitos burials (n = 4), plotted on Figure 5 by Holly Smith (1984, from Huckell and Huckell 1988).

The Arizona State University Dental Anthropology System scale of wear is a five-stage (0–4) system, and it was also used for a general analysis of wear. The majority of the teeth of the Matty Canyon burials had wear between Grade 1 (dentin exposed on one or more cusps) and Grade 2 (cusps worn off). There were some teeth worn to Grade 3 (exposed pulp) of those individuals noted with extreme wear, and only a few teeth at Grade 4 (root stump functional).

The unusual wear on the upper and lower right central incisors of Burial 1 from Los Ojitos (Fig. 7.2, probably a female aged 25 to 35 years) deserves further discussion. Use of the teeth as tools has been demonstrated in studies of various populations (Turner and Cadien 1969; Molnar 1972; Merbs 1983). Dental wear resulting from certain extramasticatory activities involving the teeth has been observed in living and prehistoric groups (Schulz 1977; Hinton 1981; Larsen 1985; Milner and Larsen 1991). It has been suggested that the wear pattern described for Burial 1 results from using the teeth as a clamping device for activities such as holding a net with the teeth while fishing, holding the mouth-piece of a bow-drill between the anterior teeth, or the processing of fibrous materials (Merbs 1983; Lukacs and Pastor 1988; Milner and Larsen 1991). The type of notching observed on the central incisor of

Burial 1 has been recorded for several individuals from two southeastern United States skeletal series (Larsen and Thomas 1982; Blakely and Beck 1984). Interestingly, all the individuals from these two populations noted for this wear were females.

Enamel Chipping

Approximately 13 tooth crowns, from 7 individuals, show enamel chipping. This represents a considerable amount of chipping in a dental analysis of only 12 individuals. The majority of the chipping is in the premolar and first molar regions. These locations suggest the teeth were used for breaking small animal bones, nut hull fragments, or seeds; in food preparation techniques; or for gripping and holding (Hartnady and Rose 1991; Turner and Cadien 1969). These different ways in which chipping could occur are not necessarily mutually exclusive. Enamel chipping has been suggested as more prevalent in meat-eating populations than in groups with an intensive agricultural subsistence.

Abscesses

The areas of the alveolar bone in which abscessing was observed were primarily in the molar and premolar regions. Those individuals with intermediate to extreme wear were more susceptible to this pathology because of pulp chamber exposure from attrition (Clarke and Hirsch 1991). Evidence of abscessing was recorded for 7 of the 12 dentitions examined, rendering a frequency of 58 percent.

Additional Observations

No teeth exhibit any cultural treatment such as filing or inlay. The majority of the individuals from both sites have ellipsoid dental arches. There does not appear to be any congenital absence of the third molars. In the observable cases, the third molars of the mandible and maxilla frequently did not come into occlusal contact.

The deposition of calculus, which may suggest high carbohydrate intake, was observed on some dentitions. A quantified analysis was not performed, because the deposition did not appear to be related to carbohydrate intake. Substantial calculus was observed on the teeth of Burial 8 at Los Ojitos, yet this individual had caries on only one tooth. Burial 1 at that site had seven caries but no calculus deposition. Other factors may contribute to calculus deposition, such as the amount of calcium carbonate in the local water source.

In general, the dental health of the individuals from the Donaldson Site and Los Ojitos appears to have been good. None of the frequencies for pathologies, although greatly influenced by small sample size, indicate otherwise.

In a comparative analysis of the dental pathologies of the agricultural Hohokam of southern and central Arizona, Hawkey (1995) observed differences between the two groups in the frequencies of abscessing, enamel chipping, calculus deposition, and enamel hypoplasia. Although the caries frequencies for both groups were similar (southern, 10.5%; central, 14.3%), Hawkey noted that the southern Hohokam had pathology frequencies that were more consistent with a hunter-gatherer model than with an agricultural model. The southern Hohokam had higher frequencies for abscessing and enamel chipping, whereas the central population had higher frequencies of calculus deposition and enamel hypoplasia. Based on her results, Hawkey suggested that possibly different subsistence strategies were used by the two groups, with the southern Hohokam consuming more gathered foods and perhaps meat than the more agriculturally dependent central Hohokam.

The frequencies for the pathologies of the Matty Canyon individuals also reflect more of a hunter-gatherer pattern than the central Hohokam. This does not diminish the fact that cultigens were being consumed at Matty Canyon, but other foods from their environment contributed substantially to their diet as well. Considering these observations, the Huckells' (1988) wear analysis, and the results of the skeletal analysis, a mixed economy of hunting and gathering with some agriculture is suggested for the Matty Canyon populations.

Dental Morphology

Five of the interments at Los Ojitos (Burials 1, 2, 6, 8, and 9) were selected for an analysis of their dental morphology (Table 7.2).

Morphologic crown traits appear as accessory ridges, tubercles, styles, and cusps expressed on the lingual, buccal, and occlusal surfaces of the teeth. These traits operate under polygenic modes of inheritance and may be absent or present. If present, the expression may range from slight to pronounced. Phenotypic differences of these traits between groups reflect temporal gene frequency changes or underlying genetic differences. These differences may be observed at the microevolutionary level, differentiating local races and tribal pop-

Table 7.2. Grades of Expression of Dental Morphological Traits for Burials at Los Ojitos

Traits and location	Burial Number				
	1	2	6	8	9
Maxillary dentition	*Grade of Expression*				
Shoveling I1	6	4	2	2	1
Shoveling I2	2	5		1	0
Double Shoveling I1	1	3	1	1	1
Tuberculum Dentale I1	4	2	0	1	0
Tuberculum Dentale I2	2	5		1	0
Uto-Aztecan Premolar P1	0	0	0	0	0
Hypocone M1	4		4	5	5
Hypocone M2	4	2		5	3.5
Hypocone M3	0	3	0	3	0
Cusp 5 M1	0		0	0	0
Cusp 5 M2	0	3		0	0
Cusp 5 M3	0	0	0	0	0
Carabelli's trait M1	0	0	0	0	0
Carabelli's trait M2	0	0	0	0	0
Carabelli's trait M3	0	0	0	0	0
Enamel extension M1	1	0	1	0	2
Enamel extension M2	1	1	1	0	0
Enamel extension M3	1	1	0	0	2
Mandibular dentition					
Groove pattern M1		X	X	Y	
Groove pattern M2	X	X	X	X	X
Groove pattern M3	X	X	Y	X	X
Protostylid M1	0	0		1	0
Protostylid M2	0	0		0	1
Protostylid M3	0	0	1	0	1
Cusp 5 M1	0			4	4
Cusp 5 M2	4		0	2	
Cusp 5 M3	5		1	3	5
Cusp 6 M1	0			0	0
Cusp 6 M2		0	0	0	0
Cusp 6 M3	2	0	2	0	0
Cusp 7 M1	0	0		0	0
Cusp 7 M2	0	0	0	0	0
Cusp 7 M3	0	0	0	0	0
Enamel extension M1	1	2	1	0	0
Enamel extension M2	1	2	2	0	2
Enamel extension M3	1	1	2	0	2

NOTE: Blank cells indicate information is not available.

ulations. The observation of discrete dental morphological traits has been used successfully in microevolutionary studies to identify various prehistoric and living groups of Native Americans (Nichol 1990; Turner 1969; Scott and Dahlberg 1982).

The observational standards that were used for examining the Los Ojitos individuals are those defined in the Arizona State University Dental Anthropology System (Turner, Nichol, and Scott 1991). Ideal sample size for statistically significant comparisons should be 100 individuals. This group of 5 persons representing the Cienega phase of southeastern Arizona is too small to compare to other populations at this time or to propose any measure of relatedness. The analysis was made, however, to make the information available for combining with similar populations as more Early Agricultural period sites are excavated.

The following brief general descriptions of the examined traits and the Grades of Expression in Table 7.2 may be of interest to students of prehistoric dental anthropology.

The expression of Shoveling on the incisors was trace to intermediate with the exception of Burial 1. The Uto-Aztecan Premolar was absent for all individuals as well as any expression of Carabelli's Trait. Expression of the Hypocone was intermediate. Of the 13 molars examined, Expression of Cusp 5 of the maxillary molars was observed on only one second molar. Enamel extensions were commonly observed on both the maxillary and mandibular molars for all individuals with the exception of Burial 8. The Groove Pattern for almost all the mandibular molars was X. Three of the individuals demonstrated Grade One Expression (buccal pit) of the Protostylid. Cusp 5 of the mandibular molars was commonly observed. Cusp 6 was minimally expressed on 2 of the 12 molars examined. Cusp 7 was absent for all individuals.

CHAPTER EIGHT

Early Agricultural Period Subsistence and Settlement in Matty Canyon and Beyond

The 1983 investigations at the Donaldson Site and Los Ojitos, conducted 25 years after Frank Eddy's pioneering work in the Matty Canyon area, have fundamentally changed our understanding of the settlement and subsistence strategies of societies in southeastern Arizona during the mid to late first millennium before Christ. Not only does this new knowledge permit a fine-grained look at one part of the Cienega Creek Basin, but it also informs us in broader ways about the processes by which Early Agricultural period socioeconomic systems developed across the Southwest. Of particular importance is the evidence of how agriculture became integrally woven into the fabric of these societies. By at least 500 B.C., the basic elements of the mixed farming-foraging economy that typified the next 2000 years of Southwestern prehistory were clearly present.

The archaeological systematics of the Early Agricultural period provide a framework for structuring this new knowledge of the Matty Canyon sites and for broadening its perspective throughout southeastern Arizona and the rest of the Southwest. By considering the subsistence ecology and mobility organization of the Early Agricultural period inhabitants in the Cienega Valley, we expand our understanding of late preceramic cultural ecology throughout southeastern Arizona and the Southwest.

EARLY AGRICULTURAL PERIOD SYSTEMATICS

Although culture history is no longer the sole goal of archaeological research, it remains true that cultural taxonomies still serve a useful function as frames of reference and aids to communication and thought. By grouping and differentiating cultural entities on a variety of scales (time, space, ecology), taxonomic schemes represent our conceptions of the past and provide organizational frameworks for discussion and research.

Particularly for a science like archaeology, which focuses on the past, taxonomies are subject to vagaries of historical accidents of discovery and investigation as we sample the archaeological record. Investigation of new sites, the application of new investigative techniques, and the accumulation of knowledge require changes in taxonomies, particularly when the phenomena being investigated have been little studied, cover a long time span, and may be comparatively uncommon in the archaeological record. These conditions apply to the Archaic period in the Southwest, but as our knowledge has grown, the existing cultural taxonomies have not kept pace.

In Chapter 1, I suggested that continued use of the term "Archaic" for the late preceramic period of southeastern Arizona was inaccurate in an ecological sense and had the potential to create confusion and foster miscommunication at the regional level. "Early Agricultural period" is a label that encompasses the shifts in subsistence and settlement that followed the arrival of agriculture across most of the Southwest, and it subsumes both the late preceramic Basketmaker II of the Colorado Plateau and the late preceramic cultures south of the Mogollon Rim. In southeastern Arizona, two temporally distinct phases of the period are identified: San Pedro and Cienega. The term "Archaic" is redefined as the preagricultural, broad-spectrum foraging adaptation that preceded the Early Agricultural period throughout the Southwest. Figure 8.1 presents a simple chart of the Early Agricultural period and its components. This proposed revision to preceramic systematics is not intended to be a major focus of this monograph, but it is necessary to briefly consider some of the issues involved with it.

Taxonomically separating that portion of the preceramic period after 1500–1000 B.C. from the preceding part achieves a more realistic recognition of the apparently marked changes in subsistence and settlement that occurred following the arrival of agriculture. Through-

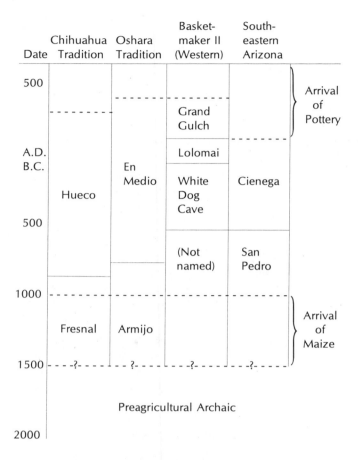

Figure 8.1. Phases of the Early Agricultural period in the southwestern United States. (Information from Irwin-Williams 1973; Matson 1991; MacNeish 1993.)

out most of the Southwest, one can recognize changes in settlement type, composition, size, and location once agriculture has been incorporated into the subsistence strategy. Thus, both the Archaic and Early Agricultural periods are defined primarily on the basis of ecology and secondarily on time rather than solely on time. Use of the term Early Agricultural period carries no assumptions regarding the degree of dependence on agriculture, which varies across the Southwest with particular environmental conditions, population densities, access to arable land, and other cultural and natural factors.

A second benefit of using Early Agricultural period is that it can serve as a broad geographic umbrella for designating the later part of the preceramic period in the Southwest. It functions at the same level as the Southwestern Archaic, recognizing the presence of broad regional patterns of similarity but permitting retention and development of subregional cultural entities and se-

quences. By embracing Basketmaker II as well as what was formerly San Pedro Cochise, En Medio Oshara, and a portion of the Fresnal and Hueco phases of the Chihuahua tradition, it may help to dispel the confusion that results from using "Late Archaic" on the Colorado Plateau to designate the final part of the preagricultural preceramic period and using "Late Archaic" in the southern portion of the Southwest to designate the earliest mixed farming and foraging societies. These disparate meanings call for a reorganization of preagricultural Archaic taxonomy for the southern Southwest, but beyond the changes offered here, that is a task for future consideration.

Some sites fit chronologically into the Early Agricultural period but lack evidence of agriculture. Coffee Camp, located a short distance northwest of the Cienega Basin, dates between approximately 300 B.C. and A.D. 100 (Halbirt and Henderson 1993). Despite intensive flotation and pollen sampling, no evidence of agriculture was detected there. Where does it fit in the Early Agricultural period? In my opinion, Coffee Camp may have been a seasonally occupied gathering location used by a group that practiced agriculture elsewhere, or it may represent occupation by a group that did not adopt agriculture. In either case, the absence of evidence of cultigens at this site is probably not unique, and other such sites likely will be found. Within the proposed schema, two strategies may be used to deal with such sites. First, they may be assigned to the Early Agricultural period on the presumption that they represent seasonally or functionally discrete occupations by groups who farmed elsewhere but at which no cultigens were consumed. As shown in Figure 8.1, the boundary between the preagricultural Archaic period and the Early Agricultural period is time transgressive; in various parts of the Southwest effective agricultural practices developed much later than in others. Secondly, then, Coffee Camp, located at the northeastern edge of the arid Papagueria, may represent the persistence of a purely foraging adaptation in an area that did not meet the optimal conditions for farming that existed in southeastern Arizona. "Late Archaic" may be an appropriate classification for these sites. To clarify such situations, it will be critical to look for the presence of cultigens at these sites, and it will also be important to develop an understanding of the subsistence-settlement patterns at a regional scale.

The Early Agricultural period in southeastern Arizona is divided into two phases. The San Pedro phase is estimated to date between 1500–1000 B.C. and 500 B.C., followed by the Cienega phase that extends from

500 B.C. to perhaps A.D. 100–200. Flaked stone projectile points, architecture, aspects of the ground stone assemblage, and possibly the forms and materials of shell jewelry provide a basis for their separation.

San Pedro Phase

The San Pedro phase, as first recognized by Sayles at the Fairbank and Charleston sites and as augmented by more recent research at Milagro, Fairbank, and the West End sites (B. Huckell 1990), is typified by the shallow side-notched or corner-notched San Pedro point. The notches tend to be broad and rounded, directed more or less perpendicularly to the long axis of the point. Often these points are made on coarse-grained raw materials. The small sample of domestic architecture so far recorded consists of structures with oval to egg-shaped, basin floor plans, excavated to a shallow depth below ground surface (Sayles 1945; B. Huckell 1990). Maximum dimensions range from 2.5 m to 3.0 m long by 1.5 m to 2.5 m wide. Prominent intramural features are a single, often large, bell-shaped pit and a hearth. The bell-shaped pit is positioned at the presumed back wall of the structure; the hearth is nearer the center a short distance inside what is probably the entryway. Postholes have not been consistently recognized and do not seem to form patterns. Ground stone artifacts are dominated by utilitarian seed milling equipment (manos, metates, pestles, mortars) and a few other forms with less obvious functions (cruciforms and small discs). Shell jewelry is limited to simple *Olivella* beads and square to rectangular *Pinctada* or *Pteria* beads, based on current information. Fired clay anthropomorphic figurines are present and probably continue in the succeeding Cienega phase.

Cienega Phase

The Cienega phase is defined on the basis of investigations at the Donaldson Site and Los Ojitos. This definition will be significantly augmented by reports on the Santa Cruz Bend and Stone Pipe sites recently excavated along Interstate 10 in the Tucson area (Mabry and others 1995). The two excavated domestic structures at the Donaldson Site are round in plan with nearly vertical pit walls and level floors. One exhibited a ring of wall postholes around the perimeter of the floor at the base of the pit walls and one contained a hearth. At the Santa Cruz Bend Site, Mabry and his colleagues (1995)

discovered hundreds of such structures, varying in diameter from slightly over 2 m to as much as 9 m; most are less than 5 m. Some contain numerous intramural cylindrical pits and a few bell-shaped pits. Rings of postholes encircling the floor are present in some structures and, rarely, shallow grooves connect the postholes. Other structures lack obvious posthole patterns. At the Matty Canyon sites, a distinctive corner-notched projectile point style appears, with relatively long, narrow notches driven at a diagonal angle to the long axis of the point. Fine-grained siliceous raw materials were favored for its manufacture. The Cienega point, as it has been named, may or may not completely replace the San Pedro point; some younger sites in southeastern Arizona contain both San Pedro and Cienega points, as well as points that seem to be stylistically intermediate between the two. The abundance of Cienega points at the Donaldson Site indicates that by 500–200 B.C. this style may heavily predominate lithic assemblages at certain settlements. With the advent of the Cienega phase, the ground stone industry becomes greatly elaborated. In particular, well-made perforated stone rings, discoidals, trays and other forms of stone vessels, cruciforms, and pendants become prominent parts of the assemblage. Some of these items may not have been local products. Shell jewelry undergoes an elaboration as well, with new species being used to produce beads, pendants, and perhaps bracelets.

Our understanding of the San Pedro and Cienega phases, and the Early Agricultural period as a whole, is still in its infancy. Continued fieldwork and analysis undoubtedly will require some changes in the composition and dating of this period and its component phases.

SUBSISTENCE ECOLOGY IN THE CIENEGA VALLEY

There is currently much debate concerning the relative dietary importance of agriculture for preceramic societies in the Southwest and a growing awareness that it varied significantly across the region as a whole. Mixed farming-foraging subsistence systems appeared in southeastern Arizona by 1500–1000 B.C. Maize farming was a critical component of that subsistence strategy in the San Pedro phase (B. Huckell 1990), but extensive use of hunted and gathered wild resources from the surrounding biotic communities continued to be indispensable. Let us examine the evidence from the two Matty Canyon sites to evaluate the contributions of farming and foraging to the overall diet in the Cienega phase.

The Role of Agriculture

To what degree did the late preceramic inhabitants of the Cienega Valley rely on agriculture? Specifying a percentage of the diet that was filled by agricultural products is impossible with current information, but the question may be evaluated in a qualitative way using macrobotanical and bioarchaeological evidence. The obvious starting place is the macrofossil record.

Macrobotanical Evidence

As documented in Chapter 5, all 11 Donaldson Site flotation samples yielded carbonized maize cob fragments and all but one produced kernels. Moreover, samples with volumes of less than 4 liters routinely yielded hundreds of cupules (Table 5.2). The screen washing of the saturated cultural deposit at Los Ojitos produced nearly 100 cob fragments picked from the ¼ –inch and $\frac{1}{16}$–inch mesh screens. In addition, analysis of three samples of "concentrate" from the $\frac{1}{16}$–inch mesh screens also revealed thousands of maize cupules, kernels, and glumes from one excavation unit in the Los Ojitos midden (Table 5.4). Such figures of maize abundance are truly impressive for preceramic sites and greatly exceed those commonly reported from Hohokam sites more than a millennium younger.

Gasser (1982) has reported that ubiquity values (the percentage of samples containing a particular taxon) for maize at Gila-Salt Basin Hohokam sites range from a low of 8 percent to a high of 69 percent. Other researchers have documented a range at Tucson Basin Hohokam sites of between 17 percent and 67 percent (Gasser 1985; L. Huckell 1986; Miksicek 1986a, 1986b). By comparison, the value of 100 percent for the samples from the Donaldson Site (Table 5.6) seems extraordinarily high, particularly because it is derived from a much older site. However, other late preceramic sites have produced similar figures: the Mission Road Site in Tucson has a ubiquity value of 91 percent (10 of 11 samples; Miksicek 1987), and the Fairbank Site has a value of 90 percent (9 of 10 samples; B. Huckell 1990). The parts-per-liter figures for maize at the Donaldson Site are also notably high (Tables 5.7, 5.8). Thus, the inference that maize agriculture was an important part of the subsistence base of the late preceramic people of southeastern Arizona is well founded. But does an abundance of evidence necessarily translate into evidence of abundance?

Other factors may have influenced these large quantities of maize macrofossils; preservation is one of them. Because the Donaldson Site and Los Ojitos are buried under more than 5 m of alluvium, is the observed abundance a function of rapid burial and excellent preservation? There is no doubt that preservation at these two sites is exceptional and surpasses that at other open sites, but examination of Tables 5.7 and 5.8 reveals that other plant taxa recorded for the Donaldson Site are not present in the same kind of superabundance (as measured in parts per liter) as maize. Some wild plants, represented by the columnar-celled seed coat fragments and the chenopod-amaranth group, reach similar levels of ubiquity but they are not consistently present in the same quantities as maize, suggesting that the abundance of maize is the result of something more than the conditions of preservation alone. Maize also may be well represented in the archaeological record because it leaves behind a large waste product, the cob, which made an excellent fuel. Still, to find so many maize cob fragments and cupules again suggests a plentiful supply. Prehistoric storage and processing practices may partially explain the abundance of maize macrofossils. If maize ears were stored in bell-shaped or other in-ground storage pits, cobs suitable for use as fuel would have been a consistently available by-product as the ears were removed, shelled, and processed for consumption. Ethnographic observations and archaeological evidence indicate maize was stored on the cob in underground pits (as described in Chapter 3), but to achieve the levels of abundance recorded from the excavated deposits, it is inescapable that the quantities of maize ears at these settlements were exceptional.

A recent examination of the capacities of bell-shaped storage pits (Huckell and others 1994) suggests that they could have held remarkable quantities of ears of late preceramic maize. This exercise was based on the estimated size and volume of a "typical" ear of maize as calculated from two complete ears from Tularosa Cave prepottery levels (Martin and others 1952, Fig. 172, two specimens at lower right). Scaled measurements suggest that an average of the two would be an ear 8.43 cm long by 2.85 cm wide. Computing a volume from these measurements, allowing for a lining of grass or juniper bark as known from ethnographic storage in bell-shaped pits, and assuming some inefficiency of packing, it can be calculated that a pit with an effective capacity of 0.5 cubic meters could have held as many as 9,200 ears of maize. Assuming that each ear might yield approximately 22 g of kernels, 202.4 kg of kernels would be available. Maize has about 3,600 calories per kilogram (Minnis 1985b), so 202.4 kg would represent some 728,640 calories. Using an adult nutritional requirement of 2,000 calories per day (Wetterstrom 1986), further computations suggest that approximately 364 person-days of food would be represented by this quantity of maize. Although all of the eight bell-shaped pits reported by Eddy (1958, Table 1) from the Donaldson Site have volumes less than 0.50 cubic meters, they still have capacities that would accommodate the storage of at least 4,000 to 7,000 ears of maize in each. This is not to say that only maize was stored in these pits, but rather to emphasize that considerable quantities of maize could be stored in them.

Since its discovery at Bat Cave nearly 50 years ago, early Southwestern maize has been described as "primitive" (Mangelsdorf and Smith 1949) and usually viewed as unproductive (Ford 1981). This low productivity has only been assumed, never demonstrated. Certainly the ears were smaller than those of later cultivars, but size alone is not necessarily a good measure of productive potential. How many ears were borne by each plant: one, two, four? Did the plants produce single stalks, or did they tiller, with each stalk bearing one or more ears? Moreover, how large were fields, and how many maize plants did they contain? How many fields were associated with a given settlement? The figures of abundance for maize from the Matty Canyon sites, as well as the capacities of the bell-shaped storage pits, should give us pause for thought. Either this maize was far more productive than we have given it credit for being, or the level of labor being invested in its cultivation was much greater than we have previously suspected.

Aside from the macrofossil evidence, pollen profiles from noncultural settings in both Matty Canyon and Cienega Creek yielded maize pollen in strata that correlate to the late preceramic period (Schoenwetter 1960; Paul Schultz Martin 1963, Figs. 17, 18). Maize pollen does not travel far and may not preserve well because of its large size and thin walls. Its presence suggests the existence of floodplain maize fields of sufficient size or numbers to contribute to the natural pollen rain at a level that can be recognized in randomly chosen exposures of sediment away from archaeological sites.

In the absence of other compelling alternative explanations for the abundance of maize, it seems appropriate to accept the evidence presented above as a true reflection of the importance of maize in the subsistence strategy. Although we cannot specify the percentage of maize in the diet, this abundance of maize does imply that the Cienega phase residents of Matty Canyon were committed farmers and that during some parts of the year, perhaps winter and spring, stored maize must have been of crucial importance for their subsistence.

Although maize is the cultigen to which the Cienega phase farmers devoted their principal efforts, Los Ojitos reveals that possibly squash was also cultivated. Squash has a much lower probability of being recognized in the archaeobotanical record because it leaves behind relatively fewer waste products likely to be carbonized than does maize. Even so, most Southwestern farmers during the recent past planted far greater quantities of maize than they did squash or other plants, and this pattern may have its roots in the Early Agricultural period.

Bioarchaeological Evidence

In addition to the maize remains, there are other indications that these people relied on farming. By the beginning of the 1980s, archaeologists learned that human bone tissue could record the presence and perhaps relative importance of maize in the prehistoric diet. Extraction of collagen from bones and measurement of the isotopic composition of the carbon it contained permitted researchers in the eastern United States to assess the times at which maize arrived in that region and when it became an important part of the total diet (B. D. Smith 1989). In the Southwest, this technique has proven useful in assessing the importance of agriculture in early Christian era Basketmaker II populations in southeastern Utah (Matson and Chisholm 1991; Matson 1991). At least by the first century A.D., Basketmaker II populations apparently relied on maize only slightly less than their Puebloan descendants in the same area, although this interpretation of the isotopic data has been questioned (Wills 1992). No such analysis was performed on the Matty Canyon skeletons, nor have such tests been conducted on any southern Arizona burial populations. Application of the technique has been limited by biological issues (such as the presence of wild plants whose isotopic signatures are like that of maize) and by sensitivity to the concerns of Native Americans.

Other aspects of the human skeletal remains provide insights into the importance of agriculture in the prehistoric diet in a less direct and nondestructive way. B. Holly Smith (1984) published a study of the patterns of dental attrition in populations of known hunter-gatherers and agriculturalists. Her work demonstrated that the patterns of molar wear differed markedly between the two groups and could be used to evaluate diet and food preparation methods. She discovered that the flatness of molar wear was one key; hunter-gatherers exhibited more nearly flat wear on their molars whereas agriculturalists tended to develop more obliquely angled wear patterns. Bivariate regression (least squares) showed increasing obliquity of wear with increasing stage of wear for both, but the molars of agriculturalists showed significantly more obliquity as tooth wear progressed (B. H. Smith 1984, Fig. 5).

Smith's approach was used to evaluate the dental wear patterns in the Los Ojitos burial population (Chapter 7; Huckell and Huckell 1988). Four individuals with intact dentition were selected (Burials 1, 2, 8, and 9) and observations were made on the lower right first molar. The results indicate that the Los Ojitos individuals clearly plot with the agricultural populations (Fig. 7.6). The small sample size naturally limits confidence in the slope of the regression line, but it is significant that for all four individuals, the plots of angle measurements by stage of attrition clearly fit within the range for agriculturalists. Smith concluded that the reason for the increased angle of wear relates to the toughness or fibrousness of the food being consumed. The reduction in these properties is probably a function of an increasingly thorough milling of foodstuffs, particularly cultigens, by agriculturalists. Thus, the observed patterns may relate to the type of food being processed, the thoroughness of the processing, or some combination of the two.

In Chapter 7, Penny Minturn and Lorrie Lincoln-Babb report that caries and abscesses were present in several of the dentitions of Matty Canyon residents, and that tooth loss in older individuals was prominent. The incidence of caries and abscesses is consistent with a population consuming relatively large amounts of carbohydrates, although the sources of the carbohydrates are probably both cultivated and wild plants. Minturn and Lincoln-Babb conclude that the patterns of dental disease are consistent with an inferred mixed farming-foraging strategy. The same conclusion may be drawn from the frequencies of trauma and porotic hyperostosis.

Human skeletal material from the Archaic period of southeastern Arizona is rare and fragmentary (Haury 1950; Sayles 1941, 1983; Waters 1986), and no well-preserved remains of securely dated preagricultural age are available for comparative dental examination. Compounding the comparison problem is the fact that the later Hohokam populations in the area generally cremated their dead and the teeth rarely survived intact. Despite the lack of comparative populations, results of this analysis strongly suggest that the late preceramic inhabitants of Los Ojitos were reliant on maize or on finely milled flour from maize and other seeds for much of their diet. When coupled with the macrobotanical and palynological information, it does not seem risky to postulate a substantial degree of reliance on agriculture by these people.

Wild Plants in the Diet

The importance of wild plants in the Cienega phase subsistence strategy should not be underestimated. The macrobotanical records from the Donaldson Site and Los Ojitos provide evidence that numerous wild plants were important contributors to the diet of these late preceramic people. As recognized by Frank Eddy (1958), the localized abundance of plant foods and the ready access to other biotic communities afforded diverse gathering opportunities for the inhabitants of Matty Canyon settlements.

Among the plant parts identified by Lisa Huckell are columnar-celled seed coat fragments, possibly representing some large-seeded member or members of the legume family, and the chenopods, amaranths, and undifferentiated cheno-ams. These taxa all had ubiquity values of 100 percent at the Donaldson Site (Table 5.6), suggesting their dietary importance. Without knowing the precise species of the plant or plants represented by the columnar-celled seed coat fragments, it is difficult to say much about what this apparently important food plant was or where it was obtained.

The positive identification of both mesquite pod fragments and seeds from the Donaldson Site and Los Ojitos demonstrates that this plant was used. Today it grows along Cienega Creek and all of the ephemeral drainages that are its tributaries. Although probably less abundant in the past, it must have been available in relatively close proximity to the settlements. Walnuts, also recovered from both sites, likely were obtained from along Cienega Creek or its tributaries.

Chenopods and amaranths thrive in the disturbed soil conditions along floodplains or agricultural fields and probably represent plants available in the immediate vicinity of the settlements. *Portulaca* and *Trianthema* were present in over half of the analyzed samples from the Donaldson Site, and like chenopods and amaranths, they favor the disturbed habitats along stream channels, floodplains, and agricultural fields. Cyperaceae achenes and *Juncus* are abundant among the samples and presumably were obtained from along the channel of Cienega Creek or from the margins of a nearby cienega. At Los Ojitos, seeds apparently from *Rumex* represent another plant sharing that same habitat. Gramineae caryopses were identified in more than three-fourths of the Donaldson Site samples and may have been derived from the floodplain of Cienega Creek and the piedmont slope or terraces of the Cienega Valley. Several species of grass, including *Sporobolus*, are present at both sites.

Also abundant were acorn nut shell fragments, occurring in nearly 90 percent of the Donaldson Site samples and in all three of the Los Ojitos samples. Acorns from *Quercus emoryi* (definitely used at both sites), *Q. arizonica*, or *Q. obongifolia* could have been obtained from the oak woodland community located in the surrounding Santa Rita or Whetstone mountains. Oak trees could be reached within 2 km to 4 km (2.5 miles) of the Matty Canyon and Cienega Creek confluence, although they are more abundant 10 km (6 miles) away. Other plants from either the higher parts of the semidesert grassland or the oak woodland are agave (*Agave palmeri*) and yucca, both of which today grow on the slopes of Matty Canyon about 2 km (1.2 miles) east of the Donaldson Site. Los Ojitos yielded a small quantity of alligator juniper (*Juniperus deppeana*) seeds, which probably were obtained from the oak woodland. Like agave, a few individual one-seed junipers are located within 2 km of the site today. The late preceramic occupants of these settlements would have made use of plant products from these higher, nearby communities in season.

One cannot attach much significance to the few saguaro seeds from both sites other than to note that today it would be necessary to travel nearly 20 km (12 miles) to reach saguaro populations of sufficient density to make harvesting a large quantity of the fruits an efficient enterprise. Perhaps the fact that so few seeds were recovered is a reflection of this distance, or it may be the product of sampling bias.

The evidence is clear that numerous kinds of wild plants were utilized for food, and that certain plants were of critical importance in the diet.

Hunting and Meat in the Diet

Hunting also provided a significant proportion of the diet, and the patterns of animal exploitation indicate that species inhabiting the surrounding biotic communities were taken. Artiodactyls form the largest part of the archaeological samples from the Donaldson Site. Deer (*Odocoileus)* were the preferred targets; mule deer (*O. hemionus*) was the only species positively identified in 1983, but a few white-tailed deer (*O. virginianus*) elements were reported by Eddy (1958). Both species occur in the area today, but white-tailed deer prefer the oak woodland and mule deer the lower elevation grasslands and desertscrub. The pronghorn antelope (*Antilocapra americana*) was second quantitatively in Eddy's

faunal sample, but only one definite pronghorn element was recovered in 1983. Eddy identified four elements as possibly elk (*Cervus* sp.); they are the only reported occurrence of this animal from a prehistoric site below the Mogollon Rim in Arizona. Three bighorn (*Ovis canadensis*) elements were recovered by Eddy and three were identified in 1983. Several additional elements classified to the order Artiodactyla were present in the 1983 sample.

The large mammals undoubtedly were hunted both in relatively close proximity to the settlement and at some distance away from it. Mule deer and antelope are the species likely to have been present along Cienega Creek and in the semidesert grasslands bordering it. The white-tailed deer may have been taken locally or may have been hunted in the oak woodland communities of the nearby Santa Rita, Whetstone, or Empire mountains. Bighorn sheep do not occur near the Cienega Valley today; the closest extant population is in the Santa Catalina Mountains some 70 km (44 miles) away. They favor brushy, rocky terrain in the mountains, and in prehistoric times may have been present in the higher elevations of the Santa Ritas or Whetstones. Hohokam sites less than 1000 to 1200 years old near Rosemont in the northern Santa Rita Mountains also produced bighorn sheep remains (Glass 1984).

Most of the large mammal elements represent portions of the lower legs or head, pieces that contain little meat, which may indicate that entire carcasses were being brought to the settlement. This pattern is most evident in the 1983 sample for deer, but extends to antelope and bighorn also. The counts of unidentifiable bone (Table 6.3) show that fragments of large mammal bones far outnumber fragments assigned to the other size classes. Probably the larger elements (humerus, radius, femur, tibia) were being intentionally broken to extract the marrow. Eddy (1958) did not report element identifications, and it is not possible to determine whether this pattern was present in his sample.

Smaller mammals, primarily rabbits, were also hunted. The jackrabbit (*Lepus* sp., *L. californicus*, and *L. alleni*) is nearly twice as abundant as the cottontail (*Sylvilagus*) in the prehistoric sample. Although their status as food is open to question, other small animals, including rodents and birds, were reported from the 1983 excavations (Chapter 6).

With this array of animals, hunters must have spent time in the valley bottoms, in the grasslands, and in the surrounding mountain ranges. In all of these biotic communities, they focused their attention on the large mammals. This is consistent with patterns identified by Speth and Scott (1989) and by Szuter and Bayham (1989). These authors have observed a tendency for more sedentary human populations to concentrate their hunting efforts on large animals, particularly when such populations are located in upland environments where large mammals are more numerous.

Discussion

The late preceramic people of the Matty Canyon area were, in many ways, ideally situated to pursue a mixed farming and foraging economy. A similar conclusion was reached by Eddy (1958) with respect to the hunting and gathering opportunities afforded by the area and, on the basis of the 1983 work, can be extended to agricultural potential as well.

As reconstructed from sedimentological, geomorphic, and palynological information, the settlements in Matty Canyon were occupied at a time when the water table was high, the Cienega Creek floodplain was aggrading, and cienegas were present along the channel nearby (Eddy and Cooley 1983: 46, Fig. 4.1b). The Cienega Creek floodplain at and upstream of the Matty Canyon confluence is broad, and extensive areas of high-quality arable land must have been available to the prehistoric residents. Field locations were probably on the Cienega Creek floodplain at the margins of the stream channel or cienegas; the high water table near cienega margins would have been particularly attractive and productive for subirrigated fields. If the technology of floodwater farming was known, the distributary fan of Matty Wash also may have been farmed. There is no evidence of late preceramic irrigation, but simple ditch systems or container ("pot" is not apropos) irrigation may have been used; dry farming would have been more risky. Modern climatic records suggest that the length of the growing season at this elevation of roughly 1,200 m probably averaged 165 to 175 days, an adequate interval in most years.

It has been proposed that agriculture may help to make foraging more efficient in certain ways. Wills (1988a) suggested that in the Mogollon highlands, cultivation would have allowed late preceramic farmer-foragers to preview the developing crops of wild plant resources so that they could better position themselves to harvest these foods in late summer and fall. Ford (1984) believed that cultivated and abandoned agricultural fields may have greatly increased supplies of wild annuals. Too, the advent of in-ground storage technology (bell-shaped storage pits are not now known from archaeological sites earlier than the late pre-ceramic period) associated with agriculture would have permitted more efficient utilization of wild plants (B. Huckell 1990). Storage technology, by making possible an extension of the period of availability of a particular resource, could have acted to encourage the collection of seeds or fruits with good storage properties in much larger quantities than was practiced by earlier populations with direct return economies that minimized storage. One effect of agricultural adoption, which emphasized delayed consumption through storage, may have been to encourage use of the same tactic on wild plant resources, thus shifting treatment of some portion of these resources from direct to delayed return (Woodburn 1980). Wild resources of the Cienega Basin amenable to storage include acorns, chenopods and amaranths, walnuts, mesquite pods, and agave. The high ubiquity values for acorns, cheno-ams, and columnar-celled seed coat fragments that perhaps represent a large-seeded legume (L. Huckell, Chapter 5) may reflect this sort of storage-aided intensification of wild plant utilization.

Despite this rosy picture of the agricultural and hunting-gathering potential of the Matty Canyon environs, the reality faced by these late preceramic populations was without question occasionally harsh. Unpredictable, climatically induced fluctuations in wild and domesticated resource production are endemic in arid and semiarid environments, and the impacts of drought can be severe (Minnis 1985b; B. Huckell 1990). The enamel hypoplasia detected on the dentition of one of the Los Ojitos burials may testify to intermittent dietary stress. Integration of agriculture with foraging provided a more secure subsistence base than hunting and gathering alone, but not an infallible one. Still, testimony to the success of this mixed strategy in southeastern Arizona is revealed not only in the rich archaeological record of later, ceramic-producing societies in this region, but also in the structure, size, and content of Los Ojitos and the Donaldson Site. These features of the sites imply a certain residential stability promoted by this adaptation to the semiarid environment of the region, and it is a consideration of that stability to which I now turn.

SEDENTISM AND MOBILITY IN THE CIENEGA VALLEY

The extent, thickness, and contents of the midden at the Donaldson Site suggested long-term or intensive occupation to Eddy (1958), just as these same attributes of the Fairbank Site prompted Sayles (1941, 1983) to ponder occupational strategies there. Neither Eddy nor Sayles had any simple way to establish the existence or importance of preceramic agriculture in the 1940s or 1950s. The 1983 Matty Canyon investigations, and work at the Fairbank Site in 1989 (Huckell and Huckell 1990; B. Huckell 1990), demonstrate that agriculture was an important factor influencing the character of the occupations at both settlements.

A commitment to agricultural production may entail a corresponding commitment to a particular place on the landscape where suitable land, water, climate, and other resources occur together. Groups with mixed farming-foraging economies may face a dilemma posed by the labor demands associated with the cultivation of crops, which necessitate staying near the fields for some part of the growing and harvest seasons, and the need to travel, sometimes over considerable distances, to procure wild resources as they become available. This potential conflict requires people to decide how best to balance and organize their efforts to resolve differing spatial and temporal demands on their labor. The Early Agricultural period occupants of southeastern Arizona apparently chose a solution that resulted in prolonged occupation of residential settlements and an attendant decrease in the frequency of residential moves (B. Huckell 1988, 1990; Roth 1989, 1992). It is important to consider how the Cienega phase residents of Matty Canyon organized their settlement-subsistence system to solve the conflicting pressures associated with hunting and gathering and cultivation. The nature of these residential settlements is considered first.

A Composite View of the Donaldson Site

The Donaldson Site is a good representative of a residential base with evidence for prolonged occupation. Neither the 1957 investigations by Frank Eddy nor the 1983 excavations reported herein explored more than a small portion of it, which, based on fuller exposure by Matty Wash, we now know extended continuously along 140 m of the stream banks. Together, however, the two studies and the kinds of features that were excavated provide the first substantial look at a Cienega phase residential settlement.

Figure 8.2 presents a composite map of the 1957 and 1983 investigations at the Donaldson Site. Unfortunately, none of Eddy's original control points survived the intervening 25 years of continual channel erosion, so the spatial relationships of the excavated features are estimated. Between the two projects, 53 features, representing nine basic feature types, were excavated (Table 8.1). The two samples help balance our understanding of the contents of the site.

Examination of Figure 8.2 and Table 8.1 reveals several important characteristics of the site that reflect the nature of the late preceramic occupation. The Donaldson Site exhibits a large variety of features and these features are present in high densities. The 1955–1957 excavations investigated 65 square meters and the 1983 work encompassed 48 square meters, a total of 113 square meters. An approximate density of features for the two samples is one feature for every two square meters.

There are indications of spatial clustering of certain kinds of features. For example, there are six human burials just north of Eddy's Test 2 within 4 m of one another; Eddy's Test 3 contains a group of four bell-shaped pits (Fig. 1.3). The contemporaneity of the features in these groupings is difficult to assess, but intra-settlement space was probably apportioned and organized into functionally specific areas. Features frequently intrude or overlie other features (Figs. 3.10–3.13). These intrusive or superposed features often are of different types, suggesting that occupation of the settlement was sufficiently intensive and temporally extensive that the use of space changed over the course of its occupation. Once they had outlived their original purpose, pit features, in particular, usually served for refuse disposal or inhumation of the dead. Areas of the Donaldson Site changed roles as the midden grew and developed in thickness during its occupation.

One might reasonably ask for what length of time the Donaldson Site was occupied. Assessing this question using radiocarbon dates is not as straightforward as it might first appear. Eddy obtained a range of dates that spanned more than 1,300 years; however, all of those were solid carbon assays and, based on a more sophisticated understanding of radiocarbon dating methods, are of questionable reliability. I believe the four dates from the 1983 investigations better reflect the true age and temporal span of the occupation, and they are used in preference to Eddy's dates. These four assays, however, constitute a small sample from this large site.

By using dendrochronological–carbon-14 calibration, it is possible to accurately translate radiocarbon years into years in the Christian calendric system (Taylor 1987). Calibration of the four Donaldson Site dates produces an apparent span of as much as 600 years at the 2 sigma level of confidence (Table 3.1), despite the fact that the mean dates in radiocarbon years before present imply an occupational span of as little as 200 years. The

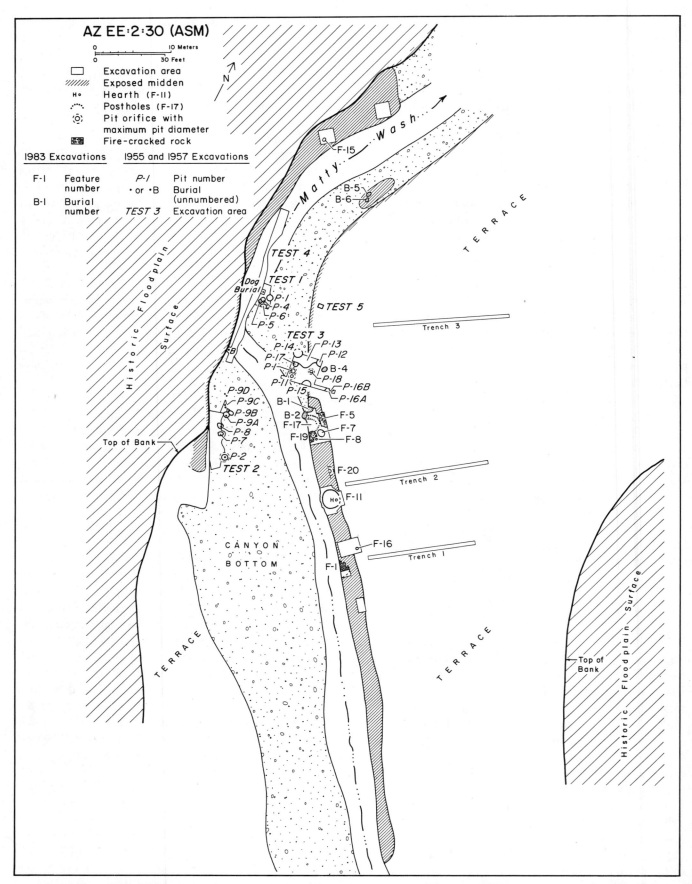

Figure 8.2. Composite map of the Donaldson Site, showing features excavated in 1955–1957 (in italics) and in 1983.

Table 8.1. Excavated Features at the Donaldson Site (AZ EE:2:30 ASM)

Feature	1955–1957	1983	Total
Structure	1	2	3
Human burial	8	5	13
Dog burial	1		1
Roasting pit		1	1
Bell-shaped pit	8	1	9
Straight-sided pit	7	1	8
Rock cluster	5	7	12
Small pit		5	5
Irregular pit		1	1
Total	30	23	53

Sedentary Settlements?

Feature and artifact densities indicate that occupation was intensive and probably long-term at the Donaldson Site and Los Ojitos, approaching "sedentary." This term provokes strong reactions in some archaeologists, and the concepts of mobility and sedentism have been much in the thoughts of Southwesternists in recent years. How one explores the issues of settlement permanence, seasonality, patterns of mobility on an annual scale, and how these might be identified or measured in the archaeological record are questions that are not only current topics but have been of interest to scholars for many decades.

Mobility and sedentism are difficult to separate conceptually, for both involve the frequency, distance, and organization of the movement of people within defined environmental and societal contexts. Mobility and sedentism are strategies by which societies or groups within a society choose to deal with problems of temporal and spatial discontinuities in resource distribution and abundance. Each is multifaceted, involving a number of specific tactics to solve discrete problems. Traditionally, hunter-gatherer societies have been described in terms of mobility, and agricultural societies have been discussed in terms of sedentism, although both sedentary hunter-gatherers and mobile agriculturalists have been identified among historic societies. Perhaps ironically, recent assessments have considered the notion that later, ceramic-producing Southwestern societies were not as sedentary as once thought, and that late preceramic societies were not as mobile as previously believed (Rocek 1993). The Matty Canyon sites may be viewed productively from the perspectives of both sedentism and mobility.

The concept of what sedentary means has been reviewed by Rafferty (1985), Kelly (1992), and Rocek (1993); agreement over terminology and usage remains elusive. Sedentism achieves meaning in part by being contrasted with mobility and is actually a reduction in or cessation of mobility. As defined by Rice (1975), it reflects a condition in which a settlement is inhabited by at least some part of the population for the entire course of a year. Rafferty (1985) and Kelly (1992) note that some portion of the population may still be mobile during certain parts of the year, but Rice's definition does contain a sort of threshold by applying the notions of time (a full year) and cessation of movement (by at least some part of the population). However, the definition is problematic when applied to real-world archaeological situations. How does one determine whether or not a

basis of this apparent contradiction lies in what are known as the de Vries effects, one form of secular variation in the atmospheric abundance of carbon-14 (see Taylor 1987: 30–33 for a description). Paired radiocarbon and dendrochronological dates have revealed that during some periods in the past, the de Vries effect results in radiocarbon years actually spanning a much broader range of calendric years than during other periods. The standard deviation, or measurement error, of a radiocarbon date exacerbates the difficulty by increasing the uncertainty and thus the calibrated age range (Taylor 1987: Fig. 2.12). Unfortunately, the millennium between approximately 2400 B.P. and 2500 B.P. was one such time (see Pearson and Stuiver 1986: 847, Fig. 2A). As a result, a radiocarbon date in this interval can actually represent any part of several centuries in the first millennium before Christ. This situation effectively compromises the effort to accurately measure the duration of the Donaldson Site occupation. Even with more radiocarbon dates, little could be done to solve this problem. The Donaldson Site may have been occupied for a maximum of 600 years, but I suspect that the actual duration of habitation was half that amount or less.

Los Ojitos represents a similar occupation. Although the 1983 investigations did little more than test a small part of it, the results indicate that it, too, was intensively occupied. The remarkable cluster of burials implies the existence of a discrete cemetery area, and the Feature 4 multiple secondary burial suggests that at least four individual burials were disturbed and reinterred, possibly when a portion of this cemetery or another was impacted by a change in the intrasettlement use of space. Coupled with the thickness and high artifact density of the midden, these observations support the likelihood that Los Ojitos was an intensively occupied residential settlement for several decades, at least.

settlement was occupied on a year-round basis or if the population was in continuous residence for the full year?

Wills and Windes (1989), in an examination of the Basketmaker III site of Shabik'eschee Village, note that for many Southwestern archaeologists sedentism has not only structural but organizational meaning. In discussing the rise of sedentary settlements in the Mogollon area, Lightfoot and Feinman (1982) use the term "village" to mean a place characterized not only by pit houses, storage pits, and possibly one or more nonresidential community structures, but by a type of social organization believed to be "simple egalitarian" with one level of suprahousehold integration. Certainly the establishment and maintenance of a sedentary community required some organizational hierarchy to resolve conflicts and to perform integrative functions of a political or religious nature to ensure the social stability of the community. An individual leader may have filled such a function, as envisioned by Lightfoot and Feinman (1982), or some social organizational shift may have occurred to integrate people into larger descent groups or decision-making bodies (Wills and Windes 1989).

How does one recognize a sedentary settlement in the archaeological record? Wills and Windes (1989) observe correctly that there are no unambiguous archaeological indicators of sedentism. Rafferty (1985) expresses a similar opinion, but offers a list of eight potential indicators of sedentary sites: more substantial houses; evidence of community planning; the presence of mounds or ceremonial structures or areas; reliance on agricultural subsistence; large, heavy artifacts; presence of storage facilities; development of deep, dark midden deposits; and flora or fauna indicative of multiseasonal occupation. No one of these features is positive proof of sedentism in and of itself; they must be present in combination. Ideally, Rafferty suggests, the identification of sedentism should involve entire settlement patterns rather than just single sites.

The Donaldson Site and Los Ojitos exhibit several of Rafferty's indicators of sedentism, although not all are straightforward or simple to interpret. A good case in point are domestic structures. Pit structures at the Donaldson Site are small and round. They were built in pits excavated into the underlying Pleistocene Unit 100 sediments, and one (Feature 17) incorporated substantial and numerous wall posts set at close intervals. Because none of the structures burned, it is uncertain whether they were of simple pole and thatch construction or whether they were earth-covered or clay-plastered. Both their small size, less than 3.0 m in diameter, and round

floor plans are architectural attributes that occur among historic and recent nonsedentary societies. Whiting and Ayres (1968) reported that slightly less than two-thirds of recent societies that constructed houses of curvilinear form (round or elliptical) were nomadic or seminomadic; only 35 percent of sedentary societies built such houses. Moreover, their small size is unusual among sedentary societies during the recent past. Gilman (1987) has suggested that among recent groups in nontropical settings, pit houses are indicators of seasonal mobility rather than sedentism. In her view, pit houses represent winter habitations when populations subsisted on stored resources. Do the Donaldson Site pit structures constitute the "more substantial houses" expected at sedentary sites? Recent excavations at two other Cienega phase sites in the Tucson Basin demonstrate that this type of house is typical for the phase, although slightly greater average diameters seem to characterize structures at those sites (Mabry and others 1995). With only a small sample of excavated structures available from the Donaldson Site, we should perhaps view them as indicators of reduced mobility during at least some part of the year, but whether year-round remains open to question.

Community planning, another of Rafferty's indicators of sedentism, is difficult to determine from the distribution of features within the limited exposures at the Donaldson Site and Los Ojitos. The distributions of burials at the Donaldson Site and at Los Ojitos suggest the existence of cemeteries, areas within the community set aside for the interment of the dead. In some areas of the Donaldson Site, the use of space changed over time; one area contains a pit structure overlying a burial and intruded by and overlain with pits and fire-cracked rock dumps (Figs. 3.10–3.13). Even if there was planning, decisions regarding the use of space were subject to reconsideration through time. Geologic evidence suggests that the settlement was positioned atop a low terrace and that physiographic constraints may have limited the total amount of space available within the settlement. The Donaldson Site deposit is complex, and the length or intensity of its occupation, coupled with a small excavated area, make assessments of settlement planning impossible.

The exposed portions of the Matty Canyon sites contained no mounds, ceremonial structures, or ceremonial areas. However, excavations in 1994 at the Santa Cruz Bend Site revealed a pit structure 9 m in diameter, posited to be a community structure in a Cienega phase settlement containing more than 180 pit houses (Mabry and others 1995). Thus, community structures, possibly serving ceremonial uses, may be expected during this period.

To continue with Rafferty's indicators of sedentism, both archaeobotanical measures of maize abundance at all locations tested in Matty Canyon and evidence from dental wear patterns indicate agriculture was notably important in the lives of these preceramic people. What percentage of the diet agricultural products may have formed at Matty Canyon is not ascertainable at present, but indications are that it was substantial.

The evidence of large, heavy artifacts at the Matty Canyon sites is far less compelling. Mobile societies are unlikely to encumber themselves with artifacts that are not easily transported, whereas sedentary societies produce and use such objects because they do not have to travel great distances with them. Rafferty also observes, however, that even mobile societies may manufacture large, heavy artifacts and leave them at or near the place where they can be used in the future. This indicator of sedentism is thus problematic to apply with much confidence. The single complete basin metate (Fig. 4.6a) at the Donaldson Site is indeed large and heavy, but no similar artifacts were recovered.

Storage facilities, on the other hand, are much more numerous. Bell-shaped pits were discovered both by Eddy and during the 1983 excavations at the Donaldson Site; they continue to be exposed today as erosion causes the left bank of Matty Wash to retreat. Their functions may be debated, but many must have served as storage features. Eddy's (1958) interpretation centered on their use as roasting pits. Once abandoned, regardless of original function, these bell-shaped pits quickly became receptacles for trash disposal; when excavated, their contents may not reflect their original function. Storage also could have occurred in other kinds of pits as well as in perishable containers such as large, coarsely woven granaries or hide bags. In-ground storage pits also may be a reflection of seasonal mobility (DeBoer 1988). Subterranean storage may be a tactic not only for the preservation of food but also for the concealment of such resources from marauders who might enter the settlement while the occupants are away. Storage pits certainly reflect reduced mobility during some part of the year, but may also suggest abandonment of the settlement during other seasons.

The Donaldson Site is marked by a dark, rich cultural deposit averaging some 40 cm in thickness whose minimum extent is 140 m on a north-south axis, thus meeting another of Rafferty's indicators. To accumulate such a uniformly thick deposit over so large an area implies the likelihood of a population in residence

for long periods of time. The Los Ojitos midden is structurally similar; although its total length is unknown, the linear extent is at least 50 m and its composition and thickness are comparable to the Donaldson Site. Both middens contain abundant artifacts, animal bones, fire-cracked rocks, and carbonized plant materials that bespeak long or intensive use of the settlement. Deposits of this kind form as a product of either intensive short-term use or less intensive occupation during a long period of time. Available chronological information from the Donaldson Site suggests an occupational span of perhaps as much as six centuries, although I speculate that the actual duration may have been half that or less.

Finally, Rafferty proposes that seasonal indicators among the plant and animal remains from a site might reflect sedentary occupation. Both Matty Canyon sites yielded plant remains that show a predominance of species available in the late summer and fall (maize, amaranth, purslane, horse purslane, carpetweed, bulrush, dropseed, saltbush, acorn, and walnut) and lesser amounts of late spring or possibly spring plants (sedges, stickleaf, chenopods, mesquite, agave, and saguaro). Agave is at its best during the spring before flowering stalks begin to grow, but it can be collected during much of the year. Missing from the record are early spring plants such as tansy mustard, cholla buds, and chia; however, these desert plants were not necessarily available in the Cienega Valley. Storage pits suggest that stored food reserves, including maize, were being consumed during the winter.

In addition to Rafferty's indicators of sedentism, attention must also be given to the burial populations at both the Donaldson Site and Los Ojitos. The two limited excavations revealed 13 individuals at the Donaldson Site and 10 individuals at Los Ojitos (not including isolated elements of subadults), representing but a small sample of the total burial population. The likelihood of an individual dying at a settlement occupied for a short period of time is small; with increasing occupational duration, the chances for a death at a residential settlement rise. The presence of so many primary burials and one secondary multiple burial at Los Ojitos, strongly suggests that people were in residence at these settlements for much of the year.

In summary, the Matty Canyon sites exhibit many of the attributes expected of sedentary settlements, but indications for some type or degree of mobility are also present. Let us briefly consider that evidence and what it may suggest regarding subsistence-settlement strategies during the Cienega phase.

Mobility

The term mobility covers a multitude of economic strategies and tactics to solve problems of temporal and spatial discontinuities in the distribution of resources and people (R. L. Kelly 1983, 1992). Mobility may take many forms, but two basic strategies are recognized: moving people to places where desired resources are located (foraging) or moving desired resources to where people are located (collecting).

Foragers are generally residentially mobile, exploiting the resources of a particular area until the returns from gathering, hunting, or both diminish such that search and processing costs exceed the energetic returns from the resources. They then move, as a group, to a new locus and repeat the cycle. Foraging societies often live in environments that lack marked seasonal change and that contain relatively uniform resource types and distributions. Collectors, on the other hand, tend to remain at a given location for a longer period of time and send task groups to obtain resources from some distance away, bringing them back to the residential base. They are, in Binford's (1980) terms, logistically mobile. Collectors typically live in more strongly seasonal climates and patchy environments in which resources are not evenly distributed. Most societies practice a mixture of these different strategies, obtaining some resources through residential mobility and others through logistic mobility.

Using ethnographic data, Binford (1982) has proposed the existence of economic zonation around a residential settlement, with particular zones associated with different procurement strategies. Of significance to this discussion are the foraging zone and the logistic zone. The foraging zone is defined by a radius of approximately 10 km (6.2 miles), representing the maximum distance that can be comfortably covered in a day-long, out-and-back trip. Beyond this extends the logistic zone, from which resources are procured by trips that include at least one overnight camp. Although it specifically addresses hunter-gatherer subsistence and settlement, Binford's concept is probably applicable also to farmer-foragers.

It is primarily the distribution and relative density or abundance of resources, coupled with societal technology, that determine the ways in which a society uses mobility in a settlement-subsistence system. As described above for the Matty Canyon sites, some resources were obtained by the residents of these settlements from areas at least 2 km to 20 km (about a mile to more than 13 miles) distant. Acorns and agave are available within 2 km to 15 km of the settlement; they could easily have been obtained by task groups and taken back to the residential area for processing, storage, and consumption. Such task groups may have been composed of family units or women and children. The absence of early spring plants such as cholla buds and tansy mustard seeds, however, may suggest that the settlements were largely or completely abandoned at that time of the year, with people moving north and west into the desertscrub community.

Hunting, particularly of large mammals, is commonly a logistically organized task involving small groups that search for game away from the settlement. Among the large mammal remains at the Matty Canyon sites, deer are the most abundant. As noted, mule deer inhabit the area around the sites, and white-tail deer range near the sites but are more common some 10 to 15 km (6 to 9 miles) away in the Santa Rita and Whetstone mountains. The hunting of antelope might have involved trips of similar or greater length into the semidesert grassland south of the settlement. To obtain bighorn sheep, the higher elevation, rougher terrain of the surrounding mountains would have to be reached. Osteological evidence suggests that entire carcasses of large mammals, not just selected portions, were brought to the residential settlements. Antelope and perhaps rabbits could have been obtained by communal hunting techniques involving large numbers of people.

The archaeological evidence indicates that logistic mobility strategies were being used by the residents of the Donaldson Site for the procurement of certain wild plant and animal resources. If one applies Binford's ideas of economic zonation around the Matty Canyon settlements, it appears that many of the important resources could have been obtained by simple foraging trips. However, logistic mobility strategies might have been necessary to reach areas of the *encinal* with greater concentrations of oaks, to reach the semidesert grassland for agave harvesting and roasting, and to reach the Sonoran desertscrub for saguaro fruit gathering. If so, the remnants of short-term gathering camps should be present in these biotic communities.

Some or all of the population residing in the Matty Canyon settlements may have moved to any one of these communities during the spring and summer. The Sonoran desertscrub, with its early spring bounty, may have attracted family or extended family groups to hunt and gather during that season. The procurement of white-tailed deer, antelope, and bighorn most likely would have required logistically organized trips in any case, but the greatest concentrations of these animals today occur more than 10 km (6 miles) away from the Matty Canyon sites. Again, small camps associated with hunting may be expected in the mountains or the grassland.

Settling Down

Domestic structures, agricultural products, storage pits, a thick and culturally rich midden deposit, and plants representing multiple seasons all suggest that late preceramic people were in residence at the Donaldson Site and probably at Los Ojitos for a major portion of the year, if not the entire year, an interpretation additionally supported by the large burial population, the areal extent of the cultural deposit, and the density of features. Yet, it is clear that these people also retained some degree of mobility to procure resources at varying distances from home. The substantive nature of this evidence supports the reasonable conclusion that the Matty Canyon settlements were sedentary. In my opinion, they may be considered villages inhabited both intensively during the course of a year and for periods of time best measured in decades, if not centuries.

Two factors promoted the development of late preceramic villages in Matty Canyon: the agricultural potential of Cienega Creek and access to a wide range of economically important resources. There was an abundant, dependable, and perennial supply of water, one of the most critical resources in any arid or semiarid environment. Lithic materials suitable for the manufacture of flaked and ground stone implements occurred in large quantities and in suitable sizes as lag gravels along the terraces bordering Cienega Creek. Firewood and construction materials were available from mesquite, oak, juniper, cottonwood, willow, and other nearby trees.

Within a few kilometers of the Donaldson Site and Los Ojitos there were three major biotic communities: the riparian community, including the cienegas, along Cienega Creek; the semidesert grassland occupying the floor of the valley; and the oak woodland on the flanks of the Santa Rita, Whetstone, and Empire mountains. The oak-pine woodland is not much farther up the slopes of these ranges. Each of these communities offered economically significant resources that could be obtained without much travel or search time. When these two significant costs of foraging are reduced and more time is devoted to collecting and processing the resources, foraging becomes more efficient. Rafferty (1985), citing Flannery and Coe (1968), has observed that a more settled lifeway is possible when settlements

are located on or near the boundaries where several microenvironments meet; the Matty Canyon settlements were so positioned.

It is unfortunate that we do not know more of the overall settlement pattern in the Cienega Creek Basin during this time. Knowledge of other kinds of sites and site locations would enhance our ability to understand the role of the Donaldson Site and Los Ojitos in the Cienega phase subsistence-settlement system. The ANAMAX-Rosemont Project, carried out in the foothills of the Santa Rita Mountains (Fig. 1.2), investigated three Early Agricultural period sites or components of sites (B. Huckell 1984a). The multicomponent Split Ridge Site (AZ EE:2:103), located 13 km (8 miles) to the west in the foothills of the Santa Rita Mountains (B. Huckell 1984), contained one badly rodent-damaged pit house, an array of small rock-filled cooking pits, a deep, cylindrical storage pit, and a few Cienega and San Pedro points. A radiocarbon date of approximately 2500 B.P. was obtained from a carbonized walnut hull from the fill of the storage pit. Carbonized plant remains were limited to walnuts, grass stems, and a single chenopod seed, and the few animal bones were those of deer. Artifact density was high. This information suggests the possibility of a single family in residence during the summer; today walnuts are available in July. Whether the site represents a seasonal occupation by a family from a large settlement such as Los Ojitos or Donaldson or a longer occupation by a family living independently of the larger villages cannot be determined. One other site in the Rosemont area, the Wasp Canyon Site (AZ EE:2:62), also contained a single pit house dated to 1990 ± 370 B.P. (calibrated at one sigma from 400 B.C. to A.D. 430, A-3103). It, too, was a multicomponent occupation, probably used primarily during the Archaic period; no Cienega points were recovered. One probable San Pedro phase hunting camp (AZ EE:2:81) documented in the Rosemont area consisted exclusively of flaked stone, including four San Pedro points and fewer than 40 other implements and pieces of debitage. This site is likely the product of a hunting party.

These are the kinds of sites that reflect other aspects of the late preceramic utilization of the Cienega Creek Basin. Their relationships to the larger sites along Cienega Creek remain uncertain. Research into the overall settlement pattern in the valley is needed to help clarify the organization of mobility during this period. If we remain uncertain about the nature of the Early Agricultural period settlement for the Cienega Basin as a whole, there is little doubt that large residential sites along the floodplain of the Cienega Creek played a pivotal role in that system for several centuries.

The Persistence of Late Preceramic Settlements

There is good evidence that the advantages of the Matty Canyon–Cienega Creek area were recognized by its inhabitants near the beginning of the Early Agricultural period. This evidence takes the form of three different habitation sites that represent a stratigraphically and probably chronologically consistent sequence of settlements.

The series begins with AZ EE:2:35 (ASM), a site on the east bank of Cienega Creek discovered and tested by Frank Eddy (1958). It is the least known of the three, but Eddy recorded it as a "buried trash zone," 40 cm thick, extending along 60 m of the east bank of Cienega Creek just 1 km (0.6 mile) upstream of the confluence with Matty Wash (Fig. 1.2); it contained five rock-filled pit hearth features. It was subsequently dated to around 1000–800 B.C., placing it within the San Pedro phase, and it was enclosed in sediments of one of the earliest of the late Holocene alluvial units identified in this part of the valley. In September of 1994, with the aid of Bill Robinson, Lisa Huckell and I relocated this site. It was nearly completely obscured by a thick, laterally extensive talus deposit at the base of a 6-m vertical bank. A flotation sample from one small exposure of the deposit produced carbonized maize, demonstrating that this site may have been one of the earliest agricultural communities in the Cienega Creek Basin. From Eddy's description, the "trash zone" was a cultural deposit or midden similar, if not identical, to middens encountered at Los Ojitos and the Donaldson Site. It is unclear whether Eddy observed the maximum extent of this site or simply an edge of it. Considering the thickness of the deposit, it is likely that AZ EE:2:35 represents a settlement occupied either intensively, or for a lengthy period of time, or perhaps both. The apparent rapidity with which alluvium was accumulating along Cienega Creek means that it could not have been occupied for too long a time before the threat of frequent inundation or the rising water table forced its inhabitants to relocate to higher ground.

On stratigraphic evidence, Los Ojitos may have been the place where the people from AZ EE:2:35 relocated their settlement. Los Ojitos is only 0.4 km south of AZ EE:2:35 (Fig. 1.2), and although exposed today by the eroded channel of Matty Canyon, prehistorically it was positioned on top of the eroded surface of Unit 100,

probably on the east side of the channel of Cienega Creek. Again, we know little of the size or occupational duration of this locus, but the thick cultural deposit, abundant artifacts and other refuse, and the burials all point to an occupation with the same suite of characteristics as the Donaldson Site or AZ EE:2:35. However, in time, the aggrading floodplain and rising water table must have again forced the people to move.

The locality of the Donaldson Site may have been their next choice, where a settlement was constructed on top of a low erosional terrace that had developed on the Pleistocene Unit 100, only 0.2 km southeast of Los Ojitos (Fig. 1.2). From stratigraphic data, Los Ojitos is clearly older than the Donaldson Site, although the radiocarbon dates from the two sites suggest the opposite (Chapter 3). Regardless of the true age of Los Ojitos, there is no doubt of the intensity of occupation at the Donaldson Site, and it was home to numerous people for a considerable length of time.

The continuity of settlement history in this area extends into the early ceramic period. Only 0.2 km upstream (east) of the Donaldson Site in Matty Canyon, Eddy excavated part of a pit house that yielded plain ware, red ware, and one incised sherd (Eddy 1958: 65–67; Eddy and Cooley 1983: 23–24). This site, AZ EE:2:10 (ASM), he labeled as Vahki-Estrella phase Hohokam, and estimated its age as A.D. 1 to 300. There were no radiocarbon samples dated from the locus, and little can be said of its size or occupational duration or intensity. Eddy noted that the site was in exactly the same stratigraphic position as the Donaldson Site, although the eroded surface of Unit 100 is a few meters higher in elevation at AZ EE:2:10 than it is at the Donaldson Site.

The area around the confluence of Matty Wash and Cienega Creek was a popular place for several centuries and perhaps much longer. Cooley's (Eddy and Cooley 1983: 35–36) estimates of the rates of deposition for various stratigraphic units at a series of localities show that Unit 3, which overlies the surfaces on which rest the Donaldson Site and Los Ojitos, accumulated quickly. At one profile locality near Los Ojitos, MC-5, (Eddy and Cooley 1983, Fig. 5.1), Cooley estimated 0.46 cm of accumulation per year. No estimates were made for Unit 4, which is in part coeval with Unit 3. At AZ EE:2:35, the average rate of deposition for the entire 5.6 m stack of alluvium was estimated to be 0.15 cm per year. Cooley noted that these estimates do not include "missing" alluvium removed by erosion. The rapid aggradation of the floodplain meant that the mud and water lapping at their doorsteps forced the inhabitants to move their settlement at least three times, but this filling of the valley created an ever-widening expanse of potentially arable land for their farming. The continuity of settlement demonstrated that the economic benefits of life in Matty Canyon outweighed the moving costs.

FORAGING, FARMING, AND SEDENTISM IN SOUTHEASTERN ARIZONA

Following the introduction of agriculture, the Cienega Basin was home to relatively stable village communities during the first millennium B.C. The Tucson Basin and the San Pedro River Valley contained settlements of similar kind and age. Because these communities all postdate the arrival and successful integration of agriculture into the economy, they do not provide direct information about the transition from purely foraging economies to mixed farming-foraging ones. The nature of the preagricultural Archaic utilization of southeastern Arizona that immediately preceded the Early Agricultural period has important implications for understanding the nature, magnitude, and rate of change that occurred after maize arrived.

The high resource diversity and relatively high resource accessibility of the river basins and mountain ranges of southeastern Arizona created an attractive environment for late Holocene, preagricultural foragers. At present, knowledge of this post-2500 to 1000 B.C. interval is poor and confined primarily to surface sites with little or no preservation of organic remains. The few buried sites with better preservation along arroyos or in sand dunes have received little attention; investigations by Frank Bayham and his colleagues (1986) in the Picacho dune field of south-central Arizona are the only significant exception. As a consequence, our understanding of preagricultural forager subsistence-settlement organization is slight, and archaeologists have relied on theoretical treatments of hunter-gatherer ecology and on the nature and distribution of resources.

Preagricultural Archaic societies have been perceived as highly mobile for most of the year, obtaining resources from several biotic communities over a wide area, operating in small social groups, and perhaps remaining in certain settlements for extended periods of time during the winter or during periods of temporary resource abundance. However, the possibility has been raised that more intensive exploitation of certain key resources could have underwritten the creation of long-term residential sites in particular parts of southeastern Arizona.

The Case for Preagricultural Sedentism

Paul and Suzanne Fish and John Madsen have proposed that sedentary or nearly sedentary communities, supported by intensification of hunting and gathering and food storage, may have existed in the Tucson Basin (and other parts of the Southwest) prior to the appearance of maize cultivation (S. Fish and others 1990, 1992; S. Fish and Fish 1991). They observe that certain wild resources are reasonably reliable and predictable, can occur in great abundance, and are potentially storable. They argue for a "high degree of pre-agricultural sedentism in favorable locales in the Tucson Basin," based on redundancy or diversity of wild resources such as mesquite, saltbush, cacti, and higher elevation resources, all available within relatively short distances of permanent water sources (S. Fish and others 1992: 14). The high topographic, pedologic, edaphic, and accompanying biotic diversity of the Tucson Basin area could have, in prime locations near permanent water, "led to no more than biseasonal movement and even year-round residence." Further, they observe that the highly mobile, early historic foragers in arid lands long used for ethnographic analogs and models do not necessarily adequately encompass the range of potential subsistence-settlement adaptations to these environments in prehistory. Preagricultural foraging economies predicated on intensive harvesting and storage of seasonally abundant resources could have developed long-term, stable residential bases. They also reiterate Haury's (1962) suggestion that the tending and encouragement of indigenous annual plants also may have been practiced, further enhancing their productive capacity.

What might the archaeological appearance be of a preagricultural community? We should expect such a site to be marked by a relatively high density and diversity of artifacts in a midden-like deposit, by domestic structures, by numerous extramural and perhaps intramural storage pits, by numerous extramural processing features (hearths, roasting pits, fire-cracked rock accumulations), and, of course, by an absence of maize. The site would exhibit a narrow range of radiocarbon dates and be located either along a stream terrace or near a spring. Plant and animal remains would be taxonomically diverse and represent at least one if not both of the major seasons of production.

The only sites now known in southeastern Arizona that display these attributes have all yielded maize. Although we can identify preagricultural sites that exhibit some of these features, there are none that we can confidently term sedentary or semisedentary communities. For example, the Lone Hill Site (Agenbroad 1970) is a large settlement located near a spring on the eastern bajada of the Santa Catalina Mountains. It has a high density of artifacts and scattered features, but the projectile points recovered from it span at least the last two millennia of the Archaic period before the Early Agricultural period. Nearly identical sites reported by Whalen (1971) and by Phillips and others (1993) from the eastern bajada of the Whetstone Mountains have similarly produced artifacts spanning several thousand years of occupation. In south-central Arizona, Bayham and others (1986) have reported two buried sites that contained relatively well-developed middens. One of these, Locus L of the Arroyo Site, produced a fairly high density of artifacts and animal bones, and it was inferred to be a spring or summer occupation adjacent to a cienega in a dune field. However, three radiocarbon dates from this locus span a 900–year period, suggesting that the site was likely the scene of repeated seasonal occupations during a lengthy interval. These sites, then, are probably the products of repeated, short-term, seasonal occupations, perhaps by large aggregates of people.

Elsewhere in the Southwest, there are preagricultural sites with structures. Patrick Hogan informs me that in both the San Juan Basin and the Rio Grande–Puerco River area a few small sites contain round structures, 3.5 m to 4.0 m in diameter or less, that date between roughly 2000 and 1000 B.C. These lack evidence of agriculture, and he interprets them to be short-term, probably winter, habitations. Excavation of the Keystone Dam Site near Las Cruces (O'Laughlin 1980) revealed similar structures, generally low densities of artifacts, and only a few small extramural pits. Radiocarbon dates spanned about 800 years, suggesting repeated short-term, probably seasonal occupations.

Short-term residential stability is not incompatible with a subsistence-settlement strategy that emphasizes frequent residential moves over most of the year. Multi-seasonal occupation of a residential settlement is typically only possible with a resource base composed of one or more extraordinarily productive species (oak trees in California, for example), access to terrestrial and marine or freshwater resources, or a highly diverse suite of resources available over a considerable portion of the year. In the Tucson Basin and southeastern Arizona, localized seasonal abundance of particular resources would have permitted longer occupations of particular settlements with easy access to those resources and to water. The duration of such occupations, however, might best be measured in terms of weeks rather than months and would coincide with the period of maximum availability of the resources. Moreover, as described below, there is considerable variation in the production of wild resources from season to season and year to year. The resource supply is therefore subject not only to predictable seasonal rhythms, but also unpredictable, climatically linked swings. For example, a superabundance of mesquite pods one year can be followed by a paucity of them the next year.

In my opinion, the one absolutely critical tactic necessary to support long-term (multi-month) settlement in southeastern Arizona or elsewhere in the Southwest is storage. One feature lacking in known preagricultural sites is the large storage pit, and it is difficult to envision any sedentary community without considerable storage capacity. Even at the short-term residential sites along the Rio Grande where pit features have been discovered, they are always shallow, basin-shaped pits of small diameter. If such pits did serve storage needs, their capacities appear insufficient for sustained habitation. Even though storage may have occurred during the preagricultural period in hide containers or above-ground granaries, I doubt that the scale or intensity of such storage was more than a small fraction of that seen in Early Agricultural period sites with their large, bell-shaped pits.

The possibility of an incipient horticultural economy based on Southwestern native annual plants deserves some consideration. In eastern North America, the cultivation of chenopod (*Chenopodium berlandieri* ssp. *jonesianum*), marsh elder (*Iva annua*), and sunflower (*Helianthus annuus*) was well established between 2000 and 1000 B.C. (B. D. Smith 1989, 1992). These plants show evidence of change in seed size or seed coat thickness or color, demonstrating human selection for desired properties in these plants during the several millennia they were cultivated. Between 250 B.C. and A.D. 200, along the rivers and streams of that region, there arose permanent villages and the beginnings of complex societies based on this native agriculture. When introduced into that region around A.D. 200, maize seems to have been unenthusiastically received; stable carbon isotopic study of human bone has revealed that dependence on maize did not occur until some six to eight centuries after its introduction.

In the Southwest, the carbonized seeds of chenopod, amaranth, and other similar annuals are routinely recovered from preagricultural and later agricultural period sites, but it is not until nearly A.D. 1000 that any of these seeds show demonstrable differences from their wild relatives. Climatic conditions in the arid Southwest are not as favorable for the cultivation of annual plants as they are in the more mesic eastern United States. The tending of wild annuals might not have had a sufficiently consistent payoff to warrant labor investment by preagricultural foragers, particularly if it interfered with other aspects of subsistence and mobility. By contrast with the East, maize in the Southwest was embraced and integrated rapidly into the subsistence base almost from its initial appearance. This observation may mean that no substantial wild plant horticulture occurred in the Southwest and that maize and its fellow Mesoamerican cultigens were the first plants to be husbanded here.

Environmental Variability and Agriculture

The Matty Canyon information underscores the importance of agriculture in the economic base that supported Early Agricultural period villages. Why would agriculture have been integrated into a foraging economy that operated in the richness and biotic diversity of the southern Basin-and-Range Province of southeastern Arizona? Several explanations have been offered for the Southwest as a whole, including dietary stress fueled by population growth, increased uncertainty or risk in obtaining food, climatic or environmental change, or simply the opportunity to add something new to the diet without risk or stress (Wills 1988a; Minnis 1985a, 1992; Hard 1986; Hunter-Anderson 1986).

Because it directly impacts technologically and organizationally simple societies, climatic variability must have played a role in structuring the choices faced by preagricultural Southwestern foragers. Dean and others (1985) have shown that variability can occur in the form of high frequency processes (those operating at scales of one human generation or less) and low frequency processes (those that operate on scales longer than a human generation). Although low frequency processes such as arroyo cutting or filling and falling or rising water tables can have effects of great magnitude, most human societies are probably adapted to deal with high frequency processes.

For southeastern Arizona, I have examined the possible effects of high frequency climatic variability as part of a study of the spread of agriculture into southeastern Arizona. Specifically, I have proposed that agriculture could have served to increase subsistence predictability and to dampen the impacts of climatically induced variation in wild resource production (B. Huckell 1990). With the onset of the late Holocene some 4,000

years ago, essentially modern climatic conditions were established. Therefore, late preceramic societies probably coped with patterns of variation in precipitation and aridity similar to those recorded in southeastern Arizona during the past 100 years. Examination of historic climatic records permits some insights into variation in resource productivity and serves as a basis for evaluating the potential effects of that variability on hunting-gathering populations. Within that context, the utility of agriculture as a coping strategy to ameliorate the effects of that variation can be analyzed.

Southeastern Arizona enjoys a biseasonal precipitation regime, which delivers approximately 55 to 65 percent of the annual total during the summer and the remainder during the winter. This biseasonal pattern creates two pulses of plant production, one in the spring and another in the late summer through fall, separated by a two- to three-month late spring-early summer drought, and a four-month winter. As is true of arid lands everywhere, amounts of seasonal and annual precipitation vary greatly, as do temperature, wind, and humidity. The Palmer Drought Severity Index (PDSI) serves as a measure that integrates "antecedent precipitation conditions and the accumulated weighted differences between precipitation, evapotranspiration, moisture recharge, and runoff" (Brazel 1985: 79). PDSI is thus a better measurement of growing conditions than precipitation alone. Positive PDSI values indicate wet conditions, negative values drought conditions; the higher the positive or negative value, the greater the surplus or deficit in moisture. Table 8.2 shows the years when winter (as reflected by PDSI values for May) or summer (as indicated by PDSI values for September) PDSI values fell more than one standard deviation above or below the seasonal mean. In southeastern Arizona, severe (PDSI > −3.0) winter droughts have a recurrence interval of about 10 to 11 years, with a standard deviation of approximately 11 years; severe summer droughts have a recurrence interval of 6 to 7 years with a standard deviation of around 10 years. Further, extremely wet winter seasons (those with PDSI > 3.0) recur approximately every 8 years with a standard deviation of 6 to 7 years; wet summers have recurrence intervals of approximately 10 to 11 years with a standard deviation of 4 years. Both dry and wet seasons can occur consecutively, and may persist for periods from as short as one season to 2 or 3 years (Table 8.2). Thus, while the seasonality of precipitation is predictable, the amount likely to fall in a given season or year is not. Drought, flood, or more "normal" conditions between these extremes can occur in any year.

Table 8.2. Significant Deviations in the Palmer Drought Severity Index for Southeastern Arizona, 1895–1986

May		September	
> -1 SD	> +1SD	> -1 SD	> +1 SD
1896 -3.55			
1900 -3.56		1900 -4.53	
1901 -3.90		1901 -3.92	
1902 -4.56		1902 -4.53	
1904 -4.77		1904 -3.33	
	1905 6.54		1905 5.68
	1906 4.73		1906 3.96
	1907 3.54		1907 3.49
		1910 -2.73	
	1915 5.25		1915 4.50
	1916 4.23		1916 3.86
			1919 6.81
	1920 6.21		
			1931 4.75
	1932 3.83		
1934 -3.20			
	1941 4.41		1941 3.25
1943 -3.93		1943 -2.82	
		1945 -2.84	
1946 -3.20			
1947 -3.59		1947 -4.74	
1948 -3.98		1948 -4.44	
		1950 -2.82	
		1951 -3.26	
		1953 -3.05	
		1956 -4.30	
		1957 -3.03	
			1958 2.83
	1966 4.14		1966 5.02
	1968 4.24		
1971 -3.15			
	1973 5.94		
1974 -3.33			
	1978 4.14		
	1979 7.34		
	1983 5.39		1983 6.90
	1984 5.54		1984 6.85
	1985 7.36		1985 5.91
	1986 3.18		

NOTE. Data from B. Huckell (1990, Table 2.6).

Another source of climatic variation is catastrophic winter freezes, defined as the persistence of very cold (20-26 degrees F) temperatures for intervals of 12 to 20 consecutive hours (Bowers 1980). Six, or possibly seven, catastrophic freezes were recorded between 1895 and 1980. They recur on average every 13 years, with a standard deviation of roughly 6 years. Such freezes are serious enough to damage or kill young and mature saguaros and other cacti, mesquites, palo verdes, and woody perennial plants that are not frost tolerant. A 1978 freeze killed most of the limbs on mature mesquite trees across much of southeastern Arizona, and oak acorn production was greatly reduced in this area and in northeastern Sonora (Jones 1980). The effects of a freeze may be felt over a broad area and across biotic communities. Finally, catastrophic freezes occur during those winters when PDSI values do not exceed 1 standard deviation, reflecting normal conditions. Thus, their impacts may be felt independently of aridity.

Climatic variability impacts plants in significant ways. Naturally, wet years may result in an abundance of food for both animals and humans. However, droughts have the opposite effect and may be particularly hard on annual plants. Annual plant productivity and rainfall are highly correlated (r = .83–.94) in arid environments (Le Houerou and others 1988), and often the variability in annual plant production is on the order of 1.5 times the variability in rainfall because of edaphic factors, soil properties, vegetation condition, and the photosynthetic efficiency of particular species. Thus the impact of a drought during which only 50 percent of the mean seasonal precipitation total is received could be a 50 to 75 percent reduction in seasonal annual plant production.

Perennial plants suffer less from single season droughts, although they still are impacted. Variation in perennial plant productivity is better correlated with the previous season's or year's precipitation. Catastrophic freezes, however, can decimate perennial plant productivity. In southeastern Arizona, severe reductions or outright failures in mesquite and other tree legume pod crops following such freezes (including noncatastrophic ones) have been reported by Felger (1977), and reductions of up to 80 percent in cholla bud and saguaro fruit production were observed by Steenbergh and Lowe (1977) after a 1971 catastrophic freeze. McPherson (1992), citing data collected by Sanchini (1981), reported a complete failure of Emory and Arizona oak acorn production in 1979, following the catastrophic freeze of 1978. Such freezes not only decimate environmental production of important perennial plants for the year, but by killing productive tree branches or saguaro arms they can have long lasting effects that might span years or decades.

The effects of such dramatic downturns in plant productivity would be felt by humans, particularly since both droughts and catastrophic freezes impact not just localized areas but potentially much of the Southwest. Human populations would be confronted by high frequency downturns in wild resource availability, possibly on the scale of once or more per decade, and the effects of such downturns would be felt at a regional level.

Foragers may cope with the risk of fluctuations in environmental production in a number of ways. Perhaps the most common is sharing food, a practice observed in most recent hunter-gatherer societies on at least some level (Low 1990; Hawkes 1992). Other coping mechanisms include intensification, storage, information sharing, or population control (Redding 1988; Kaplan and Hill 1992). Intensification may involve increasing diet breadth to include additional species, attempting to increase the production of certain species (Steward 1933: 247-248; Lawton and others 1976), or emphasizing the use of certain less variable resources. Storage of particular resources can help lessen the magnitude of swings in temporal variation in abundance. Increased sharing of information about resource distributions and abundances among groups of hunter-gatherers can help guide population movements in lean times. Population control, including infanticide and long birth spacing, can help to ensure that human numbers will not exceed some expectable minimum level of resource availability.

The responses of preagricultural Archaic foragers in southeastern Arizona to recurrent subsistence stress remain unknown. An increased scale and frequency of mobility and a shift to lower-ranked resources are probably the most predictable responses, but the persistence of drought conditions for more than one season could have had disastrous effects on foragers. Recurrent subsistence stress would have been a fact of life for Archaic populations in the Tucson Basin and in fact the whole Southwest. The development of preagricultural sedentism in southeastern Arizona is thus a complicated problem. In order to capitalize on the bounty of the Sonoran Desert and its surrounding biotic communities, these people first had to learn how to deal with the fluctuations in that bounty.

Following the advent of agriculture, it appears that a greater degree of economic security was obtained. The advantages of agriculture are four-fold, and cultivation can offset the effects of drought, perhaps not completely, but by reducing the magnitude of its impact. First and most basic is that the introduction of maize and other cultigens added a new source of food to the diet, above and beyond what was available from the natural environment. Second, to a significant degree, agriculture is under human control; this distinguishes it from wild plant and animal resources that are solely dependent on climatic conditions. Where to plant, how much to plant, how much labor to invest in the

fields, and how to use the produce are all decisions made by people. Agriculture is thus a flexible strategy that can be adjusted to the perceived needs of a group. A third advantage is that maize, in particular, has an immense productive capacity; the planting of a single kernel can produce a plant yielding hundreds of kernels. This high yield per seed is typical of many annual plants such as chenopods or amaranths, but maize produces relatively large seeds rich in carbohydrates. Finally, maize is a highly storable commodity. Storage allows delayed consumption of foods, which in turn eases problems of spatial and temporal variability and predictability of wild food resources. Reliance on delayed consumption lessens the amplitude of variations in the food supply. Of course, this same storage technology could be applied as well to certain wild resources with good storage characteristics.

Once the decision to integrate agriculture into the economy is made, farming's productive potential quickly becomes an important aspect of subsistence. The initial labor investment in agriculture is substantial; clearing and preparing the field areas, perhaps creating simple irrigation ditch systems, and digging storage pits. However, as Earle (1980) noted, the advantage of agricultural production systems is that they are less costly to intensify and have far greater intensification potential than do hunting and gathering. Once in place, the marginal costs associated with increasing agricultural production are less than those for hunting or gathering and the yield is unlimited (at least in theoretical terms). With respect to the arid Southwest, agriculture is carried out principally along stream floodplains where the highest quality soils and greatest access to water exist. The trend in stream behavior over the last 3000 to 4000 years in southeastern Arizona has been toward aggradation and the creation of fertile floodplain soils and high water tables (B. Huckell 1992). Such conditions are well documented by Cooley (1958; Eddy and Cooley 1983) for the Cienega Basin and the rest of southeastern Arizona. By growing maize and other crops, farmers in southeastern Arizona took advantage of the fact that they are summer annuals, growing during the part of the year when more than half of the total annual precipitation is likely to fall. Further, maize was grown in floodplains where the effects of variation in direct precipitation could be buffered either through access of the plant roots to the water table or by supplemental irrigation.

In summary, the integration of agriculture into late preceramic economies was a critical strategy that either permitted or enhanced the development of sedentism in southeastern Arizona. On a theoretical level, the problems associated with climatic variability and attendant fluctuations in wild resource productivity sketched above had to be overcome in some fashion in order to permit sedentism prior to agriculture. Whether preagricultural foragers sufficiently intensified and reorganized their subsistence efforts to permit the development of sedentary communities must await archaeological verification. But there should be little doubt that once maize agriculture was present, the progress toward sedentary villages in southeastern Arizona was rapid. The integration of agriculture should be viewed not as a step toward specialization but rather as one toward subsistence diversification. That it became a critical component of the economies of later societies, some of which devoted greater amounts of labor to it, is testimony to the initial success of its melding with foraging by Early Agricultural period societies.

BEYOND THE CIENEGA BASIN

The Matty Canyon sites are part of a pattern of Early Agricultural period farming-foraging village sites that can be traced across southeastern Arizona during the second millennium B.C. E. B. Sayles first discovered such sites when he and Emil Haury were surveying the San Pedro River in the mid-1930s. One was the Fairbank Site (Sayles 1941), which covered a distance of 120 m along the west bank of the river and extended at least 60 m west up a tributary arroyo. The cultural deposit was 50 cm thick in places and rich in artifacts and fire-cracked rocks. Bell-shaped pits, hearths, and pit houses were identified in the excavations. Recent investigations (B. Huckell 1990) demonstrate that this site contains abundant maize remains and is at least 2,800 years old. The Charleston Site (Sayles 1941, 1945), 10 km (6 miles) south of Fairbank, exhibited a cultural deposit that was structurally and compositionally similar to that seen at Fairbank; it was one of the first two sites at which pit houses were excavated by Sayles (1945). In 1989 when I returned to the site, the 25-cm thick cultural deposit covered a horizontal distance greater than 30 m, having been truncated on its east end by the entrenched channel of the San Pedro River. Carbonized maize from it dated approximately 2,300 to 2,500 years old. Limited investigations at AZ EE:4:1 (ASM), located west of St. David and reported to the Arizona State Museum in the early 1950s, revealed an extensive cultural deposit with pits, bell-shaped pits, and a burial (Sayles 1983). When I relocated this site in the late

1980s, the area was nearly obscured by a thick growth of tamarisk trees on a low inset terrace. The deposit was traced for approximately 65 m on the east bank of the San Pedro; it averaged about 25 cm in thickness and contained dispersed fire-cracked rocks and artifacts. A complete San Pedro point was recovered from the deposit and a flotation sample revealed carbonized maize; it has not yet been dated.

In 1991 another buried Early Agricultural period site was discovered approximately 13 km (8 miles) south of St. David. Designated AZ EE:4:20, this 100 m-long deposit contained carbonized maize, but no phase-specific diagnostic artifacts were observed. Thus, at least four large, Early Agricultural period residential settlements have been documented along the San Pedro River alone. More undoubtedly exist.

Since the initial investigations by Sayles and his Gila Pueblo colleagues, the Sulphur Spring Valley has received little research devoted to Early Agricultural period sites. Large residential sites of San Pedro phase age are present in that area; several San Pedro sites were identified in the Gila Pueblo survey of Whitewater Draw (Sayles 1941, Fig. 4). Sayles (1945) discovered one of the first San Pedro domestic structures at AZ FF:6:2 ASM (Pearce 8:4 in the Gila Pueblo site survey system), an areally extensive site located approximately 8 km (5 miles) north of Double Adobe. Slightly farther west, another San Pedro phase surface site was recorded as AZ FF:5:3 (ASM). It was approximately 150 m in diameter and contained a burned rock mound at one edge. Highway salvage excavations at the large, multicomponent Fairchild Site (AZ FF:10:2 ASM) adjacent to Double Adobe revealed a substantial San Pedro component (Windmiller 1973). Although no domestic structures were located, one large bell-shaped pit was discovered in a backhoe trench. These three examples strongly suggest that Early Agricultural period residential sites occur in this part of southeastern Arizona as well. Other San Pedro sites, including large "residential camps," are known from surface survey in the vicinity of Willcox Playa (Waters and Woosley 1990).

Whether similar residential settlements exist farther east in the San Bernardino Valley and northeast in the San Simon Valley is an open question. San Pedro phase sites exist in those general areas, and many preceramic sites of undetermined age were recorded by Sayles (1983, Fig. 6.2) along San Simon Creek. Cave Creek Village, a small pit house community of early ceramic period age, was excavated by Sayles (1945) near the mouth of Cave Creek at the northeastern end of the Chiricahua Mountains.

In the Tucson Basin there are a few more Early Agricultural period villages. Milagro, located atop a low terrace overlooking Tanque Verde Creek, is a near-surface site with small pit houses, numerous bell-shaped pits, and other features (more than 60 have been excavated) that cluster within an area 70 m in length by at least that in width. Some of the abundant carbonized maize from this site has produced radiocarbon dates of about 1200 to 1000 B.C., placing it in the San Pedro phase (B. Huckell 1990; B. Huckell and others 1994).

At the far southeastern end of the Tucson Basin and just north of the Cienega Basin, E. Thomas Hemmings and his collaborators (1968) described the Pantano Site. As exposed by Pantano Wash, this settlement was marked by a cultural deposit that was 150 m long and up to 1.5 m thick; it was rich in artifacts, animal bones, fire-cracked rocks, charcoal, and features. Hemmings and others reported two burials from the site, and in the 1970s, I observed two more. Two radiocarbon dates place the site in the early centuries A.D. (B. Huckell 1988, Table 1). The Pantano Site was never the subject of detailed investigations, and, regrettably, the October 1983 flood buried the exposure.

Younger late preceramic settlements are represented along the Santa Cruz River. One set is a closely related group of three sites named the San Agustin Mission Site (AZ BB:13:6, ASM), the Brickyard Site, and the Mission Road Site (AZ BB:13:7, ASM). The San Agustin Mission Site and a portion of the Brickyard Site were excavated in 1949 but never formally reported in the literature (see B. Huckell 1984b: 140 for a description). In addition to large numbers of burials, perhaps as many as 50, one preceramic pit house was excavated a short distance to the south. In 1986, test excavations at the Mission Road Site (Elson and Doelle 1987) revealed pit houses that were radiocarbon dated by accelerator assays on maize to 400–100 B.C. The full size of the settlement was not determined, but as revealed in testing it measured nearly 150 m by at least 50 m. One wonders whether the burials discovered at the Brickyard Site are part of a cemetery associated with this community, which probably fits within the Cienega phase.

Farther south, at the Valencia Site near Mission San Xavier del Bac, at least three late preceramic pit structures were discovered within a large Hohokam pit house village. They produced dates between 1000 to 200 B.C. on wood charcoal and may represent a portion of another late preceramic community (Bradley 1980; Doelle 1985). The extensive Hohokam occupation makes it difficult to discern details about the late preceramic component.

Barbara Roth (1989, 1992) investigated the Cortaro Fan Site, which appears to contain both preagricultural Archaic and Early Agricultural period occupations. The site is positioned at the toe of the bajada of the Tortolita Mountains on the eastern edge of the Santa Cruz floodplain. Because it was only shallowly buried, preservation of features and organic materials is poorer than at other Tucson Basin sites of comparable age. Roth recovered carbonized maize and other plant remains from pit hearths; radiocarbon dates on wood charcoal and maize yielded conflicting results, with the maize actually dating older than charcoal from the same feature. Nevertheless, the Early Agricultural period occupation clearly falls in the first millennium B.C., with both San Pedro and Cienega points present. Two-thirds of the projectile points are of the Cortaro style, which may predate the San Pedro phase (Roth and Huckell 1992). This site may have been a residential base of considerable size, but neither pit structures nor bell-shaped storage pits were encountered during investigations.

In 1993 and 1994, two large Cienega phase villages were excavated along the Santa Cruz River floodplain within what is today the Interstate 10 right-of-way in the vicinity of the Prince Road and Miracle Mile intersection (Mabry and others 1995). One of these, the Santa Cruz Bend Site, contained more than 180 round pit structures, numerous extramural pit features, and a few burials; these impressive totals reflect exposure of only a portion of the settlement. Dating between about 400 and 200 B.C., this site is the largest Cienega phase village yet discovered and results from excavations there will be extremely enlightening. The Stone Pipe Site, a short distance to the southeast, contained more than 65 pit houses and both Cienega phase and Early Ceramic period components. Dates of the Cienega phase component are similar to those from the Santa Cruz Bend Site, and only a small portion of it, too, was unearthed.

This list of sites suggests that by at least 1000 B.C., late preceramic people practicing a mixed farming-foraging economy were creating settlements that were occupied during much, if not all, of the year. AZ EE:2:35 may be the earliest such community in the Cienega Creek Basin; after 800 B.C. these settlements were increasingly common throughout southeastern Arizona.

CONCLUDING THOUGHTS

Limited though they were, the investigations conducted at the Donaldson Site and Los Ojitos offer a greatly expanded view of the late preceramic period of southeastern Arizona. The 1983 research has helped to resolve the conundrum faced by Ted Sayles, Frank Eddy, and Bill Robinson when they first discovered and attempted to understand the significance of extensive, buried preceramic sites in the Cienega Basin and San Pedro River Valley. The discovery of the presence and importance of maize, in addition to a broad range of wild resources, is probably the most significant contribution of the 1983 research. The emerging picture of late preceramic life in this region is one of stable, sedentary village communities along the permanent streams of southeastern Arizona, supported by a well-balanced farming-foraging subsistence economy. From these riverine villages in the basins, people were easily able to access the resources of different biotic communities in the surrounding mountains. Agriculture was a crucial element in their lives, underwriting the creation of these villages and helping to sustain them. In recognition of this economic strategy, it is appropriate to separate the terminal 1,500 to 2,000 years of the preceramic period and designate it as the Early Agricultural period.

The arrival of agriculture in this region no longer seems a trivial event, although debate will continue about the time and mode of its arrival as well as the speed and nature of its impact. The Matty Canyon sites do not provide information about the first appearance of agriculture in southeastern Arizona; that event occurred at least 500 years before the Donaldson Site and Los Ojitos were occupied. What they do show us is how agriculture was integrated into the subsistence strategy of this region by the mid-first millennium B.C. Available information from San Pedro phase sites like Milagro in the Tucson Basin and Fairbank in the San Pedro Valley suggest that a mixed farming-foraging economy was present in southeastern Arizona by the end of the second millennium B.C. Thus, the transition from a purely foraging existence to one also incorporating cultivation must be sought at earlier sites.

It is not my intention to convey the impression that the Donaldson Site and Los Ojitos represent Early Agricultural period settlements that are typical of the rest of the Southwest. The Matty Canyon sites are the product of decisions made by Cienega phase farmer-foragers about how best to utilize the Cienega Basin within the limits of their technology and understanding of the environment. Recent work in the Tucson Basin and San Pedro Valley suggests that similar kinds of subsistence-settlement systems arose in other parts of southeastern Arizona that afforded similar resources in similar distributions over the landscape. In other parts of the Southwest, however, we should expect to see other solutions to the problems of subsistence, and it is likely that these will not include the creation of villages like those in Matty Canyon. For example, research on the Colorado Plateau thus far has not revealed these kinds of settlements. The same mixed farming-foraging economy was adopted by the Basketmaker II people who occupied that region, but perhaps because of the large, unbroken expanses of Great Basin desertscrub and piñon-juniper woodland and the limitations of those wild resources, their settlements appear to be smaller and less permanent.

Our perception of the Early Agricultural period across the Southwest is still in its infancy. As the Matty Canyon Project demonstrates, we can benefit by returning to sites investigated by earlier archaeologists and building on their good work with new analytical technologies. We have witnessed an exciting expansion of our knowledge of preceramic subsistence during the last decade and a half, but the Southwestern landscape is liberally sprinkled with sites of this age and much more awaits our discovery, study, and understanding.

References

AGENBROAD, LARRY D.
1970 Cultural Implications from the Statistical Analysis of a Prehistoric Lithic Site in Arizona. MS, Master's thesis, Department of Anthropology, University of Arizona, Tucson.

AGOGINO, GEORGE, AND FRANK C. HIBBEN
1958 Central New Mexico Paleo-Indian Cultures. *American Antiquity* 23(4): 422–425.

ALEXANDER, HUBERT G., AND PAUL REITER
1935 Report on the Excavation of Jemez Cave, New Mexico. *School of American Research Monograph 4.* Albuquerque: University of New Mexico and Santa Fe: School of American Research.

ALLRED, KELLY W.
1993 *A Field Guide to the Grasses of New Mexico.* Department of Agricultural Communications, College of Agriculture and Home Economics. Las Cruces: New Mexico State University.

ALVAREZ DEL CASTILLO, CARLOS, AND JOEL BRIFFARD
1978 Estudio Morfológico de los Tipos de Maíz Encontrados en la Cueva El Riego, Tehuacán, Puebla. In "Arqueobotánica, Métodos y Aplicaciones," edited by Fernando Sánchez Martínez. *Colección Científica* 63: 17–24. Mexico City: Instituto Nacional de Antropología e Historia.

ANDERSON, JAMES E.
1965 Human Skeletons of Tehuacan. *Science* 148: 496–497.

ANTEVS, ERNST
1955 Geologic-Climatic Dating in the West. *American Antiquity* 20(4, Part 1): 317–355.

ASHWORTH, A., P. F. MILNER, AND J. C. WATERLOW
1973 Absorption of Iron from Maize (*Zea mays L.*) and Soya Beans (*Glycine hispida Max.*) in Jamaican Infants. *British Journal of Nutrition* 29: 269–278.

BAHRE, CONRAD JOSEPH
1991 *A Legacy of Change: Historic Human Impact on Vegetation in the Arizona Borderlands.* Tucson: University of Arizona Press.

BASS, WILLIAM M.
1971 *Human Osteology: A Laboratory and Field Manual of the Human Skeleton.* Columbia: Missouri Archaeological Society.

1987 Human Osteology: A Laboratory and Field Manual. 3d Edition. *Special Publication* 2. Columbia: Missouri Archaeological Society.

BAYHAM, FRANK E.
1982 *A Diachronic Analysis of Prehistoric Animal Exploitation at Ventana Cave.* Doctoral dissertation, Arizona State University. Ann Arbor: University Microfilms.

BAYHAM, FRANK E., DONALD H. MORRIS, AND M. STEVEN SHACKLEY
1986 Prehistoric Hunter-Gatherers of South Central Arizona: The Picacho Reservoir Archaic Project. *Anthropological Field Studies* 13. Tempe: Office of Cultural Resource Management, Department of Anthropology, Arizona State University.

BEAN, LOWELL J., AND KATHERINE S. SAUBEL
1972 *Temalpakh: Cahuilla Indian Knowledge and Usage of Plants.* Banning, California: Malki Museum, Morongo Indian Reservation.

BELL, WILLIS H., AND EDWARD F. CASTETTER
1937 The Utilization of Mesquite and Screwbean by Aborigines in the American Southwest. *University of New Mexico Bulletin* 314, *Biological Series* 5(2). Albuquerque: University of New Mexico.

1941 The Utilization of Yucca, Sotol, and Beargrass by the Aborigines in the American Southwest. *University of New Mexico Bulletin* 372, *Biological Series* 5(5). Albuquerque: University of New Mexico.

BENNETT, KENNETH A.
1987 *A Field Guide for Human Identification.* Springfield, Illinois: C. C. Thomas.

BENSON, LYMAN
1982 *The Cacti of the United States and Canada.* Palo Alto: Stanford University Press.

BENZ, BRUCE F.
1986 *Taxonomy and Evolution of Mexican Maize.* Doctoral dissertation, University of Wisconsin, Madison. Ann Arbor: University Microfilms International.

BERGGREN, GRETA
1969 *Atlas of Seeds and Small Fruits of Northwest-European Plant Species with Morphological*

BERGGREN, GRETA (*continued*)

Descriptions. *Part 2, Cyperaceae.* Stockholm: Swedish Natural Science Research Council.

BERRY, CLAUDIA F., AND MICHAEL S. BERRY

1986   Chronological and Conceptual Models of the Southwestern Archaic. In "Anthropology of the Desert West: Essays in Honor of Jesse D. Jennings," edited by Carol J. Condie and Don D. Fowler. *University of Utah Anthropological Papers* 110: 253–327. Salt Lake City: University of Utah Press.

BERRY, MICHAEL S.

1982   *Time, Space, and Transition in Anasazi Prehistory.* Salt Lake City: University of Utah Press.

1985   The Age of Maize in the Greater Southwest: A Critical Review. In "Prehistoric Food Production in North America," edited by Richard I. Ford. *Museum of Anthropology, Anthropological Papers* 75: 279–307. Ann Arbor: University of Michigan.

BINFORD, LEWIS R.

1968   Post-Pleistocene Adaptations. In *New Perspectives in Archeology*, edited by Sally R. Binford and Lewis R. Binford, pp. 313–336. Chicago: Aldine.

1980   Willow Smoke and Dogs' Tails: Hunter-Gatherer Settlement Systems and Archaeological Site Formation. *American Antiquity* 45(1): 4–20.

1982   The Archaeology of Place. *Journal of Anthropological Archaeology* 1(1): 5–31.

BIRD, ROBERT MCK., AND JUNIUS B. BIRD

1980   Gallinazo Maize from the Chicama Valley, Peru. *American Antiquity* 45(2): 325–332.

BLAKELY, ROBERT L., AND LANE BECK

1984   Tooth-tool Use Versus Dental Mutilation: A Case Study from the Prehistoric Southeast. *Midcontinental Journal of Archaeology* 9(2): 269–284.

BOHRER, VORSILA L.

1972   Paleoecology of the Hay Hollow Site, Arizona. *Fieldiana: Anthropology* 63(1): 1–30.

1975   The Prehistoric and Historic Role of the Cool-Season Grasses in the Southwest. *Economic Botany* 29(3): 199–207.

1983   New Life from Ashes: The Tale of the Burnt Bush (*Rhus trilobata*). *Desert Plants* 5(3): 122–124.

BOHRER, VORSILA L., AND KAREN R. ADAMS

1977   Ethnobotanical Techniques and Approaches at Salmon Ruin, New Mexico. *Contributions in Anthropology* 8(1). Portales, New Mexico: Eastern New Mexico University.

BOWERS, JANICE

1980   Catastrophic Freezes in the Sonoran Desert. *Desert Plants* 2(4): 232–236.

BRADLEY, BRUCE

1980   Excavations at Arizona BB:13:74, Santa Cruz Industrial Park, Tucson, Arizona. *Complete Archaeological Service Associates Paper* 1. Oracle, Arizona: Complete Archaeological Service Associates.

BRAZEL, ANTHONY J.

1985   Statewide Temperature and Moisture Trends, 1895–1983. *Arizona Climate, the First Hundred Years*, edited by William D. Sellers, Richard H. Hill, and Margaret Sanderson-Rae, pp. 79–84. Tucson: University of Arizona.

BROOKS, RICHARD H., LAWRENCE KAPLAN, HUGH C. CUTLER, AND THOMAS W. WHITAKER

1962   Plant Material from a Cave on the Rio Zape, Durango, Mexico. *American Antiquity* 27(3): 356–369.

BROTHWELL, DON R.

1963   The Macroscopic Dental Pathology of Some Earlier Human Populations. In *Dental Anthropology*, edited by Don R. Brothwell, pp. 271–288. New York: Pergamon Press.

BROWN, DAVID E.

1982a   (Editor) Biotic Communities of the American Southwest—United States and Mexico. *Desert Plants* 4(1–4).

1982b   Semidesert Grassland. In "Biotic Communities of the American Southwest—United States and Mexico," edited by David E. Brown. *Desert Plants* 4(1–4): 123–131.

1982c   Madrean Evergreen Woodland. In "Biotic Communities of the American Southwest—United States and Mexico," edited by David E. Brown. *Desert Plants* 4(1–4): 59–65.

BROWN, DAVID E., AND CHARLES H. LOWE

1981   Biotic Communities of the Southwest. *USDA Forest Service General Technical Report* RM-78, Map. Fort Collins, Colorado: Rocky Mountain Forest and Range Experiment Station.

BRYAN, KIRK

1925   Date of Channel Trenching (Arroyo Cutting) in the Arid Southwest. *Science* 62(1607): 338–344.

BRYAN, NONABAH G., AND STELLA YOUNG

1940   *Navajo Native Dyes.* Division of Education, Bureau of Indian Affairs. Washington: U.S. Department of the Interior.

BURNS, K. R., M. A. MAPLES, AND W. R. MAPLES

1976   Estimation of Age from Individual Adult Teeth. *Journal of Forensic Sciences* 21(2): 343–356.

BUSKIRK, WINFRED

1986   *The Western Apache, Living with the Land Before 1950.* Norman: University of Oklahoma Press.

CALLEN, ERIC O.

1967   Analysis of the Tehuacan Coprolites. In *The Prehistory of the Tehuacan Valley.* Vol. 1, *Environment and Subsistence*, edited by Douglas S. Byers, pp. 261–289. Austin: University of Texas Press.

CAMPBELL, JOHN M., AND FLORENCE H. ELLIS

1952   The Atrisco Sites: Cochise Manifestations in the Middle Rio Grande Valley. *American Antiquity* 17(3): 211–221.

CASHDAN, ELIZABETH, EDITOR
1990 *Risk and Uncertainty in Tribal and Peasant Economies*. Boulder: Westview Press.

CASTETTER, EDWARD F.
1935 Uncultivated Native Plants Used as Sources of Food. *University of New Mexico Bulletin* 266, *Biological Series* 4(1). Albuquerque: University of New Mexico.

CASTETTER, EDWARD F., AND WILLIS H. BELL
1942 *Pima and Papago Agriculture*. Albuquerque: University of New Mexico Press.
1951 *Yuman Indian Agriculture: Primitive Subsistence on the Lower Colorado and Gila Rivers*. Albuquerque: University of New Mexico Press.

CASTETTER, EDWARD F., AND RUTH M. UNDERHILL
1935 Ethnobiological Studies in the American Southwest II: The Ethnobiology of the Papago Indians. *University of New Mexico Bulletin, Biological Series* 4(3): 3–84. Albuquerque: University of New Mexico.

CASTETTER, EDWARD F., WILLIS H. BELL, AND ALVIN R. GROVE
1938 Ethnobotanical Studies of the American Southwest VI: The Early Utilization and Distribution of Agave in the American Southwest. *University of New Mexico Bulletin* 6(4). Albuquerque: University of New Mexico.

CATTANACH, GEORGE S., JR.
1966 A San Pedro Stage Site near Fairbank, Arizona. *The Kiva* 32(1): 1–24.

CHAMBERLIN, RALPH V.
1911 The Ethnobotany of the Gosiute Indians of Utah. *Memoirs of the American Anthropological Association* 2 (Part 5): 331–405.

CLARKE, NIGEL G., AND ROBERT S. HIRSCH
1991 Physiological, Pulpal, and Periodontal Factors Influencing Alveolar Bone Loss. In *Advances in Dental Anthropology*, edited by Marc A. Kelley and Clark Spencer Larsen, pp. 241–266. New York: Wiley-Liss.

COHEN, MARK NATHAN
1977 *The Food Crisis in Prehistory: Over-Population and the Origins of Agriculture*. New Haven: Yale University Press.

COOKE, RONALD U., AND RICHARD W. REEVES
1976 *Arroyos and Environmental Change in the American Southwest*. Oxford: Clarendon Press.

COOLEY, M. E.
1958 Recent Alluvial Geology of Cienega Valley in the Area at the Confluence of Matty Wash with Cienega Creek, Pima County, Arizona. In "A Sequence of Cultural and Alluvial Deposits in the Cienega Creek Basin, Southeastern Arizona," by Frank W. Eddy. MS, Master's thesis, Department of Anthropology, University of Arizona, Tucson.

CORDELL, LINDA S.
1984 *Prehistory of the Southwest*. New York: Academic Press.

COVILLE, FREDERICK V.
1897 Notes on the Plants Used by the Klamath Indians of Oregon. *Contributions to the U.S. National Herbarium* 5(2): 87–108. Washington.

COWAN, C. WESLEY, AND PATTY JO WATSON, EDITORS
1992 *The Origins of Agriculture, An International Perspective*. Smithsonian Institution Series in Archaeological Inquiry. Washington: Smithsonian Institution Press.

CRANE, H. R., AND JAMES B. GRIFFIN
1958 University of Michigan Radiocarbon Dates, Part 3. *Science* 128: 1117–1122.

CROSSWHITE, FRANK S.
1980 The Annual Saguaro Harvest and Crop Cycle of the Papago, with Reference to Ecology and Symbolism. *Desert Plants* 2(1): 4–61.

CURTIN, L. S. M.
1984 *By the Prophet of the Earth: Ethnobotany of the Pima*. Reprinted. Tucson: University of Arizona Press. Originally published 1949, Santa Fe: San Vicente Foundation.

CUTLER, HUGH C.
1966 Corn, Cucurbits, and Cotton from Glen Canyon. *University of Utah Anthropological Papers* 80. Salt Lake City: University of Utah.

CUTLER, HUGH C., AND THOMAS W. WHITAKER
1961 History and Distribution of the Cultivated Cucurbits in the Americas. *American Antiquity* 26(4): 469–485.

DART, ALLEN
1986 Archaeological Investigations at La Paloma: Archaic and Hohokam Occupations at Three Sites in the Northeastern Tucson Basin, Arizona. *Institute for American Research Anthropological Papers* 4. Tucson: Institute for American Research.

DEAN, JEFFREY S., ROBERT C. EULER, GEORGE J. GUMERMAN, FRED PLOG, RICHARD H. HEVLY, AND THOR V. N. KARLSTROM
1985 Human Behavior, Demography, and Paleoenvironment on the Colorado Plateaus. *American Antiquity* 50(3): 537–554.

DEBOER, WARREN R.
1988 Subterranean Storage and the Organization of Surplus: The View from Eastern North America. *Southeastern Archaeology* 7(1): 1–20.

DIBARTOLOMEO, JOSEPH R.
1979 Exostoses of the External Auditory Canal. *Annals of Otology, Rhinology, and Laryngology, Supplement* 61.

DICK, HERBERT W.
1965 Bat Cave. *School of American Research Monograph* 27. Santa Fe: School of American Research.

DI PESO, CHARLES C.
1951   The Babocomari Village Site on the Babocomari River, Southeastern Arizona. *Amerind Foundation* 5. Dragoon, Arizona: Amerind Foundation.

DOBYNS, HENRY F.
1981   From Fire to Flood: Historic Human Destruction of the Sonoran Desert Riverine Oases. *Ballena Press Anthropological Papers* 20. Socorro, New Mexico: Ballena Press.

DOEBLEY, JOHN F.
1984   "Seeds" of Wild Grasses: A Major Food of Southwestern Indians. *Economic Botany* 38(1): 52–64.
1990   Molecular Evidence and the Evolution of Maize. *Economic Botany* 44(3) Supplement: 6–27.

DOEBLEY, JOHN F., MAJOR M. GOODMAN, AND CHARLES W. STUBER
1983   Isozyme Variation in Maize from the Southwestern United States: Taxonomic and Anthropological Implications. *Maydica* 28: 97–120.
1985   Isozyme Variation in the Races of Maize from Mexico. *American Journal of Botany* 72(5): 629–639.

DOELLE, WILLIAM H.
1985   Excavations at the Valencia Site, a Preclassic Hohokam Village in the Southern Tucson Basin. *Institute for American Research Anthropological Papers* 3. Tucson: Institute for American Research.

DONGOSKE, KURT E.
1993   Burial Population and Mortuary Practices. *Archaic Occupation on the Santa Cruz Flats: The Tator Hills Archaeological Project*, edited by Carl D. Halbirt and T. Kathleen Henderson, pp. 173–181. Flagstaff: Northland Research.

DOWNUM, CHRISTIAN E., ADRIANNE G. RANKIN, AND JON S. CZAPLICKI
1986   A Class III Archaeological Survey of the Phase B Corridor, Tucson Aqueduct, Central Arizona Project. *Arizona State Museum Archaeological Series* 168. Tucson: Arizona State Museum, University of Arizona.

DRAKE, ROBERT J.
1959   Nonmarine Molluscan Remains from Recent Sediments in Matty Canyon, Pima County, Arizona. *Bulletin of the Southern California Academy of Sciences* 58(3): 146–154.

EARLE, TIMOTHY K.
1980   A Model of Subsistence Change. *Modelling Change in Prehistoric Subsistence Economies*, edited by Timothy K. Earle and Andrew L. Christenson, pp. 1–29. New York: Academic Press.

EBELING, WALTER
1986   *Handbook of Indian Foods and Fibers of Arid America*. Berkeley: University of California Press.

EDDY, FRANK W.
1958   A Sequence of Cultural and Alluvial Deposits in the Cienega Creek Basin, Southeastern Arizona. MS, Master's thesis, Department of Anthropology, University of Arizona, Tucson.

EDDY, FRANK W., AND M. E. COOLEY
1983   Cultural and Environmental History of Cienega Valley, Southeastern Arizona. *Anthropological Papers of the University of Arizona* 43. Tucson: University of Arizona Press.

EL-NAJJAR, MAHMOUD Y., DENNIS J. RYAN, CHRISTY G. TURNER II, AND BETSY LOZOFF
1976   The Etiology of Porotic Hyperostosis Among the Prehistoric and Historic Anasazi Indians of Southwestern United States. *American Journal of Physical Anthropology* 44(3): 477–487

ELSON, MARK D., AND WILLIAM H. DOELLE
1987   Archaeological Assessment of the Mission Road Extension: Testing at AZ BB:13:6 (ASM). *Institute for American Research Technical Report* 87–6. Tucson: Institute for American Research.

FELGER, RICHARD S.
1977   Mesquite in Indian Cultures of Southwestern North America. In "Mesquite, Its Biology in Two Desert Ecosystems," edited by B. B. Simpson. *US/IBP Synthesis Series* 4: 150–176. Stroudsburg, Pennsylvania: Dowden, Hutchinson, and Ross.

FELGER, RICHARD S., AND MARY BECK MOSER
1985   *People of the Desert and Sea: Ethnobotany of the Seri Indians*. Tucson: University of Arizona Press.

FISH, PAUL R., SUZANNE K. FISH, AUSTIN LONG, AND CHARLES H. MIKSICEK
1986   Early Corn Remains from Tumamoc Hill, Southern Arizona. *American Antiquity* 51(3): 563–572.

FISH, SUZANNE K., AND PAUL R. FISH
1991   Comparative Aspects of Paradigms for the Neolithic Transition in the Levant and the American Southwest. *Perspective on the Past, Theoretical Biases in Mediterranean Hunter-Gatherer Research*, edited by Geoffrey A. Clark, pp. 396–410. Philadelphia: University of Pennsylvania Press.

FISH, SUZANNE K., PAUL R. FISH, AND JOHN H. MADSEN
1990   Sedentism and Settlement Mobility in the Tucson Basin Prior to A.D. 1000. *Perspectives on Southwestern Prehistory*, edited by Paul E. Minnis and Charles L. Redman, pp. 76–163. Boulder: Westview Press.
1992   Early Sedentism and Agriculture in the Northern Tucson Basin. In "The Marana Community in the Hohokam World," edited by Suzanne K. Fish, Paul R. Fish, and John H. Madsen. *Anthropological Papers of the University of Arizona* 56: 11–19. Tucson: University of Arizona Press.

FISH, SUZANNE K., PAUL R. FISH, CHARLES H. MIKSICEK, AND JOHN H. MADSEN
1985   Prehistoric Agave Cultivation in Southern Arizona. *Desert Plants* 7(2): 107–112.

FITTING, JAMES E.
1973 An Early Mogollon Community: A Preliminary Report on the Winn Canyon Site. *The Artifact* 11(1–2).

FLANNERY, KENT V.
1973 The Origins of Agriculture. *Annual Review of Anthropology* 2: 271–310. Palo Alto: Annual Reviews.
1986 (Editor) *Guila Naquitz, Archaic Foraging and Early Agriculture in Oaxaca, Mexico.* New York: Academic Press.

FLANNERY, KENT V., AND MICHAEL D. COE
1968 Social and Economic Systems in Formative Mesoamerica. In *New Perspectives in Archeology*, edited by Sally R. Binford and Lewis R. Binford, pp. 267–283. Chicago: Aldine.

FORD, KAREN COWAN
1975 Las Yerbas de la Gente: A Study of Hispano-American Medicinal Plants. *Museum of Anthropology, Anthropological Papers* 60. Ann Arbor: University of Michigan.

FORD, RICHARD I.
1975 Re-Excavation of Jemez Cave, New Mexico. *Awanyu* 3(3): 13–27.
1981 Gardening and Farming before A.D. 1000: Patterns of Prehistoric Cultivation North of Mexico. *Journal of Ethnobiology* 1(1): 6–27.
1984 Ecological Consequences of Early Agriculture in the Southwest. *Papers on the Archaeology of Black Mesa, Arizona*, Vol. 2, edited by Stephen Plog and Shirley Powell, pp. 127–138. Carbondale: Southern Illinois University Press.
1986 Reanalysis of Cucurbits in the Ethnobotanical Laboratory, University of Michigan. *The Missouri Archaeologist* 47: 13–31.

FRITZ, JOHN M.
1974 The Hay Hollow Site Subsistence System, East Central Arizona. MS, Doctoral dissertation, Department of Anthropology, University of Chicago.

FRY, GARY F.
1976 Analysis of Prehistoric Coprolites from Utah. *University of Utah Anthropological Papers* 97. Salt Lake City: University of Utah.

GALINAT, WALTON C.
1970 The Cupule and its Role in the Origin and Evolution of Maize. *Agricultural Experiment Station Bulletin* 585. Amherst: University of Massachusetts.
1985 Domestication and Diffusion of Maize. In "Prehistoric Food Production in North America," edited by Richard I. Ford. *Museum of Anthropology, Anthropological Papers* 75: 245–278. Ann Arbor: University of Michigan.
1988 The Origin of Maiz de Ocho. *American Anthropologist* 90(3): 682–683.

GALLAGHER, MARSHA V.
1977 Contemporary Ethnobotany Among the Apache of the Clarkdale, Arizona Area, Coconino and Prescott National Forests. *Forest Service Report* 14. Albuquerque: Southwestern Region, U.S. Department of Agriculture.

GASSER, ROBERT E.
1981 The Plant Remains from the Escalante Ruin Group. In "Late Hohokam Prehistory in Southern Arizona," by David E. Doyel. *Gila Press Contributions to Archaeology* 2: 84–89. Scottsdale.
1982 Hohokam Use of Desert Plant Foods. *Desert Plants* 3(4): 216–234.
1985 Plant Remains. In "Excavations at the Valencia Site, a Preclassic Hohokam Village in the Southern Tucson Basin," by William H. Doelle. *Institute for American Research Anthropological Papers* 3: 225–234. Tucson: Institute for American Research.
1987 Macrofloral Analysis. In "The Archaeology of the San Xavier Bridge Site (AZ BB:13:14), Tucson Basin, Southern Arizona," edited by John C. Ravesloot. *Arizona State Museum Archaeological Series* 171: 303–318. Tucson: Arizona State Museum, University of Arizona.

GASSER, ROBERT E., AND E. CHARLES ADAMS
1981 Aspects of Deterioration of Plant Remains in Archaeological Sites: The Walpi Archaeological Project. *Journal of Ethnobiology* 1(1): 182–192.

GEBAUER, ANNE BIRGITTE, AND T. DOUGLAS PRICE
1992 Transitions to Agriculture in Prehistory. *Monographs in World Archaeology* 4. Madison, Wisconsin: Prehistory Press.

GEHLBACH, FREDERICK R.
1981 *Mountain Islands and Desert Seas, a Natural History of the U.S.–Mexican Borderlands.* College Station: Texas A & M Press.

GENOVESE, SANTIAGO
1967 Proportionality of Long Bones and Their Relation to Stature among Mesoamericans. *American Journal of Physical Anthropology* 26(1): 67–78.

GENTRY, HOWARD S.
1982 *Agaves of Continental North America.* Tucson: University of Arizona Press.

GIFFORD, E. W.
1971 California Balanophagy. *The California Indians*, compiled and edited by Robert F. Heizer and M. A. Whipple, pp. 237–241. Berkeley: University of California Press.

GILLESPIE, WILLIAM B.
1989 Faunal Remains from Four Sites along the Tucson Aqueduct: Prehistoric Exploitation of Jack Rabbits and Other Vertebrates in the Avra Valley. In "Hohokam Archaeology along Phase B of the Tucson Aqueduct, Central Arizona Project, Volume 1, Syntheses and Interpretations, Part 1," edited by

GILLESPIE, WILLIAM B. (*continued*)
> Jon S. Czaplicki and John B. Ravesloot. *Arizona State Museum Archaeological Series* 178 (1, Part 1): 171–237. Tucson: Arizona State Museum, University of Arizona.

GILMAN, PATRICIA A.
1987   Architecture as Artifact: Pit Structures and Pueblos in the American Southwest. *American Antiquity* 52(3): 538–564.

GILPIN, DENNIS
1992   Salina Springs and Lukachukai: Late Archaic/Early Basketmaker Habitation Sites in the Chinle Valley, Northeastern Arizona. Paper presented at the 57th Annual Meeting of the Society for American Archaeology, Pittsburgh.

GLADWIN, HAROLD S., EMIL W. HAURY, E. B. SAYLES, AND NORA GLADWIN
1937   Excavations at Snaketown: Material Culture. *Medallion Paper* 25. Globe, Arizona: Gila Pueblo.

GLASS, MARGARET
1984   . Faunal Remains from Hohokam Sites in the Rosemont Area, Northern Santa Rita Mountains. In "Hohokam Habitation Sites in the Northern Santa Rita Mountains," by Alan Ferg, Kenneth C. Rozen, William L. Deaver, Martyn D. Tagg, David A. Phillips, Jr., and David A. Gregory. *Arizona State Museum Archaeological Series* 147(2): 823–915. Tucson: Arizona State Museum, University of Arizona.

GOODMAN, ALAN H., AND JEROME C. ROSE
1991   Dental Enamel Hypoplasias as Indicators of Nutritional Status. In *Advances in Dental Anthropology*, edited by Marc A. Kelley and Clark Spencer Larsen, pp. 279–293. New York: Wiley-Liss.

GOODMAN, ALAN H., G. J. ARMELAGOS, AND JEROME C. ROSE
1980   Enamel Hypoplasias as Indicators of Stress in Three Populations from Illinois. *Human Biology* 52(3): 515–528.

GUERNSEY, SAMUEL J.
1931   Explorations in Northeastern Arizona. Report on the Archaeological Fieldwork of 1920–1923. *Papers of the Peabody Museum of American Archaeology and Ethnology* 12 (1). Cambridge: Harvard University.

GUERNSEY, SAMUEL J., AND ALFRED V. KIDDER
1921   Basket-Maker Caves of Northeastern Arizona. Report on the Explorations, 1916–1917. *Papers of the Peabody Museum of American Archaeology and Ethnology* 8(2). Cambridge: Harvard University.

GUNN, CHARLES R.
1981   Seed Topography in Fabaceae. *Seed Science and Technology* 9: 737–757

GUNTHER, ERNA
1973   *Ethnobotany of Western Washington*. Seattle: University of Washington Press.

HALBIRT, CARL D., AND T. KATHLEEN HENDERSON, EDITORS
1993   *Archaic Occupation on the Santa Cruz Flats: The Tator Hills Archaeological Project*. Flagstaff: Northland Research.

HALBIRT, CARL D., ANNICK KALER, AND KURT E. DONGOSKE
1993   Pit Features from Coffee Camp: An Evaluation of Form and Function. *Archaic Occupation on the Santa Cruz Flats: The Tator Hills Archaeological Project*, edited by Carl D. Halbirt and T. Kathleen Henderson, pp. 129–171. Flagstaff: Northland Research.

HARD, ROBERT J.
1986   *Ecological Relationships Affecting the Rise of Farming Economies: A Test from the American Southwest*. Doctoral dissertation, University of New Mexico, Albuquerque. Ann Arbor: University Microfilms

HARGRAVE, LYNDON L.
1970   Feathers from Sand Dune Cave: A Basketmaker Cave near Navajo Mountain, Utah. *Museum of Northern Arizona Technical Series* 9. Flagstaff: Northern Arizona Society of Science and Art.

HARRIS, DAVID R., AND GORDON C. HILLMAN, EDITORS
1989   Foraging and Farming, the Evolution of Plant Domestication. *One World Archaeology* 13. London: Unwin Hyman.

HARTNADY, PHILLIP, AND JEROME C. ROSE
1991   Abnormal Tooth-Loss Patterns among Archaic-Period Inhabitants of the Lower Pecos Region. *Advances in Dental Anthropology*, edited by Marc A. Kelley and Clark Spencer Larsen, pp. 267–278. New York: Wiley-Liss.

HASTINGS, JAMES R., AND RAYMOND M. TURNER
1965   *The Changing Mile: An Ecological Study of Vegetation Change with Time in the Lower Mile of an Arid and Semi-arid Region*. Tucson: University of Arizona Press.

HAURY, EMIL W.
1950   *The Stratigraphy and Archaeology of Ventana Cave, Arizona*. Albuquerque: University of New Mexico Press and Tucson: University of Arizona Press.

1957   An Alluvial Site on the San Carlos Indian Reservation, Arizona. *American Antiquity* 23(1): 2–27.

1962   The Greater American Southwest. In "Courses Toward Urban Life: Archaeological Considerations of Some Cultural Alternates," edited by Robert J. Braidwood and Gordon R. Willey, pp. 106–131. *Viking Fund Publications in Anthropology* 32. New York: Wenner-Gren Foundation.

1976   *The Hohokam: Desert Farmers and Craftsmen. Excavations at Snaketown, 1964–1965*. Tucson: University of Arizona Press.

1983 Concluding Remarks. In "The Cochise Cultural Sequence in Southeastern Arizona," by E. B. Sayles. *Anthropological Papers of the University of Arizona* 42: 158–166. Tucson: University of Arizona Press.

HAWKES, KRISTEN
1992 Sharing and Collective Action. *Evolutionary Ecology and Human Behavior*, edited by Eric Alden Smith and Bruce Winterhalder, pp. 269–300. New York: Aldine de Gruyter.

HAWKEY, DIANE
1995 Assessment of Subsistence Strategy through Dental Pathology: Classic Period Southern and Central Arizona Hohokam. MS, Department of Anthropology, Arizona State University, Tempe.

HEIZER, ROBERT F., AND ALBERT B. ELSASSER
1980 The Natural World of the California Indians. *California Natural History Guides* 46. Berkeley and Los Angeles: University of California Press.

HEMMINGS, E. THOMAS, M. D. ROBINSON,
AND R. N. ROGERS
1968 Field Report on Pantano Site (AZ EE:2:50). MS on file, Arizona State Museum Library, University of Arizona, Tucson.

HENDRICKS, DAVID M.
1985 *Arizona Soils.* Tucson: College of Agriculture, University of Arizona.

HENDRICKSON, DEAN A., AND W. L. MINCKLEY
1984 Ciénegas—Vanishing Climax Communities of the American Southwest. *Desert Plants* 6(3): 131–175.

HILL, W. W.
1938 The Agricultural and Hunting Methods of the Navajo Indians. *Yale University Publications in Anthropology* 18. New Haven: Yale University Press.

HINTON, ROBERT J.
1981 Form and Patterning of Anterior Tooth Wear Among Aboriginal Human Groups. *American Journal of Physical Anthropology* 54(4): 555–564.

HOFFMEISTER, DONALD F.
1986 *Mammals of Arizona.* Tucson: University of Arizona Press and Phoenix: Arizona Game and Fish Department.

HRDLIČKA, ALEŠ
1935 Ear Exostoses. *Smithsonian Miscellaneous Collections* 93(6): 1–101.

HUBBARD, R. N. L. B.
1980 Development of Agriculture in Europe and the Near East: Evidence from Quantitative Studies. *Economic Botany* 34(1): 51–67.

HUCKELL, BRUCE B.
1973 The Hardt Creek Site. *The Kiva* 39(2): 171–197.
1983 Additional Chronological Data on Cienega Valley, Arizona. Appendix C in "Cultural and Environmental History of Cienega Valley, Southeastern Arizona," by Frank W. Eddy and M. E. Cooley. *Anthropological Papers of the University of Arizona* 43: 57–58. Tucson: University of Arizona Press.
1984a The Archaic Occupation of the Rosemont Area, Northern Santa Rita Mountains, Southeastern Arizona. *Arizona State Museum Archaeological Series* 147(1). Tucson: Arizona State Museum, University of Arizona.
1984b The Paleo-Indian and Archaic Occupation of the Tucson Basin: An Overview. *The Kiva* 49(3–4): 133–145.
1988 Late Archaic Archaeology of the Tucson Basin: A Status Report. In "Recent Research on Tucson Basin Prehistory: Proceedings of the Second Tucson Basin Conference," edited by William H. Doelle and Paul R. Fish. *Institute for American Research Anthropological Papers* 10: 57–80. Tucson: Institute for American Research.
1990 *Late Preceramic Farmer-Foragers in Southeastern Arizona: A Cultural and Ecological Consideration of the Spread of Agriculture in the Arid Southwestern United States.* Doctoral dissertation, Arid Lands Resource Sciences, University of Arizona, Tucson. Ann Arbor: University Microfilms.
1992 Mid-Late Holocene Stream Behavior and the Transition to Agriculture in Southeastern Arizona. Paper presented at the 57th Annual Meeting of the Society for American Archaeology, Pittsburgh.

HUCKELL, BRUCE B., AND LISA W. HUCKELL
1984 Excavations at Milagro, a Late Archaic Site in the Eastern Tucson Basin. MS on file, Cultural Resource Management Division, Arizona State Museum, University of Arizona, Tucson.
1988 Crops Come to the Desert: Late Preceramic Agriculture in Southeastern Arizona. Paper presented at the 53rd Annual Meeting of the Society for American Archaeology, Phoenix.
1990 The Adoption of Agriculture in the Arid Southwest: New Investigations at the Fairbank Site, San Pedro River Valley. Paper presented at the 55th Annual Meeting of the Society for American Archaeology, Las Vegas.

HUCKELL, BRUCE B., LISA W. HUCKELL,
AND SUZANNE K. FISH
1994 Investigations at Milagro, a Late Preceramic Site in the Eastern Tucson Basin. *Center for Desert Archaeology Technical Report* 94-5. Tucson: Center for Desert Archaeology.

HUCKELL, BRUCE B., MARTYN D. TAGG,
AND LISA W. HUCKELL
1987 The Corona de Tucson Project: Prehistoric Use of a Bajada Environment. *Arizona State Museum Archaeological Series* 174. Tucson: Arizona State Museum, University of Arizona.

HUCKELL, LISA W.

1984 Archaeobotanical Remains from Archaic Sites in the Rosemont Area, Santa Rita Mountains, Arizona. In "The Archaic Occupation of the Rosemont Area, Northern Santa Rita Mountains, Southeastern Arizona," by Bruce B. Huckell. *Arizona State Museum Archaeological Series* 147(1): 267–274. Tucson: Arizona State Museum, University of Arizona.

1986 Botanical Remains. In "The 1985 Excavations at the Hodges Site, Pima County, Arizona," edited by Robert W. Layhe. *Arizona State Museum Archaeological Series* 170: 241–269. Tucson: Arizona State Museum, University of Arizona.

1987 Archaeobotanical Remains. In "The Corona de Tucson Project: Prehistoric Use of a Bajada Environment," by Bruce B. Huckell, Martyn D. Tagg, and Lisa W. Huckell. *Arizona State Museum Archaeological Series* 174. Tucson: Arizona State Museum, University of Arizona.

1993 The Shell Assemblage from Coffee Camp. *Archaic Occupation on the Santa Cruz Flats: The Tator Hills Archaeological Project*, edited by Carl D. Halbirt and T. Kathleen Henderson, pp. 305–316. Flagstaff: Northland Research.

1994 Paleoethnobotanical Analysis. In "Investigations at Milagro, a Late Preceramic Site in the Eastern Tucson Basin," by Bruce B. Huckell, Lisa W. Huckell, and Suzanne K. Fish. *Center for Desert Archaeology Technical Report* 94–5: 33–40. Tucson: Center for Desert Archaeology.

HUMAN SYSTEMS RESEARCH

1973 *Technical Manual, 1973 Survey of the Tularosa Basin*. High Rolls, New Mexico: Human Systems Research.

HUMPHREY, ROBERT R.

1958 *The Desert Grassland*. Tucson: University of Arizona Press.

HUNTER-ANDERSON, ROSALIND L.

1986 *Prehistoric Adaptation in the American Southwest*. Cambridge, England: University of Cambridge Press.

IRWIN-WILLIAMS, CYNTHIA

1967 Picosa: The Elementary Southwestern Culture. *American Antiquity* 32(4): 441–457.

1973 The Oshara Tradition: Origins of Anasazi Culture. *Contributions in Anthropology* 5(1). Portales, New Mexico: Eastern New Mexico University.

1979 Post-Pleistocene Archeology, 7000–2000 B.C. *Handbook of North American Indians*, William C. Sturtevant, general editor, Vol. 9, *Southwest*, edited by Alfonso Ortiz, pp. 31–42. Washington: Smithsonian Institution.

1985 Review of "Time, Space, and Transition in Anasazi Prehistory," by Michael S. Berry, published by the University of Utah Press, Salt Lake City. *The Kiva* 51(1): 44–48.

IRWIN-WILLIAMS, CYNTHIA, AND S. TOMPKINS

1968 Excavations at En Medio Shelter, New Mexico. *Contributions in Anthropology* 1(2). Portales, New Mexico: Eastern New Mexico University.

JOHNSON, ALFRED E.

1960 The Place of the Trincheras Culture of Northern Sonora in Southwestern Archaeology. MS, Master's thesis, Department of Anthropology, University of Arizona, Tucson.

JONES, WARREN

1980 Effects of the 1978 Freeze on Native Plants of Sonora, Mexico. *Desert Plants* 1(1): 33–36.

KAPLAN, HILLARD, AND KIM HILL

1992 The Evolutionary Ecology of Food Acquisition. *Evolutionary Ecology and Human Behavior*, edited by Eric Alden Smith and Bruce Winterhalder, pp. 167–201. New York: Aldine de Gruyter.

KEARNEY, THOMAS H., AND ROBERT H. PEEBLES

1960 *Arizona Flora*. Second Edition. Berkeley: University of California Press.

KELLEY, J. CHARLES

1959 The Desert Cultures and the Balcones Phase: Archaic Manifestations in the Southwest and Texas. *American Antiquity* 24(3): 276–288.

KELLY, ROBERT L.

1983 Hunter-Gatherer Mobility Strategies. *Journal of Anthropological Research* 39: 277–306.

1992 Mobility/Sedentism: Concepts, Archaeological Measures, and Effects. *Annual Review of Anthropology* 21: 43–66.

KELLY, WILLIAM H.

1977 Cocopa Ethnography. *Anthropological Papers of the University of Arizona* 29. Tucson: University of Arizona Press.

KENNEDY, G. E.

1986 The Relationship Between Auditory Exostoses and Cold Water: A Latitudinal Analysis. *American Journal of Physical Anthropology* 71(4): 401–415.

KIDDER, ALFRED V.

1924 An Introduction to the Study of Southwestern Archaeology, with a Preliminary Account of the Excavations at Pecos. *Papers of the Southwestern Expedition* 1. New Haven: Published for Phillips Academy, Andover, by Yale University Press.

KIDDER, ALFRED V., AND SAMUEL J. GUERNSEY

1919 Archaeological Explorations in Northeastern Arizona. *Bureau of American Ethnology Bulletin* 65. Washington: Smithsonian Institution.

1922 Part II, Notes on the Artifacts and on Foods. In "A Basket Maker Cave in Kane County, Utah," by Jesse L. Nusbaum, pp. 54-153. *Indian Notes and Monographs*. New York: Museum of the American Indian, Heye Foundation.

KIRK, DONALD R.
1975 *Wild Edible Plants of the Western United States.* Healdsburg, California: Naturegraph Publishers.

LARSEN, CLARK S.
1985 Dental Modifications and Tool Use in the Western Great Basin. *American Journal of Physical Anthropology* 67(4): 393–403.

LARSEN, CLARK S., AND DAVID H. THOMAS
1982 The Anthropology of St. Catherines Island: Vol. 4, The St. Catherines Period Mortuary Complex. *Anthropological Papers of the American Museum of Natural History* 57: 271–341. New York: American Museum of Natural History.

LAWTON, HARRY W., PHILIP J. WILKE, MARY DEDECKER, AND WILLIAM J. MASON
1976 Agriculture among the Paiute of Owens Valley. *The Journal of California Anthropology* 3(1): 13–50.

LEBLANC, RAYMOND
1992 Wedges, Piéces Esquillées, Bipolar Cores, and Other Things: An Alternative to Shott's View of Bipolar Industries. *North American Archaeologist* 13(1): 1–14.

LE HOUEROU, HENRI N., R. L. BINGHAM, AND W. SKERBEK
1988 Relationship between the Variability of Primary Production and the Variability of Annual Precipitation in World Arid Lands. *Journal of Arid Environments* 15(1): 1–18.

LEHR, J. HARRY
1978 *A Catalogue of the Flora of Arizona.* Phoenix: Desert Botanical Garden

LEONARD, ROBERT D., PETER H. MCCARTNEY, MELISSA GOULD, JAMES CARLUCCI, AND GILBERT D. GLENNIE
1983 Arizona D:11:449. In "Excavations on Black Mesa, 1983, A Descriptive Report," edited by Andrew L. Christenson and William J. Parry. *Center for Archaeological Research Paper* 46: 124–154. Carbondale: Southern Illinois University.

LEVEY, M., AND NOURY AL-KHALEDY
1967 *The Medical Formulary of al-Samargandi and the Relation of Early Arabic Samples to Those Found in the Indigenous Medicine of the Near East and India.* Philadelphia: University of Pennsylvania Press.

LIBBY, WILLARD F.
1955 *Radiocarbon Dating.* (Second Edition.) Chicago: University of Chicago Press.

LIGHTFOOT, KENT G., AND GARY M. FEINMAN
1982 Social Differentiation and Leadership Development in Early Pithouse Villages in the Mogollon Region of the American Southwest. *American Antiquity* 47(1): 64–86.

LISTER, ROBERT H.
1958 Archaeological Excavations in the Northern Sierra Madre Occidental, Chihuahua and Sonora, Mexico. *University of Colorado Studies, Series in Anthropology* 7. Boulder: University of Colorado.

LOCKETT, H. CLAIBORNE, AND LYNDON L. HARGRAVE
1953 Woodchuck Cave, A Basketmaker II Site in Tsegi Canyon, Arizona. *Museum of Northern Arizona Bulletin* 26. Flagstaff: Northern Arizona Society of Science and Art.

LONG, AUSTIN B., F. BENZ, D. J. DONAHUE, A. J. T. JULL, AND L. J. TOOLIN
1989 First Direct AMS Dates on Early Maize from Tehuacán, Mexico. *Radiocarbon* 31(3): 1035–1040.

LOTHROP, JONATHAN C., AND RICHARD MICHAEL GRAMLY
1982 *Piéces Esquillées* from the Vail Site. *Archaeology of Eastern North America* 10: 1–22.

LOVEJOY, C. OWEN
1985 Dental Wear in the Libben Population: Its Functional Pattern and Role in the Determining of Adult Skeletal Age at Death. *American Journal of Physical Anthropology* 68(1): 47–56.

LOW, BOBBI S.
1990 Human Responses to Environmental Extremeness and Uncertainty: A Cross-Cultural Perspective. *Risk and Uncertainty in Tribal and Peasant Economies*, edited by Elizabeth Cashdan, pp. 229–255. Boulder: Westview Press.

LOWE, CHARLES H.
1964 *The Vertebrates of Arizona.* Tucson: University of Arizona Press.
1981 The Vegetation and Flora of the Sycamore Canyon Area and Deering Spring Area in the Santa Rita Mountains, Arizona. In "An Environmental Inventory of the Rosemont Area in Southern Arizona, Vol. 3, The 1981 Supplemental Report," assembled by E. Lendell Cockrum, pp. 21–61. MS on file, Arizona State Museum, University of Arizona, Tucson.

LUKACS, JOHN R., AND ROBERT F. PASTOR
1988 Activity-Induced Patterns of Dental Abrasion in Prehistoric Pakistan: Evidence from Mehrgarh and Harappa. *American Journal of Physical Anthropology* 76(3): 377–398.

MABRY, JONATHAN B., AND JEFFERY J. CLARK
1994 Early Village Life on the Santa Cruz River. *Archaeology in Tucson* 8(1): 1–5. Tucson: Center for Desert Archaeology.

MABRY, JONATHAN B., DEBORAH L. SWARTZ, HELGA WOCHERL, JEFFERY J. CLARK, GAVIN H. ARCHER, AND MICHAEL LINDEMAN
1995 Archaeological Investigations of Early Village Sites in the Middle Santa Cruz Valley: Descriptions of the Santa Cruz Bend, Square Hearth, Stone Pipe, and Canal Sites. *Center for Desert Archaeology Anthropological Papers* 18. Tucson: Center for Desert Archaeology.

MACHETTE, MICHAEL N.
1985 Calcic Soils of the Southwestern United States. *Geological Society of America Special Paper* 203.

MacNeish, Richard S.
1964   Ancient Mesoamerican Civilization. *Science* 143 (3603): 531–537.
1992   *The Origins of Agriculture and Settled Life*. Norman: University of Oklahoma Press.
1993   (Editor) Preliminary Investigations of the Archaic in the Region of Las Cruces, New Mexico. *Historic and Natural Resources Report* 9. Fort Bliss: Cultural Resource Management Program, Directorate of the Environment, U.S. Army Air Defense Artillery Center.

Mandel, Irwin D.
1976   Nonimmunologic Aspects of Caries Resistance. *Journal of Dental Research* 55: C22-C31.

Mangelsdorf, Paul C.
1974   *Corn: Its Origin, Evolution, and Improvement*. Cambridge: The Belknap Press of Harvard University Press.

Mangelsdorf, Paul C., and Robert H. Lister
1956   Archaeological Evidence on the Diffusion and Evolution of Maize in Northern Mexico. *Botanical Museum Leaflets* 17(6): 151–178.

Mangelsdorf, Paul C., and Richard G. Reeves
1939   The Origin of Indian Corn and Its Relatives. *Texas Agricultural Experiment Station Bulletin* 574. College Station: Agricultural and Mechanical College of Texas.

Mangelsdorf, Paul C., and E. Earle Smith, Jr.
1949   New Archaeological Evidence on Evolution in Maize. *Botanical Museum Leaflets, Harvard University* 13(8): 213–247.

Martin, Alexander C.
1946   The Comparative Internal Morphology of Seeds. *The American Midland Naturalist* 36(3): 513–660.

Martin, Alexander C., and William D. Barkley
1961   *Seed Identification Manual*. Berkeley: University of California Press.

Martin, Paul Schultz
1963   *The Last 10,000 Years: A Fossil Pollen Record of the American Southwest*. Tucson. University of Arizona Press.
1983a   Vegetation. In "Cultural and Environmental History of Cienega Valley, Southeastern Arizona," by Frank W. Eddy and M. E. Cooley. *Anthropological Papers of the University of Arizona* 43: 4–5. Tucson: University of Arizona Press.
1983b   Pollen Profile from the East Bank of Cienega Creek. In "Cultural and Environmental History of Cienega Valley, Southeastern Arizona," by Frank W. Eddy and M. E. Cooley. *Anthropological Papers of the University of Arizona* 43: 42–44. Tucson: University of Arizona Press.

Martin, Paul Schultz, and James Schoenwetter
1960   Arizona's Oldest Cornfield. *Science* 132(3418): 33–34.

Martin, Paul Schultz, James Schoenwetter, and Bernard C. Arms
1961   *The Last 10,000 Years: Southwest Palynology and Prehistory*. Tucson: Geochronology Laboratories, University of Arizona.

Martin, Paul Sydney
1943   The SU Site: Excavations at a Mogollon Village, Western New Mexico, Second Season, 1941. *Field Museum of Natural History Anthropological Series* 32(2), *Publication* 526. Chicago: Field Museum of Natural History.

Martin, Paul Sydney, and Fred Plog
1973   *The Archaeology of Arizona: A Study of the Southwest Region*. New York: Doubleday-Natural History Press.

Martin, Paul Sydney, and John B. Rinaldo
1950   Sites of the Reserve Phase, Pine Lawn Valley, Western New Mexico. *Fieldiana: Anthropology* 38(3). Chicago Natural History Museum.
1951   The Southwestern Co-tradition. *Southwestern Journal of Anthropology* 7(3): 215–229.

Martin, Paul Sydney, John B. Rinaldo, and Elaine Bluhm
1954   Caves of the Reserve Area. *Fieldiana: Anthropology* 42. Chicago Natural History Museum.

Martin, Paul Sydney, John B. Rinaldo, Elaine Bluhm, Hugh C. Cutler, and Roger Grange, Jr.
1952   Mogollon Cultural Continuity and Change: The Stratigraphic Analysis of Tularosa and Cordova Caves. *Fieldiana: Anthropology* 40. Chicago Natural History Museum.

Mason, Herbert L.
1957   *A Flora of the Marshes of California*. Berkeley and Los Angeles: University of California Press.

Matson, R. G.
1991   *The Origins of Southwestern Agriculture*. Tucson: University of Arizona Press.

Matson, R. G., and Brian Chisholm
1991   Basketmaker II Subsistence: Carbon Isotopes and Other Dietary Indicators from Cedar Mesa, Utah. *American Antiquity* 56(3): 444–459.

McLaughlin, Steve, and Willard Van Asdall
1977   Flora and Vegetation of the Rosemont Area. In "An Environmental Inventory of the Rosemont Area in Southern Arizona, Vol. 1, The Present Environment," edited by Russell Davis and Joan R. Callahan, pp. 64–98. MS on file, Arizona State Museum, University of Arizona, Tucson.

McPherson, Guy R.
1992   Ecology of Oak Woodlands in Arizona. In "Ecology and Management of Oak and Associated Woodlands," coordinated by Peter F. Ffolliott, Gerald J. Gottfried, Victor Manuel Hernandez C., Alfredo Ortega-Rubio, and R. H. Hamre. *USDA*

Forest Service General Technical Report RM–218: 24–33. Fort Collins, Colorado: Rocky Mountain Forest and Range Experiment Station.

MCWILLIAMS, KENNETH R.
1971 A Cochise Human Skeleton from Southeastern Arizona. *The Cochise Quarterly* 1(2): 24–30.

MEALS FOR MILLIONS/FREEDOM FROM
HUNGER FOUNDATION
1980 *O'odham I:waki, Wild Greens of the Desert People.* Tucson: Meals for Millions/Freedom from Hunger Foundation.

MERBS, CHARLES F.
1983 Patterns of Activity-Induced Pathology in a Canadian Inuit Population. *Archaeological Survey of Canada Paper* 119. Ottawa: National Museums of Canada.

MERRILL, RUTH EARL
1970 *Plants Used in Basketry by the California Indians.* Ramona, California: Acoma Books.

MIKSICEK, CHARLES H.
1986a Plant Remains. In "Archaeological Investigations at the West Branch Site: Early and Middle Rincon Occupation in the Southern Tucson Basin," by Frederick W. Huntington. *Institute for American Research Anthropological Papers* 5: 289–314. Tucson: Institute for American Research.
1986b Plant Remains from the Tanque Verde Wash Site. In "Archaeological Investigations at the Tanque Verde Wash Site: A Middle Rincon Settlement in the Eastern Tucson Basin," edited by Mark D. Elson. *Institute for American Research Anthropological Papers* 7: 371–394. Tucson: Institute for American Research.
1987 Archaic Plant Remains from AZ BB:13:6. In "Archaeological Assessment of the Mission Road Extension," by Mark D. Elson and William H. Doelle. *Institute for American Research Technical Report* 87–6: 66–69. Tucson: Institute for American Research.

MILNER, GEORGE R., AND CLARK SPENCER LARSEN
1991 Teeth as Artifacts of Human Behavior: Intentional Mutilation and Accidental Modification. *Advances in Dental Anthropology*, edited by Marc A. Kelley and Clark Spencer Larsen, pp. 357–378. New York: Wiley-Liss.

MINCKLEY, W. L., AND DAVID E. BROWN
1982 Wetlands. In "Biotic Communities of the American Southwest—United States and Mexico," edited by David E. Brown. *Desert Plants* 4(1–4): 224–287.

MINNIS, PAUL E.
1985a Domesticating People and Plants in the Greater Southwest. In "Prehistoric Food Production in North America," edited by Richard I. Ford. *Museum of Anthropology, Anthropological Papers* 75: 309–339. Ann Arbor: University of Michigan.
1985b *Social Adaptation to Food Stress, A Prehistoric Southwestern Example.* Chicago: University of Chicago Press.
1992 Earliest Plant Cultivation in the Desert Borderlands of North America. In "The Origins of Agriculture, An International Perspective," edited by C. Wesley Cowan and Patty Jo Watson, pp. 121–141. *Smithsonian Institution Series in Archaeological Inquiry.* Washington: Smithsonian Institution Press.

MOLNAR, STEPHEN
1972 Tooth Wear and Culture: A Survey of Tooth Functions among Some Prehistoric Populations. *Current Anthropology* 13(5): 511–526.

MONTERO, LAURENE G., AND T. KATHLEEN HENDERSON
1993 Ground Stone Implements from the Tator Hills Archaeological Project. *Archaic Occupation on the Santa Cruz Flats: The Tator Hills Archaeological Project*, edited by Carl D. Halbirt and T. Kathleen Henderson, pp. 253–278. Flagstaff: Northland Research.

MORRIS, EARL H., AND ROBERT F. BURGH
1954 Basket Maker II Sites Near Durango, Colorado. *Carnegie Institution of Washington Publication* 604. Washington: Carnegie Institution.

MORSE, DAN
1969 Ancient Disease in the Midwest. *Reports of Investigations* 15. Springfield, Illinois: Illinois State Museum.

NABHAN, GARY P., CHARLES W. WEBER,
AND JAMES W. BERRY
1979 Legumes in the Papago-Pima Indian Diet and Ecological Niche. *The Kiva* 44(2–3): 173–190.

NATIONAL RESEARCH COUNCIL
1984 *Amaranth: Modern Prospects for an Ancient Crop.* Washington: National Academy Press.

NATIONS, DALE, AND EDMUND STUMP
1981 *Geology of Arizona.* Dubuque: Kendall/Hunt.

NICHOL, CHRISTIAN R.
1990 *Dental Genetics and Biological Relationships of the Pima Indians of Arizona.* Doctoral dissertation, Arizona State University, Tempe. Ann Arbor: University Microfilms.

NUSBAUM, JESSE L.
1922 A Basket-Maker Cave in Kane County, Utah. *Indian Notes and Monographs* 29. New York: Museum of the American Indian, Heye Foundation.

O'LAUGHLIN, THOMAS C.
1980 The Keystone Dam Site and Other Archaic and Formative Sites in Northwest El Paso, Texas. *El Paso Centennial Museum Publications in Anthropology* 8. El Paso: University of Texas.

PARKER, KITTIE F.
1972   *An Illustrated Guide to Arizona Weeds*. Tucson: University of Arizona Press.

PASE, CHARLES P., AND DAVID E. BROWN
1982   Interior Chaparral. In "Biotic Communities of the American Southwest—United States and Mexico," edited by David E. Brown. *Desert Plants* 4(1–4): 95–105.

PEARSON, GORDON W., AND MINZE STUIVER
1986   High-Precision Calibration of the Radiocarbon Time Scale, 500–2500 B.C. *Radiocarbon* 28(2B): 839–862.

PEILE, A. R.
1979   Colours that Cure. *Hemisphere* 23: 214–215, 217.

PEPPER, GEORGE H.
1902   The Ancient Basket Makers of Southeastern Utah. *Supplement to the American Museum Journal* 2(4), *Guide Leaflet* 6. New York: American Museum of Natural History.

PFEIFFER, SUSAN
1977   The Skeletal Biology of Archaic Populations of the Great Lakes Region. *National Museum of Man Mercury Series, Archaeological Survey of Canada Paper* 64. Ottowa: National Museum of Man.

PHILLIPS, DAVID A., MARK C. SLAUGHTER, AND SUSAN BIERER
1993   Archaeological Studies at Kartchner Caverns State Park, Cochise County, Arizona. *SWCA Archaeological Report* 93-26. Tucson: SWCA.

RAFFERTY, JANET E.
1985   The Archaeological Record on Sedentariness: Recognition, Development, and Implications. *Advances in Archaeological Method and Theory*, Vol. 8, edited by Michael B. Schiffer, pp. 113–156. New York: Academic Press.

RANERE, A. J.
1975   Toolmaking and Tool Use among the Preceramic Peoples of Panama. *Lithic Technology: Making and Using Stone Tools*, edited by Earl H. Swanson, pp. 173–209. The Hague: Mouton Publishers.

REDDING, RICHARD W.
1988   A General Explanation of Subsistence Change: From Hunting and Gathering to Food Production. *Journal of Anthropological Archaeology* 7(1): 56–97.

REED, CHARLES A., EDITOR
1977   *Origins of Agriculture*. The Hague: Mouton.

REINHART, THEODORE R.
1967   The Rio Rancho Phase: A Preliminary Report on Early Basketmaker Culture in the Middle Rio Grande Valley, New Mexico. *American Antiquity* 32(4): 458–470.

RICE, GLEN E.
1975   A Systematic Explanation of a Change in Mogollon

Settlement Patterns. MS, Doctoral dissertation, Department of Anthropology, University of Washington, Seattle.

RINDOS, DAVID
1980   Symbiosis, Instability, and the Origins and Spread of Agriculture: A New Model. *Current Anthropology* 21(6): 751–772.
1984   *The Origins of Agriculture, An Evolutionary Perspective*. New York: Academic Press.

ROBERTS, FRANK H. H., JR.
1929   Shabik'eshchee Village: A Late Basket Maker Site in the Chaco Canyon, New Mexico. *Bureau of American Ethnology Bulletin* 92. Washington: Bureau of American Ethnology.

ROCEK, THOMAS R.
1993   Sedentism and Mobility in the Southwest. Paper presented at the 57th Annual Meeting of the Society for American Archaeology, St. Louis, Missouri.

ROGERS, DILWYN
1980   *Edible, Medicinal, Useful and Poisonous Plants of the Northern Great Plains–South Dakota Region*. Sioux Falls: Augustana College.

ROTH, BARBARA J.
1988   Recent Research on the Late Archaic Occupation of the Northern Tucson Basin. In "Recent Research on Tucson Basin Prehistory," edited by William H. Doelle and Paul R. Fish. *Institute for American Research Anthropological Papers* 10: 81–85. Tucson: Institute for American Research.
1989   *Late Archaic Settlement and Subsistence in the Tucson Basin*. Doctoral dissertation, University of Arizona, Tucson. Ann Arbor: University Microfilms.
1992   Sedentary Agriculturalists or Mobile Hunter-Gatherers? Evidence on the Late Archaic Occupation of the Northern Tucson Basin. *The Kiva* 57(4): 291–314.

ROTH, BARBARA J., AND BRUCE B. HUCKELL
1992   Cortaro Points and the Archaic of Southern Arizona. *The Kiva* 57(4): 353–370.

ROZEN, KENNETH C.
1984   Flaked Stone. In "Hohokam Habitation Sites in the Northern Santa Rita Mountains," by Alan Ferg, Kenneth C. Rozen, William L. Deaver, Martyn D. Tagg, David A. Phillips, Jr., and David A. Gregory. *Arizona State Museum Archaeological Series* 147(2): 421–604. Tucson: Arizona State Museum, University of Arizona.

RUSSELL, FRANK
1908   The Pima Indians. *Twenty-sixth Annual Report of the Bureau of American Ethnology, 1904–1905*. Washington: Bureau of American Ethnology.

SANCHINI, P. J.
1981   *Population Structure and Fecundity Patterns in*

Quercus emoryi and Q. arizonica *in Southeastern Arizona.* Doctoral dissertation, University of Colorado, Boulder. Ann Arbor: University Microfilms.

SAYLES, E. B.
1941   Archaeology of the Cochise Culture. In "The Cochise Culture," by E. B. Sayles and Ernst Antevs. *Medallion Papers* 29: 1–30. Globe, Arizona: Gila Pueblo.
1945   The San Simon Branch, Excavations at Cave Creek and in the San Simon Valley. I: Material Culture. *Medallion Papers* 34. Globe, Arizona: Gila Pueblo.
1983   The Cochise Cultural Sequence in Southeastern Arizona. *Anthropological Papers of the University of Arizona* 42. Tucson: University of Arizona Press.

SAYLES, E. B., AND ERNST ANTEVS
1941   The Cochise Culture. *Medallion Papers* 29. Globe, Arizona: Gila Pueblo.

SCHMUCKER, B. J.
1985   Dental Attrition: A Correlative Study of Dietary and Subsistence Patterns. MS, Masters thesis, Arizona State University, Tempe.

SCHOENWETTER, JAMES
1960   Pollen Analysis of Sediments from Matty Wash. MS, Master's thesis, Department of Botany, University of Arizona, Tucson.

SCHULTES, RICHARD EVANS
1976   *Hallucinogenic Plants*. New York: Golden Press.

SCHULZ, PETER D.
1977   Task Activity and Anterior Tooth Grooving in Prehistoric California Indians. *American Journal of Physical Anthropology* 46(1): 87–91.

SCIULLI, PAUL W.
1978   Developmental Abnormalities of the Permanent Dentition in Prehistoric Ohio Valley Amerindians. *American Journal of Physical Anthropology* 48(2): 193–198.

SCOTT, G. RICHARD, AND ALBERT A. DAHLBERG
1982   Microdifferentiation in Tooth Crown Morphology Among Indians of the American Southwest. *Teeth: Form, Function, and Evolution*, edited by Bjorn Kurten, pp. 259–291. New York: Columbia University Press.

SCOTT, G. RICHARD, AND CHRISTY G. TURNER II
1988   Dental Anthropology. *Annual Review of Anthropology* 17: 99–126.

SELLERS, WILLIAM D., AND RICHARD H. HILL, EDITORS
1974   *Arizona Climate, 1931–1972*. Second Edition. Tucson: University of Arizona Press.

SHOTT, MICHAEL J.
1989   Bipolar Industries: Ethnographic Evidence and Archaeological Implications. *North American Archaeologist* 10(1): 1–24.

SIMMONS, ALAN H.
1986   New Evidence for the Early Use of Cultigens in the American Southwest. *American Antiquity* 51(1): 73–89.

SKINNER, MORRIS F.
1942   The Fauna of Papago Springs Cave, Arizona. *Bulletin of the American Museum of Natural History* 80: 143–220.

SMILEY, F. E., AND WILLIAM J. PARRY
1990   Early, Intensive, and Rapid: Rethinking the Agricultural Transition in the Northern Southwest. Paper presented at the 55th Annual Meeting of the Society for American Archaeology, Las Vegas.

SMILEY, F. E., WILLIAM J. PARRY, AND GEORGE J. GUMERMAN
1986   Early Agriculture in the Black Mesa/Marsh Pass Region of Arizona: New Chronometric Data and Recent Excavations at Three Fir Shelter. Paper presented at the 51st Annual Meeting of the Society for American Archaeology, New Orleans.

SMITH, BRUCE D.
1989   Origins of Agriculture in Eastern North America. *Science* 246: 1566–1571.
1992   *Rivers of Change, Essays on Early Agriculture in Eastern North America*. Washington: Smithsonian Institution Press.

SMITH, B. HOLLY
1984   Patterns of Molar Wear in Hunter-Gatherers and Agriculturalists. *American Journal of Physical Anthropology* 63(1): 39–56.

SMITH, ERIC ALDEN, AND BRUCE WINTERHALDER, EDITORS
1992   *Evolutionary Ecology and Human Behavior*. New York: Aldine de Gruyter.

SMITH, H. V.
1956   The Climate of Arizona. *Agricultural Experiment Station Bulletin* 279. Tucson: University of Arizona.

SPETH, JOHN D., AND SUSAN L. SCOTT
1989   Horticulture and Large Mammal Hunting: The Role of Resource Depletion and the Constraints of Time and Labor. In *Farmers as Hunters, The Implications of Sedentism*, edited by Susan Kent, pp. 71–79. Cambridge: Cambridge University Press.

STEENBERGH, WARREN F., AND CHARLES H. LOWE
1977   Ecology of the Saguaro, 2: Reproduction, Germination, Establishment, Growth, and Survival of the Young Plant. *National Park Service Scientific Monograph Series* 8. Washington: Department of the Interior.

STEWARD, JULIAN H.
1933   Ethnology of the Owens Valley Paiute. *University of California Publications in American Archaeology and Ethnology* 33(3). Berkeley: University of California.
1955   Theory of Culture Change: The Methodology of

STEWARD, JULIAN H. (*continued*)
 Multilinear Evolution. Urbana: University of Illinois Press.

STIGER, MARK A.
 1979 Mesa Verde Subsistence Patterns from Basketmaker to Pueblo III. *The Kiva* 44(2–3): 133–144.

STUIVER, MINZE, AND PAULA J. REIMER
 1993 Extended ^{14}C Data Base and Revised CALIB 3.0 ^{14}C Age Calibration Program. *Radiocarbon* 35(1): 215–230.

SWANSON, EARL H., JR.
 1951 An Archaeological Survey of the Empire Valley, Arizona. MS, Master's thesis, Department of Anthropology, University of Arizona, Tucson.

SZUTER, CHRISTINE R.
 1986 Taxonomic Richness and Animal Utilization at La Paloma. In "Archaeological Investigations at La Paloma: Archaic and Hohokam Occupations at Three Sites in the Northeastern Tucson Basin," by Allen Dart. *Institute for American Research Anthropological Papers* 4: 155–165. Tucson: Institute for American Research.

SZUTER, CHRISTINE R., AND FRANK E. BAYHAM
 1989 Sedentism and Animal Procurement among Desert Horticulturalists of the North American Southwest. *Farmers as Hunters: The Implications of Sedentism*, edited by Susan Kent, pp. 80–95. Cambridge, England: Cambridge University Press.

TAGG, MARTYN D., AND BRUCE B. HUCKELL
 1984 The Sycamore Canyon Sites. In "Miscellaneous Archaeological Studies in the ANAMAX-Rosemont Land Exchange Area," by Martyn D. Tagg, Richard G. Ervin, and Bruce B. Huckell. *Arizona State Museum Archaeological Series* 147(4): 61–106. Tucson: Arizona State Museum, University of Arizona.

TAYLOR, R. E.
 1987 *Radiocarbon Dating: An Archaeological Perspective*. Orlando: Academic Press.

TIXIER, JACQUES
 1963 Typologie de l'épipaléolithique du Maghreb. *Centre de Recherches Anthropologiques Préhistoriques et Ethnographiques, Algiers Mémoires* 2. Paris: Arts et Métiers Graphiques.

TOYNBEE, J.
 1849 Osseous Tumors Growing from the Walls of the Meatus Externus and on the Enlargement of the Walls Themselves, with Cases. *Providence Medical Surgery Journal* 14: 533–537.

TURNER II, CHRISTY G.
 1967 The Dentition of Arctic Peoples. MS, Doctoral dissertation, Department of Anthropology, University of Wisconsin, Madison.
 1969 Cranial and Dental Features of a Southeastern Arizona Cochise Culture Burial. *The Kiva* 34(4): 246–250.
 1979 Dental Anthropological Indications of Agriculture among the Jomon People of Central Japan. *American Journal of Physical Anthropology* 51(4): 619–635.
 1986 The First Americans: The Dental Evidence. *National Geographic Research* 2: 37–46.
 1987 Affinity and Dietary Assessment of Hohokam Burials from the Site of La Ciudad, Central Arizona. In "Specialized Studies in the Economy, Environment, and Culture of La Ciudad," edited by Jo Ann Kisselburg, Glen E. Rice, and Brenda Shears. *Anthropological Field Studies* 20: 215–230. Tempe: Office of Cultural Resources Management, Arizona State University.

TURNER II, CHRISTY G., AND J. D. CADIEN
 1969 Dental Chipping in Aleuts, Eskimos, and Indians. *American Journal of Physical Anthropology* 31(3): 303–310.

TURNER II, CHRISTY G., C. R. NICHOL, AND G. R. SCOTT
 1991 Scoring Procedures for Key Morphological Traits of the Permanent Dentition: The Arizona State University Dental Anthropology Scoring System. In *Advances in Dental Anthropology*, edited by Marc A. Kelley and Clark Spencer Larsen, pp. 13–31. New York: Wiley-Liss.

TURNER, NANCY J.
 1978 Food Plants of British Columbia Indians, Part 2: Interior Peoples. *British Columbia Provincial Museum Handbook* 36. Vancouver: British Columbia Provincial Museum.

UCKO, PETER J., AND GEORGE W. DIMBLEBY, EDITORS
 1969 *The Domestication and Exploitation of Plants and Animals*. London: Duckworth.

UPHAM, STEADMAN, RICHARD S. MACNEISH, WALTON C. GALINAT, AND CHRISTOPHER M. STEVENSON
 1987 Evidence Concerning the Origin of Maiz de Ocho. *American Anthropologist* 89(2): 410–419.

VESTAL, PAUL A.
 1952 Ethnobotany of the Ramah Navaho. *Papers of the Peabody Museum of American Archaeology and Ethnology, Harvard University*, 40(4). Cambridge: Harvard University.

WATERS, MICHAEL R.
 1986 The Geoarchaeology of Whitewater Draw, Arizona. *Anthropological Papers of the University of Arizona* 45. Tucson: University of Arizona Press.

WATERS, MICHAEL R., AND ANNE I. WOOSLEY
 1990 The Geoarchaeology and Preceramic Prehistory of the Willcox Basin, SE Arizona. *Journal of Field Archaeology* 17(2): 163–175.

WELLHAUSEN, E. J., L. M. ROBERTS, AND E. HERNANDEZ X
 1952 *Races of Maize in Mexico: Their Origin, Character-*

istics, and Distribution, in collaboration with Paul C. Mangelsdorf. Cambridge: Bussey Institution, Harvard University.

WENDORF, FRED, AND TULLY H. THOMAS
1951   Early Man Sites near Concho, Arizona. *American Antiquity* 17(2): 107–114.

WETTERSTROM, WILMA
1986   Food, Diet, and Population at Prehistoric Arroyo Hondo Pueblo, New Mexico. *Arroyo Hondo Archaeological Series* 6. Santa Fe: School of American Research Press.

WHALEN, NORMAN M.
1971   Cochise Culture Sites in the Central San Pedro Drainage, Arizona. MS, Doctoral dissertation, University of Arizona, Tucson.
1973   Agriculture and the Cochise. *The Kiva* 39(1): 89–96.

WHITE, T. D.
1991   *Human Osteology*. San Diego: Academic Press.

WHITING, ALFRED F.
1939   Ethnobotany of the Hopi. *Museum of Northern Arizona Bulletin* 15. Flagstaff: Northern Arizona Society of Science and Art.

WHITING, JOHN W., AND BARBARA AYRES
1968   Inferences from the Shape of Dwellings. *Settlement Archaeology*, edited by Kwang-chih Chang, pp. 117–133. Palo Alto: National Press Books.

WILCOX, R. W.
1911   *Pharmacology and Therapeutics*. Philadelphia: Blackiston.

WILLEY, GORDON R., AND PHILIP PHILLIPS
1958   *Method and Theory in American Archaeology*. Chicago: University of Chicago Press.

WILLS III, W. H.
1985   The Chronology and Stratigraphy of Early Maize at Bat Cave, New Mexico: Regional Implications. Paper presented at the 50th Annual Meeting of the Society for American Archaeology, Denver.
1988a   *Early Prehistoric Agriculture in the American Southwest*. Santa Fe: School of American Research Press.
1988b   Early Agriculture and Sedentism in the American Southwest: Evidence and Interpretations. *Journal of World Prehistory* 2(4): 445–488.
1990   Cultivating Ideas: The Changing Intellectual History of the Introduction of Agriculture in the American Southwest. *Perspectives on Southwestern Prehistory*, edited by Paul E. Minnis and Charles

L. Redman, pp. 319–331. Boulder: Westview Press.
1992   Plant Cultivation and the Evolution of Risk-Prone Economies in the Prehistoric American Southwest. In "Transitions to Agriculture in Prehistory," edited by Anne Birgitte Gebauer and T. Douglas Price. *Monographs in World Archaeology* 4: 153–176. Madison: Prehistory Press.

WILLS III, W. H., AND BRUCE B. HUCKELL
1994   Economic Implications of Changing Land-Use Patterns in the Late Archaic. *Themes in Southwest Prehistory*, edited by George J. Gumerman, pp. 33–52. Santa Fe: School of American Research Press.

WILLS III, W. H., AND THOMAS C. WINDES
1989   Evidence for Population Aggregation and Dispersal during the Basketmaker III Period in Chaco Canyon, New Mexico. *American Antiquity* 54(2): 347–369.

WILSON, GILBERT L.
1987   *Buffalo Bird Woman's Garden, Agriculture of the Hidatsa Indians*. St. Paul: Minnesota Historical Society Press.

WINDMILLER, RIC C.
1973   The Late Cochise Culture in the Sulphur Spring Valley, Southeastern Arizona: Archaeology of the Fairchild Site. *The Kiva* 39(2): 131–169.

WINTER, MARCUS C.
1976   The Archaeological Household Cluster in the Valley of Oaxaca. *The Early Mesoamerican Village*, edited by Kent V. Flannery, pp. 25–31. New York: Academic Press.

WOODBURN, JAMES
1980   Hunters and Gatherers Today and Reconstruction of the Past. *Soviet and Western Anthropology*, edited by Ernest Gellner, pp. 95–117. London: Gerald Duckworth.

WOODBURY, RICHARD B.
1993   *60 Years of Southwestern Archaeology, A History of the Pecos Conference*. Albuquerque: University of New Mexico Press.

WOODBURY, RICHARD B., AND EZRA B. W. ZUBROW
1979   Agricultural Beginnings, 2000 B.C. – A.D. 500. *Handbook of North American Indians*, William C. Sturtevant, general editor, Vol. 9, *Southwest*, edited by Alfonso Ortiz, pp. 43–60. Washington: Smithsonian Institution.

Index

Abstract

In 1983 personnel from the Arizona State Museum excavated a pair of buried late preceramic sites located within the Matty Canyon–Cienega Creek drainage 60 km (37 miles) southeast of Tucson. Site AZ EE:2:30 (ASM), named the Donaldson Site in 1983, was the locale of investigations by Emil W. Haury and Frank W. Eddy from the University of Arizona in the mid 1950s; the other site, Los Ojitos (AZ EE:2:137 ASM), lay undiscovered until 1983.

A history of the archaeological, geological, and palynological investigations in the area provides an understanding of the intellectual context of those times and details the developing archaeological interest in the transition from hunting and gathering to a mixed, farming-foraging economy in the southwestern United States. To better reflect both ecological and culture historical relationships across the Southwest between approximately 1500 B.C. and A.D. 200, it is proposed that the final portion of the preceramic period, usually designated the Late Archaic period in southeastern Arizona, be reconfigured as the Early Agricultural period. This period is subdivided into two phases, San Pedro and Cienega, and the Matty Canyon sites are used to define the Cienega phase.

A description of the modern environmental setting of the Cienega Creek Basin includes the physiographic characteristics of the basin, the climatic conditions that typify it, and the biotic communities it contains, and documents the environmental changes that began in the late 19th century. The lushness of this setting underscores the diversity of plant and animal life available to the prehistoric inhabitants.

The 1983 excavations documented small, round, domestic structures, roasting and storage pits, shallow hearths, fire-cracked rock concentrations, and human burials. Radiocarbon dates place the occupation of the Donaldson Site in the mid first millennium B.C. Two radiocarbon dates from Los Ojitos suggest a slightly younger age but violate the alluvial stratigraphic relationships between the two sites. The high artifact densities and abundance of features in these thick cultural deposits are noteworthy and are at odds with the kinds of deposits normally associated with preceramic period sites. The flaked and ground stone artifact descriptions highlight the unusual variety of forms of ground stone implements, and a new projectile point style, Cienega, is defined.

Resumen

En 1983, el personal del Arizona State Museum excavó dos sitios precerámicos tardíos localizados en el drenaje de Matty Canyon–Cienega Creek, 60 km (37 millas) al sureste de Tucson. El sitio AZ EE:2:30 (ASM), llamado Donaldson Site en 1983, fue investigado por Emil W. Haury y Frank W. Eddy de la Universidad de Arizona a mediados de la década de los años 50; el otro sitio, Los Ojitos (AZ EE:2:137 ASM) no fue descubierto hasta 1983.

La historia de las investigaciones arqueológicas, geológicas, y palinológicas en el área provee una visión del contexto intelectual de aquellos tiempos y detalla el desarrollo del interés arqueológico en la transición de la caza y recolección a una economía mixta de agricultura y forraje en el Suroeste de los Estados Unidos. Para reflejar mejor las relaciones ecológicas e históricas en el Suroeste entre aproximadamente 1500 años A.C. y 200 años D.C., se propone que la parte final del período precerámico, usualmente llamado Arcaico Tardío en el suroeste de Arizona, sea reconfigurado como período Agrícola Temprano. Este período se divide en dos fases, San Pedro y Cienega, y los sitios en Matty Canyon se utilizan para definir la fase Cienega.

Una descripción del medio ambiente moderno en la cuenca de Cienega Creek incluye las características fisiográficas de la cuenca, las condiciones climáticas típicas, y sus comunidades bióticas. También se documentan los cambios medio ambientales que empezaron al fin del siglo XIX. La riqueza de esta área enfariza la diversidad de plantas y animales disponibles para sus habitantes prehistóricos.

Las excavaciones de 1983 documentaron pequeñas estructuras domésticas circulares, pozos de almacenamiento, hornos, fogones, concentraciones de piedra rota por el fuego, y enterramientos humanos. Fechados radiocarbónicos indican que esta ocupación en el sitio Donaldson data de la mitad del primer milenio antes de Cristo. Dos fechas radiocarbónicas de Los Ojitos sugieren una edad poco más reciente pero no corresponden con las relaciones estratigráficas aluviales entre los dos sitios. La alta densidad artefactual y abundancia de rasgos en estos depósitos culturales profundos se destacan por ser diferentes a aquellos usualmente asociados con sitios precerámicos. La descripción de artefactos de piedra tallada y pulida detalla la inusual variedad morfológica de la piedra pulida; se define un nuevo estilo de punta de proyectil, el estilo Cienega.

Archaeobotanical analysis of flotation samples and macrobotanical specimens documents a surprising abundance of carbonized maize at both sites, significant quantities of a wide assortment of wild plant remains, and possibly the presence of squash at Los Ojitos. Examination of the faunal remains from the Donaldson Site suggests that hunters from that settlement focused their attention on large mammals such as deer, antelope, and bighorn, although the remains of jackrabbits and cottontails are also common. Both the plant and animal remains indicate that the varied wild resources from at least three biotic communities within 15 to 20 km (9 to 12 miles) of the settlements enriched the subsistence of the prehistoric inhabitants.

Study of the human remains from the sites provides the first systematic description of late preceramic populations from southeastern Arizona and more evidence of a subsistence strategy incorporating both food production and foraging. The degree to which these people relied on maize farming and hunting and gathering is considered in the final chapter, along with evidence relating to the development of preceramic sedentism in southeastern Arizona. The Matty Canyon sites demonstrate that significant economic reorganization, apparently fueled by a commitment to agriculture within a system featuring a diversified farming-foraging base, permitted the rise of sedentary residential communities by 1000 to 500 B.C. across much of southeastern Arizona.

El análisis arqueobotánico de muestras de flotación y especímenes macrobotánicos documenta una sorpresiva abundancia de maíz carbonizado en ambos sitios, cantidades significativas de plantas silvestres variadas, y posiblemente la presencia de calabaza en Los Ojitos. El análisis de restos faunísticos del sitio Donaldson sugiere que los cazadores de este sitio se enfocaron en fauna mayor, como venado, antílope, y borrego cimarrón, aunque los restos de liebre y conejo también son comunes. Tanto los restos de plantas como de animales indican que los recursos explotados se obtuvieron en por lo menos tres comunidades bióticas en un radio de 15 a 20 km (9 a 12 millas) de los habitantes prehistóricos.

Estudios de los restos humanos de estos sitios proveen la primera descripción sistemática de las poblaciones precerámicas tardías en el suroeste de Arizona y más evidencia de una estrategia de subsistencia que incorporó agricultura y forraje. El capítulo final considera el grado en el que esta gente dependió de la producción de maíz, caza, y recolección. También se discute la evidencia relacionada con el desarrollo del sedentismo prehistórico en el sureste de Arizona. Los sitios de Matty Canyon demuestran que una reorganización económica significativa aparentemente influenció la adopción de la agricultura dentro de un sistema de producción mixta diversificada, permitiendo la aparición de comunidades sedentarias hacia los años 1000 a 500 A. de C. en casi todo el sureste de Arizona.

ANTHROPOLOGICAL PAPERS OF THE UNIVERSITY OF ARIZONA

44. Settlement, Subsistence, and Society
in Late Zuni Prehistory.
Keith W. Kintigh. 1985.

45. The Geoarchaeology of Whitewater Draw, Arizona.
Michael R. Waters. 1986.

46. Ejidos and Regions of Refuge in Northwestern
Mexico.   N. Ross Crumrine and
Phil C. Weigand, eds. 1987.

47. Preclassic Maya Pottery at Cuello, Belize.
Laura J. Kosakowsky. 1987.

48. Pre-Hispanic Occupance in the Valley of
Sonora, Mexico.   William E. Doolittle. 1988.

49. Mortuary Practices and Social Differentiation
at Casas Grandes, Chihuahua, Mexico.
John C. Ravesloot. 1988.

50. Point of Pines, Arizona: A History of the
University of Arizona Archaeological
Field School.   Emil W. Haury. 1989.

51. Patarata Pottery: Classic Period Ceramics of the
South-central Gulf Coast, Veracruz, Mexico.
Barbara L. Stark. 1989.

52. The Chinese of Early Tucson: Historic Archaeology
from the Tucson Urban Renewal Project.
Florence C. Lister and Robert H. Lister. 1989.

53. Mimbres Archaeology of the Upper Gila,
New Mexico.   Stephen H. Lekson. 1990.

54. Prehistoric Households at Turkey Creek Pueblo,
Arizona.   Julie C. Lowell. 1991.

55. Homol'ovi II: Archaeology of an Ancestral Hopi
Village, Arizona.   E. Charles Adams
and Kelley Ann Hays, eds. 1991.

56. The Marana Community in the Hohokam World.
Suzanne K. Fish, Paul R. Fish,
and John H. Madsen, eds. 1992.

57. Between Desert and River: Hohokam Settlement
and Land Use in the Los Robles Community.
Christian E. Downum. 1993.

58. Sourcing Prehistoric Ceramics at Chodistaas
Pueblo, Arizona   María Nieves Zedeño. 1994.

59. Of Marshes and Maize: Preceramic Agricultural
Settlements in the Cienega Valley, Southeastern
Arizona   Bruce B. Huckell. 1995.

UNIVERSITY OF ARIZONA PRESS

1230 North Park Avenue, Tucson, Arizona 85719